GENERAL
OFFICE PROCEDURES

FOR COLLEGES

PATSY J. FULTON, Ph.D., CPS

President
Brookhaven College
Farmers Branch, Texas

Published by
K73 **SOUTH-WESTERN PUBLISHING CO.**

CINCINNATI   WEST CHICAGO, IL   CARROLLTON, TX   LIVERMORE, CA

Copyright © 1988
by SOUTH-WESTERN PUBLISHING CO.
Cincinnati, Ohio

ISBN: 0-538-11732-X

Library of Congress Catalog Number: 86-63580

456789W43210

Printed in the United States of America

By choosing a career in office occupations, you have selected a field which offers numerous job opportunities and promises increased job opportunities through the mid 1990s. During this period, office occupations will be challenging and ever-changing because of the growth in technology. As new technologies are developed, the way in which the office worker does the job will be affected. Therefore, as an office worker you must commit yourself to continual learning in order to do your job effectively. The skills that you will learn in this course are merely the beginning.

If you are to take advantage of the opportunities that will come your way, you must continue learning throughout your career. The changes that will occur during your career demand that you be flexible and creative. Change can be exciting and rewarding but only if you adopt an attitude that welcomes change. Another area in which you need to continue to grow and learn after you leave this course is in your communication and human relations skills. During your work life, you will encounter all types of people. These people may have very different backgrounds from your own and view the world in very different ways. If you are to work effectively with them, you must continue to develop and expand your knowledge of communication and human relations skills.

IMPORTANT SKILLS TO DEVELOP DURING THIS COURSE

As you progress through *General Office Procedures for Colleges* and complete the projects assigned by your instructor, you will learn

- How change has impacted the business world.
- How to communicate more effectively with others.
- How to improve your listening techniques.
- How the computer has influenced the office of today.
- How word processing is used in businesses.
- How reprographics is being used today.
- How to write an effective business letter.
- How to prepare various business documents.
- How to effectively use telecommunications equipment.
- How to handle incoming and outgoing mail.
- How to prepare financial records.
- How to store and find records.
- How to apply for a job.
- How to be successful on the job.

WHO CAN USE THIS BOOK *1988* *adult level*

This text/workbook is written for postsecondary vocational, community college, and university students who are interested in office careers. It is not only designed for those students who are entering postsecondary education directly from high school but for those adults who are returning to school after a number of years away or who are upgrading their skills for future job opportunities.

Although your instructor will be an able assistant as you proceed through this course, it is up to you to determine that you will use your abilities to the fullest. If you are to learn and grow to your maximum, you must make a commitment to study the information in the text and do the projects assigned outside of class. The old adage "you get out of something what you put into it" is especially true of learning. You, as a learner, must take an active role if you are to be successful in this course and are able to apply the knowledge and skills learned to a job in the future.

TEXT/WORKBOOK ORGANIZATION

The 15 chapters in this text are divided into five parts, with each part having three chapters. The parts are as follows:

- Preparing for Employment
- Processing Information
- Communicating Information
- Managing Information
- Securing the Right Job

Each of the chapters in this book contains aids to help you learn the knowledge presented in the chapter and develop the necessary skills to use this knowledge. At the beginning of each chapter, *General Objectives* are given so that you will understand what you are expected to achieve. At the end of each chapter, a *For Your Review* section is included to help you in reviewing the important points of the chapter. A case about a realistic office situation is presented in the *Professional Forum* section. From analyzing the case, you will learn how to deal with problem situations in the office. At the end of each chapter, a *For Your Understanding* section lists several questions for you to answer. After answering these questions, you will have a better understanding of the material presented in the text.

As culminating activities in each unit, you will find *Office Applications* that will challenge you and help you solve problems such as those you will encounter on the job. These tasks are directly related to the general objectives at the beginning of each unit. As you complete these office applications, you will be working for **RJ Computer Corporation.** A history of the company and your duties are explained at the beginning of the *Office Applications* section.

TESTING

To test your knowledge of what you have learned in each part, five true/false, multiple-choice, matching, and short answer tests are available in K73A. Your instructor may choose to use these tests as they are written or develop additional testing instruments to add to these tests. Whatever testing procedures are used in this course, it is your responsibility to learn the material and develop the skills so that you may demonstrate your proficiency.

APPENDICES

Eight appendices on pages 241–270 will furnish you with a ready source of reference to basic information. These appendices are

Appendix A	Grammar
Appendix B	Punctuation and Capitalization
Appendix C	Numbers
Appendix D	Business Math
Appendix E	Selection of Stationery
Appendix F	Proofreading
Appendix G	Care of Typewriter, Error Correction, and Shortcut Techniques
Appendix H	Filing Rules

ABOUT THE AUTHOR

Patsy J. Fulton is president of Brookhaven College, a community college located in Dallas, Texas. Her past experiences include teaching a variety of business education subjects on the high school and community college levels, including *keyboarding, shorthand, office machines, office procedures, business communications, business law, general business, bookkeeping,* and *vocational office education.* In addition to her teaching experiences, she has held numerous administrative positions including *Business/Social Science Division Chairperson* and *Vice President of Instruction.* Prior to entering the educational field, she worked for six years as a secretary and holds the CPS certification. Her educational credentials include a B.B.A., an M.B.Ed., and a Ph.D. One of her most recent honors was being selected as *Who's Who Among Scholars in Community and Junior Colleges.*

A FINAL WORD

As you prepare for employment in the challenging office field, it is hoped that you will find this course exciting and beneficial. It is also hoped that you are able to take advantage of the opportunities that await you in the business world. May your success be great.

Patsy Fulton

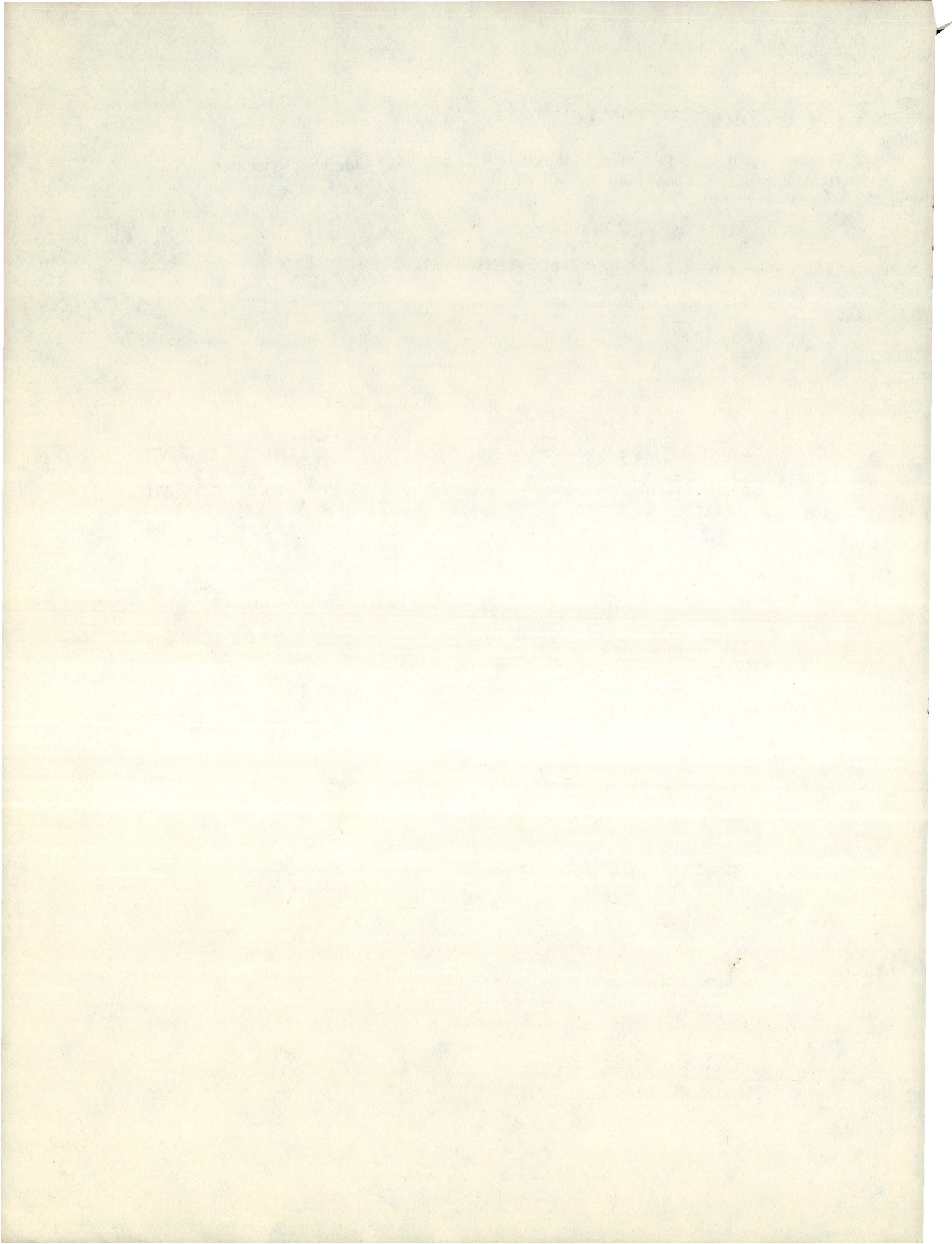

CONTENTS

PART 1

PREPARING FOR EMPLOYMENT

CHAPTER 1

The Changing Business World

We live in an age in which there have been numerous technological advances, and these advances have brought about the greatest amount of change in the last one hundred years that our world has ever known. Think for a moment about some of the changes that have occurred in our world. Numerous advances have been made in the medical world, with transplants of body parts occurring with relative frequency. Artificial hearts are also being implanted in humans—a technological advance not even dreamed of by most of us a few years ago. Space travel is almost commonplace. We are no longer surprised by the live television coverage of a space vehicle being placed into orbit. Satellites circle the earth constantly receiving and forwarding information to all points of the world. Computers have become smaller and smaller. Today we can carry a computer with us from place to place in a briefcase. Electronic calculators the thickness of a credit card can be carried in our pockets. Our homes are equipped with computer-controlled alarm systems, microwave ovens, videocassette recorders, battery-powered telephones, and numerous other devices which are the direct result of technological advances.

The changes in our society have affected the office world also. If you are to work in this office world, you need to understand and accept change. What can you expect from today's office world? What changes have occurred? What are the office worker's duties? What skills do you need in order to succeed? This chapter will help you answer these questions.

GENERAL OBJECTIVES

Your general objectives for this chapter are to

1. Become familiar with the business world of today.
2. Understand the role that change plays in the business world and how to deal with change.
3. Become knowledgeable about office positions available today.
4. Become familiar with the competencies needed in order to succeed.

THE BUSINESS WORLD OF TODAY

Two factors that have had a major impact on the business world of today are advances in technology and changes in the composition of the work force. If it were necessary to describe what is happening in technology in the business world in one word, that word would be "computers." Computers have affected not only the way in which we do our work but also the

3

types of jobs which are available. Women have become a significant part of the work force with more and more women working today than ever before. And, the number is expected to increase in the future. The educational level of the work force has increased, thus contributing to a more sophisticated group of workers than ever before.

Technological Growth. Although the first computer was built as early as 1830 by Charles Babbage, he was years ahead of his time, and very little was done with the computer until the 1960s when IBM introduced the Model 360. This system was large and costly. Just twenty years later, IBM introduced its first personal computer which was a fraction of the size and cost of the machine built twenty years earlier. Similarly, the first word processor was built by IBM in the 60s. The first word processor with a display screen was introduced by Lexitron in the early 70s. Today we have far more advanced word processors which are smaller in size and available at a cost of approximately one-third of the original word processors.

Courtesy of International Business Machines Inc.

Illustration 1-1. IBM 360

What does the future hold? Much of the technology is now in place for a springboard into the 1990s. Office workers will be employed in

workstations tailored to individual job needs and to accommodate the tools of the electronic age. And, we will come even closer to the "paperless office" which has been suggested for the past several years — an office in which correspondence may be stored in the memory of a computer and viewed on a screen. However, we will probably not give up paper since it is too convenient for us to make notes, to put into briefcases, and so on.

Illustration 1-2. Personal Computer

Technological innovations available through the 1990s will make office work easier, faster, and more creative. Office functions will exist wherever business information is created, stored, reproduced, and distributed. In the office of the future, multiple office functions will occur simultaneously and permit office personnel to utilize all kinds of business information (data, text, image, and voice) in a single application with little or no difficulty.

Work Force of Today and Tomorrow. The growth of the work force, the age of the work force, and the educational level of the population will affect employment opportunities through the mid 1990s. A fourth factor affecting employment is the number of women in the labor force. Women will continue to be an increasing part of the work force through the mid 1990s.

Work Force Growth. The labor force will grow through the mid 1990s. However, it will grow at a slower rate than in the 1970s and 1980s. From 1970–80, the average annual growth rate of the work force was in excess of 2 percent. In the 1990s, the percent of growth is expected to be only 1 percent. Notice Illustration 1-3 which depicts this growth. By 1995, it is anticipated that the work force will be about 131 million people, an increase of approximately 19 percent from the mid 1980s.

Age. Due to lower birth rates, the number of people age 16 to 24 in the work force through the mid 1990s is expected to decline. However, the number of people age 25 to 54 is expected to increase from about two-thirds of the labor force in the mid 1980s to nearly three-fourths of the labor force by 1995. Since more people are retiring early, the number of people age 55 and over in the work force is projected to decline slightly. Illustration 1-4 reflects these declines and increases.

Education. The educational level of our population continues to rise. Today approximately 40 percent of all individuals between the ages of 18 to 65 have at least one year of college. Among individuals age 25 to 35 today, nearly half have completed at least one year of college. And, 21 percent of all workers have a college degree today compared to 11 percent in 1964. This statistic is depicted in Illustration 1-5.

Education is extremely important in the work force; that importance is shown directly when looking at employment rates. Consistently, those individuals with one or more years of college have higher employment rates than those individuals with four years of high school or less. A college or postsecondary education does not guarantee success in the job market; however, it does provide a much greater opportunity for success.

Working Women. Women are a dominant part of our work force. In fact, the most dramatic shift in the labor force today is the unprecedented entry of large numbers of women into the work force. More than half of all women of

Comparing to pieces of information

Labor force growth will slow through the mid-1990's.

Average annual percent increase

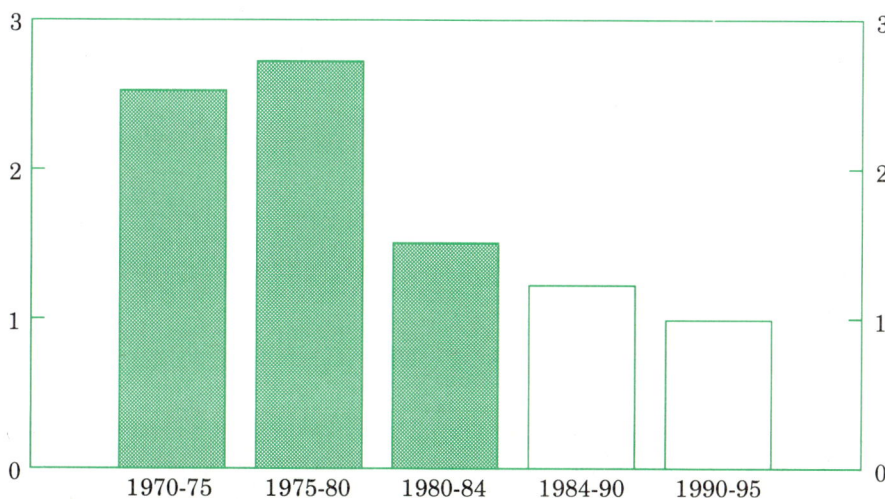

Source: Bureau of Labor Statistics

Illustration 1-3. Work Force Growth

**The number of workers in the prime working ages
will grow dramatically through the mid- 1990's.**

Labor force (millions)

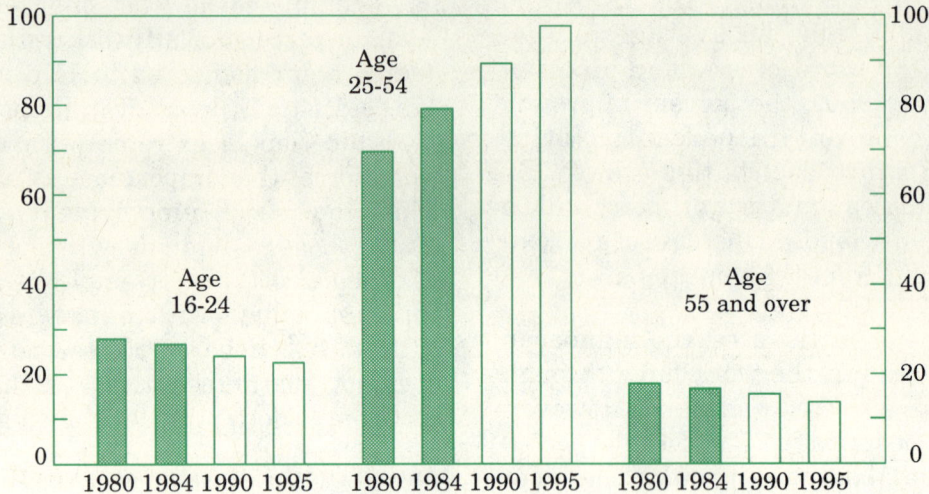

Source: Bureau of Labor Statistics

Illustration 1-4. Number of Workers by Ages

working age are in the labor force compared with 37.7 percent in 1960. By 1995, the number of women in the work force is likely to grow to more than 60 percent. Also, more and more women with children are working today. Approximately 60 percent of all women with preschool or school-age children are working presently. This percentage contrasts sharply with 1970 when only 40 percent of women with

children were in the work force. And, most employed women work at full-time jobs — jobs at which they spend 35 or more hours a week at work.

YOUR FUTURE

What do all these occurrences mean to you? The future will require office workers to have higher and higher levels of skills and knowledge. It will require that the office worker continue to learn by taking courses in school, by reading professional journals, and by participating in seminars and workshops. With a greater number of people 55 years of age or older in our society, there will be an increase in jobs in the health services. Also, with more people retiring at an early age, there may be a greater demand for recreational and leisure type activities; job opportunities in businesses engaged in satisfying the demand of the recreational market will probably increase. As more and more women continue to enter the work force, job opportunities for women will be found in diverse positions.

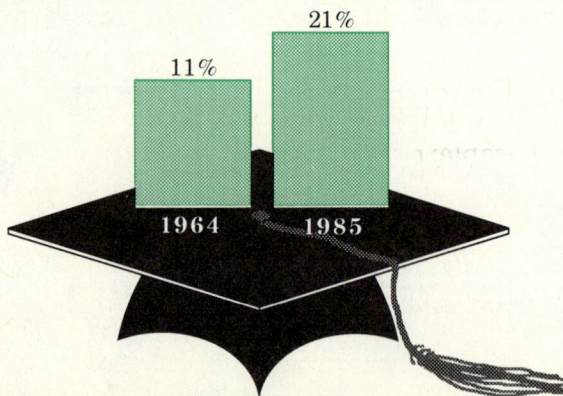

Source: Bureau of Labor Statistics

Illustration 1-5. Education of Work Force

Each of these occurrences means change; and, as a prospective office worker, you must be prepared to deal with that change. You must be willing to learn new skills and to adapt to new situations and people in our ever-changing world. The office is an active place, and its future is dynamic. It will not stand still; neither can you.

Change as a Constant. Since change is a constant now and is an anticipated constant for the future, you need to look at how you deal with change. Do you reject it? Do you accept it? Does change make you fearful? Or anxious? Most of us have differing reactions to change based on what the particular change is and how it will affect our lives.

Anxious. If you have ever had "butterflies" or "knots" in your stomach right before you try something that you have never tried before, you understand how anxiety relates to change. Anxiety is that vague, unpleasant feeling that suggests that something bad is about to happen. Anxiety is defined as a state of uneasiness and distress about future uncertainties. Some of the symptoms of anxiety are sweating, difficulty sleeping, and a faster heart rate. Anxiety is one type of response to change.

Fearful. Another type of response to change is fear. That fear may be related to the fear of failure. For example, if you are changing jobs, you may become fearful of the change due to not knowing if you will be able to succeed on the new job. This fear of failure prevents many of us from trying new things.

Resistant. A third response related to change may be resistance. Resistance is refusal to go along with a change. An example of resistance to change involves the 55 mile-per-hour speed limit. More than half of all motorists in the nation resist this change and exceed the speed limit.

In an office situation, resistance to change may occur when new work methods are introduced. For example, when an electronic filing system is introduced in an office, an office worker may resist the change and continue to file manually. People who resist new methods many times forget that risks associated with change also involve new opportunities. In the electronic filing system example, an employee has to be willing to risk learning a new method and must be willing to invest the time that such learning takes. However, once the method is learned, new opportunities may become available for the employee in the form of increased job responsibilities and even promotion. Individuals who resist new methods often limit their opportunities for growth.

Change Strategies. Since change will continue to play such an important role in the office world, how can you learn to cope with it? How can you reduce your anxiety and control your fear?

Accept and Prepare for Change. First of all, you can accept change as inevitable. Recognize that it will occur and try to predict the changes that you will face. One of the things that you do know is that technological changes will continue. Be prepared to deal with that technology. Take courses in school that give you the skills necessary to operate information processing equipment such as computers and word processors. Be prepared to continue to learn on the job. Know that continual changes in equipment will require continued learning.

Be Creative and Flexible. Creativity can be defined as the ability to combine existing ideas or things in new ways. When a change occurs, it is usually possible to connect that change to some already existing idea or way of doing something. For example, if your office installs an electronic filing system, the rules of filing which you learned in a manual system are still applicable; but you use these rules in new ways. Sometimes we think of creativity as existing only in individuals who have composed great music, written great plays, or produced magnificent works of art. However, creativity exists in all of us and can be released if we are sensitive to new possibilities.

Creativity demands flexibility. The flexible person is able to see that multiple options exist in most situations and is free to choose from a wide variety of options. Through being creative and flexible—being willing to try new ideas and to experience new situations—you can deal with change successfully. With such an approach, change becomes an opportunity or challenge rather than something to be feared and resisted.

Here are some steps which you can take that will help you deal with change.

1. Understand why it is necessary to change; determine what circumstances have occurred which have necessitated change.
2. Determine what objectives will be achieved by the changes which are proposed.
3. Establish guidelines for achieving these objectives.
4. Determine the benefits or rewards that will occur as a result of the change.
5. Once the change has occurred, evaluate the effectiveness of the change and your effectiveness in working through the change.

As you study for an office position, view the ability to deal with change as an important trait to develop.

OFFICE POSITIONS

Now that you have considered some of the changes that are taking place in the business world today, consider a few of the positions which are available in the office support area. Some of the job titles in this area are bookkeepers, computer operators, secretaries, receptionists, accounting clerks, and so on. There are numerous jobs available in the office area today, and the future is expected to bring an increase in job opportunities. In fact, this field is expected to grow more rapidly in the number of jobs available than the average for all other occupations through the mid 1990s. Four office positions which might interest you are given here with the main job duties and the job outlook for the future.

Receptionists. The day-to-day duties of receptionists vary depending on where they are employed. However, their major role is to greet customers and other visitors to a company. Many receptionists keep records of callers, the times at which they called, and the persons to whom they were referred. When receptionists are not busy greeting callers, they may operate the switchboard, file, or keyboard information. Some receptionists also handle the mail and do simple bookkeeping.

The job openings for receptionists are expected to exceed the average for all other occupations through the mid 1990s. More and more firms are recognizing the importance of human relations and thus the importance of the receptionist in promoting good public relations.

Bookkeepers and Accounting Clerks. Bookkeepers and accounting clerks handle the business transactions of a company. They record these transactions in journals, on ledgers, and on computers. They also prepare periodic financial statements. Bookkeepers may prepare and mail customers' bills and answer telephone requests concerning information about orders and bills.

Although job opportunities through the mid 1990s are projected to be good, employment in this area is expected to grow more slowly than the average for all occupations. The volume of business transactions is expected to grow rapidly, but the need for workers in this area is not expected to increase as fast because of the use of more and more computers in the accounting area.

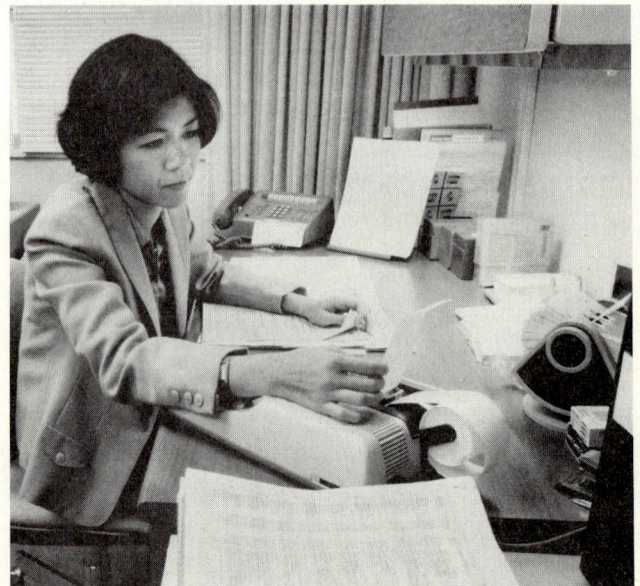

Illustration 1-6. An Accounting Clerk

Secretaries. Secretaries perform a variety of administrative and clerical tasks including scheduling appointments, giving information to callers, organizing and maintaining files, transcribing dictation, handling the mail, answering the telephone, writing letters, doing research, and preparing statistical reports. The secretarial field is one of the largest occupations in the United States economy. Employment of secretaries is expected to increase about as fast as the average for all occupations through the mid 1990s. Opportunities are also excellent for temporary or part-time work in the secretarial field. Although technological advances will continue to impact the secretarial world, automated equipment cannot substitute for the personal skills of a secretary essential to many jobs.

Word/Information Processing Specialists. The title of this position is in a state of flux today. There continue to be advertisements in the paper for word processing operators or word processors. However, with the continual integration of word and data processing, the term "information processing specialist" is becoming the more appropriate title, since the person processes both words and data on some type of electronic equipment. The information processing specialist must have the ability to operate various types of computers and word processing equipment. The person must possess excellent keyboarding/typewriting and proofreading skills and have a superior knowledge of grammar punctuation, and spelling. The information processing specialist is responsible for formatting documents (letters, memorandums, reports, and so on), inputting the information into the computer or word processor, and revising the documents. Many companies require the information processing specialist to meet certain productivity standards which have to do with the number of documents that the specialist can prepare in a certain period of time. Job opportunities for information processing specialists are expected to increase faster than the average for all occupations through the mid 1990s.

Illustration 1-7. Word/Information Processing Specialist

ESSENTIAL COMPETENCIES

Because of higher salaries and higher costs of services, office costs are increasing. Consequently, business is requiring higher standards for initial employment and advancement. Your employer will not expect you to equal the production of experienced employees when you begin. However, if you have mastered the essential knowledge and skills, you will soon be producing the desired quality and quantity of work.

English. Competency in English is the foundation of success in any office position. You may have felt that as long as you could talk well enough to be understood, that was all that was necessary. That is not true. One mark of the educated person is the precise use of English. If you have an excellent knowledge of composition and English literature, you will accomplish more and win respect from your superiors. Part of the mastery of English, of course, is an understanding of sentence structure and parts of speech. An equally important part is the ability to use the word that conveys the exact meaning.

Read worthwhile articles and books. When you find words that are new to you, look up their meaning, be sure of their spelling, and practice them in your conversation. Develop a little curiosity about words and you will find your work much more interesting. Don't limit your curiosity to your specialized field. Be curious about all words that are new to you.

In your college preparation-for-work program, develop as large and as varied a vocabulary as you can. You may be interviewed for a job by people in many different kinds of businesses and with varied educational backgrounds. The possibility of your getting the particular job you want will be much better if you are competent in English.

Spelling. Spelling is an essential tool for the efficient office worker. To many students, spelling is often nothing more than a necessary evil, something to be shunned rather than to be studied. Rather than being trivial, spelling is very important. Be sure that the business papers, reports, and letters you prepare are carefully checked for correct spelling.

Your work will probably be checked by a supervisor. You can be sure that no supervisor is going to tolerate misspelled words and incorrect grammar very long. You are responsible for your own errors, and you must be doubly careful if you are to win the respect of your superiors.

Many students feel that the dictionary will answer all their spelling problems. It should be used as an aid for spelling unusual words or determining the meaning or division of a word. You should not have to spend much of your day, and incidentally the employer's time, looking up words that you should have learned in school. The dictionary will answer many of your spelling problems if you know how to

Illustration 1-8. Checking Spelling

use it—but to use it efficiently, you must know how to spell.

Math. You may not need to have mastered geometry or calculus, but you do need to have mastered basic arithmetic. You need to be thoroughly comfortable with problems dealing with addition, subtraction, multiplication, division, and percentages. You will probably have calculators to use. However, if you do not understand the process, you will not be able to put the figures in the machine correctly or interpret them correctly.

Office Equipment. As an office worker, you need to have skills in operating various office equipment. You need to be able to operate electronic calculators, copying machines, word processors, and computers. Although electronic calculators and copying machines are easy to learn and to use, word processors and computers require much training time and effort. Before you become proficient on a computer or word processor, you must first develop keyboarding skill.

Keyboarding/Typewriting. As an office worker you will be expected to prepare many kinds of reports, memorandums, letters, and business forms. You must have good keyboarding or typewriting skill. In previous years, the office worker learned the keyboard of a typewriter; and the skill was referred to as typing skill. However, today you may never use a typewriter. You may learn keyboarding skills in school by using a computer or a word processor. Once you get on the job, you may continue to use a computer or word processor.

Although typewriters are still manufactured, typewriter sales have decreased drastically with the advent of the computer. Thus, typing is not necessarily the most appropriate term to use when referring to inputting information, since inputting may be done on a computer or word processor. Keyboarding is the more appropriate term to use today.

It is important that you be able to keyboard at a high rate of speed. The average college or business school student can keyboard at approximately 60 words-per-minute after two years of instruction. It is important that you build your skill as high as possible — to 70, 80, or even 90 words-per-minute. Any added skill you possess will help you in getting a better job and even in being promoted to a higher level position. Many executives today are using computers and need a high level of keyboarding skill in order to be as productive as possible.

Experience has shown that the office worker needs more than just the ability to keyboard at a high rate of speed. You must be able to produce work accurately, in the proper format, and with correct spelling, punctuation, and grammar. You also must be able to follow directions, to think through problems, and to be resourceful. Your work must be neat and organized.

Record Keeping. A knowledge of record keeping is useful to all office workers. You may be expected to keep certain records for the business and for your employer. Office workers in small offices, for example, may be required to keep all the records, to prepare the payroll, and to perform other duties where a knowledge of accounting is useful. Most programs of study in school require some accounting. If you are taking a program that does not require accounting, it is still a good idea to take one or two courses in the subject so that you will be prepared for future responsibilities and opportunities.

Note Taking. Although a skill in note taking is not as crucial as it was several years ago due to extensive use of dictating equipment, there are still some offices that require office workers to have note-taking ability. You may use a symbol or an alphabetic shorthand system for taking notes. Your school probably offers courses in one or both of these methods of shorthand.

Your goal in developing note-taking skill is to take notes rapidly and accurately. Speed requirements in dictation vary greatly. You may work for an individual who thinks and speaks rapidly; thus you need a high degree of note-taking skills. Or, you may work for an individual who rarely dictates; and when he or she does, the speed of dictation is quite slow. However, the ability to take dictation at a high rate of speed will provide you with the ability to work for anyone and in any situation.

Transcribing. Transcribing refers to preparing the shorthand notes you have taken or the dictation from a machine into a hard-copy form. You may use a typewriter, a computer, or a word processor in transcribing your notes. Whatever equipment you use, you are expected to be able to transcribe your notes accurately and quickly. You are also expected to transcribe them free of grammatical and punctuation errors. When transcribing notes, you put a number of your skills together — your keyboarding skill, English skill, spelling skill, and equipment skill. With a high level of keyboarding skill and equipment skill, and an excellent knowledge of English and spelling, you will be able to transcribe all types of correspondence effectively and efficiently.

Handwriting. Since you will have many occasions when the use of a typewriter, computer, or word processor will not be practical, your handwriting must be neat and legible. Remember that although you may be able to read your own handwriting, others may not be able to do so. Your handwritten office papers or records must frequently be read by others. Often the handwritten record becomes the basis for transferring information to computers. Errors in handwriting can cause delay in processing information and can be very costly.

Accuracy. As an office worker, whether you are dealing with figures or words, it is essential that you be accurate. Words should be proofread carefully to see that there are no errors. It is usually a good idea to proofread twice — once for content and once for keyboarding errors. Figures are used more and more in business today. You may have frequent calculations to make and totals to check. You may have columns of figures in a letter or report which are to be checked for accuracy. Whatever the task, it is essential that your work be prepared accurately.

Knowledge About Sources of Information.
Those who work in offices should know how to use various reference books. Such books as *Roget's Thesaurus,* handbooks for office workers, specialized reference manuals, trade journals, and a dictionary should be available for ready reference. You should know how to use each of these reference sources efficiently. If your company has an office manual, study it carefully.

Oral and Written Communication.
Office workers spend the majority of their time communicating with others. Such communication may be in the form of written letters and memorandums, telephone calls, or face-to-face conversations. Regardless of the form it takes, you must be extremely proficient in the communications area. You must express yourself accurately and concisely in written correspondence. You must communicate your needs clearly and tactfully in verbal communications.

Human Relations.
As an office worker, you will come in contact with a number of people. Within the company, you will work with co-workers, your supervisor, and executives. Contacts outside your company will include salespeople and customers. All these people will be different; they will have different backgrounds and experiences. But you will need to accept, understand, and work effectively with them. The ability to understand and apply human relations skills is essential.

Decision Making.
Increased use of technology in the office requires you to make some high-level decisions. You may be responsible for selecting the appropriate media for transmission of communications. For example, you may have to determine whether a communication should be sent by electronic mail or by regular mail. You may be responsible for selecting filing retrieval methods, for determining what equipment to use, and for developing retention methods. If you are to make the best decisions, you must determine the problem, analyze the various actions possible, and decide on the correct solution.

Table 1-1. List of Duties of Office Workers

Office Duties

1. Prepare documents.
2. Take and transcribe notes.
3. Operate calculating machines.
4. Operate word processing equipment.
5. Operate computers.
6. Use copying machines.
7. Use and prepare business forms.
8. Order office supplies.
9. Use various filing systems.
10. Open, read, sort, and classify incoming mail.
11. Prepare outgoing mail.
12. Prepare mailing lists.
13. Use the telephone.
14. Prepare envelopes.
15. Find material.
16. Plan itineraries for trips.
17. Make travel reservations.
18. Introduce callers.
19. Use reference books.
20. Take and prepare minutes of a meeting.
21. Handle banking transactions.
22. Keep accounting records.
23. Organize and key statistical reports.
24. Prepare financial statements.
25. Compose and produce letters.
26. Prepare rough drafts.
27. Figure extensions on bills, invoices, and statements.
28. Examine and sort business papers.
29. Prepare checks.
30. Weigh mail and figure postage.
31. Prepare packages for shipment.
32. Make out requisitions.
33. Organize desk for efficiency.
34. Stuff envelopes.
35. Proofread.
36. Receive and give information—communicate verbally with people inside and outside the office.
37. Schedule appointments.
38. Receive visitors.

The following review will help you remember the important points of this chapter.

1. Two factors that have had a major impact on today's business world are advances in technology and changes in the composition of the work force.

    a. Technological growth. In the last twenty years, the size and price of computers have been reduced significantly. Word processors have also become smaller and less costly. In the future, we can expect technological growth to continue, with the "paperless office" becoming closer to a reality.

    b. Work force composition. Changes in the growth, age, and educational level of the work force will affect employment opportunities. Women will continue to be an increasing part of the work force.

2. The labor force will increase approximately 19 percent from the mid 1980s to the mid 1990s; it is projected that 131 million people will be in the work force by 1995.

3. The number of people between ages 16 and 24 in the labor force is expected to decline through the mid 1990s. The number of people between the ages of 25 to 54 is expected to increase from two-thirds to nearly three-fourths of the work force during this same period of time. People will retire earlier; thus the number of people age 55 and over in the work force is projected to decline slightly.

4. The educational level of the population will continue to rise. Among individuals 25 to 35 today, nearly half have completed at least one year of college.

5. The number of women in the work force will continue to grow. By 1995, the number of women in the labor force is likely to grow to more than 60 percent. Approximately 60 percent of all women with preschool or school-age children are in the work force presently.

6. Since change is a constant now and is an anticipated constant for the future, it is important that you be able to deal with change.

Change can cause feelings of anxiety, fearfulness, and resistance.

7. To effectively deal with change, you should accept it, prepare for it, be creative, and be flexible.

8. Creativity is the ability to combine existing ideas or things in new ways. Creativity exists in all of us.

9. Flexibility can be defined as being able to see that multiple options exist in most situations and being free to choose from a wide variety of options.

10. Steps which you can take to help you deal with change are as follows:

    a. Understand why it is necessary.

    b. Determine what objectives are to be achieved.

    c. Establish guidelines for achieving the objectives.

    d. Determine the benefits associated with change.

    e. Evaluate the effectiveness of change and your ability to deal with it.

11. Office positions available include the following:

    a. Receptionists. The major role of a receptionist is to greet customers and other visitors to a company.

    b. Bookkeepers and Accounting Clerks. The business transactions of a company are handled by bookkeepers and accounting clerks. They record transactions in journals, on ledgers, and on computers; they also prepare periodic financial statements.

    c. Secretaries. Secretaries perform a variety of administrative and clerical tasks including scheduling appointments, filing, handling the mail, preparing correspondence, writing letters, and preparing reports.

    d. Word/Information Processing Specialists. These specialists operate various types of computers and word processing equipment. They must possess excellent keyboarding and proofreading skills and have a superior knowledge of grammar, punctuation, and spelling.

12. The office worker needs to develop competencies in the following areas:
    a. English
    b. Spelling
    c. Math
    d. Office equipment
    e. Keyboarding/typewriting
    f. Record keeping
    g. Note taking
    h. Transcribing
    i. Handwriting
    j. Accuracy
    k. Knowledge of reference sources
    l. Oral and written communication
    m. Human relations
    n. Decision making

PROFESSIONAL FORUM

You have worked for First State Bank for three years as a receptionist. You like your work and the people. Your immediate supervisor, Ms. Christine Hart, has just told you that a new computer has been ordered for you. You had difficulty learning to operate the computer that you now have, and you do not look forward to learning to operate another one. Ms. Hart told you that you would be given one week of training on the new computer.

You have just heard that there is a position available in the personnel department. The job is similar to the one you have now, and you would not have to learn a new machine. You like the people in the personnel department and feel you would enjoy working with them.

What should you do? Should you attempt to learn how to operate the new machine and stay where you are? Or should you apply for the job in the personnel department where you would not have to learn anything new? List the advantages and disadvantages of each position. Which job do you feel would offer the most growth for you?

FOR YOUR UNDERSTANDING

1. Discuss what is meant by, "Change is a constant in both the business world and our society today."
2. What factors have had a major impact on the business world of today?
3. How can you learn to cope with change?
4. What is the projected growth of office personnel in the future?
5. List ten competencies essential to office work.
6. How has this chapter changed your ideas of the business world and the role of the office worker?

OFFICE APPLICATIONS

On pages 273–281 are office applications that correlate with this chapter.

CHAPTER 2

Relationships

Studies show that 90 percent of the office worker's day involves working with others. It is very important that you work well with your employer and other office workers in your company. It is also important to relate effectively with people outside the company. Many times the office worker is the company's first contact with a prospective customer. The office worker's effectiveness can either give the customer a good impression, or it can convince the customer to never again call on that company. To be successful in working with others, it is important to know who you are. Take a look at yourself. What goes on inside you? What needs do you have? How do you communicate? This chapter will help you to evaluate yourself so that you can better relate and communicate with others.

GENERAL OBJECTIVES

Your general objectives for this chapter are to

1. Develop an understanding and acceptance of who you are.
2. Be aware of the relationship between your needs and the needs of your company.
3. Be able to communicate effectively with others.

YOU—A SUCCESS OR A FAILURE?

Do you know yourself? Do you accept yourself? Do you see yourself as a success or as a failure? Success and failure mean many different things to different people. So, before you attempt to answer these questions, success and failure must be defined.

Success. The successful person has a number of positive attributes. Here are some important ones.

Accepting Self. In order to be a success, you must have gained some degree of self-acceptance. Some of the most miserable people in the world are those who continually strive to be something they are not. Each of us has the ability to be a success in life. However, in the growing-up process, many people had an effect on your life—parents, brothers and sisters, classmates, etc. These people may have made you feel in some ways that you were not a capable person. Thus, you may have begun to see yourself as a failure.

Accepting yourself does not necessarily mean changing yourself. It does mean changing your mental picture of how you see yourself. Obviously you have faults and weaknesses as

15

all human beings have. However, you are not a *fault* or *weakness.* The fault or weakness may belong to you, but it does not become you. You are a worthwhile person who has both strengths and weaknesses. Accepting yourself means accepting your strengths and building on them, accepting your weaknesses but not dwelling on them. Accept yourself (all of you) for what you are — and start growing from there.

Trusting Self. Trusting self is being what you are, rather than trying to be a copy of someone else. You may not be what your best friend is or what your brother or sister is. So what? You are you — a unique person with your own special traits. Trusting self means allowing those special traits to come to the surface and realizing that you as a person have much to give to life.

Illustration 2-1. People Are Unique

Being Genuine. When you are genuine, you are a real person. You do not try to hide or ignore negative thoughts that you may have. You consciously accept these negative thoughts, but you do not allow the negativeness to consume you. For example, you realize that it is natural and normal to feel anger at times. The person who runs into trouble is the person who pretends negative feelings do not exist. The genuine person recognizes that everyone has negative feelings and accepts these feelings.

You recognize that positive feelings such as love and concern for others are natural and normal also. You are not ashamed to show open affection and concern for others when this is what you feel. Your genuineness comes through in your dealings with others in that you are sincere and straightforward.

You are not afraid to reach out and touch someone else. When is the last time you touched someone other than a girlfriend or a boyfriend or a member of your family? Most of us seem to be afraid to touch someone else in a sincere show of affection. Yet, all of us need to be touched. Studies have shown that babies need to be held and stroked. If they are denied this touching, both their physical and mental growth are retarded. We can accept touching as a need for babies, but as we grow older we sometimes feel to need touching is a weakness. It is not a weakness. The genuine person is able to touch others with sincerity.

If you are genuine, you choose goals that are important to you and try to attain these goals. You do not set goals because your family or friends see these goals as important. You realize that in setting your goals, mistakes may be made. You may set a goal and later decide that it is not a worthwhile goal. As a genuine person, you can learn from the goal-setting process.

Illustration 2-2. Touching Is Important

Being Open to Experience. To be open to your experiences means that you accept what is happening to you without letting that experience be colored by past prejudices and ideas. Your ideas and thoughts do not become set. You are willing to examine your ideas in relation to new experiences. It is not easy to be open to your experiences. To be open is to risk being threatened. You might be changed in some way. Many of us are afraid of change. We are afraid of the unknown. But growth means change.

Look for a minute at why it is not easy to be open to your experiences. Assume that your past experiences have taught you that females are more emotional and less rational in their thinking processes than males. And, assume that on every job you have held you have had a male supervisor. Now consider this situation. Your employer, who is male has been promoted recently to another position within the company, and a woman has become your boss. Immediately, upon being introduced to her, you distrust and dislike her. As the weeks go by she constantly demonstrates in her behaviors to you and others that she is extremely capable and competent. Yet, you refuse to recognize her competence due to your past experiences. Openness to experience means accepting the present, disregarding what your experiences may have been in the past. Openness isn't easy, but it is essential to personal growth.

Accepting Others. The more you accept yourself, the more you are able to accept others. Accepting others means letting other people be what they are without judging them. You do not demand that others change to fit your views. You accept them as worthy human beings with the capacity to be whatever is important to their individual needs. Appreciate them for what they are — not for what you think they should become. For you to become the very best person you can be, acceptance of others is crucial.

Failure. Since you have looked at the attributes of success, look now at these characteristics of failure.

Actions Directed Toward "Shoulds." Rather than being directed by self, the failure is di-

rected by the "shoulds" of others. For example, assume someone you admire and respect tells you that you should be an accountant. You have no interest in accounting, and you know that you do not have an aptitude for working with figures. Yet you decide to become an accountant because someone told you that you should be one. If you see yourself as a failure, you let other people provide the direction for your life since you feel your own thoughts and ideas must be inferior. You think that you have so many faults that no one will like you for yourself, so you must attempt to be something you are not.

Being Uncertain. Uncertainty is a way of avoiding mistakes and responsibility. It is based on the assumption that if no decision is made, nothing can go wrong. The failure is afraid of being wrong. If you consider yourself a failure, you have seen yourself as "wrong" so many times in life that you cannot bear being "wrong" again. Decision making becomes a life-or-death matter for you. Thus, you are continually uncertain as to what you should do. If you cannot avoid making a decision, you put it off as long as possible.

Being Lonely. The failure is lonely. If you see yourself as a failure, you use loneliness to protect yourself. You purposely cut the lines of communication with others to protect yourself against hurt. You feel that other people do not

Illustration 2-3. The Failure is Lonely

like or respect you. You are afraid of people and may often complain of having no friends.

Feeling Insecure. The failure is insecure because of feelings of inadequacy. If you feel you are a failure, you continually compare yourself to someone else and try to be what that person is. Therefore, you feel insecure because you cannot become exactly what your ideal person is. You refuse to look at your own capabilities and try to build on them. You continually measure yourself against an ideal and find yourself lacking.

YOU—A GROWING AND CHANGING PERSON

Presently, you may have more characteristics of the successful person, or you may have more characteristics of the failure. But, where you are now is not the most important point. What is important is realizing that personal growth is possible. As human beings, we do not stand still. Just as we grew in physical size from infancy to adulthood, so it is possible to grow in self-understanding and successful characteristics.

Is this growth easy? Is it quick? The answer to both questions is no. You cannot decide suddenly to become a successful person; to pluck the characteristics listed under success, and then easily attach them to yourself. Many inadequate attempts at self-growth are approached in this superficial manner. Real self-growth is a process rather than a product. It is continual.

Real self-growth implies change. As you allow new experiences to affect you, you become more aware of your feelings and also more aware of the world around you. You begin to realize that *all* trees are not green, that *all* men are not tough, and that *all* cats do not scratch. You observe a new situation as it is, rather than distorting it to fit your preconceived ideas. Such growth makes you more realistic in dealing with new people, new situations, and new problems. You become less rigid and more tolerant.

YOUR NEEDS

You can better understand yourself and other people if you understand basic human needs. According to Abraham Maslow, a noted psychologist, basic human needs fall into five categories—physical, safety, social, esteem, and self-actualization. These needs form a ladder. (See Illustration 2-4.) Unless you satisfy the lower level needs, you cannot satisfy the higher level needs. Consider these needs individually.

Physical Needs. Physical needs are at the lowest level of the ladder of needs. Examples of physical needs are hunger and thirst. You may never have known a real hunger or thirst. Many people cannot even imagine what it would be like to be hungry. Yet in parts of the world today people do go hungry. If you were hungry or thirsty, food or drink would be your most pressing need. Unless you could satisfy that hunger or thirst, you would not be thinking about such things as typing a letter in good form or helping someone with a problem. You would not be interested in learning something new. You would be trying to satisfy your deep need for food or drink.

Can this physical need be related to the office worker? In a general way, it can be. Businesses pay adequate salaries which provide money for their employees to satisfy their needs. When businesses have not paid adequate salaries, laws have been written. The minimum wage laws require businesses to pay employees what is considered an adequate wage to provide for the necessities of life.

Safety Needs. The next level of need is the safety need. You need to feel safe from physical harm. Our society has established a police force to ensure that we have law and order. None of us would want to live in a society in which we felt that physical harm might come to us at any time. You need to feel physically safe in your job also. Companies recognize this and provide such forms of security as retirement and sick leave.

In addition to the physical safety needs, an

Social Needs. The social need is third on the ladder. All of us need to feel that we are accepted by others. We need to feel that others see us as worthy, contributing persons. Companies have long recognized this need. Have you ever wondered why companies have coffee breaks; why some companies have recreation facilities for their employees; why desks are arranged in an office so that individuals are not isolated from one another? One of the main reasons is that companies recognize the social needs of their employees. Companies recognize that people need each other.

Esteem Needs. Another basic need is the need to be recognized. You need to feel that other people appreciate your opinions and ideas. Companies recognize that people have esteem needs. This is evidenced by such tangible things as private offices, names on office doors, the right to travel first-class on planes, and memberships in private clubs.

All too often, satisfying the esteem need is seen only in such tangible things as those just mentioned—in titles or privileges. If you were asked what you wanted to be, you might respond that you wanted to be an executive secretary. The executive secretarial position is considered the top rung on the secretarial ladder. It may mean to you that you have "made it" in your field. In reality, an executive secretarial job may not be any more challenging than a lower level secretarial job. In other words, the satisfaction of an esteem need should not come from a title that you may have acquired but from recognition of what you are as a person. You are unique. You may or may not want to be president of a company or an executive secretary. The important point is for you to feel successful in whatever you are doing. You do not have to be an executive secretary to be a success. In fact, you may be an executive secretary and not be successful at all. Remember the attributes of success—accept self, trust self, be genuine, be open to experience, and accept others. In order for your esteem needs to be satisfied, you must feel that you are recognized and respected.

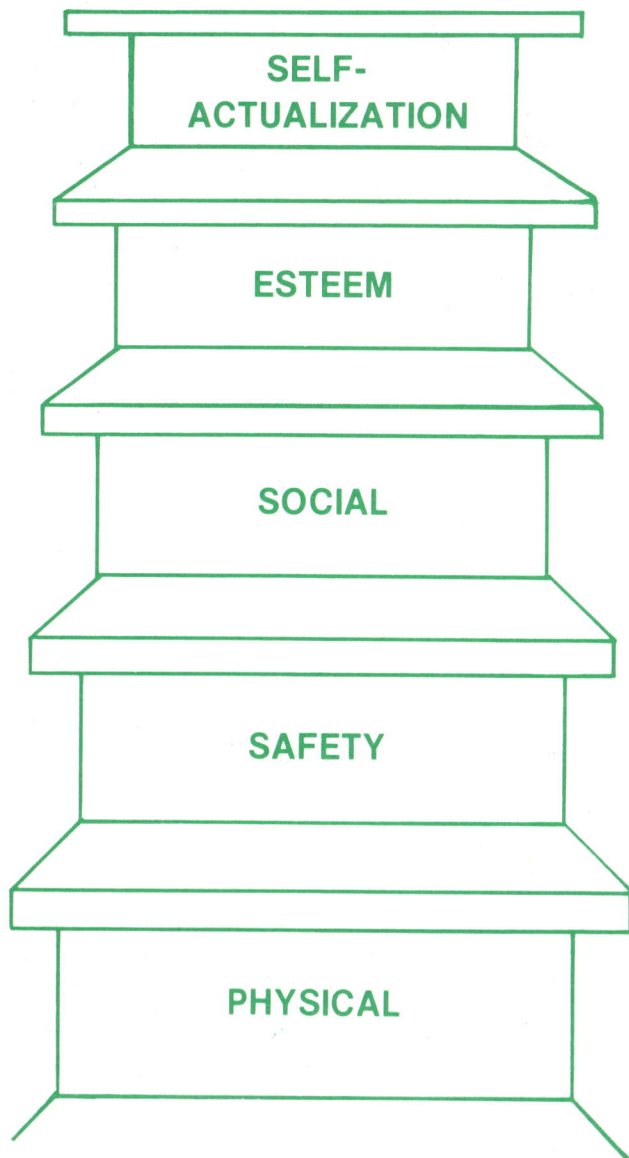

Illustration 2-4. Basic Human Needs

employee needs to feel safe and secure with the people in the company and with the company policies. You, as an office worker, can contribute to satisfying your safety needs. Assume that a new typist is hired by your company. On the first day of work or maybe even the first week or month, the employee does not feel secure in the new surroundings. You can help by explaining the rules and regulations of the company, by answering any questions about the job, and by explaining what is expected of the new employee.

Self-Actualization. The highest level of need is self-actualization. This need means that an individual is striving to be the very best person possible. This person has been able to satisfactorily meet individual needs at the lower levels and is free now to become whatever he or she can. Obviously, then, self-actualization means something different to each person. You cannot define for someone else what that person should or can be. Nor can another person define for you what you should be. Self-actualization for you may mean being the best typist you can be. To another person, it may mean pursuing creativity in music or art. The self-actualizing person is one who fulfills his or her own unique capabilities. This individual cannot be defined by what he or she is "doing," but can be defined by what he or she "is."

Unfortunately, most people do not reach this top level of needs. Most of us stop somewhere between the social and esteem needs.

YOU AND OTHERS

Now that you have considered your basic needs, consider some of the needs of others. Just as you need to satisfy your basic needs for hunger and thirst, safety, acceptance, importance, and freedom to become whatever your abilities will allow, so others have those same basic needs. In the office situation it is important that you recognize such needs.

Recognize Other Employees' Needs. The people with whom you work have needs for friendship and recognition. They need to be accepted as part of an office team — one that works together to do the best job possible. Others need to realize that you value them as worthwhile human beings and that you consider them professional friends. This statement does not mean that you are expected to socialize outside the office with other office employees. It merely means that you are capable of cooperating with other office employees to accomplish a task. It means that you work to achieve harmony in the office rather than tearing down or gossiping about others. It means that you recog-

nize other people's needs to contribute to the organization. Thus, if someone receives a promotion or some other recognition, congratulate him or her on the accomplishment, rather than being upset or jealous because you were not recognized. Recognizing others' needs means that you accept new employees into the group — that you do not form cliques or closed groups where no outsiders are welcome.

Obviously these suggestions are only a few of the many ways in which you can recognize other office workers' basic needs. The important point to remember is that these needs exist. Then you can be alert to ways of satisfying them.

Accept Others' Backgrounds and Values. Not everyone you work with in an office will have the same background or values that you have. You may have grown up in a small town, your parents may have stressed hard work as a value, and you may have been an only child. A person who works next to you in the office may have grown up in a large city. His or her parents may have stressed the fine arts as a value, and he or she may be from a large family. Because of your different backgrounds and experiences, you probably view things differently. But such different views do not make one of you "right" and one of you "wrong." They merely mean that you are different. If you are able to recognize and accept differences in other people, you will have come a long way toward becoming a successful human being.

YOU AND THE COMPANY

You have looked at who you are, at what some of your basic needs are, and at the basic needs of others. Look now at how you fit into a company.

What is a company? It is an organization with needs, and it is a collection of individuals each with needs and wants. The company's needs consist of such things as producing a product or service, making a profit, and growing and expanding. The individual needs of employees are met by such things as making enough money to provide an acceptable standard of living, satisfying social needs by being a part of a company's family, and satisfying esteem needs by having a job that is important. As you have seen previously, companies do not ignore the basic needs of a person. If a company is not helping you to satisfy your needs, you will probably not give that company your full effort.

Assume that you need to feel that you belong to the office group. Yet your desk is completely isolated from the other workers in the office. Your coffee breaks and lunchtimes are different from the other office workers. If your need to belong is not satisfied in some way, you will become unhappy on the job. You will not produce at your best level. In other words, you will become an unhappy, nonproductive employee. Thus, your need will affect the company's needs. The company needs to produce a product or service. But if you are being an inefficient, non-productive worker, you are hindering the company from producing that product or service.

In order for the company and the individual to operate at full capacity, the individual's needs and the company's needs must be compatible. Consider an example of opposing needs and then an example of compatible needs.

Opposing Needs. At 2 p.m., your supervisor asks you to get a report out by 3 p.m. After looking at it, you know it will take you at least one hour to prepare it. Your coffee break is set at 2:30 p.m. You insist on taking your coffee break rather than finishing the report. Here, your social needs are in opposition to your supervisor's need to get out the report. Your needs and your supervisor's needs are in conflict.

If this type of situation exists often, you can readily see that both you and your supervisor would suffer. The essential work of the company would not get done on time. Your supervisor would hold you responsible for not getting out the work. You might be fired. Or if you were not fired, you would suffer in that you would not get raises or promotions. Obviously when the needs of the individual and the company are in opposition, both suffer.

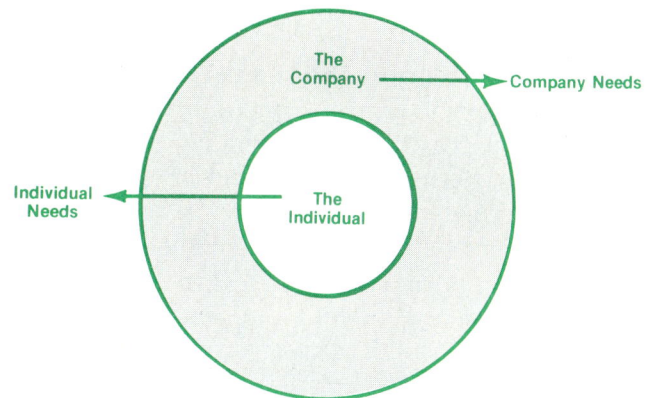

Illustration 2-5. Opposing Individual and Company Needs

Compatible Needs. Contrast that situation to one in which your needs and the company needs are compatible. Your supervisor has again asked you to complete the report by 3 p.m. before you take your coffee break. Although you have social needs, you can satisfy those needs by going to coffee at 3:15 p.m. after the report is out. Your objective is to be the best office worker you can be; you key the report and then take a break.

In this situation, there is an adjustment process. The office worker adjusted break time to satisfy the need of completing the report on time, thereby satisfying the need of being a good office worker. In a company situation, the adjusting process is essential. You will have to adjust your needs at times to meet company needs. The company will in turn have to recognize your needs and not place excessive demands on you.

When the needs of the individual and the company are compatible or can be adjusted to be compatible, both the objective of the individual and the objective of the organization are accomplished. Your objective is to be a good office worker. If you continue to operate in this manner, no doubt you will be recognized for your contributions. The objective of your employer is satisfied in that the report got out on time.

It is necessary that as an office worker you understand the relationship between your needs and the needs of the company. The company is a group of individuals operating at all levels on the ladder of needs. If your needs are continually in total opposition to the company's needs, both you and the company will suffer. You become a part of a company because you feel in some way that the company can satisfy your needs. Perhaps this satisfaction merely exists at the lowest level in that the money you make can provide you with the means for satisfying your physical needs. Or, this satisfaction may be at a high level—the esteem or self-actualization level. In any case, only when your needs and the company's needs are compatible does the greatest benefit exist for both parties. Personal objectives and organizational objectives can be accomplished at the same time.

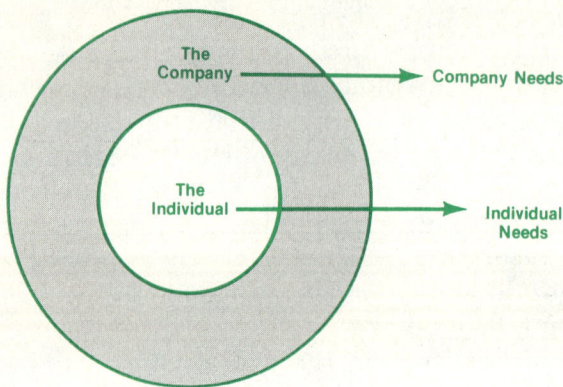

Illustration 2-6. Compatible Individual and Company Needs

COMMUNICATION

A major part of human relations is communication skill. On any job, it is essential that you communicate with your employer, your fellow workers, and people outside the company. Business today more than ever before understands the importance of satisfactory communication. Business recognizes that satisfactory communication is necessary if employees are to achieve understanding and cooperation, if employees and employers are to be able to work together, and if a desirable image of the business is to be presented to people outside the company. Communication is not tied only to a business environment. It is difficult to imagine any kind of activity involving people in which

some form of communication does not occur. Effective communication must be developed.

What is communication? Communication is a two-way process in which information is accurately received and understood in order that some action can be taken. Dissect that definition. Communication is a two-way process. Often we fail to recognize this aspect of communication. Thus, communication is often seen as one individual telling another individual his or her thoughts or feelings on a subject. The information may or may not be getting through to the person intended to receive it.

Unless you know that information is received in some way, it is not a two-way process. In other words, communication is a circular process. Notice in Illustration 2-7 that as one individual communicates with another, the second individual receives that communication and in turn responds to it.

Notice also that the definition states that "...information is accurately received and understood." Of course, you understand exactly what you are saying to the other individual. Because you understand it so thoroughly, it is difficult to realize that the other individual may not understand. Why is it so difficult for another person to understand us? What problems are involved in communications?

Illustration 2-7. Two-Way Communication

Problems in Communication. Some of the problems in communication are the following:

Hearing the Expected. All of us are guilty of sizing up an individual and then only hearing what we think that individual should say. Assume that you believe that all employers are hard-driving, demanding individuals. Your employer, in reality, may be a caring, undemanding individual. Yet, when this person gives you a job to do, you immediately assume *don't* that he or she is being demanding.

Ignoring Conflicting Information. If you already have predetermined feelings about a subject, you tend to ignore new information on the subject. This new information may be valid, but you have made up your mind otherwise. For example, assume that you believe that rock music is the only worthwhile music. You attend a music concert in which a wide range of music is presented from country, rock, popular, to the classics. You really enjoy listening to all the music, but you refuse to admit it. You have already made up your mind that all music except rock is worthless. So, you refuse to accept that you actually can enjoy other types of music.

Evaluating the Source. "The first time I met Jane Rogers I disliked her. She acted like she knew everything, and I decided she really knew nothing." *Don't prejudge allow yourself*

It is difficult for us to separate what we hear from our feelings about the person saying it. If you like the person, you tend to accept what the person says. If you dislike the person, you tend to ignore what the person is saying. *to hear them out*

Viewing Things Differently. As you have learned earlier, due to different backgrounds, values, etc., people view things differently. Consider one example. Assume that you feel that work is fun, and your friend feels that work is drudgery. Both you and your friend notice an office group in which people are laughing and enjoying life. To you, the laughter means that the office is a pleasant place to work. People are enjoying their work and much is being accomplished. However, your friend sees the same situation altogether differently and assumes that everyone in the office is "goofing off." No work is being accomplished. After all, how could you be laughing and getting any work done?

Meaning Not the Same for Everyone. The same word does not mean the same thing to everyone. Much of our meaning for words is derived from the culture and age in which we live. Consider this verse from an anonymous poet.

Remember when hippie meant big in the hips,
And a trip involved travel in cars, planes, and
   ships?
When pot was a vessel for cooking things in,
And hooked was what grandmother's rug may
   have been?
When fix was a verb that meant mend or repair,
And be in meant merely existing somewhere?
When neat meant well-organized, tidy, and clean,
And grass was a ground cover, normally green?
When groovy meant furrowed with channels and
   hollows,
And birds were winged creatures, like robins and
   swallows?
When fuzz was a substance, real fluffy like lint,
And bread came from bakeries and not from the
   mint?
When roll meant a bun, and rock was a stone,
And hang-up was something you did with the
   phone?
It's groovy, man, groovy, but English it's not.
Methinks that our language is going to pot.

Many words have several meanings as is illustrated by the verse. We certainly cannot assume that just because we attach a certain meaning to a word that the next person will attach the same meaning.

Even if the same word may not have different meanings to two persons, a statement may cause two persons to respond in two different ways. Consider this situation. Your supervisor tells you and Helen to do a certain job as quickly as you can. You have your part of the job done in 30 minutes. To you, this statement really meant that the job should be done immediately. However, Helen does not have her part of the job done until three days later. She interpreted the same statement in an entirely different manner.

Differences in Position. Breakdowns occur many times because of differences in positions.

Realize we all see things differently.

You may be hesitant to tell your supervisor that you do not understand what he or she has said to you because of your supervisor's position. You may feel that you will be considered stupid if you admit to not understanding. But if you do not understand, how can you perform? Hours of wasted time can be saved by admitting that you do not understand. Certainly you want to try to understand the first time someone tells you something. You should always listen carefully to explanations. But if you do not understand the explanation, tell the person that you do not understand. Wasting your supervisor's time and your time by doing the job incorrectly causes more problems.

Illustration 2-8. Communication Differences

Nonverbal Communication. Much of our communication is nonverbal and barriers can occur because of what we communicate nonverbally. The tone of voice we use when saying something tells the listener something about us. Our facial expressions relay our feelings. Our gestures tell the listener something about what we mean. Our physical touching or closeness to the other person says something to that person. This nonverbal part of communication is quite important. It has been said that 55 percent of our meaning in communicating with

others comes from body language. Thirty-seven percent comes from tone of voice. Eight percent comes from what we actually say. As can be seen from these percentages, our body language and the way we say something are more important to the listener than what we say.

Effective Communication. As you are aware by now, there are many communication problems. But, communication can be improved. How? Here are a few suggestions.

Listen With Openness. One of the major problems in communication is our tendency to evaluate the person who is communicating. Real communication cannot occur as long as we evaluate the person rather than what that person is saying. Real communication can only occur when we listen with openness to what the other person is saying. You need to try to understand what the other person is saying from his or her point of view. Obviously, this approach is not easy. If you listen with openness, you may find your own attitudes influenced by what the other person is saying. And, it is not easy to change our own attitudes. However, listening with openness is worth the effort for the gain in communication that results.

Be Sensitive to the Receiver's World. Whether the communication is written or oral, you need to be aware and sensitive to the receiver's point of view. Realize that the person receiving the information has needs and problems just as you do. This person may have had a difficult day and may have trouble understanding or accepting what you are communicating. Try to understand this person's needs.

Use Direct, Simple Language. It is important to use direct, simple language in both written and oral communications. It is usually easier for us to use simple language when we talk with someone than when we write. Written communication is many times sprinkled with big words and long sentences. Why? The writer is probably attempting to impress the reader with his or her large vocabulary and literary genius. However, the reverse is usually true. The reader is unimpressed. So, whether the communication is written or oral, use direct, simple language. You will get your point across easier. The listener or reader can get lost in what you are trying to say when the sentences are long and may miss your point completely.

Utilize Feedback. When communicating with someone, listen to what that person is saying. This does not mean words alone. Remember there are many ways to communicate — words, gestures, facial expressions, tone of voice. Watch for the nods of the head or the look of dismay. Hear what the other person is saying to you through that person's various means of communicating. If you do not feel the other person understands you, try to explain your point in a different manner; ask questions and pause at times to give the person an opportunity to respond. There is always danger that you may become so involved in what you are trying to communicate that you fail to hear what the other person is communicating. Remember, communication is a two-way process. Communicating takes two actively involved persons.

Repeat When Necessary. Repeating points can aid the communication process. You might be hesitant to repeat a point, but you should not be. The listener, due to involvement with his or her own problems or for many other reasons, might not be tuned in to you. You may need to repeat your major points several times. However, you should not necessarily repeat them just as you have said them previously. Repeat your points in a different way. Think about the times it has been necessary for someone to

explain a problem to you in several different ways before you understood.

Time Messages Carefully. Have you ever blurted out one of your urgent problems to your supervisor just to discover that this person was so busy with his or her problems that you were not heard? Again, you need to be aware of what is going on in the world of the receiver. We cause problems for ourselves by trying to communicate with someone when that person is not ready to receive our communication. Stop, look, and observe what is going on in the world of the receiver before you attempt to communicate.

For you as an office worker, timing messages carefully is crucial. Think for a minute about what it means. It means that you do not interrupt an important meeting with a problem that you could have handled yourself or found someone else to handle. It means that you do not rush in with an unimportant message after your employer has had an extremely trying morning. It means you realize that a badly timed message can cause confusion or irritation rather than aid communication.

As an office worker, communication is a vital part of your job. Remember, communication means that information is accurately received and understood by all individuals involved. Problems in communication are many. A few have been presented here in the hope that you will become aware of the importance and complexity of the area. You can communicate more effectively, but it takes awareness and effort on your part.

FOR YOUR REVIEW

The following review will help you remember the important points of this chapter.

1. A success: accepts self, trusts self, is genuine, is open to experience, and accepts others.
2. A failure: directs actions toward "shoulds." The failure is uncertain, lonely, and insecure.
3. Personal growth is a process; it is continual.

4. Understanding and accepting self and others is basic to good human relations.
5. The basic human needs are: physical, safety, social, esteem, and self-actualization.
6. Company needs and individual needs must be compatible if each is to be successful.
7. Communication is a two-way process in

which information is accurately received and understood in order that some action can be taken.

8. Some of the problems in communication include the following:
   a. Hearing the expected.
   b. Ignoring conflicting information.
   c. Evaluating the source.
   d. Viewing things differently.
   e. Meaning not the same for everyone.
   f. Differences in position.
   g. Nonverbal communication.
9. Communication may be improved in the following ways:
   a. Listening with openness.
   b. Being sensitive to the receiver.
   c. Using direct, simple language.
   d. Utilizing feedback.
   e. Repeating when necessary.
   f. Timing messages carefully.

Yoko Saga has just finished a two-year post-secondary program and has been employed as a stenographer for the Chamber of Commerce. Here is the problem with which Yoko is faced.

I worked hard while I was in school, and I feel I developed many valuable skills. I was selected as the most outstanding student in my class. I was excited about my new job and eager to put to work the things I had learned in school.

On the first day on my job, I was introduced to Bill Roth. Bill had worked as a secretary for the company for ten years. I was told that Bill would be happy to help me with any questions I might have. Bill was quite helpful.

After a week on the job, I felt fairly comfortable. I began to look around for things where I felt improvement could be made. I discovered that the filing system was not a good one. I knew I could make some changes that would be beneficial—changes that would enable correspondence to be located more rapidly. I was excited about making these changes. I went to Bill with my ideas. Bill immediately became almost hostile. He told me that the filing system had worked for ten years, and he was sure it would continue to work.

From what you have learned in this chapter, answer the following questions.

1. Why do you feel Bill reacted the way he did?
2. Were any of Bill's needs threatened? If so, what needs?
3. How would you have handled the situation?
4. Should the inadequate filing system have been ignored by Yoko?

1. Define success and failure.
2. Identify and discuss two characteristics which you consider most important for a successful individual.
3. Explain the importance of growth and change to an individual.
4. List and discuss the five basic human needs.
5. How do the five basic human needs affect your relationship with other office employees?
6. Distinguish between opposing and compatible needs within a company.
7. Identify five communication problems.
8. List and discuss five ways in which communication can be improved.

On pages 284–285 are office applications that correlate with this chapter.

CHAPTER 3

Effective Listening

Listening is extremely important. Studies show that the average person spends 70 percent of his or her day communicating; 45 percent of that communication time is spent listening. Since we spend such a large percent of our time listening, it is important that we do it effectively. However, most authorities agree that listening is the weakest chain in the communication process.

Hearing does not automatically imply listening. A person can hear the sounds that come from another person's mouth all day long and not understand the words. Thus, effective listening demands a concentrated effort on the part of the listener. Businesses consider listening to be an essential skill, a skill that is crucial for the office worker. A number of studies show that listening is one of the top priorities for office personnel.

Even though we spend a major part of each day listening, we are more complacent about our listening skills than most other skills. Little effort is put forth in becoming a more effective listener. This chapter is designed to help you become a better listener. You will learn about various listening barriers and how to overcome these barriers.

GENERAL OBJECTIVES

Your general objectives for this chapter are to

1. Understand what listening is.

2. Identify why listening is important to your effectiveness.
3. Recognize listening barriers.
4. Improve your listening skills through the use of effective listening techniques.

WHAT IS LISTENING?

Listening is more than the mere perception of sound. Registering sound vibrations is hearing, while listening implies making sense out of what is heard. Research studies show that most of us listen with only 25 to 50 percent efficiency. In other words, 50 to 75 percent of what we hear is never processed. Moreover, even when we do process what we hear, we may not grasp the full implications of what is meant.

Listening is the complete process by which oral language, communicated by a source, is received, recognized, attended to, comprehended, and retained. The listener attends to the oral language of the source with the intent of acquiring meaning. Thus, the main components of listening are not located in the ears, just as the main components of seeing are not located in the eyes. Our ears hear the sound vibrations to which we attend and comprehend, but our listening is based on our needs, desires, interests, previous experiences, and learning. As you can see, then, listening is a complex phenomenon that involves the total individual. As we listen, our process of thought, which is composed of many separate and independent concepts, flows into ideas and emotions and affects what we hear. We will consider three elements of the listening process—attention, comprehension, and retention—and we will note several levels of listening.

Attention. Attention refers to the awareness of stimuli. However, we cannot attend to the numerous stimuli by which we are constantly bombarded. So, we choose to respond to certain stimuli by considering three basic factors: (1) the nature of the stimuli, (2) our previous experiences or learnings, and (3) our needs, desires, and interests. We generally attend more to the things that easily fit within our expectations. Our tendency is to listen to what we want to hear and to ignore stimuli that do not fulfill our expectations or needs.

Comprehension. Comprehension is another element of the listening process. It refers to the integration of stimuli with our past experiences and learnings. Except for the very young child,

people are seldom exposed to completely new stimuli. Therefore, in most stimuli to which we attend, we can find some similarity to current or past experiences. This ability to link new stimuli with past experiences allows us to predict future results of current happenings.

Retention. A third element of the listening process is retention. Studies show that two months after a person hears something, he or she remembers only about one fourth of it. Yet, the ability to retain meanings for our own use or to reproduce meanings for others is one of the most important elements of listening. Retention can be improved through several methods, such as repeating, visualizing, and stressing main ideas. Thus, listening carefully to a speaker's main points, mentally repeating them to yourself, visualizing a picture of what is being said, and carefully observing any pictures the speaker uses can help improve your retention.

Seven Levels of Listening. Listening takes place at seven different levels. These levels are not static; they constantly change according to what is happening within the individual.

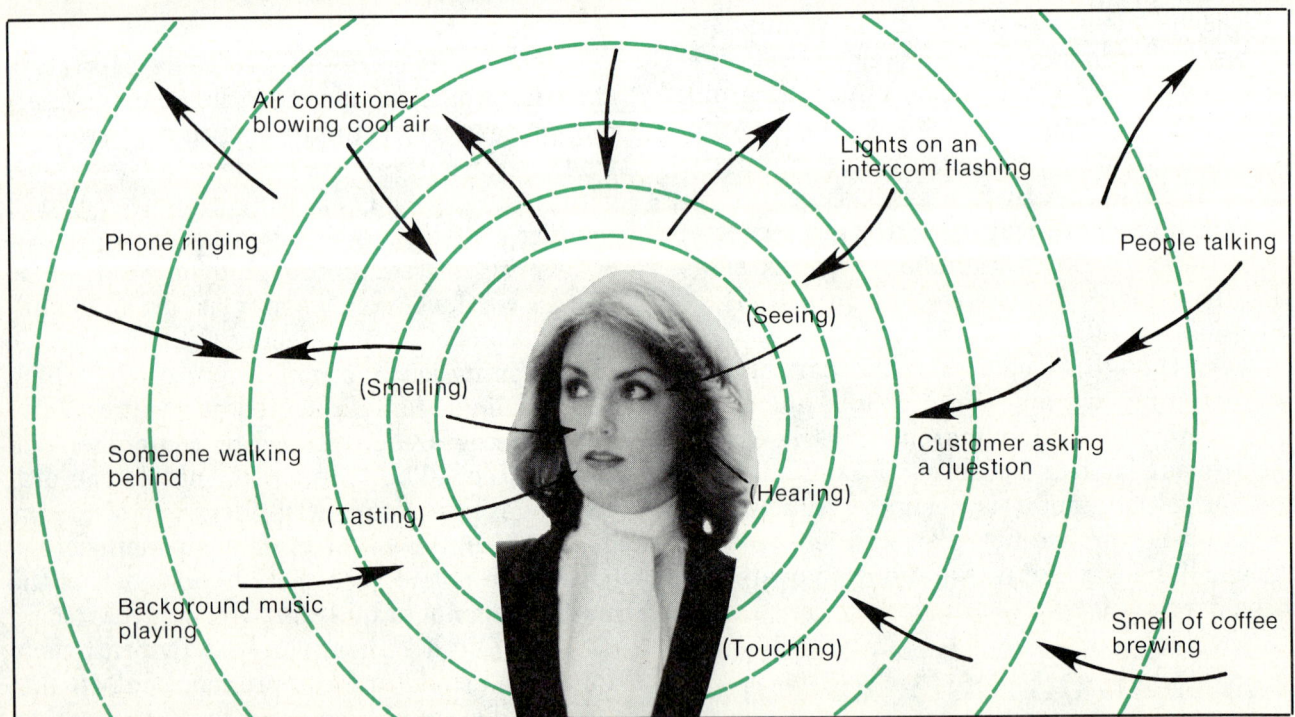

Illustration 3-1. Listening Involves the Total Individual

At the first level of listening, we isolate sounds, facts, ideas, etc. We recognize the presence of items, but make no analysis or evaluation. At the second level of listening, we identify those aspects which we have isolated. Then, at the third level, we integrate what we hear with past experiences and learnings. For example, in a debate, the successful participant relates newly presented issues with ideas previously discovered in the process of study and preparation.

At the fourth level of listening, we inspect new information. It is like fitting a new piece into a jigsaw puzzle. We examine patterns, and we note similarities and differences. Thus, we begin to evaluate. The fifth level is one in which we interpret what we hear. A person at the interpretation level translates what he or she hears into significant meaning based on his or her beliefs, judgments, and experiences. At the sixth level, mental interpolation occurs. Interpolation is the inserting of words into a conversation. Since it is impossible for any speaker to say all there is to say about a subject, a listener, at the interpolation stage, will give meaning to a speaker's words according to the message the listener thinks is intended. However, if we distort ideas or attitudes by our inaccurate or inappropriate interpolation, our listening becomes less effective than if we had remained at a lower level of noting only what the speaker said. At the seventh level of listening, we introspect; that is, we note the effect of the words on us.[1] Analyzing these levels of listening can help you become a more effective listener.

WHY LISTEN?

Now that you understand what listening is, consider why listening is so important to you.

Listening Increases Personal Effectiveness. If you listen carefully to other people's conversations, what do you hear? Many times

you hear conversations that could be called unheard dialogues, because each person talks, but neither listens. In other words, there may as well be a brick wall separating the two people. Effective listening breaks down those walls. Your ability to listen increases your personal effectiveness, because it affects what you know, what you experience, and ultimately what you become.

As you are aware from your educational experience, listening in a classroom affects your level of knowledge. Much of the information you receive in class is through verbal messages relayed by your instructors. Thus, what you learn is based on your ability to listen.

However, even in informal educational settings, knowledge is imparted through verbal means. You have already learned that as you listen you link what is being said to your past experiences, thereby predicting future directions for yourself. Ineffective listening reduces the number of linkages and thus the number of new experiences.

Listening Increases Job Effectiveness. Poor listening is responsible for a tremendous amount of waste in business. If each worker in

Illustration 3-2. Listening Increases Job Effectiveness

---

[1]Seth A. Fessenden, "Levels of Listening — A Theory," *Listening: Readings,* edited by Sam Duker (New York: The Scarecrow Press, Inc., 1966), pp. 28-33.

America made only a $20 listening mistake each year, billions of dollars would be lost. Letters would have to be retyped, appointments would have to be rescheduled, shipments would have to be reshipped, etc. Furthermore, through ineffective listening, the chain of command would lose its importance. Ideas, which can be distorted as much as 80 percent as they travel through the chain of command, would make employees and managers feel alienated and misunderstood.

Conversely, effective listening can help you on the job in the following ways:

1. Providing you with information that helps get the job done correctly.
2. Giving you increased job knowledge that allows you to learn more about your job and thus prepares you for advancement.
3. Promoting better understanding of your co-workers—understanding when they are upset, angry, and unhappy. Such understanding assists your communication with others.
4. Fostering cooperation between you and others. If you really listen to other people, they are more likely to listen to you. Effective listening allows the two of you to work closely together in completing a job.

LISTEN TO WHOM?

The obvious answer to that question is: You should listen to others—to your co-workers, your employer, your family, your friends, and all the people with whom you come in contact. The less obvious answer to that question is: You should listen to yourself.

Listen to Yourself. Know what is going on inside of you. In the last chapter you learned about the importance of knowing yourself. The level at which you know and understand yourself affects your listening ability. Listening to yourself basically means being open to your own messages, both the internal and the external ones. By listening to yourself you become more aware of your own internal biases and prejudices. You are able to answer the following questions: "What do I value?" "What are my

biases?" and "What are my prejudices?" You also become more aware of the influential and external factors in your environment such as people, noises, or surroundings. As you become more sensitive to your own frame of references and to their influence on what you hear, you will be more likely to understand another person's intent. When someone else is talking, you can ask yourself the following questions about what is being said: "How does this information relate to what I have always believed?" "Why do I believe what I believe?" "Is there a factual basis for my belief?" "Is the evidence presented here significant enough to alter my beliefs?" People who truly understand themselves can more readily listen to and accept differences in others.

Listen to Others. As an employee, you must exercise good listening skills when working with your employer, with other employees in the office, and with customers. Your willingness to listen to others on the job furthers the efficient production of the work that must be done. Effective listening also allows you to understand and relate to people in a way that ensures a more pleasant work environment.

Illustration 3-3. Listen to Others

YOUR LISTENING EFFECTIVENESS

Before you consider both ineffective and effective listening techniques, take the Listening Effectiveness Test on page 32 to determine your listening effectiveness at present. Rate yourself by checking the *Always, Sometimes,* or *Never* column.

INEFFECTIVE LISTENERS

Several characteristics produce poor listening behavior. Consider the following ineffective listeners. Are you ever guilty of such characteristics?

The Talker. Unfortunately many of us are so intent on discussing what has happened to us that we have difficulty waiting for the other person to finish talking so that we can start talking. In fact, many times the eager talker will interrupt the speaker to get his or her point across. Such individuals absorb little of what the other person says. In addition, they usually are planning their story while the other person is talking. Such behavior causes little to be heard other than the sound of the speaker's voice.

The Attention Faker. Have you ever talked to someone who made good eye contact with you while you were talking but when it came time for the person to respond you realized that she or he had not heard a word? Or have you ever sat in a classroom and intently watched the instructor during an entire lecture but were unable to answer any questions about the lesson? Most of us are good at adopting an outward posture that leads the speaker to believe we are listening when actually we are thinking of something else.

The Easily Distracted. Most people speak approximately 125 words a minute, yet it is believed that the brain can process information at about 500 words a minute. Listening allows plenty of time for the mind to wander. Unless the listener is committed to listening to the speaker, it is easy to become distracted.

Distraction can be in the form of external noises or movement, either inside or outside the room. For example, when passing a classroom, have you ever watched the number of eyes that follow you down the hall?

Distractions can also be in the form of internal noise, such as a problem that is bothering you. You may take the time in between the speaker's words to think about your problem; in doing so, you tune out the speaker for several minutes. When you finally tune back in, the speaker is usually on another point and you are lost.

The Outguesser. Have you ever known someone who would never let you finish a sentence but always finished it for you? That person may have assumed time was being saved, but on the contrary, time was actually lost. Many times the outguesser makes an inaccurate assumption concerning your message. You, therefore, have to stop and explain that what the outguesser said was not what you intended, before you can continue to say what you did intend. Such behavior causes not only a time problem, but generally an emotional problem as well. The speaker becomes upset with the listener's behavior; attempted communication often stops.

LISTENING BARRIERS IN BUSINESS

Because of the nature of businesses, certain barriers exist that foster poor listening habits. Some of these barriers are as follows.

Status. Status is the ranking of people into relative positions of prestige; certain rewards accompany such positions. Job titles provide a way of making status distinctions in business. A manager has more status than a shipping clerk; your supervisor has more status than you. Status affects the manner in which people listen to each other. For example, if your supervisor gives you job instructions, you usually are

Listening Effectiveness Test

1. When people talk to me, I find it difficult to keep my mind on the subject at hand.
   Always_____   Sometimes_____   Never_____

2. I listen only for facts.
   Always_____   Sometimes_____   Never_____

3. Certain words and ideas can prejudice me against a speaker to the point that I cannot listen objectively to what is being said.
   Always_____   Sometimes_____   Never_____

4. When I think a speaker has nothing worthwhile to say, I deliberately turn my thoughts to other things.
   Always_____   Sometimes_____   Never_____

5. I can tell by a person's appearance if he or she will have something worthwhile to say.
   Always_____   Sometimes_____   Never_____

6. When someone is talking to me, I try to make the person think I am paying attention even when I am not.
   Always_____   Sometimes_____   Never_____

7. I am easily distracted by outside sights and sounds.
   Always_____   Sometimes_____   Never_____

8. I interrupt the speaker to get my point across.
   Always_____   Sometimes_____   Never_____

9. When someone else is talking, I plan what I will say next.
   Always_____   Sometimes_____   Never_____

10. I frequently criticize the speaker's delivery or mannerisms.
    Always_____   Sometimes_____   Never_____

11. I use the difference between the talking time of the speaker and my own comprehension time to analyze and relate the speaker's points.
    Always_____   Sometimes_____   Never_____

12. I am aware of the nonverbal communication of others.
    Always_____   Sometimes_____   Never_____

13. I try to understand what the other person is feeling as he or she talks.
    Always_____   Sometimes_____   Never_____

14. I ask questions when I do not understand what the speaker is saying.
    Always_____   Sometimes_____   Never_____

How did you do? To be the most effective listener, you should have checked "never" on the first ten questions and "always" on the last four questions.

much more inclined to listen to what he or she is saying than if a co-worker gives you instructions. You also may have some built-in fear or apprehension of your supervisor since she or he usually controls your raises, your job promotion, and even your continued employment. Thus, you may not hear something correctly because the emotion of fear impedes the listening process.

Illustration 3-4. Status Can Affect Listening

Hidden Agendas. Individuals within the work environment often function on two levels: one level is what they say, the other level is what they think. An individual's aspirations can contribute to hidden agendas. For example, assume you and your co-worker are in competition for the same promotion. What you tell your co-worker and what that co-worker hears can be influenced by your desire to be promoted. Conversely what your co-worker tells you and what you hear can be influenced by your co-worker's hope for promotion.

The Grapevine. Informal communication networks which are created by friendships and social associations within the work environment form the grapevine. This informal chan-

nel of communication is very important in any organization as it provides a quick communication channel. However, the grapevine can hinder your listening process. A negative aspect of the grapevine is that it often carries rumors. Thus, each message you hear from the grapevine should be checked for accuracy before it is accepted as fact.

Social Barriers. Social barriers result from differences that are perceived because of ethnicity, age, sex, and experience. Real, or perceived, differences in the experiences and values of persons with diverse backgrounds contribute to blind spots in each person's ability to understand and tolerate others. Although differences in individuals are often not as great as is thought, blind spots can occur, as long as the perception of differences is in the individuals' minds.

Word Barriers. Words mean different things to different people. Words such as *great, small, good,* and *bad* are open to interpretation by the listener. Thus, the intended meaning of a supervisor may be misinterpreted by the employee, unless both persons use the same frame of reference. If a supervisor tells an employee that productivity must be increased to a high level, the employee may hear *high* as meaning *unrealistic.*

Technological change has also contributed to word barriers. New words such as microcomputers, silicon chips, and telecommunications are constantly entering our vocabulary. But they do not mean something to the entire population. Therefore, if you are working with a computer specialist and you have little knowledge of computers, you may have trouble listening to what he or she is saying, since you are not able to interpret the meaning of the words. Terminology that is not understood by the majority of the population should be defined by the speaker.

LISTENING CORRECTIONS

Several false assumptions exist concerning listening. You have already learned one — hearing and listening are the same. Two other faulty assumptions are (1) intelligent people listen well and (2) training in listening is unnecessary. Studies show that intelligence and listening are not highly correlated. Certainly a poor intellect has something to do with listening difficulty, but many intelligent people are poor listeners. Little emphasis is given to teaching listening in school, because it has long been assumed that if a person hears, he or she listens. There have even been skeptics who doubt the possibility of teaching listening. However, a number of studies have been done which compare those who have been pre-trained in listening with those who have been post-trained in listening. These studies show that after 12 weeks of listening training, gains in listening ability increased from 25 to 52 percent.

Listen—How? Concentrated effort on a number of different techniques can help you become a better listener.

Listen for Facts. Catalog the speaker's words. Use the differential time between how long it takes the speaker to say the words (an average of 125 words a minute) and how long it takes you to comprehend them (approximately 500 words a minute) in order to review the key ideas presented. Raise questions in your mind about the material. Relate what the speaker is saying with your own experience. Mentally repeat key ideas or associate key points with related ideas. Listening is not a passive activity in which you act as a sponge to soak up what is being said. Good listening is hard work, and it requires concentration and active participation on your part.

Listen for Feelings. Listen to what the speaker is *not* saying as well as to what he or she is saying. What is the speaker's feeling when she says, "I will be glad to do that report over for the third time."

Respect the Speaker. Appreciate the speaker's values, perceptions, cultural background, and expectations. It isn't necessary for you to accept these values and perceptions as part of your own life, but it is necessary for you to try to understand the speaker.

Withhold Evaluation. Try to understand the speaker's intended message without arguing (overtly or covertly) with the speaker. Admittedly, such behavior is difficult. If you are opposed to an idea that a person is talking about, you tend to become emotional. Therefore, work hard at being objective. Control your feelings until you have completely heard the speaker. You may find your views changed or broadened by what the speaker has said. Or you may find after listening completely to the speaker, that what the speaker said is not relevant for you. Growth will occur, however, regardless of your acceptance or rejection of what the speaker said, because you will have learned more about a subject or about another person's views.

Illustration 3-5. Withhold Evaluation

Get Ready to Listen. Stop thinking about any of the thousands of miscellaneous thoughts that constantly run through your mind. Direct all your attention to the speaker. Daydreaming is one of the leading causes of poor listening.

Make the Shift from Speaker to Listener. In a conversation, you must frequently switch roles from speaker to listener. Be sure that the switch is complete. Do not spend time preparing your next speech while the speaker is talking.

Act on What the Speaker Is Saying. Provide feedback for the speaker. Use gestures to let the speaker know that you are listening—nod, smile, laugh, frown, etc. Do not read, look at your watch, look out the window, or engage in similar activities which demonstrate a lack of interest.

Try to Understand the Words the Speaker Uses. Words have different meanings for different individuals. In fact, it has been said that the meaning of words lies within the individual. Try to understand what the speaker means by the words he or she is using. What does the speaker mean by "unreasonable," "quality," "immediately," and "good"?

Watch for Nonverbal Communication. What forms of nonverbal communication is the speaker using? Observe the speaker's eyes, hands, and body movements. Do the nonverbal communications agree with what the speaker is saying?

Illustration 3-6. Watch for Nonverbal Communication

Remove Distractions. Don't doodle, tap your pencil, shuffle papers, etc., while the speaker talks. Try to eliminate noise distractions. If a conversation is taking place in a noisy environment, move to another location. Control the physical environment as much as possible.

Be Patient. Allow the speaker plenty of time to get his or her point across. Do not interrupt. Interruptions merely serve as barriers to information exchanges.

Ask Questions. When you are not sure that you understand something that is being said, ask questions. Such questions clear up the information and show the speaker that you are interested in what is being said.

Don't Get Angry. Getting angry merely causes walls to be built inside you; this blocks your ability to think clearly.

Go Easy on Arguments and Criticism. Arguments and criticism tend to put the speaker on the defensive. Rarely does the speaker or listener benefit from an argument.

Don't Fake Attention. The same amount of time and energy that is used to fake attention can be put to good use by really paying attention.

Don't Anticipate the Speaker. If you try to anticipate the speaker, you may be wrong. Don't help the speaker by saying the next word or sentence for him or her.

Use Mnemonic Devices to Remember Key Ideas. A mnemonic device is a formula, word association, or rhyme used to assist the memory. For example, if a person says that her objections to a jogging program include boredom with the activity, exhaustion in the process, and the time required, you might develop the mnemonic device of $B\ E\ T$ to remember these ideas.

Organize What You Hear. A listener who can identify the speaker's main points and the pattern of the speaker's remarks certainly has an advantage over the listener who simply listens to the words.

Minimize Your Mental Blocks and Filters. All of us have certain biases and prejudices. However, if we are aware of these blocks, we can control them. You may have heard people say: "You can't talk to CPAs; they only know how to deal with figures," "Don't try to deal with a union person," or "Give me the old equipment any day, it was much better." In such statements, you can hear prejudices. Stereotyping is taking place—an entire group of people or things is being evaluated based on one individual, one experience, or one thing. Listening behaviors are improved if you are aware of your own blocks and filters, as well as the speaker's blocks and filters.

Stop Talking. Since most of us enjoy talking, we must constantly remind ourselves that if we are to be good listeners one of the most important rules is to *stop talking*. It is impossible to listen and talk at the same time. The nature of the listening process—receiving and attending to oral communication and comprehending and retaining that information—demands that we stop talking. Start now to concentrate on talking less and listening more.

Take Notes. When listening to a presentation or a lecture, you may find it beneficial to take notes. However, taking notes can become a listening block if it is not done properly. Have you ever found yourself so caught up in trying to take down the speaker's every word that you lost the meaning of the presentation? Note taking can distract you from listening by becoming an end in itself. Note taking can cause you to miss comments. It can interfere with your mental activity and reduce your power to analyze. Here are some suggestions for effective note taking.

1. Determine whether you need to take notes. Consider your goals, your concentration and retention abilities, and whether you will immediately use the information or use it at some later date.
2. Identify the pattern of the message. Reflect that pattern in your notes.
3. Only take down the main points of the message. Do not record each word.
4. Keep your notes clear. Avoid doodling or making other marks on your notes which may confuse you as you reread your notes.
5. Read over your notes immediately after the presentation. If you feel you need to expand on a point, do so at that time.
6. Categorize and file your notes so that they are easily found when you need them.

FOR YOUR REVIEW

The following review will help you remember the important points of this chapter.

1. Listening is the complete process by which oral language communicated by a source is received, recognized, attended to, comprehended, and retained.

2. Listening can take place at seven different levels. These levels are recognition of items, identification of items, integration with past experience, inspection of items for new information, interpretation of items, interpolation, and introspection.

3. Listening increases your personal effectiveness. It affects what you know, what you experience, and ultimately what you become.

4. Listening increases your job effectiveness. Billions of dollars are lost in business because of poor listening.

5. Effective listening on the job (1) provides information that helps you get your job done; (2) gives you ideas and information that help you learn more about your job, thereby allowing for advancement; (3) allows you to understand more about the people with whom you work; and (4) fosters cooperation between workers.

6. You should listen not only to others but also to yourself. Listening to yourself basically means being open to your own messages, both the internal and the external ones.

7. Ineffective listeners include individuals who talk constantly, who fake attention, who are easily distracted by noises, and who try to outguess what the speaker is going to say.

8. Listening barriers in business include status, hidden agendas, the grapevine, social barriers, and word barriers.

9. To help you become a more effective listener, you should
  a. Listen for facts.
  b. Listen for feelings.
  c. Respect the speaker.
  d. Withhold evaluation.
  e. Get ready to listen.
  f. Make the shift from speaker to listener.
  g. Act on what the speaker is saying.
  h. Try to understand the words the speaker uses.
  i. Watch for nonverbal communication.
  j. Remove distractions.
  k. Be patient.
  l. Ask questions.
  m. Avoid getting angry.
  n. Go easy on arguments and criticism.
  o. Avoid faking attention.
  p. Do not anticipate the speaker.
  q. Use mnemonic devices to remember key ideas.
  r. Organize what you hear.
  s. Minimize your mental blocks and filters.
  t. Stop talking.
  u. Take notes.

PROFESSIONAL FORUM

You overhear the following conversation:

Adrian: Are you ready for exams tomorrow? Personally, I feel a little sick just thinking about them.

Norma: I feel fine. You would too if you had studied.

Adrian: What do you mean? I did study, but I am still scared.

Norma: If you had studied thoroughly, you would feel as confident as I feel.

Adrian: Forgive me for even mentioning exams. Obviously you have all the answers to everything.

Norma: No, I don't have all the answers, but I do think I will do okay on the test. I have confidence in myself, which is something you don't seem to have.

Adrian: I may not have confidence, but at least I have humility—something you are not familiar with.

What went wrong? Identify the listening barriers that occurred here. How could the situation be improved?

FOR YOUR UNDERSTANDING

1. What is the difference between hearing and listening?
2. Explain attention, comprehension, and retention in relation to listening.
3. How does listening increase your job effectiveness?
4. Why is it important to listen to yourself?
5. Describe two ineffective listeners.
6. Explain how technology can be a barrier in the listening process.
7. What is meant by withholding evaluation when listening?
8. State four effective techniques in note taking.

OFFICE APPLICATIONS

On pages 286–289 are office applications that correlate with this chapter.

PART 2

PROCESSING INFORMATION

CHAPTER 4

Data Processing

We live in an age that is called the Information Society due to the tremendous explosion of knowledge that has occurred and the magnitude of the information that is available to us today. The computer is an integral part of this Information Society; in fact, the Information Society was made possible due to the advent of the computer. The computer is capable of storing vast amounts of information in its memory, of manipulating this information into new forms, of performing complicated statistical analyses in seconds, and of giving back this information on a printed page or through various other output mechanisms which we choose.

Presently, the computer has extensive impact on our lives. It assists us in making telephone calls; it controls ignition systems and fuel-air mixtures in our cars; it controls heating and cooling systems in our offices and homes; it is used to make our flight reservations; it monitors life support systems on the critically ill; it is used in depositing our pay checks directly into the bank. The list is almost endless. And, the impact that the computer will have on our lives in the future is expected to increase rather than decrease. In fact, the greatest change in our lives between now and the year 2000 is expected to be caused by the continued growth of computer access and capabilities.

As an office worker, you need to have a gen-eral knowledge of the data processing field. It is important that you have an understanding of the basic terminology used in data processing and how computers are used in offices today. This chapter will give you this basic understanding—an understanding that will enable you to be a more effective office worker.

GENERAL OBJECTIVES

Your general objectives for this chapter are to

1. Become familiar with the history of the computer.
2. Learn basic data processing terminology.
3. Understand the components of a computer system.
4. Distinguish among the following types of computer systems: mainframe, minicomputer, and microcomputer.
5. Become familiar with the commonly used computer languages.
6. Become knowledgeable of projected future directions for data processing in the office.

DATA PROCESSING DEFINED

A basic requirement of people and organizations is the processing of data. *Data processing* is the manner in which facts and figures are collected, assigned meaning, communicated to others, and retained for later use. The facts and figures are the *data*. Handling or manipulating the data in some manner is the *processing*. It is many times assumed that data processing means computers. Such is not the case. Data processing may mean manual manipulation of data. For example, a small business may record accounting transactions on journals and ledgers through a paper and pencil process. However, today when we think of data processing we usually think of the electronic processing of data which is done through the computer. The remainder of this chapter will deal with electronic data processing.

THE HISTORY OF THE COMPUTER

A review of the history of the computer helps you to better understand the field and the evolution of the computer. Blaise Pascal, the French mathematician, physicist, and religious philosopher, is widely credited with building the first digital calculating machine in 1642. It performed only addition of numbers entered by means of dials and was intended to help Pascal's father, a tax collector. In 1671 Gottfried Wilhelm von Leibniz invented a computer that could add and multiply. This computer was built in 1694, but it was not widely used. These machines built by Leibniz and Pascal remained as curiosities until more than a century later when Charles Xavier Thomas in 1820 developed the first commercially successful mechanical calculator that could add, subtract, multiply, and divide.

While Thomas was developing the calculator, Charles Babbage, a mathematics professor in Cambridge, England, was working on an automatic mechanical calculating machine. By 1822 he had built a small calculating machine which he called the "difference engine." The difference engine was a great advance conceptually, and he continued to work on it for ten years. In 1833, he lost interest in this machine and began construction on a digital computer. Digital computers operate by counting. Digital

data are represented by means of coded characters such as numbers, letters, and symbols; *characters* are the smallest elements of data processed by a computer. Babbage called the digital computer an analytical engine. The analytical machine was to be a digital machine capable of one addition per second with data entered from punched cards and a built-in storage unit. Babbage's computers were never completed, and after Babbage there was a temporary loss of interest in automatic digital computers.

In 1890 Herman Hollerith and James Powers developed devices that could automatically read information that had been punched into cards. This keypunch, sorting, and tabulating equipment allowed the 1890 U.S. census to be completed in two years as opposed to the seven years that it had taken to complete the 1880 census using manual methods. By the late 1930s, punched-card machine techniques had become so well established and reliable that Howard Hathaway Aiken, in collaboration with engineers at IBM, began construction of a large, automatic, digital computer. This computer was called the Mark I and could perform all four arithmetic operations in addition to handling logarithms and trigonometric functions. The computer was slow, requiring three to five seconds to complete a multiplication. Mark I was the first of a series of computers designed and built under Aiken's direction.

With the outbreak of World War II, there was a desperate need for computing capability, especially for the military. New weapons systems were produced for which trajectory tables and other essential data were lacking. In 1942 John Eckert, John Mauchly, and their associates at the Moore School of Electrical Engineering decided to build a high-speed electronic computer. This machine became known as ENIAC (Electrical Numerical Integrator and Calculator). Eckert and Mauchly later developed the UNIVAC-1, the first electronic computer offered as a commercial product. The UNIVAC became famous when it correctly predicted Dwight Eisenhower's victory in the 1952 presidential election. General Electric, in 1954, was the first private American company to purchase one of these computers.

Intrigued by the success of ENIAC, the mathematician John von Neumann in 1945 undertook a theoretical study of computation that demonstrated that a computer could have a very simple, fixed physical structure and yet be able to execute any kind of computation effectively by means of proper programmed control. (A *program* refers to a detailed set of instructions.) He contributed a new understanding of how fast computers should be organized and built. His ideas are often referred to as the stored-program technique and this concept became fundamental for future generations of high-speed digital computers. Because of his ideas, von Neumann is sometimes called the intellectual father of computers.

COMPUTER SYSTEMS

A *computer* is a device which (1) performs arithmetic operations on data, including addition, subtraction, multiplication, and division; (2) performs logical operations such as comparing the equality or inequality of items; (3) can run a detailed set of instructions (the program); (4) can store programs internally; and (5) can output data onto the appropriate medium. In order to perform these basic functions, the typical computer has an input unit, an output unit, a processor unit, and a storage unit. A *computer system* is the equipment or

hardware and the programs or *software* which direct the computer to perform its arithmetic, logic, storage, and input/output functions. Illustration 4-1 is a typical computer system represented schematically.

Input Media and Input Devices. Before data can be processed by the computer, it must be input into the computer on material that the computer can read. *Input media* are the materials on which programs and data are recorded. *Input devices* are the pieces of equipment that transmit the programs and data on media into the computer in machine-readable format. There are several input media and devices available; the most commonly used are given here.

Magnetic Tapes and Cassettes. Magnetic tapes and cassettes are often-used media for entry into a computer system. *Magnetic tape* is similar to the tape used in an ordinary reel-to-reel recorder. The tape is coated with a magnetically sensitive substance upon which information is placed; the information is transmitted as electronic impulses to a computer. Reels of magnetic tape are mounted on tape-drive units (input devices) for reading by the computer system. Magnetic tape has one major disadvantage. In order to reach a group of related data (called a *record*), an operator must process all the records that occur preceding the record needed. This is known as *sequential access;* that

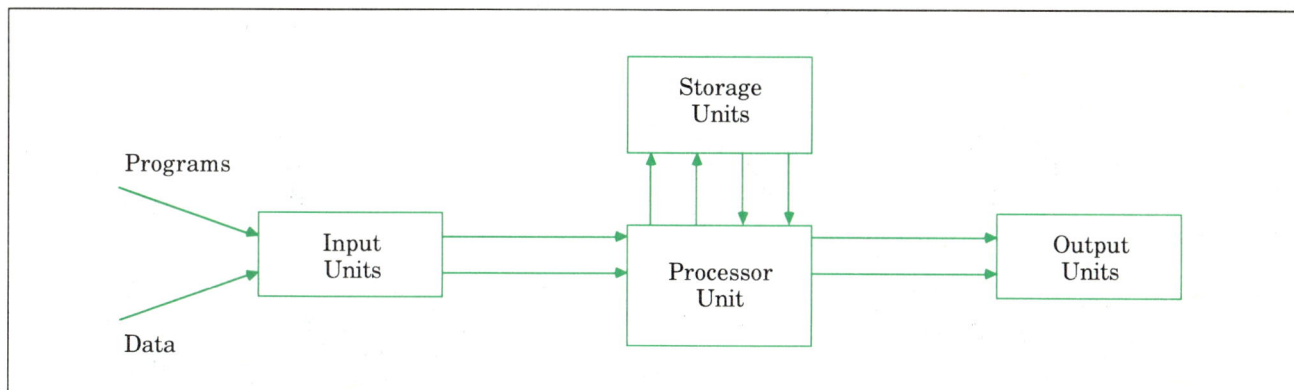

Illustration 4-1. Components of a Computer System

is, records must be processed in the same sequence as they appear on a reel of magnetic tape. Obtaining information from a tape can be time consuming if the information needed is scattered throughout the tape.

Cassette tapes are similar in appearance to the audio cassette that you would play on your home cassette player. Just as the magnetic tape has sequential access, so does the cassette. The major advantage of a magnetic cassette over a tape is that it is easier to handle. The input device for a cassette is a tape-drive unit.

Magnetic Disks and Diskettes. *Magnetic disks* are round, flat metal platters with magnetically coated surfaces; magnetic disks are also referred to as hard disks. Magnetic disks are packaged as single units or stacked together as disk packs. A *disk pack* is a collection of two or more hard disks mounted on a vertical shaft. Data stored on any one of the disks in the pack can be quickly found and read. The *diskette or floppy disk* is another widely used input medium. It is a small, flexible diskette about the size of a 45 rpm record. Floppy disks are used extensively for entering data into a microcomputer.

Whereas tapes and cassettes have sequential access, disks employ a process called random access. *Random access* allows any information to be located without having to read all the information preceding that which is desired. Thus, disks and diskettes may be processed faster than tapes or cassettes. The input device for disks and diskettes is a disk drive.

Document Readers. Magnetic tapes, cassettes, and disks require placing information onto special media before it can be read by the computer. For example, a tape must be prepared and then fed in through a tape drive to the computer. A disk must be prepared and fed in through a disk drive. Today, however, document readers are used widely to input data already existing in printed form directly into the computer. Such input methods are referred to as *source data automation.* Examples of source data automation include optical mark recognition, optical character recognition, magnetic ink character recognition, and graphics input devices such as joysticks, lightpens, and

graphics tablets. Information concerning graphics input devices is given in Chapter 8.

Optical Mark Recognition (OMR). Examples of optical mark recognition are the bar codes or "zebra-stripped" universal product codes that appear on supermarket products. Typically, a high-intensity light beam is passed over these bars. The reflected image is interpreted by a special bar code reader and is transmitted as data to a computer. These codes are product identification data. Using these data, the computer can locate the product descriptions and prices that are then displayed at the register and printed on the sales tapes.

Optical Character Recognition (OCR). OCR is one of the most common types of optical recognition systems. An OCR scanner is used to pass over the handwritten or typewritten characters which are encoded into electronic signals and read by the computer. In addition to handwritten and typewritten characters, the OCR scanner also recognizes tapes generated from an adding machine or cash register. The Post Office uses OCR to scan envelopes and sort mail by ZIP Codes, thus eliminating untold hours of hand sorting.

Magnetic Ink Character Recognition (MICR). MICR equipment is designed to read characters printed with magnetic ink. An excellent example of MICR usage is the processing of

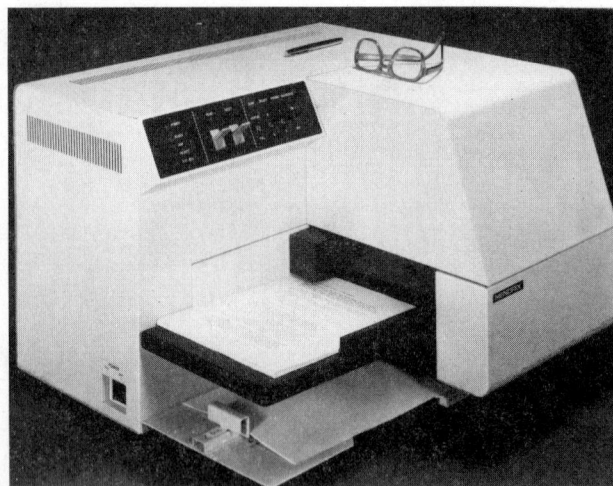

Hendrix Technologies, Inc.

Illustration 4-2. Table-top OCR

checks by banks. Preprinted at the bottom of all checks is bank routing information and the customer's account number. When the bank receives the checks that have been written, the amount of the check is encoded with MICR equipment in the bottom right portion of the check. MICR machines then transfer the check routing, account identification, and dollar amount information onto magnetic tape for subsequent entry into the computer.

Terminal Input. One of the most common methods of input into the computer today is direct input through a computer terminal. The terminal keyboard is the input medium. Keyed data can be entered directly into the computer from an on-line terminal. *On-line* refers to a terminal which is wired directly to the computer.

On-line processing consists of a terminal with a keyboard and a TV-like screen. The operator keys the information on the keyboard of the terminal; it is displayed on the screen and sent to the computer. The terminal is referred to as a *video display terminal* (VDT), and the TV-like screen is called a *cathode ray tube* (CRT).

Illustration 4-3. Video Display Terminal

Audio Input or Voice Recognition. Audio input or voice recognition is not used extensively today, but more and more research is being done in this area. *Voice recognition* means simply that computers can recognize and react to the sound of human voices. At present, applications are limited to specific vocabularies. It is anticipated, however, that in the future audio or voice input will be commonplace. One example of audio input that is used today is in voice commands to a robot. The robot can be given voice commands which are then converted into machine-language instructions which the robot understands and will follow.

INTERNAL PROCESSING OF DATA

Once data has been input into the computer through the input media (e.g., magnetic tapes, magnetic diskettes, or terminal keyboard) and input devices (e.g., tape drives, disk drives, and document readers) processing takes place in the central processing unit of the computer. This unit has three major functions; the unit and its functions are explained below.

Central Processing Unit. The *central processing unit (CPU)* is the heart of a computer system. It accepts the data from the input device, processes the data according to the program, and delivers the results through some type of output device. The *program* that the computer uses is a series of instructions directing the computer to perform a sequence of operations. For example, in performing payroll functions, the program may tell the computer to compute the number of hours that the employee has worked for a week; multiply the number of hours by the rate of hourly pay; deduct Social Security, income tax, and retirement; and print out the net pay of the employee on a paycheck. In other words, through a program the step-by-step operations are accomplished by the electronic circuitry in the central processing unit of the computer. The output devices that deliver the data will be explained later in this chapter. Notice in Illustration 4-4 that there are

three parts to the central processing unit — the memory, the control unit, and the arithmetic/logic unit.

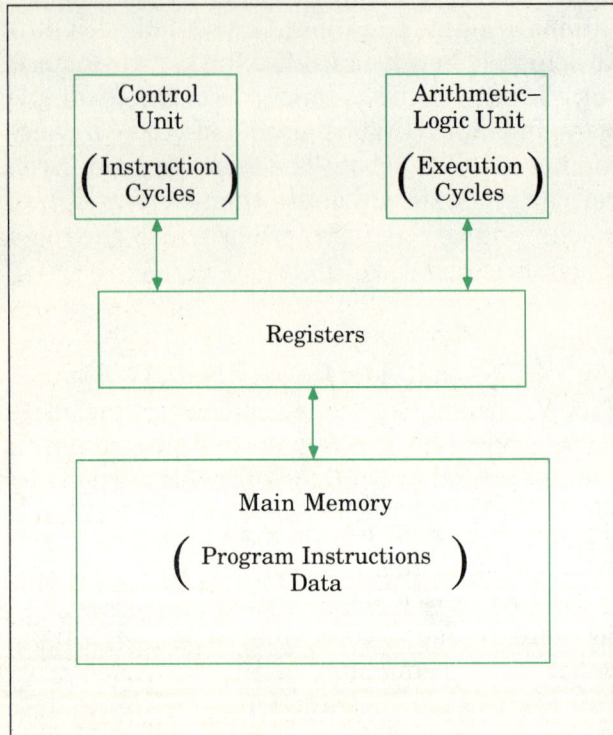

Illustration 4-4. Central Processing Unit

The Memory. Data are transferred from the input device to the memory unit. Data remain in this unit until the computer processes the data. The memory unit also holds the results of processed data until the data are transferred to an output device. Thus, the memory unit also serves as a storage unit to hold data until it is processed or to hold processed data until it is transferred to *auxiliary storage devices.* Auxiliary storage devices, such as the disk or tape drive, are on-line to the computer; i.e., directly connected to the computer. Data not currently being used by a computer can be recorded on magnetic tapes, cassettes, and disks. These media serve as secondary storage for the computer; they extend the storage capacity of the computer system.

Data within computer memory are stored in the form of a code which utilizes a 1 or a 0. These 1s or 0s are called *binary digits* or *bits*. The reason for storing pieces of data in bits is that computer circuitry is electronic in nature, and electronic devices can be turned either "on" or "off." Combinations of bits are put together to form a *byte,* which represents a character (letter, number, or symbol) in a computer. For example, eight bits are put together to form the letter "A"; these combined bits are called a byte.

The memory or storage capacity of computers is not the same; however, each computer does have a fixed memory capacity. These memory capacities are expressed by the symbol K, which represents 1,024 bytes. Thus, a memory capacity of 24K is equal to 24,576 bytes (24 × 1,024). Obviously, the size of the memory on a computer is an important purchasing consideration, since it determines how much data can be stored within the CPU.

The Control Unit. As its name implies, the control unit regulates the different functions of the computer system. All instructions to the computer are interpreted here. For example, the unit directs the input-output devices, giving them instructions as to when to input data and when to output data. It also interprets instructions for all arithmetic-logic operations. It tells the arithmetic-logic unit (ALU) when to add, subtract, multiply, and divide. The unit also tells the ALU when and how to classify and sort data, and it coordinates the transfer of data to and from the main computer storage.

The Arithmetic-Logic Unit. This unit adds, subtracts, multiplies, and divides numeric data. It also compares both alphabetic and numeric data.

Registers. In transferring data from one section of the CPU to another section, registers are used. Registers are paths or conduits that connect the arithmetic-logic unit and the control unit to the memory unit. When data is taken from the memory unit, it is placed in a register to await instructions from the control unit. And, data are also stored in registers prior to execution in the arithmetic-logic unit.

COMPUTER PROGRAMS AND LANGUAGES

The programs that occupy the computer's memory and tell the computer what to do are called *software*. To give you an understanding of how a program might work, consider this example of an accounting program. The program contains a line which says that profit is equal to income minus expenses. In the computer, the profit, income, and total expenses are stored in the memory in numbered locations which may be thought of as electronic pigeonholes. The number assigned to each location is called its *address*. The computer finds the profit, income, and expenses data stored in the electronic pigeonholes and transfers this information to the register. The computer then puts this information into the arithmetic-logic unit and tells it to find the difference. After the arithmetic-logic unit computes the information, it transfers it to another register for holding until the information is output through an output device such as a printer.

To communicate with the computer involves writing a series of instructions in special languages called programming languages. The person who designs and develops programs to direct the processing of information is called a *programmer*. The following are some of the languages that are used in preparing programs.

BASIC (Beginners All-Purpose Symbolic Instruction Code) was developed in the early 1960s by John Kemeny and Thomas Kurtz. It is an algebraic language and handles computations well. It is one of the easiest languages to learn and can be used on many different computers.

APL (A Programming Language) was developed by Kenneth Iverson in the early 1960s. It is a concise, powerful language that is simple to learn and is especially useful for computational applications.

COBOL (COmmon Business Oriented Language) was first released in 1959; one of the prime contributors to its development was Captain Grace Hopper. COBOL ranks as one of the most popular business application programming languages in use today. It is well suited for business data processing because it contains extensive features for creating, maintaining, and accessing data.

FORTRAN (FORmula TRANslator) was developed by John Backus of IBM and was released in 1957. It was designed to support scientific and engineering problems which involve complex mathematical computations.

Pascal is a programming language that was developed in the early 1970s by Niklaus Wirth of Switzerland. Pascal is a very concise, readable language, making it an increasingly popular and powerful language for microcomputers.

There was a need for a programming language that combined the business data processing features of COBOL with the computational features of FORTRAN in a single, general-purpose language. In 1963, IBM and SHARE, a group representing large-scale computer users, formed a committee to develop a programming language; and in 1966 formal specifications for PL/I (Programming Language — Version I) were released.

RPG (Report Program Generator) is a highly specialized language which was initially designed to generate programs with outputs that are business-oriented reports. RPG can be learned in only a few hours and is widely used among small businesses to process a collection of related data.

The programs in memory that are executed or run by the CPU must be in machine language, which consists of a set of binary digits that have precise meanings to the CPU. Programs that are written in the high-level languages (e.g., FORTRAN) must be translated into machine language by yet another program, either a compiler or an interpreter.

OUTPUT DEVICES AND STORAGE MEDIA

Now that you have examined input media and devices, the CPU of the computer, and computer programs and languages, consider what types of output devices and storage media are used. The most commonly used output device is a printer, and the most widely used output storage media are magnetic tapes, disks, and cassettes. However, there are additional output devices and storage media also used, and these are discussed here.

Printers. The printer is used extensively as an output device, with paper being the output medium for the printer. Paper is considered *hard copy* since it provides a permanent record of the output as opposed to output on a screen which is considered *soft copy;* i.e., no permanent record is provided. Printers are classified as either impact or nonimpact.

Impact Printers. The first printer to dominate the market was the impact printer. It utilizes a device or mechanism that prints one or more characters on paper by physically impacting or hitting the paper. An impact printer is either a serial or line printer.

Serial printers have a printing device or element that prints a character at a time. Serial print devices come in four styles: ball shaped, daisy wheel, thimble, or dot matrix. A daisy wheel printing mechanism is shown in Illustration 4-5. It utilizes 96 spokes with each having its own character. A dot matrix printhead strikes the paper with different combinations of metal pins. As the printhead moves across the paper, tiny pins in the printhead tap the paper

through a ribbon to form each character. These metal pins create dots in patterns that approximate the shape of characters. A dot matrix printer is shown in Illustration 4-6.

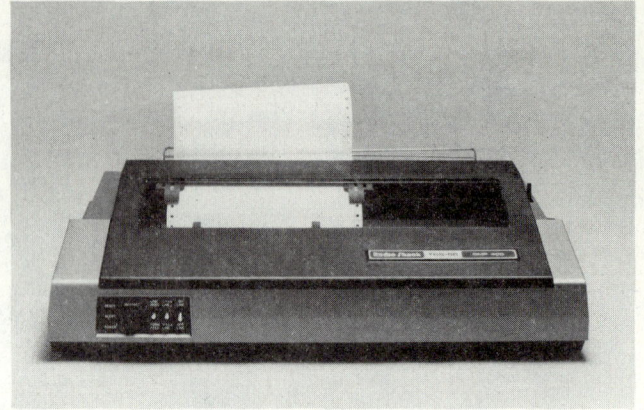

Illustration 4-6. Dot Matrix Printer

Line printers print a line at a time. Picture a long chain of characters which continually rotates at high speed in front of paper. When each character is in its proper place, a hammer strikes the chain and the line of characters prints on paper.

Nonimpact Printers. Impact printers can be noisy and subject to breakdowns. To overcome the limitations of impact printers, manufacturers such as Xerox and IBM designed mechanisms that would place marks on paper without a printing device actually contacting the paper. These printers are called nonimpact printers and shape characters through the use of light (often a laser beam) or a spray of ink. Nonimpact printers are generally cleaner, faster, and more reliable than impact printers. The major disadvantage of nonimpact printers is their high cost.

Plotters. Another type of output device is a plotter. There is a tremendous increase today in the use of computers in preparing graphs and charts for business. A *plotter* draws output using one or more pens that are controlled by instructions from the CPU. You will learn more about this usage in Chapter 8. Illustration 4-7 shows a plotter.

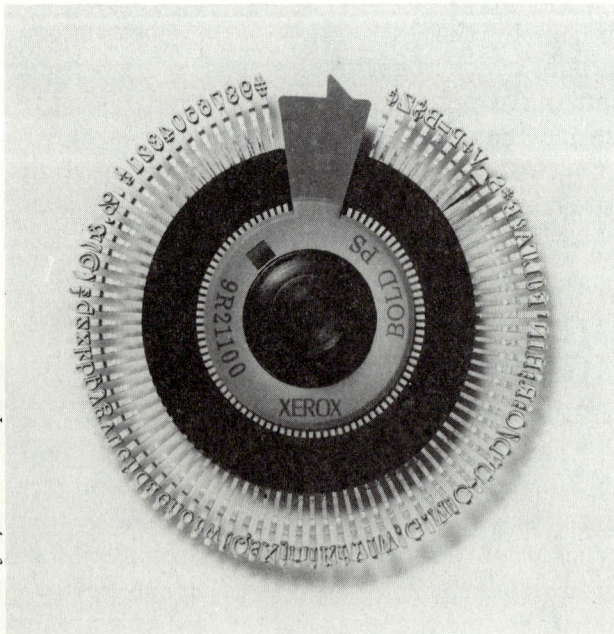

Courtesy of Xerox Corporation

Illustration 4-5. Daisy Wheel

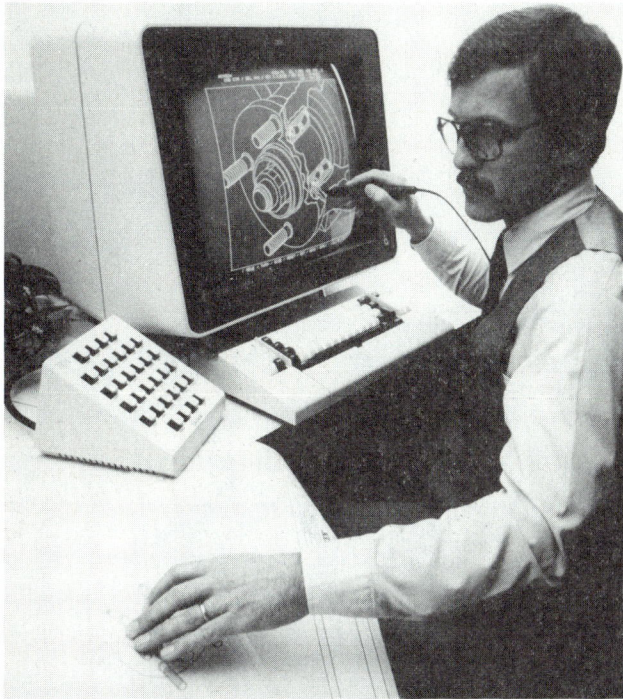

Photograph Courtesy of the Timken Co.

Illustration 4-7. Plotter

Audio Output (Speech Synthesis). Audio response is a small but growing form of output from a computer. An output device converts data into understandable audio responses by imitating the human voice. It is expected that this type of output will continue to grow in usage in the future. Some audio response applications presently used include announcement of departure times of airlines, reading machines for the blind, elevators which announce the floor, announcement of gasoline supply in a car, and certain educational toys.

Video Display Terminals. If there is no need for a hard copy of information, a video display terminal may be used as the output device. The information is displayed on the CRT. Airline employees use this method of output in making seat assignments at the departure gate or in checking flight reservations for you.

Output Storage Media. As mentioned previously, programs and data are placed in the memory of a computer and are used in the processing of the data. The computer memory is called the main memory and is reused con-

tinuously. As each processing job is completed, the programs or data that were in memory are replaced to permit the processing of other data. For most electronic data processing applications, however, programs and data need to be retained so that they can be reused. To save items for later use, storage devices are provided. Once placed on storage devices in machine-readable form, these programs and data can be retrieved and entered into memory whenever needed.

Several types of media are used for storage, including magnetic tapes, disks, and videodiscs. These media become output media for the computer and also storage media, since data held on the media are reused. These storage media are referred to as *secondary storage units*. The most common types of output and storage media are given here.

Magnetic Tapes, Cassettes, and Disks. In the earlier part of this chapter, you learned that these media are input media for the computer. They are also output and storage media. Magnetic tapes, cassettes, and disks are the most common output media used.

Videodisc. The videodisc is a highly accurate method of storing both audio and visual information. The *videodisc* is typically made of glass and coated with photosensitive resin upon which it is possible for a laser beam to record information. Computer applications of videodiscs are currently very limited. Illustration 4-8 shows a videodisc with a playback system.

3M File Management Systems

Illustration 4-8. Videodisc System

Computer Output Microfilm (COM). In order to save paper and handling costs, many large organizations have begun storing important information on a compact medium called *computer output microfilm*. With COM, standard printed computer output is photographed and stored as images on a roll of film or a flat piece of film. The roll of film may be in reel-to-reel form or in cartridge form; the flat piece of film is called a *microfiche*. Approximately 200 pages of computer printout can be stored on one microfiche which is a six-inch by four-inch card. You will learn more about COM in Chapter 12 on records management.

Illustration 4-9. Mainframe System

COMPUTER CLASSIFICATIONS

Computers may be classified by the amount of storage capacity they contain and the speed with which they operate. For purposes of clarification, consider these three classifications: (1) the large or mainframe computers; (2) the medium or minicomputers; and (3) the small or microcomputers.

Mainframe Systems. Mainframes are the largest computer systems. A *mainframe* is capable of processing large amounts of information at very fast speeds. Mainframes can support a number of auxiliary devices such as terminals, printers, disk drives, tape drives, and other input and output equipment. The components of the mainframe may all be located in the same room, on different floors of a building, or in different cities or states. For example, a large company with its central office in New York and its branch offices in California, Texas, Florida, and Colorado may have a mainframe in New York and terminals and printers in each branch office. Telephone lines connect one component of the computer to various other components at different locations. Because of their complexity and diversity, mainframes are the most expensive classification of computers. In fact, due to their expense, companies will sometimes lease or rent mainframe computers from their manufacturers rather than buy the systems.

Minicomputer System. A typical *minicomputer* is more compact in size, has a slower processing speed, and has a more limited storage capacity than a mainframe computer. However, minicomputer systems are also less expensive than mainframe systems. The smaller capability of the minicomputer system usually limits its use to smaller businesses. A company may have a centralized mainframe computer and a decentralized minicomputer at various sites such as branch locations. In such a situation, the mainframe and minicomputer are usually interfaced (interconnected) so that they can communicate with each other.

Microcomputer Systems. The microcomputer is the smallest of the computer systems. Microcomputers were made possible by the advances in technology in the 1970s which permitted the manufacture of electronic circuits on silicon chips as small as a fingernail. A single miniature chip (called a *microprocessor*) contains the circuitry and components for arithmetic, logic, and control operations. Microcomputers are also known as personal computers and are purchased for a variety of home uses in addition to being used widely in business and educational institutions. Since the first microcomputer appeared on the market in 1975, the number of users has grown rapidly; this growth is projected to continue. Microcomputers are relatively inexpensive, and the cost has been going down consistently since they were first introduced. It is anticipated that the price will go even lower in the future.

A type of microcomputer that is gaining in popularity and usage is the laptop computer. *Laptop computers* are a special type of portable computer. They are about the size of a loose-leaf notebook and weigh less than five pounds. They get their name from the fact that they can rest comfortably on the lap during use. All laptop computers are battery powered, have full typewriter-style keyboards, come with a built-in display screen, and are supplied with software permanently stored in the computer. Compactness, portability, and affordability are the laptops' main assets; small screens and limited memory are the main drawbacks. Laptop computers excel in providing computing power for the executive who travels frequently. Laptops may be used in airplanes, hotel rooms, meeting rooms, and outdoors.

Courtesy of International Business Machines Corporation

Illustration 4-10. Laptop Computer

THE FUTURE OF COMPUTERS IN BUSINESS

Distinctions have been made between mainframes, minicomputers, and microcomputers. However, the projection is that the distinction between minicomputers and microcomputers will vanish within the next few years and that microcomputers will eventually absorb most functions now done by mainframes. This projection is based on the fact that more and more power is becoming available on the microcomputer. Also, companies are finding that the advantages of centralized computer power through the use of a mainframe are offset by the flexibility and relatively low cost of a decentralized system available through the use of microcomputers.

It is projected that the microcomputer of the 1990s will be three times as powerful as the minicomputer of today. The microcomputer will be an easy-to-use electronic Goliath that sits on a desktop and stores and sorts data like a contemporary minicomputer for a fraction of the cost. The business office of the future will probably hold a powerful microcomputer.

Another projection is that before the year 2000 the CRT as we know it today will be a thing of the past. Japanese have already developed thin, flat, video screens based on liquid crystal technology, which they are marketing as TV watches in this country. It may well be that by the year 2000 even the notion of a screen at all will be obsolete. It is a virtual certainty that long before the century is over, we will be able to display not only data and graphics but full moving video images on anything from walls to tiny screens worn on the wrist.

Videodisc storage technology will allow microcomputers to utilize complex programs now only practical on mainframes. When this capacity is combined with future software developments, we may see the keyboard disappear entirely. It may be replaced by such things as plain-English voice command, a voice writer which translates spoken words into written prose, or even a think writer or telepathic computer that uses some form of biofeedback technology.

ARTIFICIAL INTELLIGENCE

Scientists are actively engaged in research designed to make machines think like humans.

Intelligence is defined as the ability to cope with change and to incorporate new information to improve performance. Thus, the challenge for scientists working in this area is to develop a computer that has the ability to "think." For now, artificial intelligence remains a potential yet to be realized. Numerous researchers are expending much energy en route to this goal. But for all their impressive abilities, computers cannot think on their own.

It is likely, however, that over the next 10 to 20 years artificial intelligence will begin providing various types of aid more sophisticated than the limited systems that have recently emerged. The next few years ought to see natural-language advise-giving programs that people can dial up and consult about travel, financial planning, investments, retirement, and medical matters. Natural-language processors will allow us to communicate with the computer just as we now communicate with another human being. Regardless of the direction that computer research takes, computers are presently a part of our every day life; and their impact will only increase in the future.

FOR YOUR REVIEW

The following review will help you remember the important points of this chapter.

1. Data processing is the manner in which facts and figures are collected, assigned meaning, communicated to others, and retained for later use.

2. Pascal built the first digital calculating machine in 1642.

3. Charles Xavier Thomas in 1820 developed the first commercially successful mechanical calculator.

4. In 1833, Charles Babbage began construction on a digital computer which he called an analytical engine.

5. In 1890, Herman Hollerith and James Powers developed devices that could automatically read information that had been punched into cards.

6. In the late 1930s punched-card machine techniques had become so well established and reliable that Aiken, in collaboration with IBM engineers, began construction of a large automatic digital computer called the Mark I. This computer could handle all four arithmetic operations in addition to handling logarithms and trigonometric functions.

7. In 1942, John Eckert, John Mauchly, and their associates at the Moore School of Electrical Engineering decided to build a high-speed electronic computer. This machine became known as ENIAC (Electrical Numerical Integrator and Calculator).

8. The first electronic computer offered as a commercial product was UNIVAC, which was developed by Eckert and Mauchly.

9. John von Neumann in 1945 undertook a theoretical study of computation that demonstrated that a computer could have a very simple, fixed physical structure and yet be able to execute any kind of computation effectively by means of proper programmed control. Because of his work, von Neumann is sometimes called the intellectual father of computers.

10. A computer is a device which (1) performs arithmetic operations on data, including addition, subtraction, multiplication, and division; (2) performs logic operations such as comparing the equality or inequality of items; (3) can be programmed with a set of instructions; (4) can store programs internally; and (5) can output information onto the appropriate medium.

11. A computer system is composed of the equipment or hardware and the programs or software which direct the computer to perform its arithmetic, logic, storage, and input/output functions.

12. Input media are the materials on which programs and data are stored.

13. Input devices are the pieces of equipment that transmit the programs and data on the media into the computer in machine-readable format.

14. Input devices include tape readers, disk drives, document readers, terminals, and audio input.

15. The following are computer input media: magnetic tapes and cassettes, magnetic disks and diskettes, and the terminal keyboard.

16. Document readers input data already existing in printed form into the computer. Such input methods are referred to as source data automation. Examples of source data automation include optical mark recognition, optical character recognition, magnetic ink character recognition, and graphics input devices such as joysticks, lightpens, and graphics tablets.

17. The central processing unit (CPU) is the heart of a computer system. It accepts the data from the input device, processes the data according to the program, and delivers the results through some type of output device.

18. There are three main parts to the central processing unit — the memory, the control unit, and the arithmetic/logic unit.

19. The memory unit is the primary storage unit of the computer. Data are transferred from the input device to the memory unit, and it also holds the results of processed data until the data are transferred to an output device.

20. The control unit regulates the different functions of the computer system. The control unit directs the input-output devices; interprets instructions for all arithmetic/logic operations; determines when to add, subtract, multiply, and divide; and coordinates the transfer of data to and from main computer storage.

21. The arithmetic-logic unit adds, subtracts, multiplies, and divides numeric data. It also compares both alphabetic and numeric data.

22. The programs that occupy the computer's memory are called software.

23. Programs in memory that are executed by the CPU must be in machine language. There are a number of languages used today; some of these languages are BASIC, APL, COBOL, FORTRAN, PL/I, RPG, and Pascal.

24. Output devices include printers, plotters, audio output, and video display terminals.

25. Output storage media consists of magnetic tapes, cassettes, disks, videodiscs, and computer output microfilm.

26. Printers are either impact or nonimpact. Impact printers utilize a device or mechanism that prints one or more characters on paper by physically impacting or hitting the paper. Nonimpact printers form characters without striking the paper.

27. There are three basic classifications of computers: mainframe systems, minicomputer systems, and microcomputer systems.

28. In the future, microcomputers used in the business office will be three times as powerful as the minicomputer of today. It is projected that before the year 2000, the CRT as we know it today will be a thing of the past. Videodisc storage technology will allow microcomputers to utilize complex programs now only practical on a mainframe system.

29. Scientists are engaged in research referred to as artificial intelligence with the purpose of making computers think like humans. As a result of research in artificial intelligence, it is expected more sophisticated systems will emerge.

PROFESSIONAL FORUM

Carlos Topia has worked for Branton, McConagle, and McQuown Law Firm for the past six months. His job consists of work which he does at home on a microcomputer and sends to the office via telephone lines. He talks with his employer about work assignments at least three times a week on the telephone. Working from his home fits Carlos' family needs, since his wife works outside the home and they have two school-age children. He is able to be at home when the children get home and can still hold a challenging job.

When Carlos was first employed by the firm, he was given a list of job expectations; and he gets direct input from his employer each week about specific assignments that are expected.

However, other than this contact with his employer, he has been given no other knowledge of the company. And, since his orientation session with his employer when he was first hired, he has had no personal contact with his employer. Carlos would like to feel more a part of the company. It would help him if he had a general overview of the directions of the company and knew some of the other employees who work for the company. Carlos has been told that the law firm has five other employees who work on computers in their homes. Carlos would like to have some contact with these employees to see if they have similar needs such as being more knowledgeable about the law firm.

1. How would you suggest that Carlos solve his problem?
    Should he talk with his employer about his concerns?
2. If he talks with his employer, what suggestions should Carlos make for improving his work situation?

FOR YOUR UNDERSTANDING

1. Describe the difference between data processing and electronic data processing.
2. What is a computer?
3. List and explain three types of input media.
4. What is OMR and how is it used?
5. List and explain the parts of the central processing unit.
6. What is BASIC?
7. Are magnetic tapes input, output, or storage media? Explain.
8. What is COM?
9. Describe a mainframe system.
10. What is the projected direction of computer usage in the office?

OFFICE APPLICATIONS

On pages 292–293 are office applications that correlate with this chapter.

CHAPTER 5

Word/Information Processing

In Chapter 4, you learned about the importance that computers have had on the office of today. An equally important advancement for the office worker is the word processor. The first word processor was developed by IBM in 1964; and since that time, this machine has had a revolutionary impact on the way in which the office worker performs his or her tasks. The first word processor was a relatively simple machine called the MT/ST (Magnetic Tape Selectric Typewriter) which allowed the office worker to store material on a tape and make revisions to the material without having to retype the document. In the last twenty years, extremely sophisticated word processors have been developed which have screens so that the office worker can read what is being keyboarded. Also, these machines can now check your spelling, add columns of figures, and alphabetize material. If you work in an office today, the chances of using some type of word processing equipment are great.

In this chapter, you will learn about the history of word processing, word processing equipment, dictation equipment, career opportunities in word processing, and future directions of word processing.

GENERAL OBJECTIVES

Your general objectives for this chapter are to

1. Become knowledgeable about the development of word processing.
2. Understand the rationale for word processing.
3. Become knowledgeable about methods of creating correspondence.
4. Become familiar with word processing equipment.
5. Understand the types of word processing environments that exist.
6. Become knowledgeable about career opportunities available in word processing.
7. Cite projected future developments in word processing.

AN INTRODUCTION TO WORD PROCESSING

Word processing, simply defined, is the process of communicating one person's ideas in the form of words to another person. Therefore, taken in its broadest form, word processing includes such activities as verbally presenting an idea to another individual, writing a handwritten note to another person, or writing and mailing a letter. However, the concept of word processing has taken on meaning that is narrower in scope but more complex in nature. Word processing as a concept is the transformation of ideas and information into a readable form of communication through the management of procedures, equipment, personnel, and the work environment. One of the most important elements of this definition is equipment. In fact, the term word processing has become synonymous with equipment.

Now that you have considered the definition of word processing, consider the evolution of word processing from the late 1800s. Before the late 1800s, much of the processing of words was done through manual methods such as longhand. Obviously, this method of processing soon became too slow and other methods were sought.

The manual typewriter was an important part of the switch from manual to mechanical methods of word processing. The first manual typewriter, invented by Christopher Sholes in 1874, was introduced as the Remington Model I. Soon other brands appeared on the market, including the Royal, L. C. Smith, and Underwood. The manual typewriter was used extensively in the office until the late 50s and early 60s, when the electric typewriter began to be used widely. Today, a manual typewriter is rarely seen in an office.

The first electric typewriter suitable for office use was introduced by IBM in 1934. This typewriter had type bars and a movable carriage similar to the manual typewriter. In 1961, IBM introduced the Selectric typewriter with a ball-shaped typing element and no movable carriage. The element moved along the platen as keystrokes were made. By 1970 most of the typewriters sold were element-type machines. Although electric typewriters are still used in offices today, electrics are rapidly being replaced by word processing equipment.

The birth of modern word processing occurred in 1964 when IBM introduced the Magnetic Tape Selectric Typewriter (MT/ST). The MT/ST not only produced documents faster than had been possible before, but it also allowed copy to be added and omitted. As copy was typed, the strokes were printed on paper and recorded on a magnetic tape. Whenever an error was made, the typist could backspace and strike over the error. The paper would show a strikeover, but the magnetic tape had been corrected in the manner a tape is erased and reused on a tape recorder. Once a document had been recorded on tape, corrections and revisions could be made without retyping the entire document. Copy could be played back on the MT/ST at 150 words per minute — nearly three times the average typing speed.

The next step in the development of word processing was the Magnetic Card Selectric Typewriter (MC/ST) introduced by IBM in the late 1960s. This typewriter used magnetic cards rather than tape. Early magnetic card models captured text on a single magnetic card that could store about one page of text. Later models had better text revision capabilities.

Today, word processors are much faster than the earlier models, have a great many more features, and cost much less than the earlier machines. Also, personal computers have become word processors with the advent of word processing software.

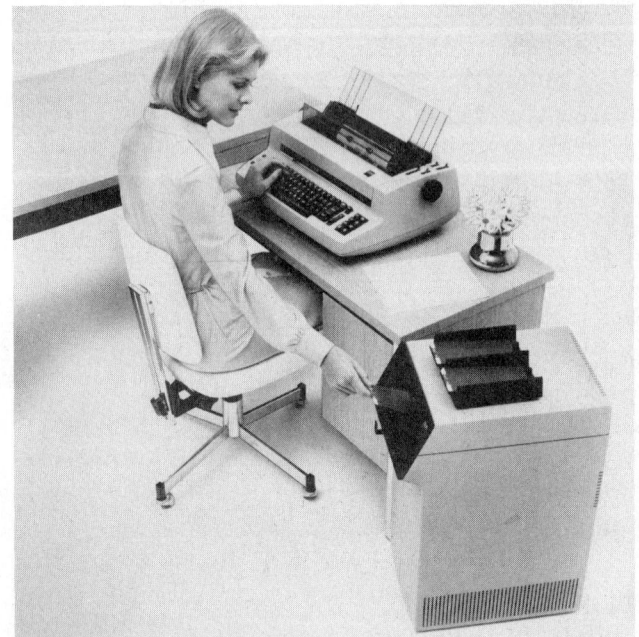

Courtesy of International Business Machines Corporation

Illustration 5-1. Magnetic Card Machine

RATIONALE FOR WORD PROCESSING

Why is word processing equipment used so extensively today? Why have businesses been willing to invest thousands of dollars in word processing equipment? What are the advantages of using word processors? Here are some of the reasons that word processors have become so important to business today.

Growth in Paperwork. We live in an information age. More information is available today than ever before, and the amount of information continues to grow. Managers in today's businesses must learn how to handle information quickly and efficiently. This handling of information means that paperwork must be read, sorted, changed, recorded, and stored; and additional paperwork must be produced. As the amount of paperwork continues to grow, the traditional methods of dealing with paperwork have become too time consuming. Word processors provide for more efficient handling of the paperwork.

Greater Productivity. It is estimated that office personnel have only been 40 to 60 percent as productive as they could be. There are a number of reasons which account for this low productivity, including frequent interruptions, waiting for other people, and revising correspondence because of changes that the originator makes, keyboarding errors, or incorrect formats. Here are some ways that word processing can increase productivity.

1. When it is necessary to revise material, productivity is increased, since it is not necessary to retype the entire document. Revisions can be made by inserting new material and/or deleting old material.
2. With the extensive use of dictating equipment, an executive does not take the office worker's time to dictate correspondence. Thus, the office worker does not have to sit and wait for the dictator to generate ideas or locate materials.
3. Since errors are corrected easily, the keyboarding speed of the word processing operator can be increased significantly.

Cost Savings. Office costs have been increasing rapidly for the past few years. Several factors have contributed to these costs including increased building and rental costs and inflation. Another factor that contributes to higher costs is the cost of labor which represents 75 to 90 percent of total office expenditures. Over the past several years, labor costs (including executive and office worker salaries) have continued to rise. With word processing equipment, the office worker can produce more work in less time, thus reducing the costs associated with processing paperwork. In addition, fewer employees can complete a greater volume of work, thus lowering the total salary expenditures for the business.

Higher Quality of Work. In an office without word processing equipment, an executive or office worker may be hesitant to change the wording of a piece of correspondence, since it will involve costly retyping. With word processing equipment, the office worker can make these changes quickly and efficiently. Thus, the executive or office worker is not hesitant to make needed changes in the correspondence. Also, the physical appearance of correspondence is of higher quality, since corrections are made before a final copy is produced; the result is a "perfect" copy.

CREATING CORRESPONDENCE

There are three main methods for creating correspondence to be processed on word processing equipment: longhand, shorthand, and machine dictation. Voice recognition, which you learned about in Chapter 4 and which will be discussed in more detail later in this chapter, is a method of the future. If voice recognition becomes available at a reasonable cost, it will eliminate the need for keyboarding information into a word processor.

Longhand. Longhand is a basic form of word creation that involves the use of pen and paper. It is the slowest and most expensive method of originating words, but it is the most widely used due to its ease and convenience. And, there are times when longhand has advantages over other methods. For example, when composing creative work such as presentations or reports, many writers need to be able to see the words. In preparing statistical copy, it is much easier to handwrite the figures than it is to try to dictate them. Also, when doing minor revisions on work, it is easier to write these revisions on the printed copy than it is to try to dictate the revisions.

In spite of the ease and convenience of longhand and the times when longhand is advantageous, as mentioned above, it has some major disadvantages. One of these disadvantages is that longhand is slow. At top speed, an individual writes only about 40 wam. When composing in longhand, the rate drops to 10 to 15 wam.

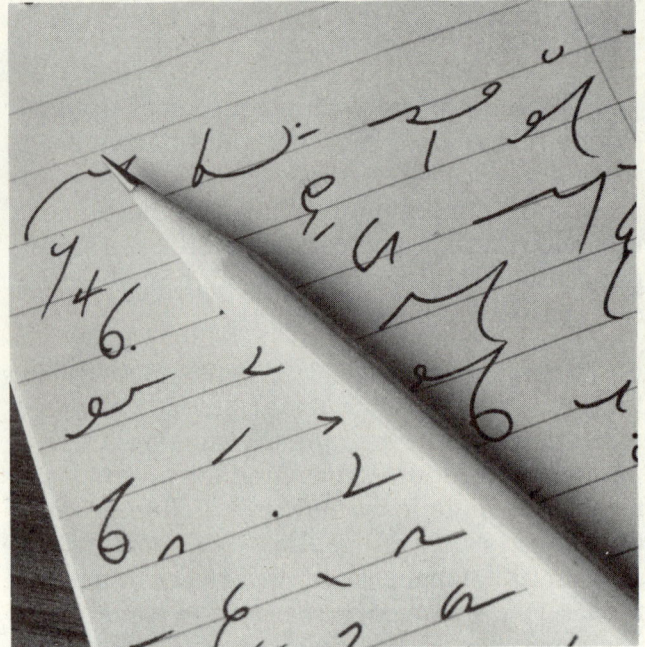

Illustration 5-2. Shorthand Dictation

Shorthand Dictation. Shorthand dictation is another method of creating correspondence. The average person when dictating correspondence speaks at the rate of 80 to 120 words per minute, and shorthand can be written easily at this speed. The main advantage of shorthand is the increased speed of recording the spoken word. However, shorthand dictation has some major disadvantages, some of which are

1. Shorthand dictation ties up the time of two people — the person giving the dictation and the office worker recording the dictation.
2. Shorthand dictation can be given only when the office worker is on duty; and this person is usually not available after working hours, although the executive may prefer to dictate then.
3. A dictator may be interrupted by a telephone call or important message, and the office worker must wait until the dictator is ready to resume the dictation.
4. Cold notes may be difficult to read if they are not written well. Most office workers prefer to transcribe shorthand notes immediately. It is also difficult for another person to read and transcribe an individual's notes.

Machine Dictation. Machine dictation is one of the more productive and cost efficient means of originating correspondence for word processing. It has numerous advantages, some of which are

1. Dictation equipment can be available whenever and wherever the dictator wants to dictate. It can be used at home or at the office and while the dictator is traveling.
2. Machine dictation ties up only one person's time during the dictation process. Thus, it is less costly than shorthand dictation.
3. Machine dictation can be transcribed at any time.
4. Dictation equipment allows the word originator to dictate, to rewind and review what has been said, to make corrections, to indicate the end of dictation, and to give the person doing the transcribing instructions.

Regardless of these advantages, there are disadvantages to machine dictation. Dictators must be taught how to dictate and how to use the equipment. The cost of buying dictation machines, installing them, and training people to use them is expensive. Time and effort must be expended in determining the most effective dictation equipment for the company. Selecting the wrong equipment can result in added expense and frustration. For example, the equipment must be compatible with other equipment in the office. Also, dictation equipment must be kept in good repair at all times.

There are basically three types of dictation equipment — portable units, desktop units, and centralized systems. So that you may understand more about this equipment, the types are explained here.

Portable Dictation Units. Portable units are very useful for people who travel frequently. They may be used in a car, in a hotel, or in an airport. Portable units are hand-sized, battery-powered, and designed to be placed in a pocket or briefcase. The media used by portables include standard cassettes, minicassettes, microcassettes, and the smallest recording medium available, the picocassette. The picocassette is about two-thirds the size of the microcassette. Most companies purchase portables that use the same recording media as their desktop or centralized systems. The dictation time available is usually from sixty minutes to three hours. Portable dictation units contain a number of

Lanier Business Products

Illustration 5-3. Portable Dictation Unit

features. Models contain LCDs (liquid crystal displays) that show users how much recording time has been used and how much is remaining. Some models let the dictator visually mark the documents and instructions on the recording media.

Desktop Dictation Units. Desktop units are so named because they are generally used on a word originator's desk. Desktop machines are available in three units — a unit for dictating only, a unit for transcribing only, or a combination unit for both dictating and transcribing. However, in most instances it is not wise to buy a unit which has both the dictation and transcription functions. Usually the operator is interested in either the dictation or transcription function, not both. And, it is more costly to buy a machine with both functions.

Desktop units use the same kinds of recording media as portables — standard cassettes, minicassettes, microcassettes, or picocassettes. The transcribing unit will accept media that is dictated on a portable unit if that media is the same size or if an adaptor (a device that makes media compatible) is used.

Desktop units include a number of special features. Some have a numerical display that informs the user how many special instructions and documents are on the media as well as their locations. Some models allow users to record telephone messages. Callers leave messages on the recording medium, and the receiver can listen to the recording upon returning to the office. Some units have a mode display which tells the user at a glance whether the machine is recording, rewinding, fast forwarding, or in telephone record or listen modes. Some models feature a special document counter that automatically measures the productivity of the transcriptionist. Another feature of some models is the media pre-end and end alarms. These alert the user when the end of the media is near.

Centralized Dictation Systems. With a centralized dictation system, one or several recording machines receive the dictation of a number of executives. The machines that receive the dictation are at a centralized area; however, the executives who dictate may be located at various places throughout the building. The correspondence is transcribed by an office worker who is probably at a different location than the executive, and the correspondence is returned to the executive for her or his signature. A centralized recording system is particularly useful to the executive who has only a small amount of correspondence to dictate and who does not need a full-time office worker.

There are two basic types of centralized dictation systems—discrete media and endless loop. The difference between the two systems is the manner in which the dictation is recorded and distributed. With discrete media systems, the dictation is recorded on magnetic media such as a cassette. The cassette is then given to the office worker who places it on a transcription unit and begins the transcription process. With an endless-loop system, no media are handled. An endless reel-to-reel tape is permanently housed in the tank of the recorder. The tape passes from the recording head to the transcribing head. An endless-loop centralized dictation system is shown in Illustration 5-4. The parts of a centralized dictation system are

1. Dictation station. This station may be a telephone or a microphone unit and is usually located in the executive's office.
2. Recorder. Recorders are located in a central transcription area. This unit records the dictation onto a magnetic medium (cassette or endless-loop tape). Because the recorders and the dictation stations are in different locations, the dictation is referred to as being remote.
3. Transcription unit. The office worker uses this piece of equipment to play back the recorded material. The transcription unit has a headset for listening to playback, a control device that either contains the discrete media (i.e., cassette) or accesses the transcribing head of an endless-loop tape, and a foot pedal.

Voice Recognition Technology (VRT).

With this technology, the message delivered by the voice is recognized by the computer through a special type of processor that converts the

Illustration 5-4. Centralized Dictation System

speech to digital impulses or signals. The digital signals are then matched to the sound patterns stored in the memory of the computer, and the computer is able to print out the words on paper. Voice-recognition technology is already being used in factory assembly and inventory applications. Vocabularies tend to be in the 40- to 100-word range and to consist of words and phrases with distinct pauses rather than continuous sentences without pauses.

Several companies are actively working on systems for office use. These systems will allow dictators to speak directly into recorders and processing terminals to convert spoken words into visual words. The systems will translate speech into computer-readable text and store the text for later output in the form of a printed copy. With one system, each user goes through a process in which a 15- to 20-minute standard script is read into the system. From this script, the system learns a user's speech pattern and the sounds used to construct words. Words the system does not recognize are spelled phonetically for later correction. The system is designed to recognize continuous, conversational speech. Words do not have to be spoken as distinct units in order for the computer to translate them into text.

It is anticipated that voice recognition technology (VRTs) will become an increasingly significant factor in dictation methods. Instead of needing both dictating machines and transcribing machines, dictators or word originators will speak directly into recorders; and processing terminals will convert spoken words into visual words or text. Editing and revising will be done verbally as well as visually and with considerably greater ease than is now possible.

INPUTTING CORRESPONDENCE

If correspondence has been created through longhand, shorthand, or machine dictation, it must be inputted onto some type of equipment. The equipment that is used most frequently today includes electronic typewriters, dedicated word processors, multistation systems, and microcomputers with word processing software. In addition to these four types of equipment on which correspondence is input, one additional method of input will be presented here — optical character recognition.

Electronic Typewriters. The keyboard is the input mechanism on the electronic typewriter for correspondence that was created through longhand, shorthand, or machine dictation. Electronic typewriters resemble an electric typewriter in appearance, although they are quite different in operation. An electronic typewriter is shown in Illustration 5-5. On an electronic typewriter, a handful of electronic chips (microprocessors) tells the machine what to do. There are almost no mechanical parts (levers, gears, springs, or screws) inside the case of the machine. You see a printing element that glides across the page.

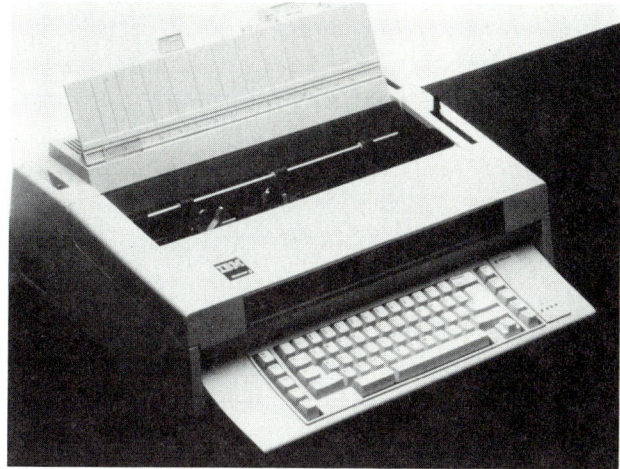

Courtesy of International Business Machines Corporation

Illustration 5-5. Electronic Typewriter

Some of the features included on electronic typewriters are

1. Automatic features such as centering, underscoring, indenting, pitch selection, error correction, carriage return, and number alignment.
2. Adjustable keyboard that can be adjusted to a low, medium, or high-angle position.
3. Storage capacity of several thousand characters which allows storage of several pages of text. Some models provide for optional plug-in memory cartridges which increase the memory capacity of the machine.
4. Several electronic typewriters will also attach to a personal computer and become a letter-quality printer for the computer.
5. A thin window where a limited amount of text is displayed as it is keyboarded (approximately one line).
6. Optional software packages such as a spelling package which can catch misspellings as they are typed and programs that aid in the use of the system.

Dedicated Word Processors. Just as the keyboard is the input mechanism on the electronic typewriter, so is the keyboard the input mechanism on a dedicated word processor. The correspondence that was created by longhand, shorthand, or machine dictation is keyboarded into the dedicated word processor.

The dedicated word processor is sometimes

referred to as a "standalone" since it can "stand alone" or operate without the aid of another machine such as a computer or a printer. All of the components necessary to produce the final document are included in the system. These components are the screen, the keyboard, the recording/storage device, the printing unit, and the intelligence/logic device.

The Screen. The early dedicated word processors did not have a screen; they were referred to as "blind word processors." Now all dedicated word processors have a screen, or video display, which allows the operator to see the text as it is being keyboarded. As text is keyboarded and appears on the screen, a cursor (indicator or pointer) marks the place of action. The operator moves the cursor to the point in the document where copy needs to be added, omitted, or moved. The operator can key in new text while the previous page is being played out by the printer. Visual displays vary as to the amount of text that can be seen on the screen at one time from partial displays with as little as six lines to full-page displays.

The Keyboard. Although the keyboard looks like that of the standard typewriter, it has additional keys which direct the movement of the cursor, provide for the deletion and insertion of copy, and allow the operator to see previous material entered on the screen. The keyboard is usually separate or detached from the screen and thus can be moved around for the comfort of the operator.

Recording/Storage Device. The dedicated word processor has some internal memory, and material is stored there temporarily as it is input into the machine. However, in order to save the correspondence for later printout, it must be transferred to permanent storage. For most dedicated word processors permanent storage is on a floppy diskette. It may be a standard diskette about the size of a 45 rpm record or a mini-diskette. The diskette is kept in an envelope which protects the surface of the diskette. This envelope is then inserted into the disk drive of the machine where information is transferred from the temporary internal storage to the disk-

ette or permanent storage. Once one diskette is filled, another diskette is inserted. Thus, there is unlimited permanent storage on diskettes.

Printing Device. The printer of a dedicated word processor is a separate piece of equipment. A word processor may have its own printer or two or three word processors may share one printer. Once the operator is ready to print a document, the appropriate command is keyed into the word processor, and the copy is printed from the diskette onto paper in the printer.

Intelligence/Logic Device. Just as a computer has a CPU (central processing unit) so does a dedicated word processor. The CPU enables the word processor to perform all of the functions that it performs, including storing information, displaying copy on the screen, adding and deleting copy, and printing the copy. In other words, it is the brain of the unit.

Courtesy of Wang Laboratories, Inc.

Illustration 5-6. Dedicated Word Processor

Multistation Systems. The term "multistation system" refers to a system in which there is more than one workstation with each station sharing a common device. Such a system may include a cluster of terminals sharing storage facilities, printers, and/or the logic/intelligence (CPU) of the system. Terminals may be either smart or dumb. A smart terminal has some intelligence and can do many functions on its own. A dumb terminal has no intelligence and depends on the CPU for its logic capabilities.

There are two basic advantages of multistation systems over single-station systems—lower costs and file sharing. By allowing several stations to share at least one device, the average price of each station is less than the same number of single stations. Several operators can also share master files (or a collection of related records) thus eliminating the need for each station to have master file diskettes. The basic disadvantage of a multistation system is that if one portion of the system goes down it affects the entire system.

Courtesy of Wang Laboratories, Inc.

Illustration 5-7. Multistation System

Microcomputers. Microcomputers with word processing software are beginning to be used more and more by businesses to perform the word processing functions of the office. There are several advantages to using microcomputers for word processing, some of which are

1. Both word processing functions and data processing functions can be performed on the same machine.
2. Numerous software packages are available at minimal cost which allow you to perform word and data processing functions on the microcomputer. The costs of these software

packages are minimal, from under $100 to several hundred dollars. You learned in Chapter 1 that the word processing operator is being called an information specialist. This change is due to the integration of word and data processing which changes the job duties of the word processor from only processing words to processing data and words. This integration is projected to continue. The word processor is also now dealing with graphic information more and more, since graphics packages are readily available for the microcomputer.

3. An executive may have a microcomputer at home and be connected to the office computer by a modem. A modem enables communication between computers through telephone lines.
4. The cost of microcomputers continues to decrease, with entire systems including the printer available for a few thousand dollars.

Since more and more executives have microcomputers in their offices, some are beginning to keyboard their letters and memos directly into the computer. The secretary may have the responsibility of making revisions, or the secretary may rarely handle the correspondence; therefore, the creation of correspondence by executives may change office roles drastically. Secretaries may become freer to perform a wider variety of tasks and participate more in decision making.

Optical Character Recognition. In Chapter 4 you learned that OCR devices are input devices for the computer. They are also input devices in word processing. For example, law firms and corporate legal departments use OCR equipment to enter briefs, contracts, wills, and trial proceedings which have been keyboarded on a standard typewriter. With the use of OCR equipment, costly rekeying of already typed information is eliminated.

An OCR scanner transfers typed text into digital signals or impulses for recording on a diskette. The diskette can then be inserted on a disk drive and be read by word processing equipment. The document is edited and printed in final form by a word processing operator.

OCR scanners improve productivity by allowing initial keyboarding to be performed on less expensive standard electric typewriters and revisions to be performed on word processors.

OCR technology has made tremendous advances over the past few years. OCR equipment was previously large and costly. The original document had to be typed with special OCR fonts. Disks and CRTs displayed many "misreads" and "can't reads" that had to be edited on screen by a tedious, time-consuming process. OCR equipment is now the size of small office copiers. Special codes are used to spot potential errors, and these can be found easily on a screen using a global-search and replace feature. The equipment searches through a document for words or sets of characters and replaces them with new ones. OCR equipment can now read standard type styles (including courier, letter gothic, prestige elite and pica, and bookfact academic) from a variety of sources such as a Selectric-like ball or a daisy-wheel print device. Some systems are even able to read handprinted characters and handwritten signatures and drawings. The devices can also handle single-, one-and-one half-, double-, and triple-line spacing, underlining, blank spaces between paragraphs, and even crooked lines. Although the capabilities of OCR equipment has increased, the price of this equipment has been reduced drastically. And, it is anticipated that prices will be even lower in the future.

Some of the advantages of OCR equipment are

1. Speed. An OCR unit can read from a typed page at 400 characters per second; the OCR can input at a rate that is 240 times faster than the average office worker can keyboard material.
2. Low error rate. The average error rate for an OCR scanner is one in 300,000 characters.
3. Expansion capability. OCR scanners can handle added office paperwork volume without having to add more word processing equipment and personnel.
4. Extended compatibility. OCR equipment can read text printed on one system and transmit it to other incompatible systems.

OUTPUTTING CORRESPONDENCE

Once correspondence has been entered into a word processor and the appropriate revisions made, correspondence is ready to be output and used. The basic method for outputting correspondence is done through the printer. However, other methods can be used; two of these methods along with the printer method are presented here.

Printer. For most information that is entered into a word processor, it is important that it appear in final form as printed copy. Therefore, the printer is the most important output device for a word processor. In Chapter 4 you learned about impact and non-impact printers. Daisy wheel printers have been used extensively in the past with word processors since they produce letter quality copy. However, with the improvement in dot matrix technology, the dot matrix printer produces near letter quality print at a much faster speed than the daisy wheel printer. And, although laser printers are relatively expensive, these printers produce letter quality output at higher speeds than either of the other two printers and with much quieter operation. The laser printer is probably the printer of the future.

Magnetic Media. Magnetic media such as disks and diskettes also become output for the word processor. For example, assume that a report is going to be revised at a later date. The report may be output on a printer and distributed to several executives to read and to revise as appropriate. Then, the report is also output to a magnetic diskette. The diskette will be used later to input the report back into the word processor where it will be revised and printed out.

Video Display Terminal. Output from a word processor can also be through a video display terminal. For example, assume that you are going to send information from one word processing unit to an individual at another word processing unit. Once the information is received by the second word processing unit, it is called up on the video display unit and read by the individual. It is not necessary to have a printed copy of the information; therefore, no information is printed. You will learn more about this type of transfer from one word processor to another which is generally called *electronic mail* in Chapter 9.

THE WORD PROCESSING ENVIRONMENT

If the word processing concept is to result in productivity in an office, there must be an environment where people feel comfortable with the equipment they use. There are two basic organizational structures that are used with word processing — centralized structures and decentralized structures.

Centralized Word Processing Structure.

When word processing structures were first created, the emphasis was on totally centralized services. Thus people, tasks, and word processing equipment were grouped together in one area which was called a word processing center. The emphasis was on producing large volumes of documents, such as memos, letters, forms, and reports. For example, if there was a long report to produce or a form letter to be sent to hundreds of addresses, the document was sent to the center where it was produced and returned to the originator for processing.

Centralization provided for specialized job functions. A word processing operator would keyboard and produce documents and not have to be interrupted with a wide variety of duties such as filing correspondence, running copies of materials, answering the telephone, and handling frequent interruptions. The individual was free to concentrate on one job duty; thus, it was anticipated that productivity would be increased. The centralized structure is still used in many companies today and can increase productivity significantly. However, such a structure does not work for all companies. A centralized word processing structure is shown in Illustration 5-8.

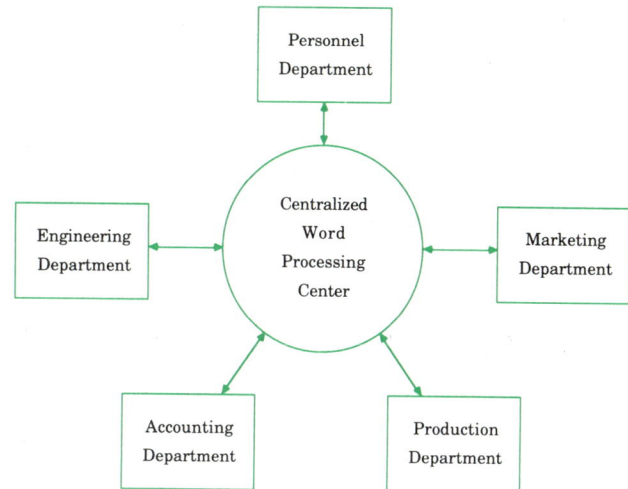

Illustration 5-8. Centralized Word Processing Structure

Decentralized Word Processing Structure.

Having several small centers where each office worker has a word processor is called a decentralized structure. In such a structure the office worker may not have all of the components of the system. For example, two or three word processing operators may share one printer as in a multistation system. Also, the word processing equipment used in a decentralized structure may be an electronic typewriter or a microcomputer with a software package rather than a dedicated word processor. As equipment has become less expensive, decentralized structures have grown. In fact, many people project that in the future all office personnel will have access to some type of word processor. One of the benefits of a decentralized structure is control. The word originator no longer has to wait his or her turn in the word processing center. The major disadvantage of a decentralized structure is cost. Even though word processing equipment is less expensive today than in the past, it is still more expensive to place equipment on or near every office worker's desk. A decentralized system is shown in Illustration 5-9.

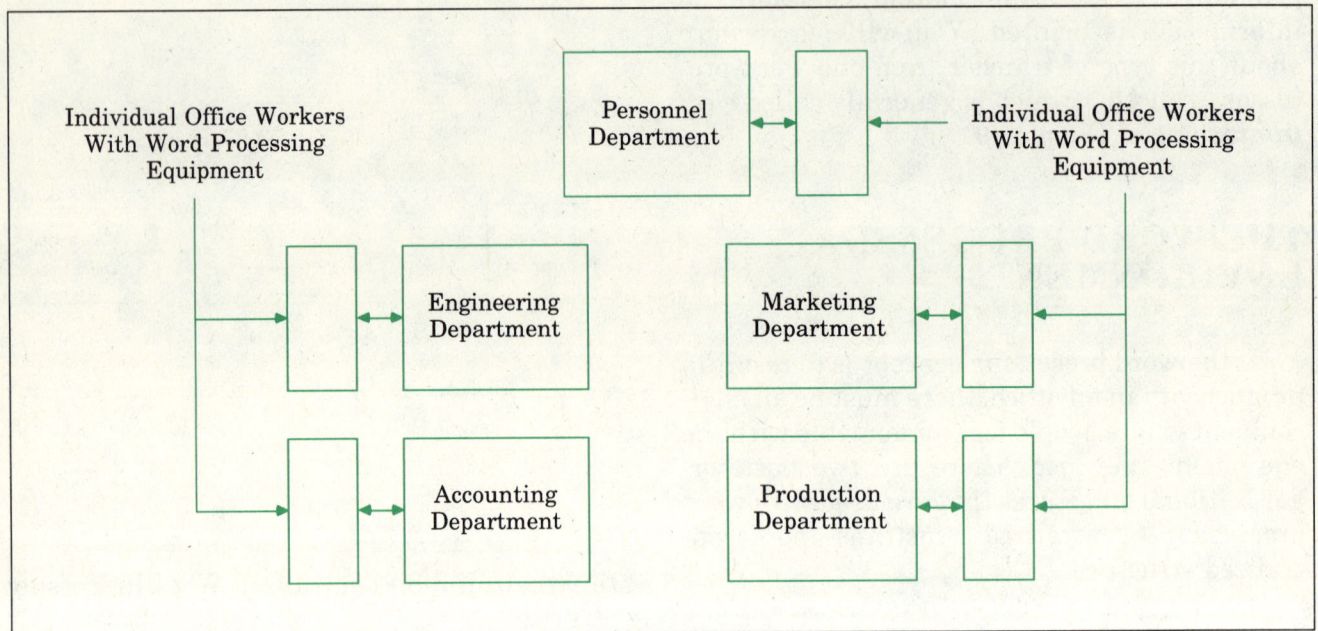

Illustration 5-9. Decentralized Word Processing Structure

Centralized/Decentralized Structure. Some companies have both a centralized and decentralized structure. The centralized structure is used to produce the heavy volume of work such as extensive reports and form letters. And, office workers have some type of word processing equipment at their workstations to produce the daily correspondence such as routine letters and memorandums.

The advantage of a centralized/decentralized structure is that it provides a centralized word processing center which produces the heavy volume of work. Individuals in the center are not interrupted by the usual demands made on the office worker; i.e., telephone calls, visitors, running errands, etc. It also provides a decentralized structure within the individual offices so that routine correspondence may be produced quickly for an individual originator without the possibility of having to wait for work from a large center. It allows the individual office worker all the advantages of word processing equipment; e.g., greater productivity, ease of revision of work, graphics capabilities, etc. The major disadvantage is cost. It is expensive for a company to set up both a centralized and a decentralized system. Usually, it is only cost effective for the mid-size to large-size company. See Illustration 5-10.

CAREER OPPORTUNITIES

There are a number of career opportunities available for people interested in the word processing field. People in entry level jobs are generally called word/information processing operators or specialists. The word/information processing specialist must possess good keyboarding and proofreading skills. He or she must also have an excellent knowledge of grammar, punctuation, and spelling. Other skills necessary are the ability to operate word processing equipment, and machine transcription. The ability to format, input, and revise complicated documents is also essential.

The office worker of today needs word processing skill. As you read the paper on job openings available in the office, you will notice that

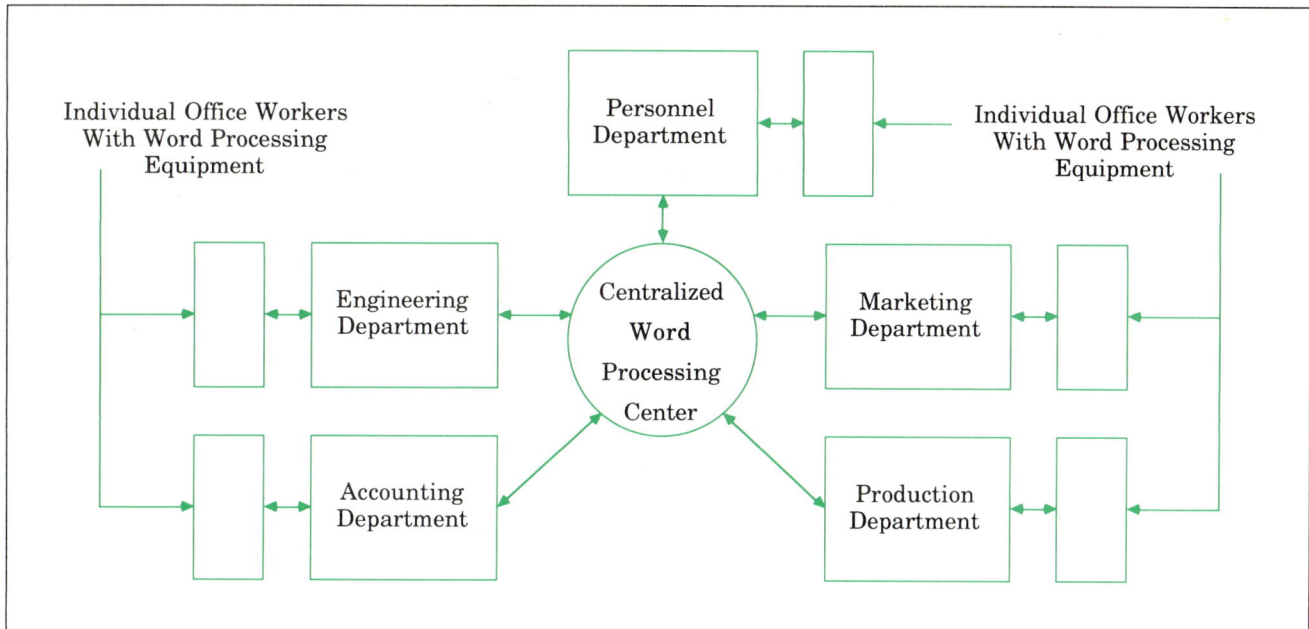

Illustration 5-10. Centralized/Decentralized Word Processing Structure

secretarial positions often require word processing skill along with various other skills. Therefore, if you plan to be an office worker you will probably need to develop skill on the word processor.

If you work for a large company that has a centralized word processing structure, other possible career opportunities include a word processing supervisor and a word processing manager. A word processing supervisor must possess work experience as a word processing operator. The supervisor assigns work to operators and is responsible for accuracy and quality of material produced by the operators. The supervisor may train new operators or existing staff on new equipment. A word processing manager must possess skills in word processing and communications. The manager is responsible for recommending staff and equipment. He or she is also responsible for setting productivity standards. The manager maintains budgets, plans for the word processing center, and evaluates and supervises personnel.

The projected future job opportunities in word processing are extremely good. In fact, re-

gardless of the type of office position you may obtain, your chances for promotion and advancement are better if you have skill in word processing.

FUTURE DIRECTIONS

Word processing technology is operating today at only a fraction of its potential. It is anticipated that word processing equipment and products will proliferate to meet the incredibly expanding needs of a marketplace that encompasses office, home, and school. Word processing has had the effect on the handling of words similar to that of the pocket calculator on the handling of numbers.

Many alternative software and hardware combinations will be designed to support the needs of a broad spectrum of users. Greater advances will be made in voice recognition and artificial intelligence. All office workers will be supported by information/word processors that will increase their efficiency in handling conventional tasks such as organizing schedules, keeping calendars, writing memos, filing electronically, preparing for meetings, tracking events and projects, managing phone communications, and coordinating efforts with other personnel. In fact, it is anticipated that widespread use of information/word processors in the office will improve individual productivity by as much as 20 percent.

Whatever the exact directions the office of the future takes, it is certain that word processors and computers will be of major importance. For you, it means that you must develop proficiency on the machines of today and expect to learn new skills and new machines as they are developed.

FOR YOUR REVIEW

The following review will help you remember the important points of this chapter.

1. Word processing involves communicating one person's ideas in the form of words to another person.

2. Word processing as a concept is the transformation of ideas and information into a readable form of communication through the management of procedures, equipment, personnel, and the work environment.

3. With the advent of the typewriter, the mechanical method of processing words came into being.

4. The birth of word processing as we know it today did not begin until 1964 with the invention of the first automated typing system that recorded keystrokes on a magnetic medium — the Magnetic Tape Selectric Typewriter (MT/ST).

5. Word processing equipment has become important to business because of the growth in paperwork that can be handled more efficiently; greater productivity; cost savings due to a greater volume of production; and higher quality of work.

6. Correspondence is created by longhand, shorthand dictation, and machine dictation.

7. Voice recognition is a computer process whereby the spoken word is converted to print. This technology is still in the experimental stage for word processing applications.

8. Some of the advantages of machine dictation are (a) dictation equipment can be available whenever and wherever the dictator wants to dictate; (b) it ties up only one person's time during the dictation process; and (c) it can be transcribed by any person trained on a transcription unit.

9. There are basically three types of dictation equipment — portable units, desktop units, and centralized systems.

10. Portable units are hand-sized, battery-powered, and designed to be placed in a pocket or briefcase. They are good units for the executive who travels frequently.

11. The most common means of dictation is the desktop unit. It is used by one originator with an office worker transcribing the material which has been dictated.

12. In a centralized system, one of several recording machines receives the dictation of a number of executives. The machines that receive the dictation are at a centralized location, while the executives who dictate the correspondence and the office workers who transcribe it are at different locations.

13. There are five basic types of equipment used in inputting correspondence, namely, the electronic typewriter, a dedicated word processor, a multistation system, a microcomputer with word processing software, and optical character recognition devices.

14. Electronic typewriters have almost no mechanical parts and operate by electronic chips which tell the machine what to do.

15. Electronic typewriters today have a variety of features including automatic error correction, carriage return, and indenting; format and phrase storage; various sizes of internal memory; removable storage through diskettes; and video display.

16. Dedicated word processors can operate

without the aid of another machine such as a computer or printer. The components of a dedicated word processor include the screen, the keyboard, the recording/storage device, the printing device, and the intelligence/logic device.

17. The term multistation system refers to a system in which there is more than one workstation with each station sharing a common device. Such a system may include a cluster of terminals sharing storage facilities, printers, and/or the logic/intelligence (CPU) of a central computer.

18. Microcomputers with word processing software are beginning to be used more and more by businesses to perform word processing functions.

19. An OCR scanner is used to input data already existing in printed form directly into the computer.

20. Advantages of OCR equipment include speed, low error rate, expansion capability, and compatibility with other machines.

21. The basic method of outputting correspondence from a word processor is through a printer.

22. There are two basic office structures used with word processing — centralized structures and decentralized structures.

23. In a centralized system, people, tasks, and word processing equipment are grouped together in one area called a word processing center.

24. In a decentralized system small centers exist at locations all around the company.

25. Numerous career opportunities exist for people with word processing skills. The entry-level position is called an information/word processing operator or specialist.

26. It is anticipated that word processing equipment and products will proliferate in the future to meet the increasing demands of the marketplace. It is projected that all office workers will be supported by information/word processors that handle a variety of office functions.

PROFESSIONAL FORUM

Your company is planning to hire two additional word processing specialists. You had two courses in word processing while you attended business college; however, you have not used your word processing skills in your present position. Your job duties now include receptionist duties, filing, handling the mail, greeting callers, and doing light typing. You feel you cannot get a promotion from your present position, and the position as a word processing specialist is attractive to you. As you consider this position, answer these questions:

1. What skills will you need in order to succeed as a word processing operator?
2. What promotional opportunities do you think you will have if you take the job?

FOR YOUR UNDERSTANDING

1. Briefly describe the development of word processing.
2. Give three reasons why word processors have become so important in business today.
3. State three methods of creating correspondence for word processing equipment.
4. Identify three advantages of machine dictation.
5. Name and describe three types of dictation equipment.
6. Distinguish between discrete dictation media and endless-loop dictation media.
7. List and describe the main types of equipment for inputting correspondence.
8. Explain the parts of a dedicated word processor.
9. Explain the difference between centralized and decentralized word processing structures.
10. What is the projected future of word processing?

OFFICE APPLICATIONS

On pages 294–295 are office applications that correlate with this chapter.

CHAPTER 6

Reprographics

The information age in which we live and work has necessitated that greater and greater numbers of copies of correspondence, reports, and other documents be produced. And, the electronic revolution that has affected data processing and word processing has also influenced the methods of reproducing or duplicating information from a computer or word processor. Numerous types of equipment for making reproductions are available. As an office worker, it will be your responsibility to determine what method of reproduction should be used. You will make decisions about the most economical way to reproduce information in the quantity and quality desired. Not all office documents demand high-quality copies, so you must choose the correct process for the situation at hand. This chapter will help you to acquire the knowledge needed for accomplishing a variety of reprographics tasks.

GENERAL OBJECTIVES

Your general objectives for this chapter are to

1. Identify the methods used to reproduce material.
2. Become knowledgeable about the types of copiers, duplicators, and printers available and how they are used.

3. Understand the copyright law.
4. Determine future directions of reprographics.

REPROGRAPHICS DEFINED

Reprographics is the process of making copies of correspondence, reports, and various other documents. The primary method of making reproductions in an office is the copying process. Copiers are commonly used to make ten or fewer copies. As an office worker, the copier will be the main piece of reprographics equipment that you will use. However, you will also need to have an understanding of the duplicating process, the carbon paper process, the printing process, and the facsimile process. All of these methods are presented in this chapter.

THE CARBON PAPER PROCESS

One of the oldest methods of producing multiple copies is the carbon paper process. In making carbon copies, you may use separate sheets of carbon paper and second sheets or carbon packs. Carbon packs include carbon paper and second sheets which are bound together at one end. With a carbon pack, once the carbon has been used it is discarded; with separate carbon sheets, the carbon may be used several times. If you are making carbon copies, you need to be knowledgeable about the types of carbon paper available, how to assemble the carbons for multiple copies, and how to store your carbon paper. Appendix E gives you additional information on carbon paper. Since the heavy usage of copying equipment has almost eliminated the use of carbon paper, little emphasis is placed on carbon paper in this chapter.

CATEGORIES OF COPIERS

Each day in the average office hundreds and even thousands of copies are made by the use of copying machines. Copying machines create exact copies from already existing originals. Almost any type of material can be reproduced on a copying machine. It is the most convenient and easiest method of reprographics in use today. There are basically four categories of copiers available—low-volume, mid-volume, high-volume, and duplicating-volume. These divisions are based on the monthly copy volumes each copier can handle. This copy volume is basically determined by the speed at which the copiers operate.

Copies can be produced on either plain or specially coated paper. As the copier market has grown, plain-paper copiers have become the preferred machine. Today, few machines use specially coated paper. In fact, copy machines are sometimes referred to as plain-paper copiers. Plain-paper copiers produce copies on regular bond paper. These machines can also make copies on colored paper, on company stationery, and on various types of business forms.

Low-Volume Copiers. Low-volume copiers can be divided into two groups: (1) copiers which produce 8 to 15 copies per minute, with monthly volumes of up to 1,000 copies; and (2) copiers which produce up to 20 copies per minute and are marketed for volume levels of up to 20,000 copies per month.

The copiers which produce 8 to 15 copies per minute are small, desktop copiers which can be moved anywhere since they weigh as little as 39 pounds. These copiers are characterized by being lightweight, portable, and virtually service free. They are the least expensive of all copiers. Much of the growth of copier sales is in this small, low-volume market. And, it is anticipated that these inexpensive copiers will maintain their growth position due to the large number of businesses in the United States with fewer than 20 employees and the decentralization of machines within the office. Copiers are being placed closer to the office worker as a productivity and convenience factor. As the costs of these copiers continue to go down, it is anticipated that the copier sales will continue to grow. A small, desktop copier is shown in Illustration 6-1.

The low-volume copier that produces up to 20 copies per minute, with monthly volumes of over 20,000 copies is slightly more expensive than the copier that produces 8 to 15 copies per month but less than mid- and high-volume copiers. These copiers are generally located strategically throughout a company or are used as the sole copier in small businesses or offices. These copiers may be either desktop models or consoles (floor models).

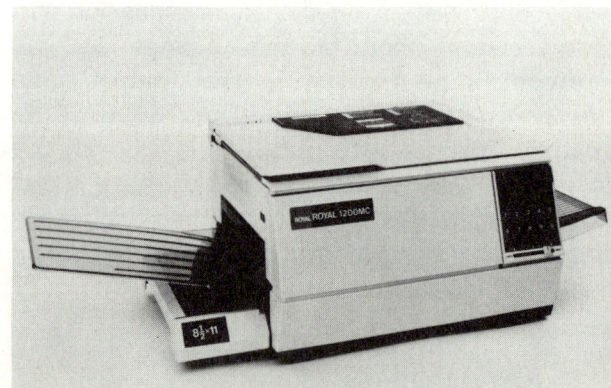

Konica Business Machines U.S.A., Inc.

Illustration 6-1. Desktop Copier

Mid-Volume Copiers. Mid-volume copiers operate at speeds of 21 to 50 copies per minute and produce up to 60,000 copies per month. Although low-volume copiers do not have many special features or options, mid-volume copiers have numerous features. Some of the features include recirculating document feeders, fully automatic duplexing, and reduction and enlargement copying modes. Mid-volume copiers are floor-console models and are found in semi-central or satellite copying locations to service walk-up users.

High-Volume Copiers.
High-volume copiers operate at speeds of 51 to 90 copies per minute and are recommended for volume levels of 50,000 to 100,000 copies per month. Automatic or recirculating document feeders, sorters, fully automatic duplexing, reduction copying, and continuous paper tray switching capabilities are standard offerings on most high-volume copiers. These units are floor-console models and are found in centralized reprographics departments or in distributed locations within large companies. A high-volume copier is shown in Illustration 6-2.

Multigraphics Division, AM International, Inc.

Illustration 6-2. High-Volume Copier

Duplicating-Volume Copiers.
Duplicating-volume copiers operate at speeds of 100 or more copies per minute and produce from 50,000 to 200,000 copies per month. Standard features on such machines include fully automatic duplexing, automatic feeding of originals, variable reduction copying, and sorting. The machines are the most expensive of the copiers, costing two to three times what a high-volume copier costs.

They also produce the highest quality copies. In fact, many of these machines produce copies that are comparable to those produced on an offset press (see page 78). These machines are placed in centralized reprographics centers where trained personnel are employed full time in producing copies. The ordinary office worker would not be operating this type of copier but would be sending work to a center to be produced by the employees operating the copier.

Intelligent Copiers.
Intelligent copiers are high- or duplicating-volume copiers that may receive input from a word processor, computer, optical character recognition unit, or pre-recorded magnetic media. For example, information can be inputted into a dedicated word processor and sent by electronic signals to the intelligent copier where the required number of copies are printed. An intelligent copier is shown in Illustration 6-3.

To be intelligent, a copier needs to have, at a minimum, a significant amount of memory. The intelligent copier uses microprocessor technology which allows it to accept input from one or more machines and to provide hard copy output. The capability to input electronic signals from other equipment and to format output (often as hard copy) in various layouts makes these copiers true information distributors.

In addition to the printing capabilities, the intelligent copier can operate as an electronic

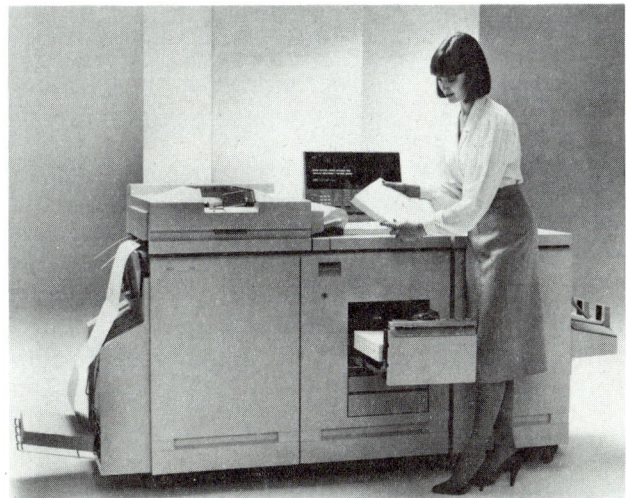

Photo Courtesy of Xerox Corporation

Illustration 6-3. Intelligent Copier

mail device. A letter prepared on a word processor can be stored in the copier. When delivery is desired, the letter can be sent via the phone lines to another intelligent copier. At the receiving end, the mail can be distributed on demand via a visual screen (CRT) or as hard copy (printed copy).

COPIER FEATURES

In addition to making copies of correspondence, reports, and other documents, copiers are able to perform numerous other functions. There are basic features that all copiers can handle, and then there are a variety of special features which are available only on some copiers. Both the basic features and several of the special features are presented here.

Basic Features. Copiers usually handle the two standard sizes of paper — 8½ by 11 inches and 8½ by 14 inches. The paper tray, which feeds the paper through the machine, may be adjusted for different paper sizes; or there may be separate trays. If there are separate trays, one size holds the 8½- by 11-inch paper and one tray holds the 8½- by 14-inch paper. The trays snap in and out of the copier for reloading the paper. If there is a single tray, the appropriate paper size for the task being performed must be placed in the tray. Some copiers are fitted with a roll of continuously fed paper that is cut to specific lengths as it is fed through the machine. Since roll-fed machines allow a variety of different size copies to be reproduced, it is especially suitable in applications where odd-size copies are required.

Another basic feature of copiers is the copy counter. Before starting to copy material, the counter is set for the number of copies needed. When the appropriate number of copies has been made, the copier will automatically stop. Also copiers are equipped with an exposure control which controls the lightness or darkness of the copies being produced. For example, if a copy is too light, a button may be pushed instructing the machine to make the copies darker.

Copiers are also equipped with features that indicate the cause of a machine malfunction.

For example, if the paper path is jammed, the copier will indicate this problem. If the paper stock is low, the copier will indicate that paper needs to be added. If the toner in the machine needs to be replaced so that clear, dark copies can be produced, the machine will let the operator know that also.

Special Features. Due to technological advances, many special features are available today on copiers. A number of these special features are explained here.

Duplexing. Duplexing, copying on both sides of a sheet of paper, is a special feature that is available on numerous copiers. Duplexing may be fully automatic or semiautomatic. If it is fully automatic, copies may be made on both sides by merely pushing the proper buttons. If it is a semiautomatic feature, the operator must turn the original over for copying on the second side. The duplexing feature is popular because of its cost effectiveness due to the paper saved.

Reduction and Enlargement. Reduction and enlargement of material being copied is possible through the use of a zoom lens. Users can select from a range of reduction or enlargement modes, usually in one percent increments. For example, an original might be reduced by 80 percent, 78 percent, or even 60 percent. This feature is helpful when material is being copied from a computer printout. Most computer paper is larger than the standard 8½- by 11-inch paper. With the reduction feature on copiers, the printout may be reduced to the standard size paper which can be placed conveniently in reports, along with other information that is being produced on the standard size paper. The standard 8½- by 11-inch paper is also easier to file.

The enlargement feature on a copier allows for material to be copied larger than the original material. For example, if there are details on the original that need to be larger for ease of reading and clarity, the enlargement feature on the copier allows for this to happen without costly retyping or reproducing of the original. A button is merely pushed on the machine, and the copy appears larger than the original.

Automatic Document Feed. The document feed on a copier may be semiautomatic or fully automatic. With semiautomatic document feed, each original must be fed into a receiving slot on the copier. The copy is then made and the original feeds out into one tray of the machine while the copies feed out onto another tray. With fully automatic document feed, a stack of originals is placed in the document handler; and each original is fed into the copier. Some document feeders can be programmed so that originals of varying sizes can be copied onto one-size paper.

Edit Feature. Some copiers now provide editing functions where the original image can be manipulated without destroying the original copy. This editing feature is a form of electronic cutting and pasting. For example, portions of the original copy may be deleted or moved to another location in the copy. Also, copy may be centered on the page through the editing feature.

Color Reproduction. Some copiers offer more than one color in the machine at any given time, allowing the operator to change colors simply by pressing a button. For example, copies can be made in black, blue, green, red, or brown which can match letterhead paper or be used for various other purposes. In addition, some copiers are capable of producing color copies of colored originals.

Collating and Stapling. Some copiers automatically sort copies in bins, while others collate internally and produce the collated copies in staggered sets. Copiers will also staple collated sets of material.

Reproducing Transparencies and Offset Masters. A number of copiers can produce transparencies which are used in presenting material on an overhead projector. Also, some copiers are capable of producing offset masters which are used in printing. In the next section of this chapter you will learn more about offset printing.

Computer Form Feeders. Since copies are often made of computer printouts, computer form feeders are found on many copiers, either as a standard in combination with other types of feeders, or as optional devices to be placed on the copier as required.

Voice Synthesis. Some copiers are equipped with voice synthesis systems which tell the operator in a simulated voice when a problem is occurring on the copier and what the problem is.

Job Recovery. Sometimes it is necessary to interrupt the copying of a large project in order to make a few copies of other material. The job recovery mode remembers how many copies have been made of the original project. And, when the operator is ready to finish the project, the copier automatically picks up where it left off and completes the required number of copies.

Message Display. Some copiers have a message display function which provides feedback on the features being used on the copier and keeps you informed of a copy job's progress.

Automatic Folding. Certain copiers will fold 11″ × 17″ copies to 8½″ × 11″. With this feature, drawings and schematics can be kept in a legible size and convenient format for handling and distribution. The fold can also be offset so that folded materials can be placed in three-ring binders.

COPYING PROCESSES

One of the early copying processes (developed after 1940) was the *diffusion transfer process*. With this process, the original document to be copied is placed against a light-sensitive negative sheet and then exposed to light. The original document is removed and the negative sheet placed on a coated light-sensitive positive paper and both sheets are run through a developer solution. The two sheets are chemically treated so that the coating on the negative sheet corresponding to the image of the original diffuses into the copy paper where it turns black to form a copy.

Soon after the diffusion transfer process was developed, 3M Corporation developed a process called *thermography*. This process is based on the principle that dark colors absorb more heat than light colors. Material to be copied is placed beneath a heat-sensitive copy sheet. Infrared light is then beamed through the sensitized copy onto the original as both sheets feed through the machine. The heat causes the dark outlines on the original to turn the sensitized paper dark in the same places, thus producing the copy. Thermography was used extensively until 1960 when Xerox introduced the 913 copier. This copier used Xerography (also called the *electrostatic process*). Since that time, copiers using Xerography have dominated the copier market. However, with the advent of the laser and fiber optics, these technologies are being used more and more today as they become more affordable.

Xerography.

This process is based on the principle that unlike electrical charges attract each other and like charges repel each other. It is also based on the principle that electrostatic coatings such as selenium have the unique property of holding an electrostatic charge in the dark and losing the charge when exposed to light such as that reflected from the white areas of an original. This method exposes a positively charged drum or cylinder surface within the copier to light reflected through lenses and mirrors from the original document. When light from the white areas of the original strikes the drum, the positive charge disappears. A negatively charged black powder or liquid called a *toner* adheres to the portion of the drum surface still charged. A sheet of plain paper that has been given a positive electrostatic charge is passed over the drum, and a copy is produced.

Lasers.

Lasers are high energy concentrated light sources which are used for scanning and recording images at high speed. Because the laser can be controlled by electronic impulses, it can be operated by digital signals from a computer, thus enabling satellite and facsimile transmission of plate images to remote printing locations. (The facsimile process is explained on p. 79.) Many of the intelligent copiers use laser beams to reflect the images.

Fiber Optics.

Fiber optics copiers have few moving parts and are small and lightweight. Rather than using mirrors and lenses to transfer electrical charges of an image to a drum, optic fibers transmit light from the original to the drum. Optic fibers are made up of rows of tiny glass fibers encased in a thin resin wafer. Each fiber functions as a miniature lens, focusing its tiny segment of the total image on the drum. Fiber optics has been used mainly in the low-volume copiers.

THE DUPLICATING PROCESS

As you have learned, a copier produces directly from an original. However, a duplicator produces copies from prepared masters and from stencils. Two types of duplicators are the spirit and stencil duplicators. In the past, these machines were used extensively because of their simple operation and low cost. However, with copiers becoming less and less expensive and providing more and more features that are simple to use, the spirit and stencil duplicators are used infrequently today. Most often you will find these machines used in schools or churches where inexpensive copies are needed and the quality of the copy is not of prime importance. Since these duplicators are used infrequently, only a limited discussion is presented here about these machines.

Spirit Duplicators.

Spirit duplicators are also referred to as *fluid* or *liquid-process duplicators*. In spirit duplication, a master is prepared by typing, writing, or drawing on a special paper that is placed against a sheet of hectograph carbon paper. After the master has been prepared, it is placed on the cylinder of the machine so that the back of the master comes in contact with the copy paper. As the cylinder is rotated, a liquid comes in contact with the dye on the back of the master and transfers the finished copy to the paper. Approximately 300 copies may be run from one master. Masters are available in five colors—purple (the most commonly used color), black, blue, red, and green. A spirit duplicator is shown in Illustration 6-4.

Illustration 6-4. Spirit Duplicator

Stencil Duplicators. The stencil duplicating process (mimeograph) involves the use of a stencil and a machine which has an inked drum. The stencil is a thin sheet of paper coated with a waxy substance. As you type, draw, or write on the stencil, the stencil is "cut." Then, when the stencil is placed on the drum of the machine, ink penetrates through the cut surface to produce a copy on plain paper. Several thousand copies can be run from one stencil. A stencil duplicator is pictured in Illustration 6-5.

Illustration 6-5. Stencil Duplicator

THE OFFSET PRINTING PROCESS

When thousands of high-quality copies are needed, one method of reproduction that may be used is offset printing. The offset printing process produces copies that resemble material that has been typeset, assuming that care has been taken in preparing the master used in printing. Since the operation of the offset press requires a degree of training, the office worker does not run an offset press. Trained personnel are employed full time in centralized printing departments to run offset presses. The task of the office worker in reproducing material on an offset press is to prepare the original copy.

The offset process is based on the principle that grease and water do not mix. The image area (the typed area) is receptive to greasy printing ink; the nonimage area is receptive to water. Thus, the outlines on the typed area hold the printing ink, while the remaining surface attracts water and repels the ink. One way the copy is produced is from a typed offset master. (Other methods are given in the next paragraph.) This master is placed on a cylinder and is inked. The ink is transferred to a rubber-blanket roll, called the offset roll, which then comes in contact with the copy paper, resulting in the finished copy. An offset printer is shown in Illustration 6-6.

The masters which are used to print the offset copy are of three basic types: paper, electrostatic, and metal.

1. *Paper or direct impression master.* This master is a smooth paper material that may be prepared by typing or writing directly on it. One paper master will run approximately 2,500 copies if handled properly.
2. *Electrostatic master.* In order to prepare this master, the original is typed on a sheet of bond paper. The original is then copied on a sensitized offset master that is inserted into an electrostatic copier. The image is transferred from the original to the offset master during copying. These masters will run approximately 5,000 copies.
3. *Metal plate.* A camera is used to produce a picture that is transferred to a metal plate.

This plate is the most expensive of the three masters and produces the greatest number of copies; it has the capability of producing approximately 50,000 copies.

A.B. Dick Company

Illustration 6-6. Offset Printer

As an office worker, you will prepare copy for the offset press by keying or writing directly on a paper master or by preparing copy on a plain sheet of paper and then having the copy run through a copier that uses the electrostatic process. However, you usually will not have the responsibility for producing copy that is to be run on a metal plate, since that copy generally contains drawings or some type of photographs.

DESKTOP PUBLISHING

Desktop publishing refers to a personal computer-based system or a dedicated workstation that uses page layout software and outputs to a laser printer. With a desktop publishing system, the business has the option of producing print-quality copy in-house rather than sending material out to be typeset. Typesetting is used for printing books, magazines, annual reports, and other widely distributed documents that must look polished rather than for preparing copies of everyday documents, such as letters and memos. Today, the most common method of setting type is phototypesetting. A *phototypesetter* uses photographic technology to set text into special styles and column widths.

The advantages of desktop publishing are cost savings, time, control, and security. For example, it may cost as much as $14 to produce a professional page of copy using an outside source. With a desktop publishing system, that same page of copy can be produced for as little as $2. Time, which equates to money, can also be saved by reducing or eliminating the turnaround time associated with work done outside the company. The company also has more control over the product since the manager can oversee all phases of production. Security becomes an advantage in that no one outside the company will have access to the information being produced until it is officially made available.

The hardware for most desktop publishing systems consists of a personal computer with a significant amount of memory. Most graphics packages and page layout programs require large amounts of RAM (random access memory). In addition to the hardware, desktop publishing systems use page-layout software. With this software, you have control over every element on the page—placement and thickness of lines and borders, selection of typestyles and sizes, position of graphics and photos, and many other elements. Page-layout programs allow you to put text into columns and link them together from one page to another. Graphics can be moved about, stretched, cropped, or trimmed to fit the exact space that is allotted. Text can be enhanced by changing typestyles and sizes. Backgrounds of varying shades of gray can be added and text placed on top in either black or white for emphasis.

The last main component of a desktop system is the laser printer. The *laser printer* uses a technology very similar to photocopiers—a laser beam scans an image onto a drum from which it is reproduced. The laser printer has the ability to produce graphics and text on the same page. At present, laser printers cannot print in color; thus, only black and white (or shades of black) are available. However, it is anticipated that color will be possible in the future.

Other components which may be used with desktop publishing systems include digitizers, tablets, and OCR devices. *Digitizers* read video signals from video cameras and change the signals into digital form which then can be manipulated by the computer. With *tablets and light pens*, a person can draw freehand images that can be read into a computer. *OCR devices* can scan printed pages of both text and graphic images and convert the information to digital form.

Presently, desktop publishing is not on the verge of displacing the typesetting industry. Typesetting equipment provides over three times the resolution or density available with the laser printer. And, this higher resolution or density means that the type is darker or clearer. Also, personal computers are no match for the larger computers used in typesetting in terms of speed and capability. However, desktop publishing can be used profitably in a variety of ways in the office. Some of these are in producing newsletters, brochures, proposals, forms, reports, training materials, artwork, manuals, advertisements, conference and seminar handouts, and documents which include photographs.

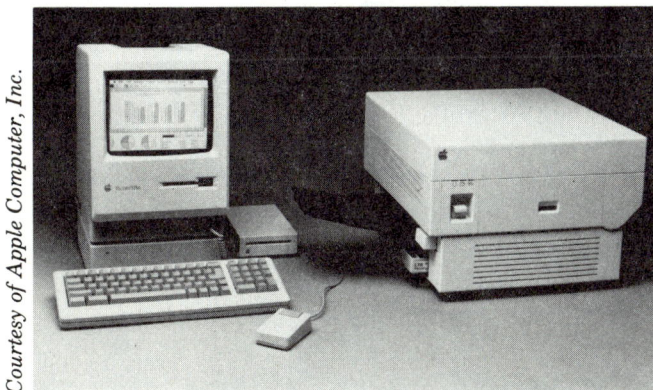

Illustration 6-7. Desktop Publishing System

THE FACSIMILE PROCESS

A facsimile device (commonly known as FAX) is a type of copier that electronically sends an original document from one location to another by producing an image replica or facsimile of that information. The distance of communication can be across the room or across the world. A facsimile machine is pictured in Illustration 6-8.

Facsimile devices combine copying technology and telephone communications. There are three basic steps in a facsimile transmission:

1. The original document is placed on a cylinder or on a platen of the facsimile machine. A light source scans the images on the document and converts the information into an electrical signal that is transmitted over telephone lines to a receiving facsimile device.
2. The receiving unit converts the electronic message to its original form.
3. A printing device produces an exact copy (a facsimile) of the received document.

The facsimile process is explained in greater detail in Chapter 9, Telecommunications.

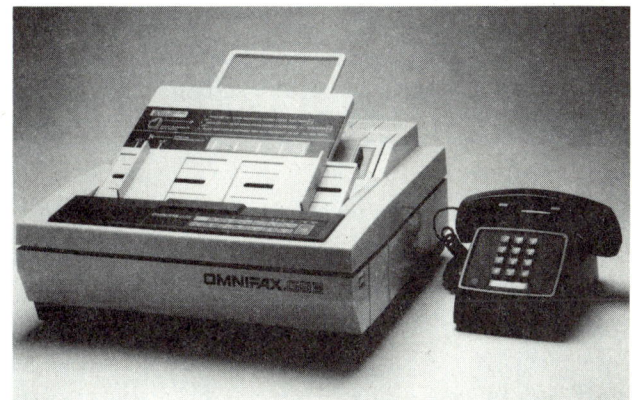

Illustration 6-8. Facsimile Equipment

COPYRIGHT LAW

The modern concept of copyright had its statutory beginnings in the British copyright law of 1710, known as the Statute of Anne, which for the first time recognized the author's right of protection. In the United States the first federal copyright act, which covered books, maps, and charts, was passed in 1790. Throughout the nineteenth century, U.S. copyright law was expanded to protect prints, music, photographs, paintings, and drawings. Because of the heavy use of copying machines, the notice of fair use was incorporated into law in the 1970s. The fair use clause allows material to be copied where the intended use is private, educational, or journalistic, and where the amount to be copied is limited. An excerpt from the law on fair use is given below. Libraries have been given certain larger copying rights, although these are also carefully spelled out.

The Federal Copyright Law
P.L. 94-553

106. The fair use of a copyrighted work including such use by reproduction in copies of phone records or by any other means specified by that section, for purposes such as criticism, comment, news reporting, teaching (including multiple copies for classroom use), scholarship, or research, is not an infringement of copyright. In determining whether the use made of a work in any particular case is a fair use, the factors to be considered shall include:

(1) The purpose and character of the use, including whether such use is of a commercial nature or is for nonprofit educational purposes;

(2) The nature of the copyrighted work,

(3) The amount and substantiality of the portion used in relation to the copyrighted work as a whole, and

(4) The effect of the use upon the potential market for or value of the copyrighted work.

Further technological advances have impacted the copyright process even more. The 1970s law, for example, did not address itself specifically to the issue of private video- and audio-tape recording. In a 1984 decision the Supreme Court ruled that neither the sale of home video recorders nor their use to record from television was a violation of the copyright law. However, movies that are leased for viewing on home video recorders are copyrighted and contain notations that they may not be copied.

Software packages present still another problem concerning copying. Almost all software is copyrighted and contains statements to the effect that under the copyright laws neither the documentation nor the software may be copied, photocopied, reproduced, translated, or reduced to any electronic medium or machine readable form without prior written consent from the company.

As you use copying machines in the office, you need to be aware of the copyright law. Many companies have legal counsel which may advise you if you have questions concerning the legality of making copies.

FUTURE DIRECTIONS

It is anticipated that copier prices will continue to decline for the next few years, while equipment performance, operability, and reliability will continue to improve. Research and development in the copier field will be aimed at making copiers more compact, easier to use, and maintenance free. Cartridges will be available to replace major components of the machine as these components wear out. Already manufacturers are attempting to make copiers less intimidating to users. Seldom-used keys are concealed behind plexiglass panels, and many manufacturers have incorporated English language messages to guide users. In the future, it is possible that copiers will use video display terminals to communicate simple directives to the user.

Industry leaders see the copier of the future as part of a fully integrated electronic office system. Systems are already being marketed that link the copier, word processor, electronic typewriter, and personal computer. You learned earlier in this chapter about intelligent copiers. These copiers interface (connect) with computers and word processors. It is anticipated that these copiers will become more sophisticated and will be used to an increasing degree. Computer-interfaced copiers will convert images to digital information. The information will then be stored in the computer's memory, transmitted over communication lines, and used to produce exact copies. If material needs to be edited, a word processor will be used to edit the material before it is copied. A system exists at present which can integrate text and graphics and then print out the copy. Line drawings, photographs, logos, and signatures can be converted into digital images. Images can be reduced, enlarged, or the density adjusted to make the image lighter or darker. The images can then be integrated with the text and printed out. A schematic of such a system is shown in Illustration 6-9. The office of the future will see more and more linkages of machines with the copier being an important element of the total system.

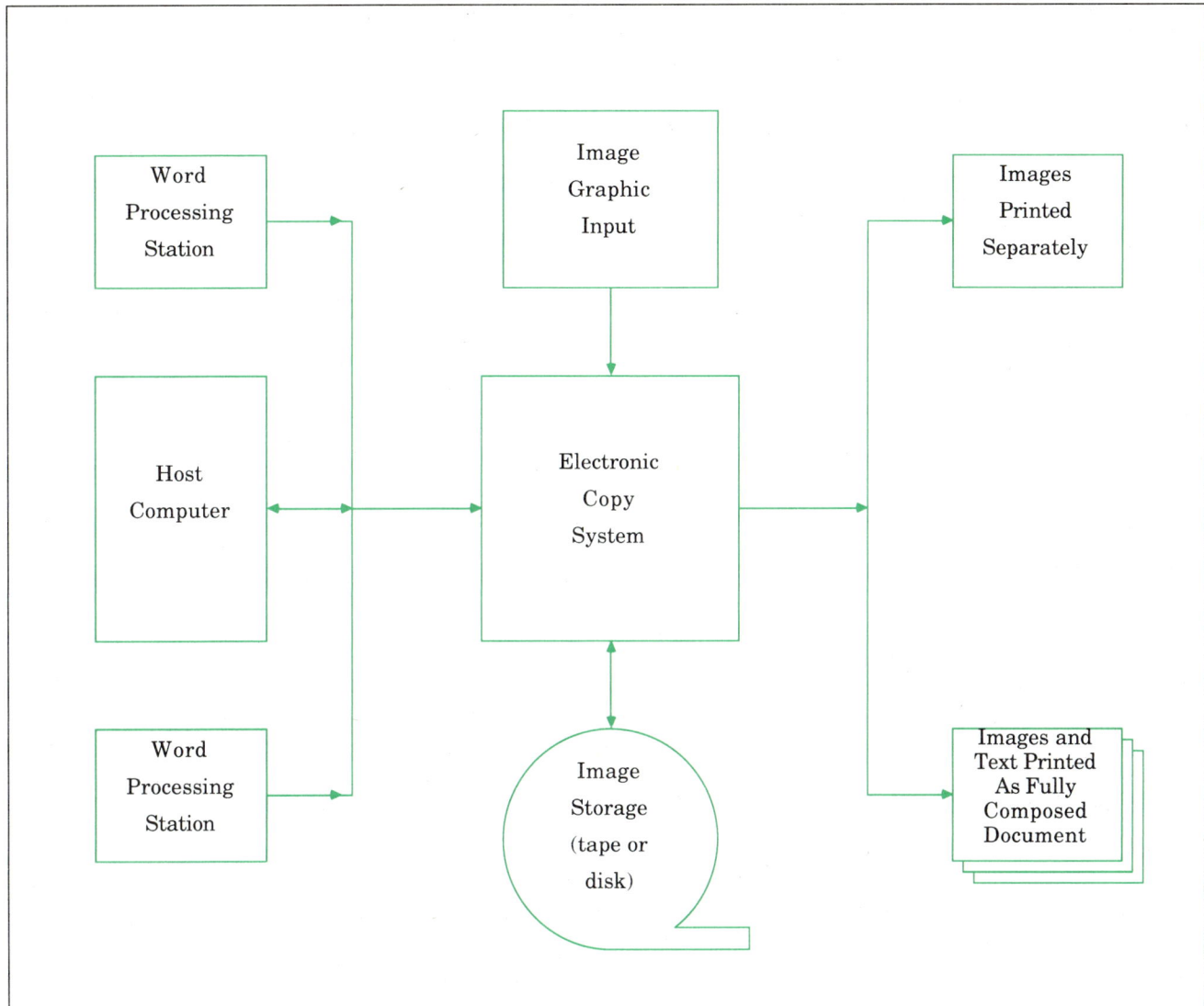

```
┌──────────────┐        ┌──────────────┐        ┌──────────────┐
│     Word     │        │    Image     │        │    Images    │
│  Processing  │───┐    │   Graphic    │        │   Printed    │
│   Station    │   │    │    Input     │        │  Separately  │
└──────────────┘   │    └──────────────┘        └──────────────┘
                   │           │                        ▲
                   ▼           ▼                        │
┌──────────────┐  ┌────────────────────┐               │
│     Host     │  │     Electronic     │               │
│   Computer   │◄─┤        Copy        ├──────────────►│
│              │  │       System       │
└──────────────┘  └────────────────────┘       ┌──────────────┐
                   │           ▲                │  Images and  │
                   ▼           │                │ Text Printed │
┌──────────────┐  ┌────────────────────┐       │   As Fully   │
│     Word     │  │       Image        ├──────►│   Composed   │
│  Processing  │─►│      Storage       │       │   Document   │
│   Station    │  │   (tape or disk)   │       └──────────────┘
└──────────────┘  └────────────────────┘
```

Illustration 6-9. Schematic of Integrated System

FOR YOUR REVIEW

The following review will help you remember the important points of this chapter.

1. Reprographics is the process of making copies of correspondence, reports, and various other documents.

2. The main reprographic equipment used in the office presently includes copiers, duplicators, offset printers, and facsimile equipment.

3. The oldest method of producing multiple copies is the carbon paper process. The advent of copying equipment has almost eliminated the use of carbon paper in the office today.

4. Copying machines create exact copies from already existing originals.

5. There are basically four categories of copiers — low-volume, mid-volume, high-volume, and duplicating-volume. These divisions are based on the monthly copy volumes each copier can handle.

6. Today, almost all copying machines use plain paper.

7. Low-volume copiers can be divided into two groups: (1) copiers which produce 8 to 15 copies per minute, with monthly volumes of up to 1,000 copies; and (2) copiers which produce up to 20 copies per minute and are marketed for volume levels of up to 20,000 copies per month.

8. Mid-volume copiers operate at speeds of 21 to 50 copies per minute and produce up to 60,000 copies per month.

9. High-volume copiers operate at speeds of 51 to 90 copies per minute and are recommended for volume levels of 50,000 to 100,000 copies per month.

10. Duplicating-volume copiers operate at speeds of 100 or more copies per minute and produce from 50,000 to 200,000 copies per month.

11. Intelligent copiers are high- or duplicating-volume copiers that may receive input from a word processor, computer, optical character recognition unit, or prerecorded magnetic media.

12. Copiers have a number of basic and special features. Some of these features are copy counters, duplexing, reduction and enlargement, color reproduction, editing, collating and stapling, and voice synthesis.

13. One of the most common copying processes used is Xerography (also called the electrostatic process). This method exposes a positively charged drum or cylinder surface within the copier to light reflected through lenses and mirrors from the original document. A sheet of plain paper is passed over the drum, and a copy is produced with the aid of a toner which is placed in the machine.

14. Fiber optics and lasers are also used in producing copies through copying machines.

15. A duplicator produces copies from prepared masters and from stencils in contrast to a copier which produces directly from an original.

16. Spirit and stencil duplicators are two means of duplicating that have been used in the past but are used infrequently today. They are presented in the text only as items of information should you encounter these methods.

17. The offset printing process is used extensively in businesses when thousands of high-quality copies are needed. The office worker does not run an offset press, since it requires considerable training. However, the office worker does prepare the master for printing on the offset press.

18. Desktop publishing refers to a personal computer-based system or a dedicated workstation that uses page layout software and outputs to a laser printer.

19. A facsimile device (commonly known as FAX) is a type of copier that electronically sends an original document from one location to another by producing an image replica or facsimile of that information. Facsimile devices combine photocopying technology and telephone communications.

20. With the heavy use of copying machines, the fair use clause was incorporated into the copyright law. The fair use clause allows material to be copied where the intended use is private, educational, or journalistic, and where the amount to be copied is limited.

21. It is anticipated that copier prices will continue to decline, while equipment performance, operability, and reliability will continue to improve. Research and development in the copier field will be aimed at making copiers more compact, easier to use, and maintenance free.

22. According to industry leaders, the copier of the future will be part of a fully integrated electronic office system. Intelligent copiers (copiers linked to computers and word processors) will become more sophisticated and greater numbers will be used in the office.

Three months ago Edna Seiber was promoted to manager of the reprographics center at A-1 Electronics. She began as an offset operator and has worked her way up. Two of the reprographics operators (Joe Dyle and Dorothy Miller) worked with Edna when she was an operator and are still working in the center. Of the eight reprographics operators in the center, Edna feels that her supervisory relationship is good with all of them except Joe and Dorothy.

Joe wanted the supervisory job which Edna now has. In fact, he told Edna that since he was the only male in the center, he felt he should have the job. He was extremely disappointed when he didn't get it. Recently, his attitude has been poor and his work inferior. When Edna tries to talk with him, he takes the attitude that no woman is going to tell him what to do.

Dorothy's problem is quite different from Joe's. She cannot seem to make the simplest decision without Edna's help. She is always apologetic about taking up Edna's time; but nevertheless, she continues to come to Edna with problems five or six times a day. Dorothy has always leaned on Edna—she asked questions constantly when Edna worked as an offset operator. It wasn't so bad then; but now that Edna is the manager, she doesn't have time to help Dorothy with every minor detail.

What would you suggest that Edna do about Joe and Dorothy?

1. Define reprographics.
2. Name and describe the four categories of photocopiers.
3. What is an intelligent copier and how is it used.
4. Explain the difference between copying and duplicating.
5. Give two basic features that are on copiers.
6. Define voice synthesis as it relates to copiers.
7. Describe Xerography.
8. Define desktop publishing.
9. Of what importance is the copyright law in making copies of material?
10. What are the future directions of reprographics?

On page 296 are office applications that correlate with this chapter.

PART 3

COMMUNICATING INFORMATION

CHAPTER 7

Business Letter Writing

In Chapters 2 and 3 you discovered the importance of effective business communication skills. You learned that effective verbal communication with your employer, fellow employees, and people outside your company is essential if you are to be effective in your job. You also learned that the ability to really listen to other people is an important part of communication.

Letters also are a major part of business communications. Depending on a letter's appearance, it can either create goodwill or ill will for a company. Thus, in addition to effective verbal and listening communication skills, you need to add still another communication skill to your list of qualifications if you are to be a truly effective office worker—the ability to write business letters.

Many letters leave the average business office each day. It may be your responsibility to prepare the printed copy for letters that your employer writes. If so, you must make sure that these letters are attractively placed on the page, that the proper format is used, and that no keyboard or grammatical errors are present. As your skills become recognized by your employer, you may be asked to compose some routine correspondence. Routine correspondence generally includes letters requesting information or services, letters ordering materials or products, and letters of goodwill. These letters should

present a favorable image of your company and of your employer. This chapter will help you attain the necessary skills to write such business letters.

GENERAL OBJECTIVES

Your general objectives for this chapter are to

1. Identify the characteristics of an effective business letter.
2. Plan the business letter.
3. Apply effective principles when composing the following types of business letters: order letters, inquiry letters, and goodwill letters.
4. Select the appropriate stationery.
5. Identify the standard letter parts.
6. Set up and produce letters and envelopes using an appropriate style.
7. Fold letters for insertion into envelopes.

THE EFFECTIVE LETTER

How do you know if a letter is effective? Probably if the letter gets results; if it serves the purpose that the writer intends. For example, an effective letter of application secures the interview; an effective sales letter sells the product; and an effective letter of inquiry receives the necessary information. All effective letters have certain common characteristics: completeness, conciseness, courteousness, accuracy, positivism, and a "you" approach. If you know how to apply these characteristics in your letter writing, your letters can get results.

Completeness.

A letter is complete if it gives the reader all the information needed so that the writer achieves the results intended. To help you achieve completeness, here are some questions to ask yourself when writing letters. As you prepare to write the letter, ask

1. Why am I writing this letter?
2. What do I hope to achieve?
3. What information do I need to write the letter?
4. What are the facts?

As you write the letter, ask

1. Who are the parties involved? Who needs to receive the letter, and who needs to get copies of the letter?
2. What dates and times need to be included in the letter? For example, if there is to be a meeting, when is the meeting to be scheduled?
3. What places or rooms need to be included? If a conference is scheduled, where is it being held?
4. Why is an event occurring? If a seminar is scheduled, why is it being held? What is its purpose? If a meeting is being canceled, why does it need to be canceled?

In order to remember these questions, use a mnemonic device; and refer to these questions as the "W" questions.

Consider the following examples of ineffective writing (the "W" questions were not asked) and the corresponding examples of effective writing (the "W" questions were asked):

Ineffective: Your order will be mailed soon. (WHEN?)
Effective: Your order will be mailed June 12.

Ineffective: There will be a conference on May 31. (WHERE AND WHAT KIND OF CONFERENCE?)
Effective: There will be an effective letter writing conference in the Executive Conference Room at 2 p.m. on May 31.

Ineffective: The sales meeting was canceled. (WHY AND WHAT?)
Effective: The sales meeting scheduled for May 5 at 2 p.m. has been canceled due to an unexpected conference that Jack Edwards, sales manager, must attend. The meeting has been rescheduled for May 8 at 2 p.m.

Conciseness.

Conciseness in letter writing means expressing the necessary information in as few words as possible. Say what you need to say without cluttering your letter with irrelevant information, needless words, or flowery phrases. Here are some suggestions to keep your letter writing concise.

1. Keep your sentences short. The longer the sentence, the more chance the reader has of misunderstanding the meaning. Readability studies show that materials written for an average American reader should contain sentences of approximately 16 to 18 words. Occasionally you may have to use longer sentences, but strive for an average of 16 to 18 words. The following example illustrates conciseness:

Long Sentence: In answer to your letter of June 12, I wish to tell you how pleased and happy I am with your asking me to speak at the meeting on July 12 and to tell you that it will give me great pleasure to speak to your group.
Shortened Sentence: I would be delighted to speak to your group on July 12.

Notice that in the shortened sentence, you do not need to call attention to the letter of June 12. Obviously you received the letter if you are responding. Why say, "I wish to tell you..."? Merely tell them. It is redundant to use both "pleased and happy."

2. Avoid unnecessary repetition. Say what you need to say without repeating words. Consider these examples.

Poor: In my opinion, I think the conference is a good one.
Better: The conference is a good idea.

It is obvious that it is *your opinion* and that *you think* that it is a good idea.

3. Eliminate excessive detail. Tell the reader what she or he needs to know, but do not give the reader confusing details that may hide the main issue.

Excessive: At this point in time, I must tell you that our plant will be closed due to the remodeling of our facilities. We have wanted to remodel our facilities for the last five years but have been unable to do so due to the large demands of our customers for products. We have every confidence in our ability to complete the remodeling and get your order out by July 15.

Concise: Since our plant will be closed for remodeling from June 1 to June 15, your order will be shipped on July 15.

Notice that in the concise statement only the information in which the reader is interested is given.

4. Avoid clichés. In many business letters, you probably have read such phrases as, "according to our records," "at your earliest convenience," and "under separate cover." These phrases are overused. The rule to remember is: Write as you talk. For example, when talking face-to-face with another person, would you say, "I mailed you the book under separate cover today"? Probably not. You would more likely say something such as, "I sent the book by air freight today." You stated what was necessary (how and when the book was sent), and you avoided using a cliché. Listed below are some additional clichéd phrases that you should avoid in letter writing. Notice how each phrase is improved.

Cliché: As per my letter
Better: When I wrote you in June

Cliché: According to our files
Better: Our files indicate

Cliché: As soon as possible
Better: On June 12 (give date)

Cliché: By return mail
Better: Mail today

Cliché: May I take the liberty (better to omit and say what you have to say)

Cliché: This is to inform you (better to omit and make the statement)

Cliché: Your kind letter (better to omit *kind* — people, not letters, are *kind*)

Cliché: At the present time
Better: Now

Cliché: In view of the fact that
Better: Because

Cliché: Until such time as
Better: When

Cliché: Enclosed please find
Better: Enclosed is

5. Do not try to impress. A business letter is not the place to impress a person with your vocabulary. The aim of a business letter is to get your purpose across in a simple, concise manner by using everyday words. If a short, easily understood word is available, use it. Don't spend time looking for a less understood word or a more impressive word.

Courteousness. Courteousness in letter writing means using good human relations skills. Treat the reader with respect and friendliness and write as if you care about the reader.

One way to express good human relations skills is to address the reader directly. Call the reader by name. Use the reader's name in the salutation, and use the reader's name again in the body of the letter. Offer to help the reader if you can. For example, you may close a letter with a statement such as, "If I can help you further, I will be happy to do so. Call me at 555-4156."

Never show your anger in a letter. You may be extremely unhappy about a situation, but to show your anger merely compounds the problem. Angry words make angry readers. Both parties end up yelling at one another through the written word; little is accomplished. Remember, anger and courtesy do not go together.

To be effective, you must be believable. If a person is asking you something, respond to the request. If you are unable to respond, explain why. If you respond negatively, also explain why. Explanations let others know that you are sincere. Whether your response is positive or negative, let the reader know that you care. Be real. Let your humanness come through on paper.

Accuracy. Although you can't be perfect all the time, you can try to be. Get the facts *before* you start to write a letter. Check your information carefully. If you are quoting prices, be sure you have the latest price list. If you are presenting dates, confirm the dates. If the letter contains columns of figures, double check the figures. The more accurate your message is, the more trust your reader will place in you.

Positivism. It's much easier to hear the word "yes" than to hear the word "no." It's much easier to accept a *concern* than it is to accept a *complaint*. Positivism gives the reader a favorable association with the person, service, or product. It helps the reader to respond the way the writer intends. A positive tone is set by the words chosen and by the way they are used. For example, some words possess positive qualities while other words possess negative qualities. Consider the following list of positive and negative words.

Positive Words	Negative Words
Congratulations	Apologize
Glad	Complaint
Immediately	Difficult
Pleasure	Error
Qualified	Disappointed
Satisfactory	No
Thank you	Inconvenient
I will	Your claim
Honest	Careless

When writing, use positive words. Avoid negative words. Don't tell the reader that you *wish* you could do something. Instead, tell the reader what you *can* do. Don't apologize for an error. Instead, tell the reader what you *will* do to correct the error.

The "You" Approach. The "you" approach requires the writer to place the reader at the center of the message. This means that the writer must place herself or himself in the shoes of the reader, and try to understand the situation from the reader's perspective. It involves using empathy in writing. If the writer is trying to sell a product or a service, the writer must look at the benefits that the product or service will offer to the reader, not the amount of sales commission the writer will receive. If the message involves something as routine as setting up a meeting, then the writer must stress the benefits of the meeting to the reader. Such writing emphasizes the "you" and "your" and de-emphasizes the "I," "we," "mine," and "ours."

To carry out the "you" approach, adhere to two words of caution: Be sincere. Do not overuse

the "you" approach to the point of being insincere and even dishonest. Your goal is not to flatter the reader; rather, your goal is to see the situation from the reader's point of view and to respond accordingly. Sincerity dictates that you tell it like it is. So, be honest and empathetic with the reader.

Notice how the following examples of writing from the "I-we" viewpoint have been changed to the "you" viewpoint. The changes are small, yet the meaning and tone are quite different. The "you" approach makes the reader's viewpoint important in contrast to the "I-we" viewpoint which ignores the reader.

"I-We" Viewpoint: We received your order for 100 seat belts today.

"You" Viewpoint: Your order for 100 seat belts was received June 10.

"I-We" Viewpoint: We sell the seat belts for $25 each.

"You" Viewpoint: Your cost for the seat belts is $25.

"I-We" Viewpoint: I will be glad to attend the conference.

"You" Viewpoint: Thank you for asking me to attend the conference. I am delighted to accept your invitation.

LETTER PLAN

Now that you understand effective letter-writing principles, consider the planning of a letter. In anything you set out to do, it is a good idea to have a plan in mind; that advice certainly holds when writing a business letter. You save yourself and the reader considerable time and effort by planning carefully what you want to say.

Gather Your Facts. Before you begin to write a letter, gather all the necessary facts. Ask yourself the "W" questions: What? Why? When? Where? and Who? Once you have answered these questions, you will have the information needed to accomplish your letter-writing purpose. For example, assume that you must handle the following situation:

The office workers at RJ Computer Corporation need help in writing effective letters.

Your employer, Jack Navarate, asks you to find a good film on the subject and to order it for viewing by the office staff. What do you need to know before you can accomplish your purpose?

1. What is the purpose of the film?
2. Who should see the film?
3. When should the film be shown?
4. What is Mr. Navarate willing to pay for rental of the film?
5. Where can letter-writing films be obtained? From what companies?

Determine What You Want to Say. Once you have gathered your facts, determine what you want to say. At this point do not be concerned with how you are going to say it or the order in which you will say it. Merely jot down the points that you want to make.

For example, here are some questions you may want to ask when ordering the film.

1. Is the film available for rental?
2. What is the rental price?
3. When is the film available?
4. How long may we keep the film?
5. Are other films available on this subject?

Decide on the Order of Presentation. The third step in writing a letter is to determine the order of the presentation. There are two basic approaches to developing a letter — the deductive approach and the inductive approach. The deductive approach goes from the general to the specific. For example, if you use the deductive approach you let the reader know that you are interested in all the films available on business letter writing. Thus, you ask for a listing of all the films that are available. You then identify your particular interest in a film and give the specific information for ordering this film. Conversely, the inductive approach goes from the specific to the general. In using this approach you give specific information on the film at the beginning of the letter and then ask for general information on all films.

The situation usually dictates whether the inductive or deductive approach is best. In a sales letter, for example, it is usually best to use the deductive approach. Your goal is to get the reader in a favorable frame of mind before trying to sell a specific product. You, therefore, begin with general statements that attempt to stimulate interest. Furthermore, letters in which the main message is bad news should usually be written deductively. Negative messages are received better when an explanation precedes them. Thus, you start the letter with a general explanation of why something is not possible and go on to the specifics of the situation. Illustration 7-1 is an example of the deductive approach when the answer is no.

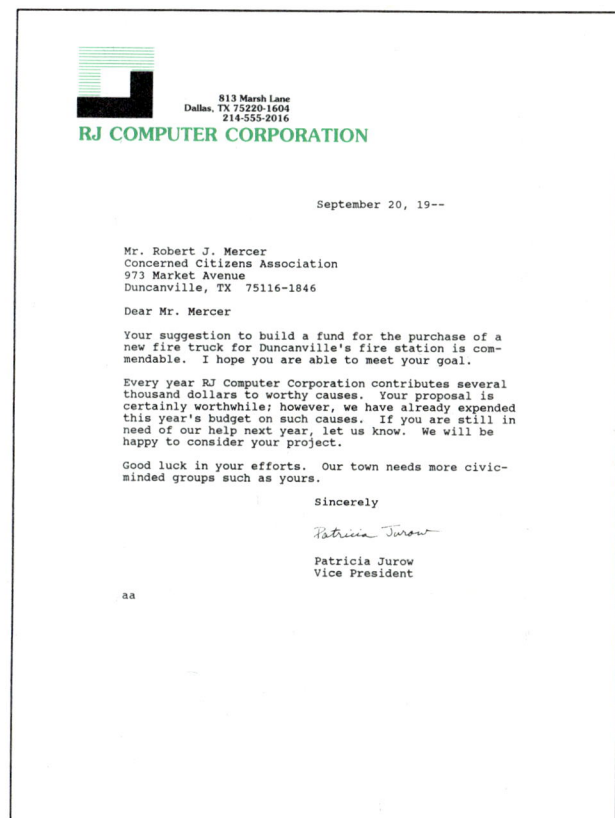

Illustration 7-1. Using the Deductive Approach

Make an Outline. You may be asking yourself, "Why should I prepare an outline? If I have all the facts, if I know what I want to say, and if I know the order in which I want to say it, then why can't I just say it? Certainly after writing for a while, you will be able to skip the outline stage. However, for the beginning writer, it is a good idea to first put your thoughts in outline form. It may seem time-consuming, but it actually saves time and money. Making an outline forces you to get your thoughts on paper; and, in the process, you may discover you do not have all the facts you need. An outline also helps you to see the relationships between topics and to determine whether your letter is in logical order. It is much easier to change an outline than it is to change a finished product.

Develop an Effective Beginning. Now that you have completed the preceding steps, you are ready to write the letter. The first paragraph is the most important paragraph of any letter. It should get the reader's attention and prepare the reader for what follows. This paragraph sets the tone for the entire letter. The effective opening emphasizes the reader's interest; it uses the "you" approach. Here is a good example of how you might start the letter to order the film.

> Will you please tell me whether your film "Writing Effective Business Letters" is available on a rental basis? Our office workers need some help in letter writing, and your film sounds as if it would be a good aid for us.

Can you see the difference in the above beginning paragraph and the following one?

> I saw your film "Writing Effective Business Letters" advertised in a company brochure. If it is available, my company would like to rent this film to show to our office workers.

The first example sets the tone from the reader's point of view; the second example addresses only the writer's needs.

Develop an Effective Ending. The closing of the letter is also important because it sets the tone for action. It should reinforce goodwill and inspire the reader to do what you are requesting. Never end a letter by expressing doubt, demanding compliance with your request, or thanking the reader in advance. Thanking the reader in advance is trite and implies that you are sure the reader will do what you ask. Note the differences between the following types of endings.

Inappropriate Ending: I regret that we cannot comply.

Appropriate Ending: May we serve you in another way?

Inappropriate Ending: Trusting you will give this matter your attention.

Appropriate Ending: Please act soon on this matter.

Inappropriate Ending: I hope you will mail your order today.

Appropriate Ending: Mail your order today to get a quick response.

Inappropriate Ending: Thank you in advance for responding to this request.

Appropriate Ending: Your immediate response will insure that the order reaches you within a week.

Here is an appropriate ending to the letter requesting information about film rental.

> Since we are eager to help our employees write more effective letters, could you let us know immediately if this film is available?

LETTERS AN OFFICE WORKER WRITES

As an office worker, the letters you will most likely write will request information, order materials, respond to requests for information and materials, and communicate goodwill. If you write these letters effectively, you will be a big asset to your company.

Writing Routine Letters. Use the same approach in writing routine letters that you would use in any letter; that is, gather your facts, determine what you need to say, decide on the order of presentation, and develop an effective beginning and ending. Also keep in mind the characteristics of a good letter — completeness, conciseness, courteousness, accuracy, positivism, and the "you" approach.

Order Letters. A routine letter that you may frequently write is the order letter. Order letters are generally written when printed purchase orders are unavailable. The order letter is a direct letter and, as such, should state clearly, concisely, and accurately what materials or products are being ordered. Before you attempt to write this letter, know exactly what materials you want, what quantity you want, and the necessary specifications. If you fail to give accurate specifications, you may receive materials which you had no intention of ordering. The following is a checklist of information that should be included in the order letter.

1. *Quantity.* Give the number of units, pounds, yards, reams, etc.
2. *Description of materials.* Give the catalog number (if available), size, color, material, weight, finish, quality, and style.
3. *Price.* List the price per unit and the total price for the items.
4. *Method of payment.* Charge to the account established or include a check.
5. *Shipment.* If you have a preference as to how the items should be shipped, state that preference.

The order of your letter presentation should be as follows: (1) direct statement of need, (2) tabulation of items, (3) shipping and payment methods, and (4) date materials are requested. Illustration 7-2 presents a sample order letter.

Inquiry Letters. Another routine letter that you may frequently write is the letter of inquiry. Such letters ask for information about prices, products, services, and people.

When writing inquiry letters, you should include the following:

1. Begin with your objective. The direct approach is convenient for the reader because it lets the reader know immediately what your concerns are, and it saves misunderstandings. You may wish to begin this letter with a question. Such an approach can be advantageous, since questions stand out and immediately call attention to your purpose.
2. Give all the necessary facts concerning your inquiry. If you do not explain in enough detail, or if you assume the reader has some knowledge that he or she does not actually have, you make it difficult for the reader to respond to your inquiry.
3. End with goodwill. Just as you would end a face-to-face inquiry with an expression of goodwill, so should you end a letter. Use specific words selected for the situation rather than a general statement of goodwill. For example, "If you can get the conference information to me by Friday, I shall be delighted" is much better than "Thank you for your prompt attention to this matter."

Illustration 7-3 is an example of a letter of inquiry.

Answering Routine Letters. Not only will you write order letters and inquiry letters, but you also will answer these letters. If your answer is positive, use the direct approach. Such an approach gives the reader what she or he wants at the beginning of the letter. However, if your answer is negative, use an indirect approach. Bad news generally is received better if an explanation precedes it. The indirect approach, therefore, allows you to give the information first and it cushions the disappointment for the reader.

Saying "Yes." To write a routine letter when the answer is positive, follow these steps.

1. Respond to the request.
2. Explain any necessary details.
3. End with a statement of goodwill.

Since "yes" is an extremely positive word, you may wish to start with it. For example, you might say:

> Yes, the management conference sounds like a challenging one. I will be happy to speak on the topic of "Listening."

In the next paragraph of a routine letter of response, you should give any additional information needed. Here is an example.

> My flight is American Airlines No. 345, arriving at 2 p.m. Thursday, October 12, at JFK. Will someone meet me at the airport? Also, do you want me to make my own reservation at the hotel or will you make it for me? My flight back to Dallas leaves at 6 p.m. on Friday, October 13. Therefore, I will need to be at the airport by 5 p.m.

Close your letter with a statement of goodwill.

> Thank you for asking me to speak. I am looking forward to a chance to talk over old times with you.

Saying "No." In almost every situation in which a negative answer must be given, there is

RJ COMPUTER CORPORATION

813 Marsh Lane
Dallas, TX 75220-1604
214-555-2016

September 24, 19--

Mrs. Rosalynn Carroll
Carroll Management Institute
52 Drayton Street, Suite 305
Fairview, NJ 07022-5739

Dear Mrs. Carroll:

Would you send me information concerning the management conference on November 12? Specifically, I need answers to the following questions:

1. Will there be a session on budgeting in addition to the session on planning?

2. Is the conference designed for the beginning or the seasoned manager?

3. Is there a discount if more than one manager from a business attends?

Can you get this information to me by November 5? Your conference could be an excellent addition to our training sessions which take place in December.

Sincerely

Jon Bendix
Manager
Finance Department

JB:aa

Illustration 7-3. Letter of Inquiry

RJ COMPUTER CORPORATION

813 Marsh Lane
Dallas, TX 75220-1604
214-555-2016

September 22, 19--

Ms. Clorita Diaz
Ramsey Manufacturing
1715 Daysprings Road
Oklahoma City, OK 73101-4236

Dear Ms. Diaz:

Please send the following items:

Quantity	Description	Price	Total
500	5 1/4" floppy disks, DSDD, 48 TPI	$ .47 ea.	$ 235.00
120	Floppy disk organizer, store up to 96 disks, wood, oak finish w/plastic removable dust cover, Unix storage AFZ-429	12.50 ea.	1,500.00
			$1,735.00

Charge these items to the account established by RJ Computer Corporation. Please ship the materials so that they are received no later than October 25.

Sincerely,

Jack Navarate
Manager, Purchasing Department

rl

Illustration 7-2. Order Letter

a reason. That reason should be explained before you say no. If the reason is stated sincerely and courteously, most readers will understand. They may not be happy, but they will be able to accept and appreciate your refusal. Here is a good plan to follow in writing a refusal.

1. Begin with a statement that acknowledges the request.
2. Explain why you must refuse.
3. Refuse.
4. Propose an alternative if one is possible.
5. End with a courteous and friendly statement.

In the previous example, a yes answer was given to a speaking engagement. Now consider the same invitation as presented in Illustration 7-4 when the answer is no.

Writing Goodwill Letters. Consider the examples of goodwill letters of appreciation and congratulations presented in Illustrations 7-5 and 7-6.

Goodwill letters give a chance to express sincerity and ingenuity. For example, Illustration 7-7 is certainly not the usual letter that is written to customers. However, the goodwill letter gives you a chance to be creatively different. As you write goodwill letters, let your creativity show, convey a positive viewpoint, and call attention to the reader by using the "you" approach.

BUSINESS LETTER PREPARATION

In addition to a letter being well written, it is also important that the letter be arranged attractively on quality stationery. When you open a letter, the first impression that you receive is based on the way the letter is placed on the page and the quality of the stationery. Since first impressions often are lasting ones, you must know how to place a letter on the page and how to select the right type of paper. In addition, as an office support employee, it is your responsibility to address the envelope correctly and properly fold and insert the letter for mailing.

Stationery Selection. The standard size of stationery used for business letters is 8½ by 11 inches, and the standard weight of paper is 20 to 24 pound paper. The weight of the paper is determined by the weight of a ream of paper which consists of 500 sheets 17 × 22 inches. Two thousand sheets of 8½ × 11 inch paper are cut from one ream. The weight of the paper is printed on the box or package. For example, if the label on the end of the ream reads "Sub 20," that particular ream is 20-pound paper. Other sizes of paper which may be used for business letters are 8½ × 5½ inches, which is referred to as baronial, and executive-size stationery which is 7¼ by 10½ inches.

The letterhead on business stationery customarily shows the name, address, and telephone number of the company. Additional features may be the logo and slogan of the company. The term letterhead is used because this information is usually placed at the top of the page. However, the information is sometimes placed at the side or even at the bottom of the stationery. Illustration 7-8 on page 98 shows several types of letterheads. White is the traditional color of stationery; however, off-white and ivory colors are used frequently. Some companies even select colors such as yellow, light brown, and blue.

Additional information concerning types of paper, second sheets, and carbon paper is given in Appendix E. With the advent of copying machines and microcomputers, fewer carbon copies are made now than in the past. However, your responsibility as an office worker is to use the most economical method of copying possible. And, if you are making only a few copies, the use of a carbon copy may be the most economical method.

Letter Placement. A letter should be well balanced on a page. In order to achieve the appropriate balance, the top, bottom, right, and left margins should resemble a frame around a picture. The right margin should be as even as possible, and all margins should appear to be an equal distance from the edge of the page. There should be as few word divisions at the ends of lines as possible, and there should never be more than two end-of-line word divisions in a row.

RJ COMPUTER CORPORATION

813 Marsh Lane
Dallas, TX 75220-1604
214-555-2016

September 23, 19--

Mr. Steven Marceau
Higgins Association
39 Belmont Avenue
Dallas, TX 75001-4839

Dear Steve

Your invitation to speak at the management conference on
October 13 is an honor. Your group is a respected one,
and I have enjoyed my association with it.

The demands on my time at work now are extremely heavy.
In addition to a new planning process that I must implement, we have recently employed two new managers who are
looking to me for assistance in learning their jobs. As
you might expect, I hardly have time to "look up." Since
I would not want to accept your invitation without having
adequate time to prepare, I must say no this time. However, if you need a speaker in the future, please don't
forget me. It is always a good experience for me to speak
to your group.

Have you met Ramona Stanley, our sales manager? She does
an excellent presentation on listening, and she might be
available to speak at your conference. Her extension is
378. Good luck with your program.

Sincerely

Jon Bendix

Jon Bendix
Manager, Finance Department

JB:jl

Illustration 7-4. Letter of Refusal

RJ COMPUTER CORPORATION

813 Marsh Lane
Dallas, TX 75220-1604
214-555-2016

September 28, 19--

Ms. Jeanne Moriarity
Aviation, Incorporated
85 Windon Place
Stamford, CT 06904-4738

Dear Ms. Moriarity

Your name ranks high among our loyal customers.
It is to friends like you that we owe our success at RJ Computers.

I sincerely appreciate your business of the last
four years. We will continue to do everything
within our power to maintain our present standards of service.

THANK YOU! It's always a real pleasure to serve
you.

Sincerely

Ramona Stanley

Ramona Stanley
Manager, Sales Department

RS:aa

Illustration 7-5. Letter of Appreciation

813 Marsh Lane
Dallas, TX 75220-1604
214-555-2016

RJ COMPUTER CORPORATION

October 3, 19--

Mr. Wayne Meredith
7026 Gratiot Avenue
Dallas, TX 75212-2349

Dear Mr. Meredith

BEFORE THE WEDDING, a man and a woman are usually
extremely thoughtful of each other. They often express
their love for each other with notes, flowers, and gifts.

AFTER THE WEDDING, the situation changes dramatically.
Too often the only notes, flowers, and gifts exchanged are
on special occasions such as Valentine's Day, Christmas,
and birthdays.

BUSINESSES are too often just like that. They solicit a
person's business with all types of sales letters and
special offers. But once they get your business, they
forget you.

WE BELIEVE we should tell you how much you are appreciated. You are a valued customer of our business. We want
to keep you happy, and we want to serve you. Thank you
for your business.

Sincerely

Ramona Stanley

Ramona Stanley
Manager, Sales Department

cs

Illustration 7-7. Letter of Goodwill

---

813 Marsh Lane
Dallas, TX 75220-1604
214-555-2016

RJ COMPUTER CORPORATION

September 27, 19--

Miss Jessica Wiggins
Fashion Group
125 Second Avenue
Dallas, TX 75116-1368

Dear Jessica

Congratulations! What a pleasure to read
in this morning's paper that you will be the
next president of Fashion Group. I can think of
no one better qualified for this important position.

Since I know of your dedication and follow
through on a job, I know you will lead the Fashion Group in a way that will benefit every
member and also be a real credit to you.

Just remember as you go about your numerous
tasks, I will be rooting for you.

Sincerely

James Rutherford

James Rutherford
President

JR:mb

Illustration 7-6. Letter of Congratulations

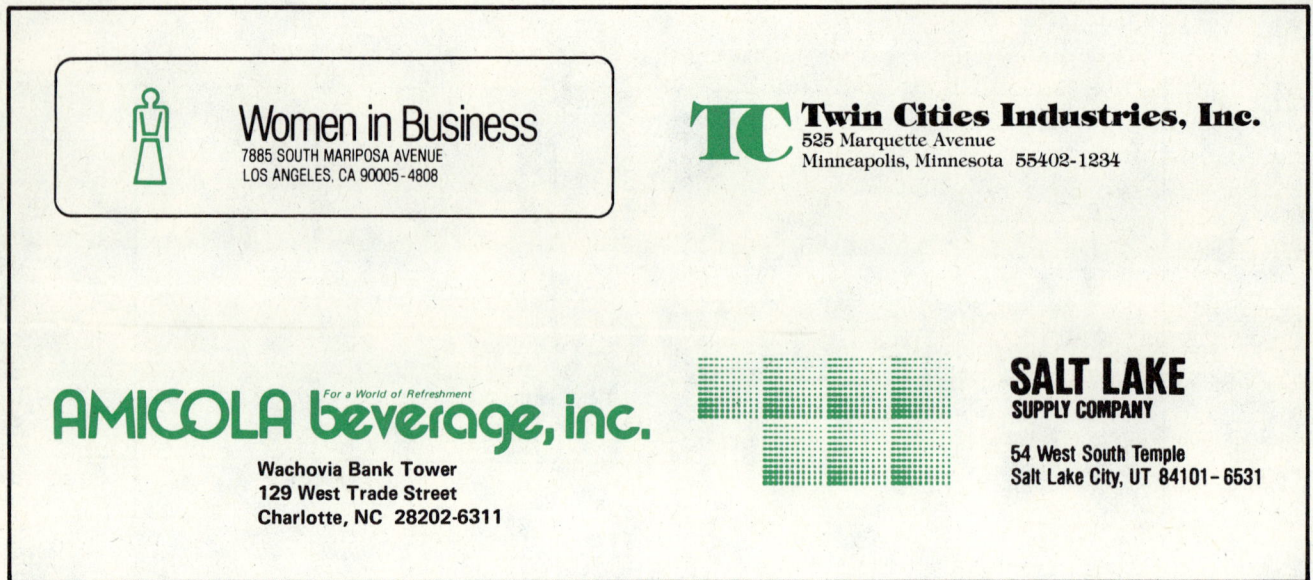

Illustration 7-8. Letterheads

Table 7-1 indicates the proper side margins for short, average, and long letters. Thus, your first step is to recognize the length of the letter. You will need some practice in making these estimates from longhand materials, shorthand notes, or from a dictating machine. You are not expected to count each word in a letter. Letter placement should become an intuitive process. However, when you first begin typing letters, you will probably need to make a rough count of the words.

Table 7-1

Letter Placement Table

Letter Length	Words in Body of Letter	Side Margins
Short	Up to 100 words	2″
Average	101-200 words	1½″
Long	201-300 words	1″
Two-Page	More than 300 words	1″ each

Basic Letter Parts. Most business letters contain a number of parts. It is important to know what these parts are and to know the correct format for them.

Dateline. Two methods for determining the placement of the date are widely used. One method is the *floating dateline*. This dateline varies in vertical placement according to the letter length. For example, in a short letter the dateline is placed on line 19 from the top edge of the paper; in an average letter, the dateline is placed on line 16; and in a long letter, the dateline is placed on line 13. The first line of the letter address is always on the fourth line below the date.

The other method for determining the placement of the dateline is called the *fixed dateline*. The fixed dateline is always keyed on the second line below the last line of the printed letterhead. However, the space between the dateline and the letter address varies depending on the length of the letter. For example, eight blank lines are left between the dateline and the letter address in a short letter; five blank lines are left between the dateline and the letter address in an average letter; and three blank lines are left in a long letter.

Letter Address. The letter address provides all the necessary information for mailing the letter. This includes the recipient's name, title, company name, street number and name, city, two-letter state abbreviation, and ZIP Code. As indicated in the preceding paragraphs, at least three to five blank lines are left between the date and the first line of the letter address for long and average-length letters. The number of lines may be increased to eight blank lines for a short letter. The keyboard operator must use judgment in placing the letter on the page so that it appears properly balanced.

Salutation. The salutation in a letter serves the same purpose as a greeting. The salutation is typed one double space below the letter address. It must agree in number with the letter address. Notice in the example below that the letter address is to an entire company and the salutation is plural in number.

Jong Equipment Corporation
134 Magnolia Avenue
Woodland, CA 91364-6784

Ladies and Gentlemen

If you are writing a letter to an individual, the most appropriate salutation to use is the individual's name. For example, if the letter is addressed to Mr. Arnold Borchgrave, the salutation should be:

Dear Mr. Borchgrave

Other appropriate salutations are as follows. One person, sex unknown:

Dear A. L. Schuster

One person, name unknown, sex unknown:

Dear Sir or Madam

One person, name unknown, title known:

Dear Personnel Manager
Dear Purchasing Agent

One woman, title preference unknown:

Dear Ms. Sabin
or
Dear Anne Sabin

Two or more men:

Dear Mr. Steel and Mr. Wallace
or
Dear Messrs. Steel and Wallace

Two or more women, titles known:

Dear Ms. Perez, Mrs. Li, and Miss Stein

If all women are married:

Dear Mrs. Perez, Mrs. Li, and Mrs. Stein
or
Dear Mesdames Perez, Li, and Stein

If all women are unmarried:

Dear Miss Perez, Miss Li, and Miss Stein
or
Dear Misses Perez, Li, and Stein

If all women use Ms.:

Dear Ms. Perez, Li, and Stein
or
Dear Mses. (or Mss.) Perez, Li, and Stein

A woman and a man:

Dear Ms. Perez and Mr. Wallace

An organization composed entirely of women:

Ladies
or
Mesdames

An organization composed entirely of men:

Gentlemen

An organization composed of women and men:

Ladies and Gentlemen

The person dictating a business letter may specify the salutation to be used, but in many offices a standard salutation is used for all routine letters. Sometimes, however, you will not be told to use a special salutation when one should be used. For example, Mr. Eric Strickland of RJ Computer Corporation may be answering a letter from Mr. Joseph D. Hall. Mr. Hall used the salutation "Dear Eric" in writing to Mr. Strickland and signed his letter "Joe." Even though the general instructions are to use a salutation, such as "Dear Mr. Hall," unless other instructions are given, you should know that a more personal salutation, such as "Dear Joe," should be used in this letter. If Mr. Hall knows Mr. Strickland well enough to address him as "Dear Eric" and to sign his letter "Joe," he certainly would not expect a reply to carry the salutation "Dear Mr. Hall."

Body. The body of a letter contains the message. It begins a double space below the salutation or a double space below the subject line (if the letter contains a subject line). The body is single-spaced, but double-spaced between paragraphs. A very short letter can be double-spaced to create a page that looks balanced. Paragraphs begin at the left margin, except for the modified block letter with indented paragraphs (see page 105). In this letter style, paragraphs are indented five spaces. An effort should be made to have at least two paragraphs in a letter, without the paragraphs being extremely long or short.

Complimentary Close. The purpose of the complimentary close is to provide a courteous ending. The most commonly used complimentary closes are "Very truly yours" and "Sincerely." Two others that are frequently used are "Yours very truly" and "Sincerely yours." The complimentary close is keyed at the left margin in the block letter or at the center of the page in the modified block letter. It is placed a double space below the end of the body with only the first letter of the first word capitalized.

Signature. The name and title of the individual writing the letter are keyed four line spaces below the complimentary close. If the name and title are short, they may be placed on the same line. But if the name and title are relatively long, the name is keyed on the first line and the title is placed on the second line. The general rule is to make the lines as even as possible.

If a letter is not prepared on company letterhead, the company name is used in the close. It is keyed a double space below the complimentary close and in all capitals, with the name and title of the writer keyed four line spaces below the company name.

Reference Initials. Reference initials are placed even with the left margin and a double space below the title of the writer. The recent trend is to key only the keyboard operator's initials in lowercase letters. However, it is also acceptable to use the dictator's initials, which are shown in all capitals, followed by a colon or

a slash, and then followed by the keyboard operator's initials. Notice the examples presented in Illustrations 7-9 and 7-10 on page 104.

Special Letter Parts. The letter parts discussed in the preceding paragraphs are found in virtually all business letters; however, certain letters have other parts.

Attention Line. If a letter is addressed to an organization, an attention line may be used to direct the letter to the proper person or department within the organization. The attention line is placed on the second line of the letter address and even with the left margin. The placement of the attention line in the block letter style is shown in Illustration 7-9.

The use of an attention line does not change the salutation. For example, if a letter is addressed to a company with an attention line of "Attention Mrs. Rice," the salutation is still "Ladies and Gentlemen," not "Dear Mrs. Rice."

Subject Line. The writer of a letter may feel that the letter will be clearer if the subject to be discussed is indicated at the beginning of the letter. In that case, a subject line is used. The subject line is placed a double space below the salutation. After the subject line, there is a double space before the body of the letter. The subject line is keyed even with the left margin if the block letter style is used. If the modified block letter style is used, the subject line may be either centered, begun at the left margin, or indented five spaces (if the paragraphs are indented). The word SUBJECT or RE may precede the subject line, but this is not necessary. The subject line can be shown in capitals, in capitals and lowercase, or in capitals and lowercase and underlined. Here are several examples of how the subject line may be keyed.

Dear Dr. Kallaus

AMERICAN MEDICAL ASSOCIATION

Dear Dr. Kallaus

SUBJECT: American Medical Association

Dear Dr. Kallaus

RE: American Medical Association

File Number. In some businesses a file or reference number is inserted at the beginning of a letter to facilitate the filing of correspondence. When such a number is used, it may be inserted a double space below the date or placed opposite the dateline, ending at the right margin. A file reference number is used in Illustration 7-9.

A company using a file reference number in a letter expects the one answering the letter to refer to the file number. This can be done in the following ways: a reference to the file number may be made in the first paragraph of the letter, or the file number may be treated as a subject and typed in the usual subject line position.

Enclosure Notation. When reference to an enclosure is made in the body of the letter, a notation of the enclosure should be made by keying "Enclosure" or "Enc." a double space below the reference initials. For example:

pjf

Enclosures 2

Copy Notation. When additional copies are made for distribution to various persons, reference to each recipient is commonly made in the copy notation so that the addressee knows to whom copies are sent. The copy notation is keyed a double space below the enclosure, if used, or the reference initials if there is no enclosure. When more than one person is to receive a copy, list each person on a succeeding line that is indented three spaces from the left margin. The notation may be keyed in any of the following ways:

cc Mr. Mack (when a carbon is used)

pc Mr. Mack (when a photocopy is used)

Copy to Mr. Mack (when a photocopy is used)

Blind Copy Notation. If the person who receives the original letter does not need to know that a copy is being sent to a particular person, a blind copy notation is used. To make

the notation, the original letter is removed from the machine and the notation is keyed on the carbon copy or on the photocopy one inch from the top of the paper at the left margin. Examples of the notation are:

bcc Ms. Turner (for carbon copy)

bc Ms. Turner (for photocopy)

Mailing Notation. When mailing notations such as SPECIAL DELIVERY and REGISTERED MAIL are keyed on the letter, they are shown even with the left margin, a double space below the date, and in all capitals. These notations may be keyed on the original and the file copy or keyed only on the file copy. Other special notations such as CONFIDENTIAL or PERSONAL are also keyed in the same location.

Postscript. Place a postscript either a double space below the reference initials or the enclosure notation, whichever is the last line. The initials "P.S." or the word "postscript" need not be used. Notice the example presented in Illustration 7-10 on page 104.

Second-Page Headings. When keying the second page of a letter, use plain bond paper. Letterhead paper is to be used for the first page only. A heading consisting of the name of the addressee, the page number, and the date is to be single-spaced, an inch (on line 6) from the top of the sheet, and in one of the following forms.

Block form (used when the letter is in block style):

Ms. Ellen Sumter
Page 2
September 12, 1987

Horizontal form (used when the letter is in modified block style):

Ms. Ellen Sumter   2   September 12, 1987

Double space between the heading and the first line of the body of the letter.

The last paragraph of the letter's preceding page should contain at least two lines, and the first paragraph of the letter's second page should contain at least two lines. A word should not be divided at the end of the first page of the letter.

Punctuation. The two common types of punctuation used in the writing of business letters are as follows:

1. *Open punctuation,* in which all punctuation is omitted after the dateline, letter address, salutation, and complimentary close.
2. *Mixed punctuation,* in which punctuation is omitted after the dateline and letter address, but the colon is used after the salutation, and the comma is used after the complimentary close.

Letter Styles. There are four basic letter styles—block style, modified block style with blocked paragraphs, modified block style with indented paragraphs, and the AMS simplified style. These letter styles are presented in Illustrations 7-9 through 7-12 on pages 104-105. In each style notice where the date, letter address, salutation, and closing lines begin.

The block and modified block styles are used more frequently than the AMS simplified style; however, this style is extremely efficient. It was adopted by the Administrative Management Society because of its timesaving features. Notice in Illustration 7-12 that the letter has no salutation or complimentary close. Notice also that a subject line is used. This subject line, keyed in all capitals, is three line spaces below the letter address. The body begins three line spaces below the subject line. The writer's name and title are positioned at least four line spaces below the body and in all capitals. The name and title are keyed on the same line.

Envelopes. Envelopes match the letterhead stationery in quality, design, and color. The address on the envelope must be correct, legible, and placed in the appropriate location. To speed the delivery of mail, the United States Postal Service has installed Optical Character Recognition (OCR) equipment in many post offices. This scanner electronically reads and sorts envelopes. Certain changes in the addressing of an envelope have occurred as a result of the OCR. The scanner starts reading from the bottom line and is programmed to read the city, state, and ZIP Code first. Therefore, any extra lines that fall below the last line of the address prevent the OCR from locating the address. Such notations as the attention line, please forward line, and a confidential notation cannot be placed in the lower left corner of the envelope. The attention line should be keyed as the second line of the letter address. The please forward and confidential notations should be typed three line spaces below the return address and even with that address. Notice the examples presented in Illustration 7-13.

To speed up scanning, the United States Post Office recommends that the address on the envelope be shown in all capitals with no marks of punctuation. If this format is used, the beam on the scanner does not have to move from uppercase letters to lowercase letters and does not have to scan punctuation marks. Although this practice is not yet followed in the majority of business offices, you need to be aware of the advantages of using this procedure. The ZIP Code is keyed two spaces after the state abbreviation. Again, notice Illustration 7-13.

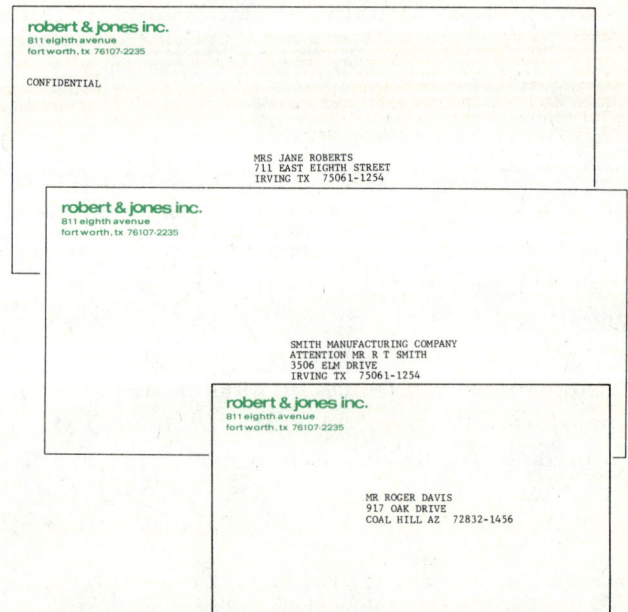

Illustration 7-13. Formats for Addressing Envelopes

Abbreviations. Two-letter state abbreviations are recommended by the United States Post Office. These recommended abbreviations are presented in Table 7-2.

Addressing Envelopes. On No. 10 envelopes (9½″ × 4⅛″) the address begins approximately 14 lines from the top and approximately five spaces from left of center. The address is keyed in block style and is single-spaced, with all lines having a uniform left margin. The No. 10 envelope is the size most commonly used in business offices. On small envelopes (6½″×3⅝″), the address begins approximately 12 lines from the top and ten spaces left of the center.

Folding and Inserting Letters. To fold a letter for a No. 10 envelope, fold slightly less than one third of the letter up toward the top. With the edges even at the sides, crease the fold. Fold down the top of the sheet to within one-half inch of the bottom fold. With the edges even at the sides, crease the fold. Insert the letter into the envelope with the last crease toward the bottom of the envelope. Illustration 7-14 shows this process. See page 106.

Even though a small envelope is infrequently used in a business office, you need to know how to fold and insert a letter into such an envelope. Fold the letter from the bottom to within one-half inch of the top. With the edges even at the sides, crease the fold. Then, fold from right to left a third of the sheet's width. Next fold another third of the sheet's width from left to right to one-half inch of the last crease. Insert the letter into the envelope with the last creased edge inserted first, as shown in Illustration 7-15. See page 106.

Table 7-2

Recommended Postal Abbreviations

Name	Standard Abbreviation	Two-Letter Abbreviation
Alabama	Ala.	AL
Alaska	Alaska	AK
Arizona	Ariz.	AZ
Arkansas	Ark.	AR
California	Calif.	CA
Colorado	Colo.	CO
Connecticut	Conn.	CT
Delaware	Del.	DE
Dist. of Columbia	D.C.	DC
Florida	Fla.	FL
Georgia	Ga.	GA
Hawaii	Hawaii	HI
Idaho	Idaho	ID
Illinois	Ill.	IL
Indiana	Ind.	IN
Iowa	Iowa	IA
Kansas	Kans.	KS
Kentucky	Ky.	KY
Louisiana	La.	LA
Maine	Maine	ME
Maryland	Md.	MD
Massachusetts	Mass.	MA
Michigan	Mich.	MI
Minnesota	Minn.	MN
Mississippi	Miss.	MS
Missouri	Mo.	MO
Montana	Mont.	MT
Nebraska	Nebr.	NE
Nevada	Nev.	NV
New Hampshire	N.H.	NH
New Jersey	N.J.	NJ
New Mexico	N. Mex.	NM
New York	N.Y.	NY
North Carolina	N.C.	NC
North Dakota	N. Dak.	ND
Ohio	Ohio	OH
Oklahoma	Okla.	OK
Oregon	Oreg.	OR
Pennsylvania	Pa.	PA
Rhode Island	R.I.	RI
South Carolina	S.C.	SC
South Dakota	S. Dak.	SD
Tennessee	Tenn.	TN
Texas	Tex.	TX
Utah	Utah	UT
Vermont	Vt.	VT
Virginia	Va.	VA
Washington	Wash.	WA
West Virginia	W. Va.	WV
Wisconsin	Wis.	WI
Wyoming	Wyo.	WY

DRISCOLL & SMITH, Inc. fine furniture

Louisville, KY 40219-8866

September 17, 19--

Mr. Jack Navarate
RJ Computer Corporation
813 Marsh Lane
Dallas, TX 75220-1604

Dear Mr. Navarate:

Several weeks ago you placed an order with us for five desks to be manufactured according to your specifications. You approved the plan we submitted and asked us to let you know when the desks would be ready for finishing.

The desks are ready for finishing. We were very fortunate in finding some unusual wood that we believe will match very closely the other furniture in your office. It was necessary for us to make some slight changes in the hardware because it was impossible to obtain exactly what you had in mind.

Will you come in within the next week so we can decide on the proper finish for the desks? We can also decide at that time whether you want any special drawer pulls. If you can telephone us and let us know what day you will come, we can be sure that our furniture expert is here at that time.

It is certainly a pleasure to work with you on this order, and we believe you will be satisfied with the finished product.

Sincerely yours,

A. H. Rice

A. H. Rice
Sales Manager

AHR:bh

If we do not hear from you soon, we will assume you are no longer interested.

Illustration 7-10. Modified Block Letter Style, Mixed Punctuation

---

ATLANTIC PAPER CO.

3500 Appalachian Avenue   Atlanta, Georgia 30325-3427

October 17, 19--   In reply, refer to
                        File No. 637-1

RJ Computer Corporation
Attention Mr. J. C. Chaney
813 Marsh Lane
Dallas, TX 75220-1604

Ladies and Gentlemen

Thank you very much for your recent fine order for corrugated boxes and wrapping paper. The shipment of the corrugated boxes will be sent within ten days.

Usually we are able to make immediate shipment on wrapping paper, but a shortage of certain types of paper pulp has resulted in manufacturing delays. We are quite sure, however, your wrapping paper can be sent within the next month.

If you are in immediate need of wrapping paper, may we suggest that you let us send a limited supply of a lighter grade? We have quite a stock of this paper on hand. If we do not hear from you, however, we shall assume that it will be satisfactory to go ahead with your order for wrapping paper and ship it next month.

Very truly yours

E. James Pullman

E. James Pullman
Manager

kr

pc Jane Kelly

Illustration 7-9. Block Letter Style, Open Punctuation

RJ COMPUTER CORPORATION
813 Marsh Lane
Dallas, TX 75220-1604
214-555-2016

September 29, 19--

Mr. John C. Walters, Sales Manager
Central States Supply Company
1609 North Meridian Street
Indianapolis, IN 46203-2247

Dear Mr. Walters

For some time I have been trying to plan a trip so that I could visit you. After Jim Conley called on you last time, he wrote me that you have several problems you want to discuss. I shall be in your city on the 25th of this month.

Your company has certainly given us a tremendous volume of business during the four years I have been sales manager. Just to satisfy my curiosity, I had someone total the volume over that period. I was surprised myself at the amount--over $500,000. We have appreciated this business more than I can tell you.

If for any reason you cannot see me on the morning of the 25th, wire or call me at my expense; I will try to come at your convenience. Enclosed are circulars giving information about two of our newest products. You may wish to look these over before I see you.

Sincerely

Ramona Stanley
Ramona Stanley
Manager, Sales Department

rv

Enclosures 2

Illustration 7-11. Modified Block Letter Style, Indented Paragraphs, Open Punctuation

---

ams
ADMINISTRATIVE MANAGEMENT SOCIETY
WILLOW GROVE, PENNSYLVANIA 19090-1256 • 215-659-4300

April 14, 19--

Ms./Mr. Office Secretary
Better Business Letters, Inc.
5 Main Street
Philadelphia, PA 19124-4534

SIMPLIFIED LETTER

There's a new movement under way to take some of the monotony out of letters given you to keyboard, Ms./Mr. Secretary. The movement is symbolized by the Simplified Letter being sponsored by AMS.

What is it? You're reading a sample.

Notice the left block format and the general positioning of the letter. We didn't write "Dear Ms./Mr. ___," "nor will we write "Yours truly" or "Sincerely yours." Are they really important? We feel just as friendly toward you without them.

Notice the following points:

1.   Date location
2.   The address
3.   The subject
4.   The name of the writer

Now take a look at the suggestions prepared for you. Talk them over with your employer. But don't form a final opinion until you've really tried The Letter. That's what our secretary did. As a matter of fact, he finally wrote most of the suggestions himself.

Our secretary is sold on this style. We hope you will have good luck with better (Simplified) letters too.

Wilma H. Latham
WILMA H. LATHAM - ADMINISTRATOR, TECHNICAL & PROGRAM SERVICE

si

cc D. M. Graff

Illustration 7-12. AMS Simplified Letter Style

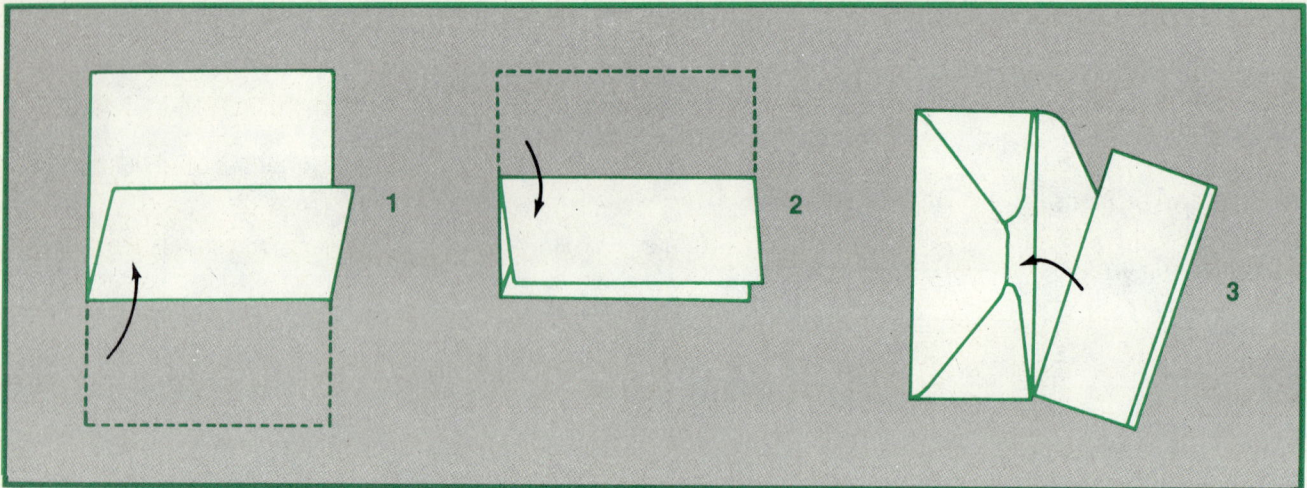

Illustration 7-14. Folding a Letter for a No. 10 Envelope

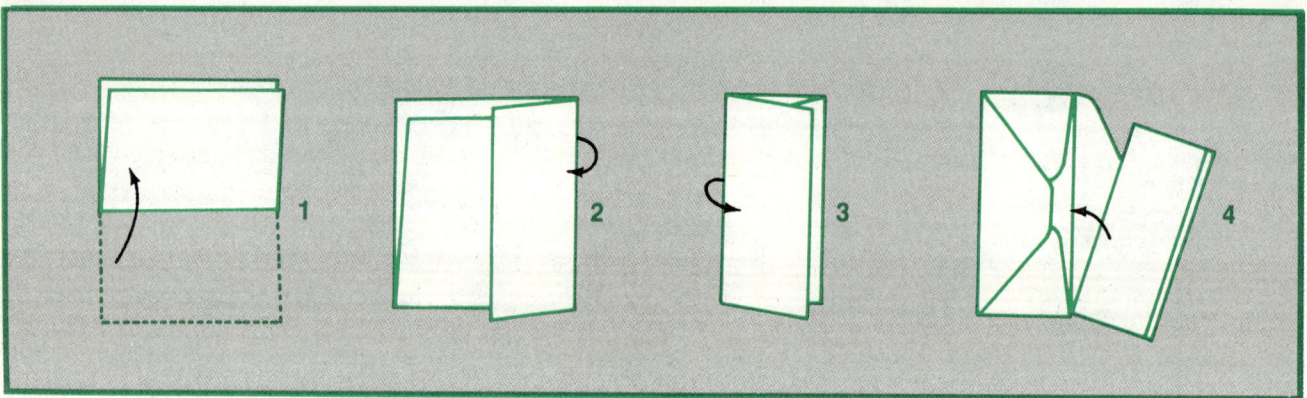

Illustration 7-15. Folding a Letter for a Small Envelope

FOR YOUR REVIEW

The following review will help you remember the important points of this chapter.

 1. The effective business letter has the following characteristics:
   a. Completeness
   b. Conciseness
   c. Courteousness
   d. Accuracy
   e. Positivism
   f. The "you" approach

 2. A planning process should exist before writing a business letter. That process includes the following:
   a. Gathering the facts.

   b. Determining what to say.
   c. Deciding on the order of presentation.
   d. Outlining.
   e. Developing an effective beginning.
   f. Developing an effective ending.

 3. Letters which an office worker might write are
   a. Order letters.
   b. Inquiry letters.
   c. Goodwill letters.

 4. An order letter should have the following information:
   a. Quantity.
   b. Description of materials.

    c. Price.

    d. Method of payment.

    e. Shipping procedures.

5. Inquiry letters should

    a. Begin with an objective.

    b. Give all the necessary facts.

    c. End with goodwill.

6. When answering a letter positively, use the inductive approach. These are the steps to follow:

    a. Respond to the request.

    b. Explain any necessary details.

    c. End with a statement of goodwill.

7. In answering a letter negatively, use the deductive approach. Here are the steps to follow:

    a. Begin with a statement that acknowledges the request.

    b. Explain why you must refuse.

    c. Refuse.

    d. Propose an alternative if one is possible.

    e. End with a courteous and friendly statement.

8. The goodwill letter should contain

    a. A personal expression of appreciation, congratulations.

    b. A strong "you" approach.

    c. A sincere expression.

    d. Use of words that convey a positive viewpoint.

9. Business letters are prepared on letterhead paper. The usual size of letterhead paper is 8½ × 11 inches. However, other sizes are available: executive — 7¼ × 10½ inches and baronial — 8½ × 5½ inches.

10. The parts of a business letter are as follows:

    a. *Dateline* — either floating or fixed.

    b. *Letter address* — name and address of the person receiving the letter.

    c. *Salutation* — "Dear Mr. _____" or "Dear Mrs. (Ms., Miss) _____" are the most common salutations used.

    d. *Body* — should be single-spaced, but double-spaced between paragraphs.

    e. *Complimentary close* — trend today is toward the less formal complimentary close, for example, "Sincerely."

    f. *Signature* — writer's name and title keyed below the complimentary close.

    g. *Reference initials* — typist's initials placed to the right of writer's initials and against the left margin, or only the typist's initials if the writer is identified in the signature.

11. Some special business letter parts include the following:

    a. *Attention line* — may be used to direct the letter to the proper person or department if a letter is addressed to an organization.

    b. *Subject line* — lets the reader know what the letter is about without reading the entire letter.

    c. *File number* — reference number inserted at the beginning of a letter and used to facilitate the filing of correspondence, as practiced in some businesses.

    d. *Enclosure notation* — a notation made if an additional item is enclosed with the letter.

    e. *Copy notation* — reference made when additional copies are made for distribution to various persons.

12. The most common forms of punctuation are open punctuation and mixed punctuation.

    a. *Open punctuation* — no punctuation after salutation and complimentary close.

    b. *Mixed punctuation* — colon after salutation and comma after complimentary close.

13. Letter styles include the following:

    a. *Block letter style* — everything typed against the left margin.

    b. *Modified block letter style with blocked paragraphs* — date and closing are centered; paragraphs are blocked.

    c. *Modified block letter style with indented paragraphs* — date and closing are centered, paragraphs are indented.

    d. *AMS simplified letter style* — salutation and complimentary close are eliminated; everything positioned against the left margin; subject line shown in all capital letters; writer's name and title typed in all capital letters.

14. The United States Post Office now uses OCR scanners to speed the processing of mail by rapid reading and sorting of envelopes.

15. Envelopes are prepared in the following manner:

    a. All lines are single-spaced.

b. The name and address are keyed in all capital letters with no marks of punctuation.

c. For a No. 10 envelope, the address is keyed

14 lines down and five spaces left of the center.

d. For a small envelope, the address is keyed 12 lines down and ten spaces left of the center.

PROFESSIONAL FORUM

You are asked to key the letter which follows. If you had the opportunity to make suggestions for improvement, what would they be?

We received your recent request to credit your account for $400 on the basis of the return of 15 seat belt retainers.

You must have made a mistake in the amount. Upon checking the sales invoice, we discovered that you were billed $375 for these seat belts. Therefore, we are crediting your account for $375 rather than $400.

If you have any questions about this transaction, please let me know.

FOR YOUR UNDERSTANDING

1. Discuss four ways of keeping business letters concise.

2. Explain how you can achieve good human relations in writing letters.

3. What does positivism mean in letter writing?

4. Illustrate the difference between the "you" approach and the "we" approach.

5. Why is it important for the beginning writer to develop a letter outline?

6. Differentiate between an inductive and a

deductive approach to letter writing.

7. If you were responding negatively to a request, would you handle it differently than a positive response? If so, how?

8. What is meant by clichéd words and phrases?

9. What are the advantages of the AMS simplified letter style?

10. What influence has the OCR had on addressing envelopes?

OFFICE APPLICATIONS

On pages 297–307 are office applications that correlate with this chapter.

CHAPTER 8

Business Documents

A large amount of written material is produced daily in the business office, including materials that are prepared and used within the office and mailed outside the office. Since business executives travel extensively today, trip arrangements must be made and itineraries showing departure and arrival information must be prepared. With numerous meetings being held monthly, agendas giving the items to be discussed at the meetings and minutes recording the events of the meetings must be prepared. A variety of reports detailing special projects of the company or reflecting new directions of the company are written. These reports often include tabulated material, charts, and graphs. With businesses engaged in purchasing and selling activities, records which reflect these operations in the form of invoices, statements of account, purchase requisitions, and purchase orders must be prepared.

As an office support employee, one of your main responsibilities is to prepare this material. You must be able to present the information given you in a format that is consistent with the requirements of the business. You must also be able to proofread the information carefully to ensure that the copy is error free. This chapter will help you develop the necessary skills in preparing business documents.

GENERAL OBJECTIVES

Your general objectives for this chapter are to

1. Become knowledgeable of air travel arrangements.
2. Prepare an itinerary.
3. Prepare agendas and minutes.
4. Become familiar with various reference sources.
5. Prepare interoffice memorandums.
6. Prepare business reports.
7. Prepare tabulated material.
8. Understand various uses of computer graphics.
9. Prepare the following business forms: invoices, statements of account, credit memorandums, purchase requisitions, and purchase orders.
10. Demonstrate knowledge of proofreader's marks and correct proofreading methods.

AIR TRAVEL

The business executive today travels great distances for conferences and meetings; for example, he or she may travel from New York to

109

California, Texas to Japan, Washington to Florida, and similar such distances frequently. Because of the distance to be covered and the importance of time to the busy executive, most business executives travel by air. As an office support employee, you will seldom if ever make arrangements for train or bus travel. However, if you do have occasion to make travel arrangements by train or bus, you may obtain information through the Amtrak WATS number (a toll free number listed in your local directory) or through your local bus lines.

Flight Arrangements. In making flight arrangements for your employer, you will usually use one of three methods: (1) a travel department in your company; (2) a travel agency secured by your company; or (3) direct contact with airlines, hotels, and car rental agencies. Whatever method you use, before making the arrangements you need to be knowledgeable concerning the destination of your employer, the preferred times of arrival and departure, type of flight service, preferences as to motel or hotel (type of accommodation, price ranges), and whether or not a rental car is desired.

Airlines have basically two classes of accommodations available: first class and coach. However, some airlines now offer another flight class called business class. Since first class is the most expensive type of service, most companies have a policy that only the chief executives (chairperson of the board, president and possibly the executive vice president) can travel first class. First-class accommodations are more luxurious than coach, the seats are wider and farther apart. Meals and refreshments, including alcoholic beverages, are served free of charge. Meals are served on china dinnerware and with tablecloths. Special service is provided through a greater number of flight attendants than are available in coach class. Coach accommodations provide snacks, soft drinks, tea or coffee, and meals free of charge. However, seats are closer together and fewer flight attendants are available to serve the needs of the customers. Business class is slightly more expensive than coach but less than first class. Accommodations include more spacious seating, headsets, complimentary alcoholic beverages, and meals served on china dinnerware and tablecloths are used.

The Itinerary. Once you have determined where and when your employer wants to travel and have made the appropriate flight, hotel or motel, and car rental arrangements, you are responsible for preparing an itinerary. The *itinerary*, a detailed outline of the trip, is a record for you and your employer of all trip arrangements. A brief itinerary covers such items as the flight number and departure and arrival times. A more comprehensive itinerary will include appointments, hotel and motel arrangements, and car rental information. An itinerary is presented in Illustration 8-1.

ITINERARY FOR MARY STANLEY

October 6-7, 19--

Trip to New York City

MONDAY, OCTOBER 6 (DALLAS TO NEW YORK CITY)

10:11 a.m.	CST	Leave Dallas--DFW Regional Airport on Delta Flight 842 (pick up ticket at airport; lunch served on plane).
2:25 p.m.	EST	Arrive New York City--LaGuardia International Airport (pick up Avis rental car at airport; hotel reservation at the Waldorf).
4:00 p.m.	EST	Appointment with Peter Wolf, Wolf and Associates, 315 Fifth Avenue, telephone: 555-5418 (correspondence file in briefcase).

TUESDAY, OCTOBER 7

10:00 a.m.	EST	Appointment with Elaine Ott, First Word Corporation, Central Tower, telephone: 555-5329 (reports in briefcase).
2:00 p.m.	EST	Appointment with Ted Martinez, Sanchez Company, One Main Place, telephone: 555-1100.
6:45 p.m.	EST	Leave New York LaGuardia International Airport on Delta Flight 871 (dinner served on plane).
9:03 p.m.	CST	Arrive Dallas--DFW Regional Airport.

Illustration 8-1. Itinerary

Notice that time zones are given on the itinerary since the executive is traveling from one time zone to another. Such indication is helpful since it indicates when a time change occurs. If the executive is not changing time zones, it is not necessary to list the time zone. The time zones are given in Illustration 8-2.

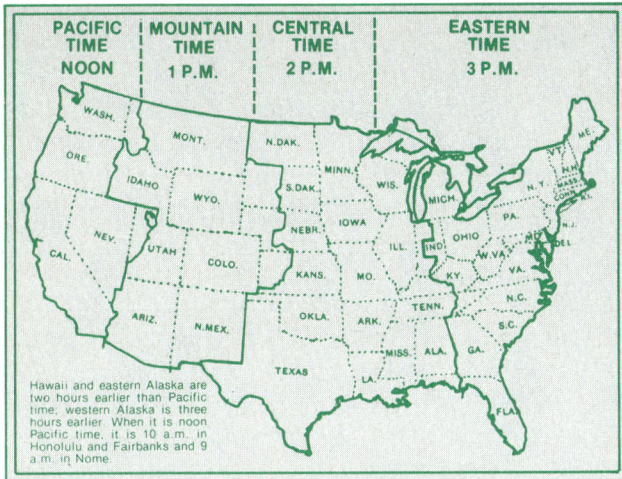

Illustration 8-2. Time Zone Map

As you start to plan a trip, it is a good idea to set up a travel folder for the trip. All information that you receive concerning the trip should be placed in the folder. Then, when you are ready to prepare the itinerary, you have all the necessary information available in one place. In addition to the itinerary, some executives prefer to have a separate appointment schedule which lists all the appointments on one form. Illustration 8-3 shows an appointment schedule.

Illustration 8-3. Appointment Schedule

MEETING PREPARATION

In addition to frequent travel, the business executive spends a considerable amount of time each week in meetings. Many of these meetings may be informal in nature and consist of your employer and one or two other individuals meeting in the employer's office. In such a case, your responsibilities as an office support employee usually include a telephone call or a memorandum to the participants to let them know the day, time, and location of the meeting. However, the business executive also attends numerous meetings of a more formal nature which require agendas and minutes. In these more formal meetings, it is your responsibility as an office support worker to prepare the agenda and the minutes.

Agenda. An *agenda* is an outline of topics to be discussed and things to be done during a meeting. The agenda is mailed to participants prior to the meeting to allow them time to review topics for the meeting. The items on an agenda will vary. However, the items generally included on the agendas of a formal meeting are as follows:

1. Call to order.
2. Review and approval of minutes.
3. Reports from officers of the company.
4. Personnel reports.
5. Financial reports.
6. Additional matters to be discussed or acted upon.
7. Adjournment.

In informal meetings of companies, the agenda usually includes

1. Reports from various company representatives.
2. Informational matters.
3. Items on which decisions must be made.
4. Future meeting times and dates.

The heading of an agenda should give the name of the entity and the date, time, and location of the meeting. The heading should be centered and presented in all caps. A 60- to 70-space line should be used. One blank line should be left after the main heading and one blank line should be left between agenda items. An agenda is shown in Illustration 8-4.

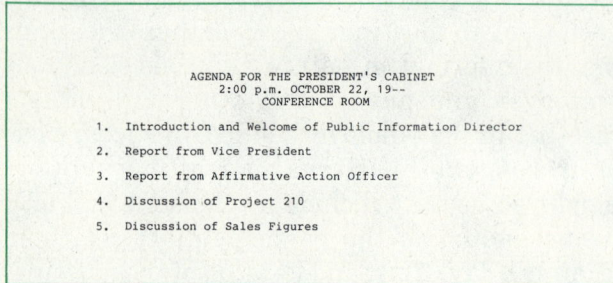

AGENDA FOR THE PRESIDENT'S CABINET
2:00 p.m. OCTOBER 22, 19--
CONFERENCE ROOM

1. Introduction and Welcome of Public Information Director

2. Report from Vice President

3. Report from Affirmative Action Officer

4. Discussion of Project 210

5. Discussion of Sales Figures

Illustration 8-4. Agenda

Minutes. When recording the proceedings of a meeting, you may wish to use a tape recorder or to take notes in shorthand or longhand. The *minutes* should contain a record of all important matters that are presented at the meeting. It is usually to your advantage to record all information presented at the meeting, although it does not have to be a verbatim transcript. It is much easier to eliminate information that is not essential when preparing the minutes than it is to try to remember information that was not recorded. Generally, the items to be included in the minutes are

1. The date, time, and place of the meeting.
2. The individual presiding at the meeting.
3. The members present and absent.
4. Approval or correction of the minutes from the previous meeting.
5. Reports of committees, officers, or individuals.
6. Motions made.
7. Appointment of committees.
8. Items on which action needs to be taken and the person(s) responsible for taking the action.
9. Adjournment of the meeting.

There are several acceptable formats in preparing minutes; general suggestions for minute preparation are given below. Illustration 8-5 shows the minutes of a meeting.

1. Minutes may be double- or single-spaced. Left and right margins should be at least

1 inch. If the minutes are to be placed in a bound book, the left margin should be 1½ inches. The top margin on the first page should be 1½ inches.

2. Capitalize and center the heading that designates the title of the group.

3. Use subject captions for ease in locating various sections of the minutes.

4. At the end of the minutes provide a signature line for the secretary of the organization or the presiding officer.

5. Complete the minutes in final form within twenty-four hours after the meeting.

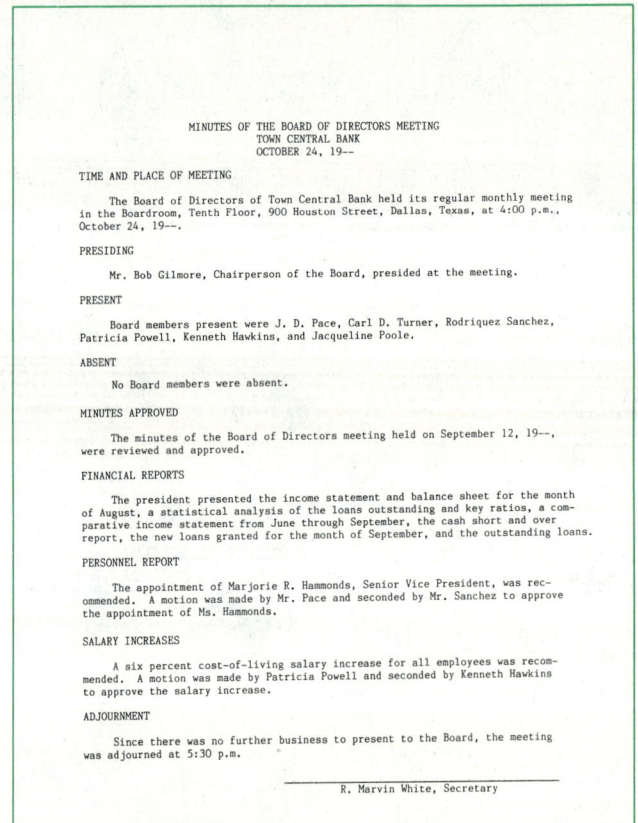

MINUTES OF THE BOARD OF DIRECTORS MEETING
TOWN CENTRAL BANK
OCTOBER 24, 19--

TIME AND PLACE OF MEETING

    The Board of Directors of Town Central Bank held its regular monthly meeting in the Boardroom, Tenth Floor, 900 Houston Street, Dallas, Texas, at 4:00 p.m., October 24, 19--.

PRESIDING

    Mr. Bob Gilmore, Chairperson of the Board, presided at the meeting.

PRESENT

    Board members present were J. D. Pace, Carl D. Turner, Rodriquez Sanchez, Patricia Powell, Kenneth Hawkins, and Jacqueline Poole.

ABSENT

    No Board members were absent.

MINUTES APPROVED

    The minutes of the Board of Directors meeting held on September 12, 19--, were reviewed and approved.

FINANCIAL REPORTS

    The president presented the income statement and balance sheet for the month of August, a statistical analysis of the loans outstanding and key ratios, a comparative income statement from June through September, the cash short and over report, the new loans granted for the month of September, and the outstanding loans.

PERSONNEL REPORT

    The appointment of Marjorie R. Hammonds, Senior Vice President, was recommended. A motion was made by Mr. Pace and seconded by Mr. Sanchez to approve the appointment of Ms. Hammonds.

SALARY INCREASES

    A six percent cost-of-living salary increase for all employees was recommended. A motion was made by Patricia Powell and seconded by Kenneth Hawkins to approve the salary increase.

ADJOURNMENT

    Since there was no further business to present to the Board, the meeting was adjourned at 5:30 p.m.

_____
R. Marvin White, Secretary

Illustration 8-5. Minutes of a Meeting

REFERENCE SOURCES

As an office worker you may be called upon occasionally to research information for your employer. In doing so, you must be familiar with the major sources of information. Several of these sources are given here.

Almanacs and Yearbooks. Almanacs and yearbooks provide a record of notable events and statistical information, such as population and production figures. Some frequently used publications are the *Information Please Almanac, Atlas, and Yearbook*; the *World Almanac and Book of Facts*; and the *Reader's Digest Almanac and Yearbook*.

Government Publications. Numerous informational and statistical publications are available from the United States government. The *Monthly Catalog of United States Government Publications* provides a comprehensive listing of all publications issued by the various governmental departments and agencies.

Some of the government publications available and a brief synopsis of what is contained in each are as follows:

- *The Statistical Abstract of the United States* gives statistics concerning population, climate, employment, military affairs, social security, banking, transportation, agriculture, and related fields.
- *The Guide to Foreign Trade Statistics* gives detailed records of the foreign commerce of the United States.
- *The Survey of Current Business* reports on the industrial and business activities of the United States.
- *The Monthly Labor Review* publishes labor statistics, standards, and employment trends.
- *International Financial Statistics Yearbook* traces financial statistics for more than 125 countries. It covers income to central governments, grants, aid, and such financial obligations as debt repayments and other financing.

Reference Guides. One of the most frequently used reference guides is the *Reader's Guide to Periodical Literature*. A selected list of magazines is indexed in each issue. It is easy to use. Articles may be looked up through subject and author indexes; there is extensive cross referencing. Another reference guide which you may find helpful is the *Business Periodicals Index*. It contains a list of articles published in selected business magazines. These listings are cataloged alphabetically by the subject of the article and the author.

Books in Print contains listings of books published since 1900. This index lists each book by author, by title, and by one or more subjects. It also gives the name of the publisher, the year of publication, and the price of the book. There are also many special guides for reference readings, some of which are the *Medical Books in Print, Scientific and Technological Books in Print*, and *Business and Economics Books in Print*.

Computer Reference Sources. Today several computer networks exist which allow you to do research through a microcomputer. Services such as Tymnet, Telenet, and Uninet allow you to dial a local number of your telephone which connects you to a communications network. A *communications network* allows the microcomputer or terminal user to access other computers in order to obtain information. If you don't live near a network number, you can connect to the network through long-distance service. From these networks, information services such as *Compuserve, Delphi, Dow Jones, and The Source* are reached. Through these information sources, huge amounts of information are available on the microcomputer. Some of the information is up-to-the-minute stock quotes, entire encyclopedias, news, periodical indexes, and reference works full of specialized scientific, legal, and economic information. Commands and keywords describing the subject you wish to reference are given to the computer. Then, the various references available on the topic requested appear on the terminal. Once you decide what references you wish to review, you can receive an abstract or summary of this reference through your terminal and print out that abstract or summary on your printer.

Airline and travel information is also available. Travel routes and schedules may be keyboarded into the computer and several possible flights are given from which to choose. The *Official Airline Guide* which lists arrivals and departures for all airlines around the world is another source available, along with the

Mobil Travel Guide to Hotels, Motels, and Inns, and a hotel reservation service.

The *Dow Jones* service can give you current quotes of stocks, with a minimum delay of 15 minutes, of securities traded on the New York, American, Midwest, and Pacific stock exchanges, as well as quotas from the national over-the-counter market, updated six times daily. This service also lets you search for stories of interest that have appeared in *The Wall Street Journal, Barron's,* and the *Dow Jones News Service.* Other offerings include corporate earnings information and weekly economic summaries. Numerous other data bases (information on various subjects in computer accessible files) are available, a few of which are *Books in Print, Reader's Guide to Periodical Literature, Standard & Poor's Blue List,* and the *Harvard Business Review.*

INTEROFFICE MEMORANDUMS

Quite frequently in the average business office, written information is sent to other departments in the business or to other company offices. Special *interoffice memorandums*, which are usually printed, are recommended for this purpose.

Ordinarily an interoffice communication form provides space for the title of the department or the name of the person to whom the memorandum is being sent. Space is also provided for the date, the message, and the signature or initials of the person writing the memorandum.

Space may also be provided for the file number or the subject of the memorandum. At least one copy should be made for the files of the person sending the memorandum. Extra copies may be needed for filing or for referring to other individuals in the office.

Many executives who use interoffice communication forms require a copy for their personal file. The reason for this is that some executives issue orders or directions by means of interoffice memorandums and periodically

like to go through their copies of the memorandums to see whether the orders have been carried out. The person preparing these memorandums should determine whether the executive wishes copies of all interoffice memorandums or whether copies of only certain memorandums are needed for the file. Illustration 8-6 shows a typical interoffice communication form.

Illustration 8-6. Interoffice Memorandum

When copies of the same interoffice communication are sent to several individuals, a number of copies of the message can be prepared either by using a copying machine or a word processor/computer printer.

The name of the person to receive each copy of the memorandum may then be inserted individually. Sometimes when two or three persons are to receive an interoffice communication, the names of all the persons are listed in the space provided for the name. A copy is made for each individual listed.

BUSINESS REPORTS

Numerous reports are prepared in the office. These reports may be informal reports of two or three pages, or they may be formal reports containing a table of contents, the body of the report (with footnotes), appendices, and a bibliography. They may be either single-spaced or double-spaced. Single spacing reduces the amount of paper needed; for this reason, many business reports are single-spaced. However, if the report is long, it is easier to read it double-spaced. The procedure for preparing a report is presented here.

Margins. With the exception of the first page, if a report is to be unbound, margins should be 1 inch on both sides and at the top and bottom. The heading for the first page begins on line 10 (pica) and 12 (elite). If the report is to be left-bound, a half inch more is provided for the binding. Thus, the left margin of a leftbound report would be $1\frac{1}{2}$ inches. If the report is to be top-bound, an additional 2 lines are added for the binding.

Headings. The main heading is prepared in all capitals and is centered. It is followed by a double space if a secondary heading is used or by a quadruple space if no secondary heading is used. Side headings are placed at the left margin and are underscored with the first letter of major words capitalized. Double space before and after a side heading. Paragraph headings are underscored and indented, with only the first word capitalized and with a period at the end. Double space before a paragraph heading. Illustration 8-7 shows the position of the title and various types of headings on an unbound report.

Page Numbers. It is not necessary to number the first page of a report, but if you choose to do so, the number is centered on line 62. On leftbound and topbound reports, the second and subsequent pages are numbered on line 6 at the right margin. The body of the report begins a double space below the page number. On topbound reports, all page numbers are centered on line 62.

Footnotes and Endnotes. Footnotes and endnotes are references used to cite the source of any quoted or paraphrased material. Footnotes may be placed on the same page of quoted or paraphrased material, or they may be placed at the end of a manuscript and then are called endnotes. If footnotes are placed on the same page, they are separated from the text by a $1\frac{1}{2}$ inch dividing line, which is preceded by a

double space and followed by a double space. The footnotes themselves are single-spaced with a double space between the footnotes. They are numbered consecutively with superior figures.

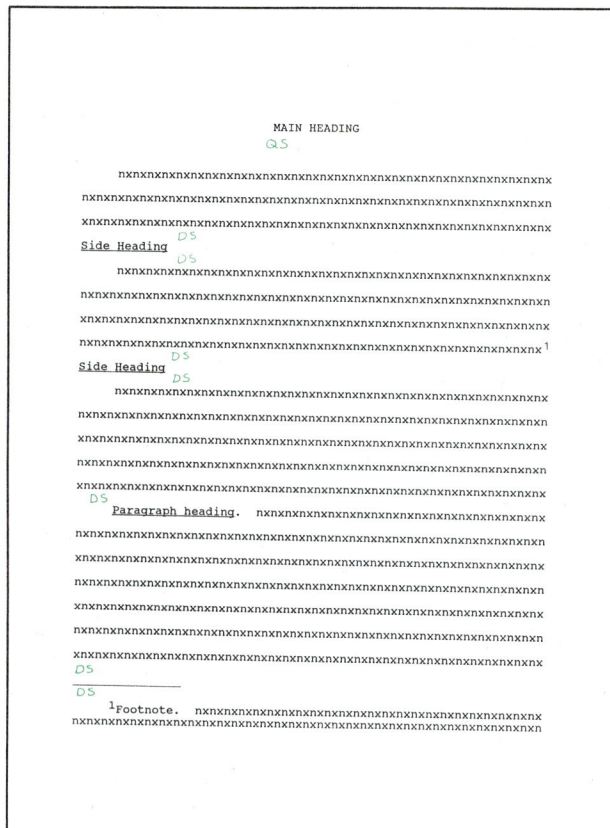

Illustration 8-7. Unbound Business Report Format

Textual Citations. A simpler method of documentation than either the footnote or endnote approach is the textual citation method. Both the footnote and endnote methods require the use of superior (raised) figures. Since electronic printers cannot accommodate a superior number at the present time, the textual citation method of documentation is the best method to use when preparing reports on computers or word processing equipment. With the textual citation method, the surname of the author, the publication date, and the page number or numbers are given in the text. An example of the textual citation method is given in Illustration 8-8. When using footnotes, a bibliography is prepared at the end of the report which lists all references cited in alphabetical order. When endnotes and textual citations are used, the word "References" is used rather than "Bibliography."

```
One of the more difficult aspects of speech preparation
is going from ideas on paper to sharing ideas aloud with
an audience.  Throughout the process of shifting through
information and organizing thoughts, it is important to
consider your impact upon the audience.  It is your aware-
ness of your audience that helps you decide how to shape
your arguments in a way that will best involve the lis-
eners (Flacks, Rasberry, 1982, 120).
```

Illustration 8-8. Textual Citation

Bibliography or References.
The bibliography or reference page identifies all sources used within the report. When preparing a bibliography or reference page, the same margins are used that are used for the first page of the report. If the report is topbound and footnotes are used, BIBLIOGRAPHY is placed on line 12 (pica) or 14 (elite). A quadruple space follows the title. When endnotes or textual citations are used, the word REFERENCES is keyed on line 12 (pica) or 14 (elite). Each entry is arranged alphabetically by the first word of the entry. Individual items are single-spaced with a double space between items. The first line of each item starts at the margin; additional lines are indented five spaces.

Table of Contents.
A table of contents, often simply titled CONTENTS, lists each major division in the report and the number of the first page of each division. When preparing the table of contents, use the same margins that are used for the first page of the report. If the report is topbound, CONTENTS is placed on line 12 (pica) or 14 (elite). The title is centered and is in all capital letters. A quadruple space is left between the title and the table itself. Leaders are used to connect the listings with the page numbers.

STATISTICAL TABLES

In order to prepare statistical tables that look attractive on the page and are arranged so that they are meaningful to the reader, you must plan carefully. You should keep these points in mind when planning and preparing tables.

Horizontal and Vertical Centering.
The finished copy must be pleasing to the eye of the reader. Therefore, to place statistical tables attractively on the page, center the table both vertically and horizontally.

Title.
The title should let the reader know what is contained in the copy. It should be complete, but care should be taken to make it as concise as possible. The title is shown in all capital letters.

Column Headings.
Each column should have an appropriate column heading. The column heading should be written in as few words as possible, and should be underlined.

Alignment of Words and Figures.
The left margin should be even when you are aligning words, and the right margin should be even when you are aligning figures. If the table contains sums of money, a dollar sign should be used with the first amount in the column and with the total.

Leaders.
Leaders (lines of periods) can be used to aid the reader in going from one column to another. An example of a table with leaders is shown in Illustration 8-9. Leaders are usually prepared with a single space between the periods and are aligned vertically.

```
            RJ COMPUTER CORPORATION

                 October 1, 19--
                 (By Department)

    Department                      Employees

    Purchasing. . . . . . . . .        12

    Sales . . . . . . . . . .          23

    Manufacturing . . . . . . .        11

    Personnel . . . . . . . . .         4
```

Illustration 8-9. Table with Leaders

Rules. If you have a table with many columns of figures, you may want to rule the table to increase the readability. Drawing vertical and horizontal rules on the typewriter is explained in Appendix G. An example of a ruled table is shown in Illustration 8-10. Tables may also be prepared on the computer. A section on computer graphics appears later in this chapter.

Footnotes. It is sometimes necessary to further explain an item in a table. This explanation is made in a footnote at the bottom of the table. An example of a table footnote is given in Illustration 8-10. Notice that a symbol (*) is used to designate a footnote rather than the superior figure used in manuscript copy. This procedure eliminates confusion when reading the data.

COMPUTER GRAPHICS

In addition to preparing simple tables, elaborate tables, charts, and graphs may be prepared on the computer. With the advent of the microcomputer and computer software packages, computer graphics applications for businesses have become readily available. Numerous types of graphics presentations are available. Illustration 8-11 shows several types of computer graphics possibilities. Notice that the illustration includes a pie chart, line graph, bar graph, drawing, and *spreadsheet* (a format for presenting statistical or accounting information). Graphics can be done in black-and-white or in color and can incorporate two or three dimensions.

RJ COMPUTER CORPORATION

1985 to 1987

Month	1984	1985	1986	1987
January	$ 75,000*	$ 130,000	$ 175,000	$ 205,000
February	85,000	135,000	178,000	220,000
March	110,000	140,000	182,000	225,000
April	115,000	142,000	190,000	230,000
May	120,000	150,000	194,000	235,000
June	122,000	170,000	195,000	240,000
July	117,000	185,000	200,000	255,000
August	128,000	155,000	210,000	260,000
September	130,000	195,000	212,000	270,000
October	132,000	187,000	214,000	280,000
November	133,000	166,000	217,000	290,000
December	127,000	153,000	215,000	290,000
Total	$1,394,000	$1,908,000	$2,382,000	$3,000,000

*Includes sales from January 15 to January 31.

Illustration 8-10. Ruled Table with Footnote

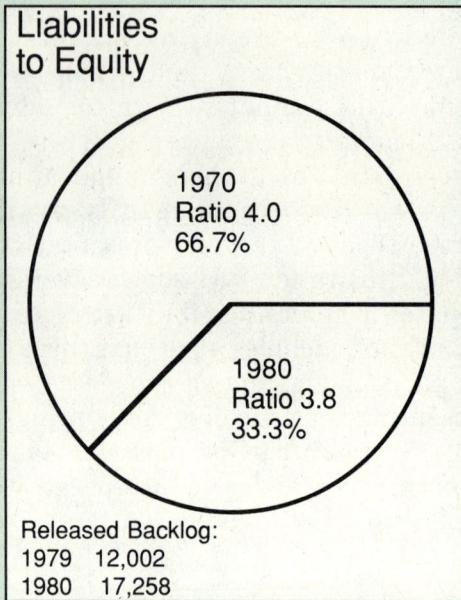

Pie Chart

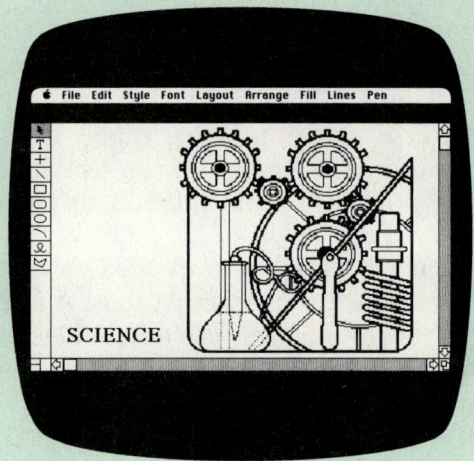

Drawing

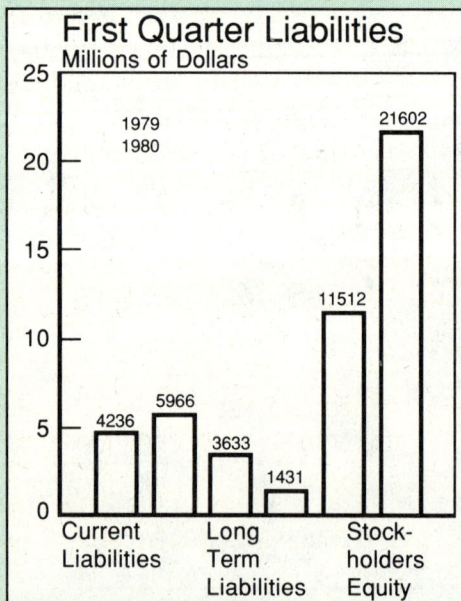

Bar Graph

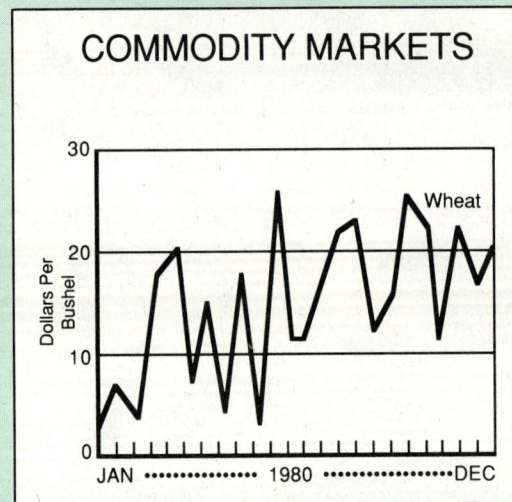

Line Graph

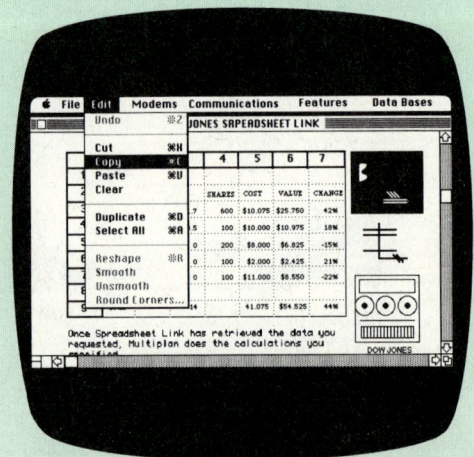

Spreadsheet

Illustration 8-11. Computer Graphics

In order to put the graphic into the computer, various input devices are used. The input device may be a standard keyboard, a *joystick* (a stick which is usually mounted on a separate box and attached to the computer by a cable), a *mouse* (a controller which moves the cursor to different locations on the computer screen), a *graphics table* (sometimes called a digitizer), and a light pen. A *graphics tablet* allows you to draw or trace a picture on the surface of the tablet, and the drawing is then displayed on the computer screen. The graphics tablet is attached to the computer by a cable. The light pen, which is also attached to the computer by a cable, resembles a ballpoint pen. *Light pens* are used to indicate locations on the computer screen. The pen contains a sensor that measures the intensity of the electron beam being shot from the rear of the monitor (also called the video display) toward the screen. These pens are called light pens because of their sensitivity to light on the screen, not because they produce light.

Still another process that allows you to read drawings and photographs directly into a microcomputer is "image processing." The input device for reading into the computer is through an optical character scanner or a video camera. The uses for image processing are many. Business reports can be accompanied by photographs, illustrations, and graphs. Realtors can add photos to computerized listings of homes. Financial institutions can verify signatures. Doctors can store patient histories together with X rays, cell slides, photos of external condition, and other diagnostic evidence.

Output devices for computer graphics systems can be divided into three main categories: film recorders, display devices and printers, and plotters. *Film recorders* in use today convert computer encoded information into human readable information on microfilm. For display on the monitor, the graphic image is presented by lighting a series of dots on the screen called *pixels* (picture elements). With a printer, the graphics are printed out just like text copy would be printed out from the computer. A *plotter* is a mechanical device which uses one or more drawing pens to produce fine-line images in several colors. You can add new colors simply by changing pens; some plotters have as many as eight built-in pens. Also, some plotters allow you to use several different types of pens for different line widths and qualities and are able to draw images on paper, vellum, or transparent plastic sheets (to be used with an overhead projector).

Computer graphics are used fairly extensively at present. And, as the cost of graphics packages continues to decline and the degree of sophistication available from these packages continues to increase, it is anticipated that business use of computer graphics will continue to grow.

BUSINESS FORMS

If you work for a large company, you may never prepare an invoice, a purchase order, a statement of account, or a credit memorandum because such forms are processed by computer. However, in many small companies these forms are still prepared on a typewriter. Regardless of whether you work for a large company or a small company, you need to have an understanding of the process involved in ordering and billing. You also need to have a working knowledge of the terminology. By studying and preparing the forms in this unit, you should gain a knowledge of the ordering and billing procedures of business.

Invoices. An *invoice* usually includes the name and address of the buyer (vendee), the name and address of the seller (vendor), the date of the invoice, the terms of the sale, the quantity and the price of each item sold, an extension (the price of an item times the number of items purchased), and the total amount of the invoice. In addition to this information, the invoice may also include the method of delivery, the order number, and the address to which the shipment is to be sent if the address is different from that of the vendee.

When invoices are prepared, several copies are usually made. The original copy may be sent to the customer; the second copy may be for the accounting department; a third copy, for the sales department; and a fourth copy, for the stock record department. Additional copies may be needed for other purposes.

When a business has occasion to make multiple copies of forms, there is frequently a great saving in time and cost of preparing them if they are purchased in pads or in continuous forms. One-time carbon snap-out forms are also widely used. Manufacturers of office forms assemble forms in multiple copies, the copies can be snapped or pulled away from a binding edge and the one-time carbon discarded. NCR (No Carbon Required) paper may also be used.

In preparing invoices, accuracy is extremely important. Amounts, prices, extensions, and terms, as well as the name and address, should be checked carefully after each invoice is prepared. A typical invoice is depicted in Illustration 8-12.

Illustration 8-12. Invoice

Every well-trained office employee should understand the meaning of credit terms as commonly used on invoices. The following are a few of the terms with a brief explanation of each:

2/10, n/30   • The invoice must be paid within 30 days. If it is paid within 10 days, a 2 percent discount is allowed.

net 30 days   • The invoice must be paid within 30 days.

2/10, EOM   • EOM means end of month. The term 2/10, EOM means that 2 percent discount is allowed if the invoice is paid within 10 days after the end of the month. For example, an invoice dated in July would be discounted if paid by August 10.

The due date for an invoice is figured from the date of the invoice and not from the date the shipment is received. An invoice dated January 15 with terms 2/10 must be paid by January 25 if a discount is to be applied. Most companies permit the discount to be taken if the payment is postmarked the day it is due. A relatively small number of companies, however, insist that the payment actually be received on or before the date the payment is due.

Statements of Account. Periodically, the accounting department of a business sends each customer a *statement of account*. Statements are usually sent out at the end of each month, but in some businesses, statements are mailed at other intervals. Businesses may send some customer statements every few days. For example, customers whose names begin with A, B, or C may be mailed statements on the first day of each month; those whose names begin with D, E, or F on the fourth day of each month, etc. The closing of customers' accounts at different times during the month and the staggered mailing of customer statements is called *cycle billing*. Cycle billing prevents the overloading of the billing clerks at the end of the month since the work load is spread out more evenly throughout the month.

The purpose of a *statement of account* is to enable a customer to check the account and to report any discrepancies. The statement of account is also designed to encourage customers to pay the account, or at least make a payment on it, at the time the statement is received. Illustration 8-13 shows a typical statement of account. A statement of account, which a customer receives at the end of a billing period, usually contains the following information:

1. The name and address of the seller.

2. The name and address of the buyer.
3. The balance due at the time the last statement was prepared.
4. The dates on which transactions occurred affecting the account.
5. Amounts that have been paid since the last statement was sent. These amounts and the amounts of any credit memorandums appear in the Credits column of the statement.
6. A list of the charges to the account since the last statement was prepared. These amounts appear in the Charges or Debits column.
7. The balance of the account, which is the sum of the original balance plus the amounts charged to the account less the amounts credited because of payments or returns.

813 Marsh Lane
Dallas, TX 75220-1604
214-555-2016
RJ COMPUTER CORPORATION

J R WHITE COMPANY
428 ALLISON AVENUE
ARLINGTON TX 76011-1203

WE RENDER MONTHLY STATEMENTS ON THE 25th OF EACH MONTH
ALL BILLS DUE 30 DAYS FROM DATE OF INVOICE 11/25/--

DATE	CHARGES	CREDITS	BALANCE
19--			
Nov. 1			74.55
7	43.60		118.15
10		74.55	43.60
16	110.40		154.00
21	28.35		182.35

Illustration 8-13. Statement of Account

Regardless of the bookkeeping system used, extra copies of statements occasionally must be prepared for customers. This work involves tabulation and accuracy on the part of the office employee. If a statement is being copied from a ledger page or a ledger card, the statement should be verified carefully. If statements are being typed and envelopes for them are being addressed, care should be exercised in placing the right statement in each envelope.

Credit Memorandums. There are times when a customer returns merchandise for credit. Such returns may be necessary because unsatisfactory merchandise or the wrong merchandise was received. When a return is made, the seller gives the customer a statement of the material returned. This statement is called a *credit memorandum.* A typical credit memorandum is shown in Illustration 8-14. A credit memorandum usually contains the following:

1. A heading of some kind to indicate that it is a credit memorandum and not an invoice. Colored paper may be used.
2. The name and address of the seller.
3. The name and address of the buyer.
4. A description of the item or items returned, with the amount of credit for each item and the necessary extensions.
5. The date on which the credit memorandum is prepared.

In addition to this information, the credit memorandum sometimes contains a number,

813 Marsh Lane
Dallas, TX 75220-1604
214-555-2016
RJ COMPUTER CORPORATION

CREDIT MEMORANDUM

No. 15

Name HMB Metals

Street 304 Ashwood Drive City Arlington, TX 76010-3052

QUANTITY	DESCRIPTION	PRICE	EXTENSION
2	Printerhead, plastic, elite 12, HX-475K	6.50	13.00

DATE	AUTHORIZED BY	REC'D IN STOCK BY	DATE OF SALE	AMOUNT OF SALE
11/4/--	ER	CF	10/14/--	13.00

Illustration 8-14. Credit Memorandum

which appears on all copies of the memorandum, and the reason why the merchandise was returned. The same care should be used in preparing credit memorandums as is used in preparing invoices.

Purchase Requisitions. Some form should be available for the stock department, department head, or other person in charge of the supplies or materials to use in notifying the purchasing department that the stock of certain materials is depleted. A *purchase requisition* is the name usually given to a form of this kind. At least two copies of this form should be made, with one copy going to the purchasing agent and one being retained by the person requesting the purchase of the goods. A purchase requisition need not be a formal printed business paper; but in large business offices where purchase requisitions are frequently used, it is advisable to have a printed form and a definite routine for preparing requisitions. Illustration 8-15 shows a typical purchase requisition.

813 Marsh Lane
Dallas, TX 75220-1604
214-555-2016
RJ COMPUTER CORPORATION

Purchase Requisition

REQUISITION NO. B-211

Date Issued November 6, 19--

Required for Department
Advise Jack Navarate on delivery

Date Required November 25, 19--

	DESCRIPTION
500	Diskette, flexible, $5\frac{1}{2}$", DS, quad density, Part No. 57-4881
200	Printwheel, metal, prestige elite 12, Part No. BA-362K

Approved by *J. C. Chaney*

Requisition placed by Marjorie Ott

PURCHASING AGENT'S MEMORANDUM

Purchase Order No. 185

Issued to Office Supply Co.

Date November 6, 19--

Dallas

Illustration 8-15. Purchase Requisition

Purchase Orders. In ordering supplies or materials, most businesses use a special form called a *purchase order*. Such a form is shown in Illustration 8-16.

Usually several copies of a purchase order are made. The original is sent to the company from which the goods are being ordered; one copy is kept in the files of the purchasing department; and one is sent to the person who prepared the purchase requisition asking that the goods be ordered. Extra copies may also be made for the receiving department and the accounting department. Frequently the copies are made on different colors of paper, with one department receiving the same colored copy for each purchase order. A purchase order usually contains the following information:

1. The purchase order number.
2. The date.
3. The name and address of the company making the purchase. (This information is usually printed on the purchase order form.)
4. The name and address of the company to which the order is being sent.
5. The quantity, description, and price of each item ordered.
6. The shipping instructions.
7. The requested delivery date.
8. The signature of the purchasing agent or other persons authorized to sign purchase orders.

813 Marsh Lane
Dallas, TX 75220-1604
214-555-2016
RJ COMPUTER CORPORATION

PURCHASE ORDER

No. 185

To OFFICE SUPPLY CO
2089 LEWISTON AVENUE
DALLAS TX 75217-4836

Date November 7, 19--
Ship Via Our Truck
FOB
Terms 2/10, n/30

Deliver November 25, 19--

QUANTITY	DESCRIPTION	UNIT PRICE	TOTAL
500	Diskette, flexible, $5\frac{1}{2}$", DS, quad density, Part No. 57-4881	2.65	1,325
200	Printwheel, metal, prestige elite 12, Part No. BA-362K	11.00	2,200
			3,525

J. C. Chaney

Illustration 8-16. Purchase Order

PROOFREADING

A good proofreader is an asset to any office—and is worth his or her weight in gold. As an office worker, you need to find all errors in material before it leaves your hands. Suggestions for helping you to become a more effective proofreader are given in this section.

You also need to be familiar with the commonly used proofreader's marks. These marks are used to indicate corrections in materials; and unless you know what these marks mean, you will not be able to make the proper corrections. The basic proofreader's marks are presented in Appendix F, along with some proofreading suggestions.

Proofreading Text Copy. When proofreading from a printed page, always proofread each page twice. The first time you should read the copy through to see that it has no grammatical errors, that it makes sense, and that there are no omissions. If you are working from a rough draft, check the copy carefully against the draft to see that all material is included. After you have read the copy through one time, read it a second time; check for any misspelled words. One method of holding your attention more closely to each specific word is to read the copy backwards (from right to left rather than left to right). Using this method, you are not as likely to skip over misspelled words. If there are figures in the copy, be sure to check the figures for accuracy. If there are columns of figures with a total given, add the figures to double check the accuracy of the total.

If you are proofreading typewritten copy, you should not take the copy out of the typewriter until it has been proofread. One method of holding your attention on each line as you proofread is to use what is called the "paper bail" method of proofreading. While your copy is still in the machine, roll it back until you have the first line of type just above the paper bail. Read the line, then move your copy up, keeping one line at a time above the paper bail.

If you are using a word processor or computer, you may have the advantage of a built-in dictionary that brings misspelled words to your attention and a mathematical package that adds figures. However, a dictionary does not automatically correct spelling errors. Neither does it notice incorrect grammar, word usage, punctuation, or capitalization. Also, a mathematical package does not notice incorrect or transposed numbers.

When preparing material on a word processor or computer, it is a good idea to replay the material on the screen and check for errors before printing the copy. In order to do so, you should scroll back to the beginning of the document. Use the cursor to call your attention to one line at a time. Proofread that line, checking for keyboarding errors, grammatical errors, punctuation errors, and number errors. Once the entire document has been replayed and proofed, print it out. Then, proof the printed document once also.

Proofreading Statistical Copy. Statistical copy is doubly hard to proofread, since a misplaced number is not as obvious as a misplaced word. Because statistical copy is difficult to proofread, it is a good idea to ask someone to proofread the figures with you. If you are proofreading from printed copy, have the other person proofread the printed copy while you read from the rough draft. If you are proofreading at the screen of a computer, ask someone to proof at the screen while you read from the rough draft. When you have been given numbers on a dictation tape, play back the tape and check the screen. If the table contains columns of figures with a total, you should add the figures on a calculator to check their accuracy unless you have a mathematical package on your word processor or computer which will add for you. Additional suggestions for proofreading are given in Appendix F.

FOR YOUR REVIEW

The following review will help you remember the important points of this chapter.

1. Flight arrangements are generally made in one of three ways: (1) a travel department within the company; (2) a travel agency; or (3) direct contact with the airlines, hotels, and car rental agencies.

2. Airlines have basically two classes of flight available: first class and coach. Some airlines now offer a business class. First class is the most expensive, with coach being the least expensive.

3. An itinerary is a detailed outline of a trip and is a record for you and your employer of

the flight, departure and arrival times, appointments, and hotel and car rental arrangements.

4. Some executives prefer to have a separate appointment schedule which lists all appointments in addition to the itinerary.

5. An agenda is an outline of topics to be discussed and things to be done during a meeting. The agenda is mailed to participants before the meeting to allow them time to review and be prepared to discuss topics on the agenda.

6. Minutes contain a record of all important matters that are presented at meetings. Several acceptable formats exist for minute preparation; however, margins should be at least one inch on all sides, with an approximate two-inch top margin on the first page.

7. The office worker may be called upon to do research and should be familiar with the basic reference sources, some of which are almanacs and yearbooks, government publications, and reference guides.

8. Today numerous computer networks exist which allow you to do research through a microcomputer. Information such as stock quotes, periodical indexes, and reference works containing specialized scientific, legal, and economic information is available.

9. Interoffice memorandums are used to send written information to other departments within the same company.

10. Numerous business reports are prepared in offices. These reports may be informal, containing two or three pages; or they may be formal, containing a table of contents, the body (with footnotes), appendices, and a bibliography. An unbound business report is prepared with top, side, and bottom margins of 1 inch except for the first page which begins on line 10 (pica) or 12 (elite). If the report is left bound, an additional one-half inch is required for the binding. If it is top-bound begin on line 12 (pica) and 14 (elite).

11. Statistical copy must be arranged in meaningful manner and placed well on the page. When keying statistical copy, keep these points in mind.

a. The copy should be centered both vertically and horizontally.

b. The title should be complete, concise, and shown in all capital letters.

c. Each column should have a concise heading.

d. Words should align on the left, and figures should align on the right.

e. Leaders may be used to aid the reader in going from one column to another.

f. Tables may be ruled to increase the readability.

g. Footnotes are used in tables to further explain an item within the table.

12. Business forms are frequently used in offices. Some of the more common forms are

a. *Invoices.* An invoice is used to record sales transactions.
   The invoice includes the following:
   Name and address of buyer
   Name and address of seller
   Date of invoice
   Terms of sale
   Quantity
   Price of each item
   Total amount of invoice
   The invoice may also include the method of delivery, the order number, and the address to which the shipment is to be sent.

b. *Statements of account.* A statement of account is sent to each customer of a business at the end of the billing period. The statement shows the transactions that have occurred during the month and the amount of money due at the billing date.

c. *Credit memorandums.* When material is returned by a buyer due to incorrect or unsatisfactory merchandise, a credit memorandum is prepared. This memorandum credits the account of the buyer for the amount of the returned merchandise.

d. *Purchase requisitions.* A purchase requisition is used by an individual department within a business to request the ordering of supplies.

e. *Purchase orders.* A purchase order is

prepared by the business and sent to the company from which the business is buying supplies.

13. All material must be proofread carefully.

Copy should be read twice, the first time for grammatical errors and to see that it makes sense, the second time for any misspelled words. All statistical copy should be checked for accuracy.

PROFESSIONAL FORUM

Your employer has given you the following projects. Explain how you would handle each project.

1. Mr. Navarate is leaving for New Orleans next Monday; you must handle the trip arrangements.

2. An important meeting has been scheduled for Friday with all company employees. A new benefits package for all employees will be discussed.

3. Your employer is making a presentation on conflict management; he has asked you to do some research on the topic.

FOR YOUR UNDERSTANDING

1. When is an itinerary prepared and what does it include?

2. What type of information is available through computer reference sources?

3. List and explain three input devices for computer graphics.

4. What is a plotter?

5. What is an invoice? How is it used?

6. What is the purpose of a statement of account?

7. What is the purpose of a purchase order?

8. Explain how text copy should be proofread.

OFFICE APPLICATIONS

On pages 309–334 are office applications that correlate with this chapter.

CHAPTER 9

Telecommunications

In the last two chapters you learned about several types of written communication, including letters, agendas, minutes of meetings, and reports. These written communications are traditional forms that we have used for years. Other forms of communication which are a result of our technological age are becoming increasingly important today. Telecommunications is the word that is used to describe these forms of communication. This word is a relatively new word in our society, not appearing in our dictionary until the mid-1960s. The word itself refers to long-distance communication with the prefix coming from the Greek word "tele" which means far off. At present telecommunication is carried out through the aid of some type of electronic equipment.

As an office worker of the future, you will be heavily impacted by telecommunications. You will be expected to be knowledgeable about the field and be able to communicate through various telecommunication devices. In this chapter you will learn about how information is transmitted electronically and the various types of telecommunication equipment available today.

GENERAL OBJECTIVES

Your general objectives for this chapter are to

1. Become knowledgeable of the telecommunications field.

2. Develop a good telephone personality.
3. Use the telephone correctly.
4. Become familiar with various types of telecommunication equipment and services.
5. Develop an understanding of the various types of written message and image communication systems.

THE TELECOMMUNICATIONS FIELD

The telecommunications field is one of the fastest growing technological fields of today. Notice Illustration 9-1 which gives expenditures in this field since 1984 and the projected expenditures through 1994. Applications for telecommunications are found in an astounding variety of industries. All major airlines in the United States use telecommunications in handling reservations. Telecommunications permits the monitoring of air traffic from control towers. Banks use telecommunications (electronic funds transfers) to reduce the enormous amount of paperwork in handling financial transactions. Newspapers transmit pages to be printed from editorial offices to printing plants by means of telecommunication devices. Insurance companies use telecommunications to check records of policyholders. Stockbrokers throughout the country transmit their buy and sell orders over communication lines to their representatives at stock exchanges.

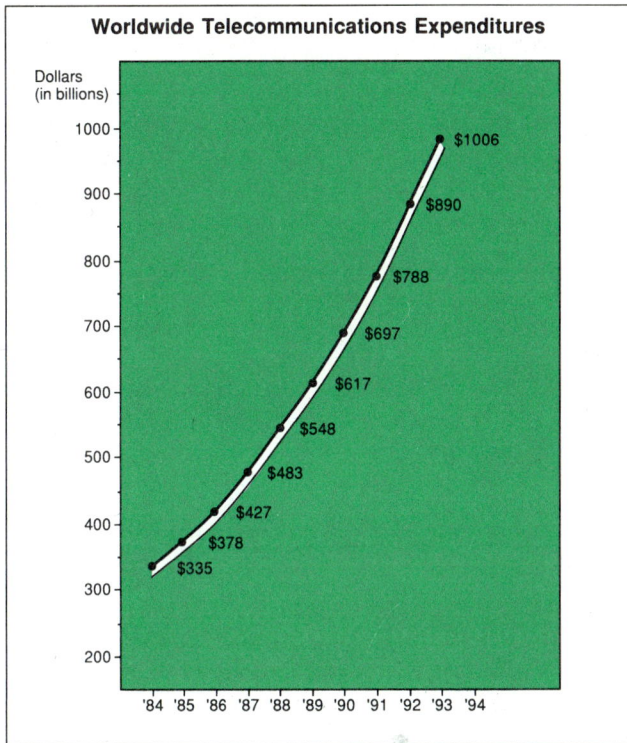

Illustration 9-1. Growth of Telecommunications Expressed in Expenditures

Telecommunications Defined. Telecommunications is the process of transmitting information over a distance by electronic impulses. These electronic impulses are sent through transmission media which may be wire cable, fiber optic cable, or wireless methods. Telecommunications involves the transmission of voice, written or text messages, and images.

Transmission Media. Although the wire cable is still the major transmission device used today, the direction is toward the use of fiber optic cable and microwave and satellite transmission. The wire transmission will be discussed here, along with fiber optic cable and wireless methods.

Wire Cable. There are two basic types of wire cable—twisted-pair wires and coaxial cable. Twisted-pair wires have been insulated and

twisted into pairs. Twisting minimizes the interference between wires that are packed or bundled into a cable. Most electronic applications require at least two wires to complete a circuit. These wires are made of a metal which has good conductive properties. The wires often consist of copper surrounded by a plastic covering. Most of these wire pairs are placed together in a circular bundle. The bundle in turn is surrounded by another plastic covering to form multiconductor cable. Twisted-pair wires are commonly used in telephone lines. The lines may be either suspended from poles or buried underground. See Illustration 9-2.

Coaxial cable consists of a single conductor (usually a small copper wire) surrounded by a plastic insulator and a braided wire sleeve. These cables can be bundled into a large cable that contains 20 coaxial cables. Coaxial cable is

Illustration 9-2. Twisted-Pair Wire Cable

used where interference (distortion or signal loss) from surrounding wires is a problem; for example, in the connection of a host computer to several remote terminals. A coaxial cable is shown in Illustration 9-3.

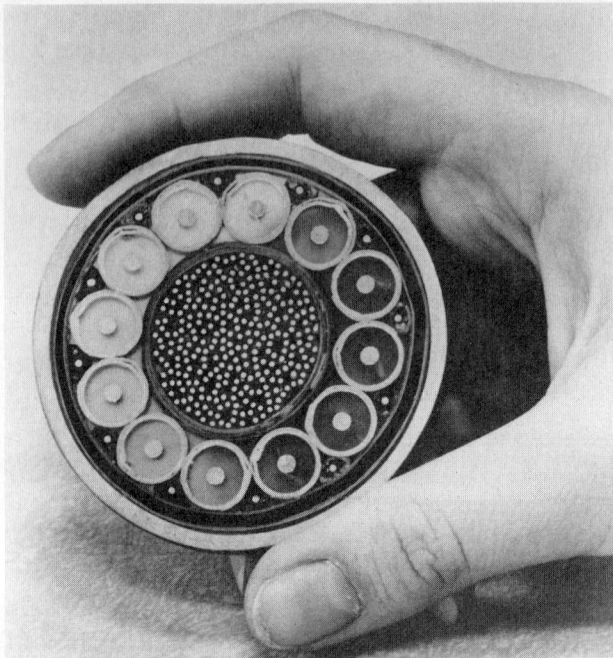

Reproduced with permission of AT&T Corporate Archives

Illustration 9-3. Coaxial Cable

Fiber Optic Cable. Multiconductor cables containing several hundred wires may be several inches thick, very heavy, and also very inflexible. In recent years, fiber optic cables have been replacing transmission devices. The fiber rod used in fiber optic cables is a nonconductor of electricity made of glass or plastic that conducts or passes light waves. See Illustration 9-4 for a fiber optic cable.

The electronic impulses from a computer or telephone must be converted to light signals which pass through the fiber optic cable at approximately the speed of light. This speed is approximately one and one-half times faster than electronic impulses pass through copper wires. Once the light impulses reach the destination, the light must be changed back to electronic impulses for processing.

The primary advantage of fiber optic cables is that many more communication channels are available in each fiber rod than on wire cable

pairs. For example, a single glass fiber only 5 thousandths of an inch thick can replace 10,000 telephone wires. These fiber rods may be grouped together much like multiconductor cables. One fiber optic cable in use today is only one-half inch in diameter, but the 144 fibers inside can handle up to 80,000 two-way voice communications. Operational fiber optics transmission systems are in use connecting various cities along the East and West Coasts of the United States and under the Atlantic Ocean connecting the United States to Europe.

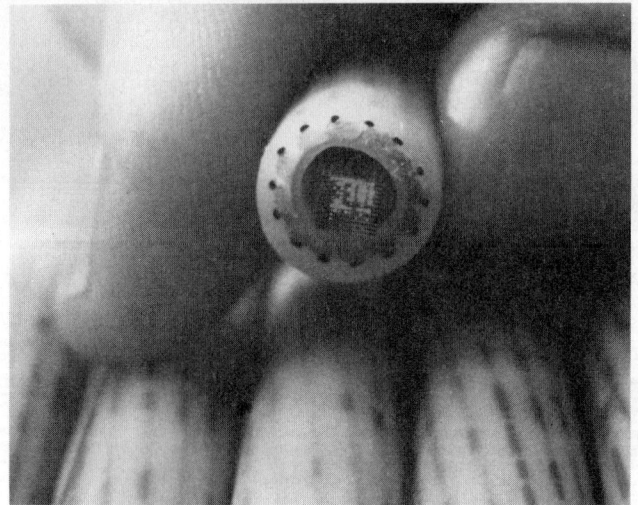

Courtesy of Bell Laboratories

Illustration 9-4. Fiber Optic Cable

Wireless Methods. Wireless methods of transporting electronic signals include land-based microwave links and satellite stations. These methods are similar in that signals are transmitted through the air to receivers located at a microwave station or a satellite at very high frequencies (above one billion cycles per second).

Microwave Transmission. Microwave transmission is land-based transmission in which an electronic signal is transmitted from the sending location through the air to a microwave tower which receives the signal and transmits it on to the next microwave tower. The receivers and transmitters on the microwave towers are called *transponders*. These transponders are high-powered amplifiers that duplicate the received signal and transmit it to the next transponder. Microwave towers are spaced approximately 40 miles apart. These towers can be readily identified as you travel along the highway because of their dishlike antennae which are mounted at the top and bottom of the towers.

Satellite Transmission. Satellite transmission is space-based microwave transmission in which an electronic signal is transmitted from the sending location through space to a satellite that orbits some 22,300 miles above our heads. See Illustration 9-5. The satellite receives the signal and transmits it to a receiving station on Earth. The satellite functions as a microwave tower in space.

Satellites resemble coffee cans with "wings." These wings are covered with solar cells to generate electrical power; the interiors are crammed with electronics, including the key electronic components called transponders. *Transponders,* similar to those used in land-based microwave transmission, receive signals from a ground station, boost their power, and rebroadcast the signals back to a different location on Earth. The cost of launching a satellite into orbit is expensive; however, the costs of extending land-based systems to remote locations are greater.

In addition to the cost savings of satellite transmission over terrestrial or land-based systems, satellite transmission is of higher quality.

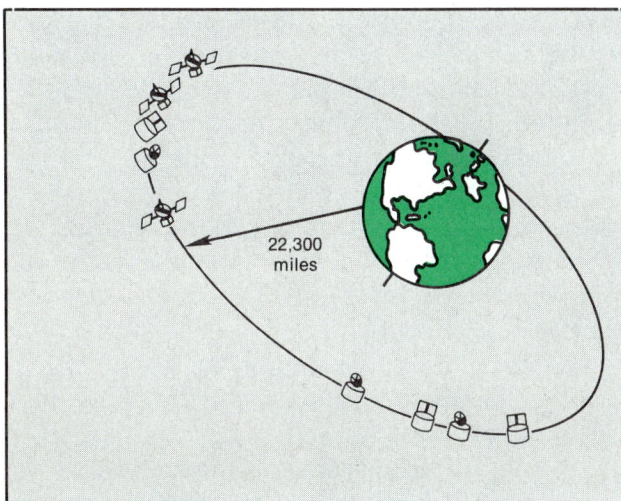

Illustration 9-5. Communication Satellite

On the traditional land-based system, a signal going from the East Coast of the United States to the West Coast must be repeated through more than 100 relay points or land-based antennae. Transmission through these various relay points causes the quality of the transmission to be lower and the costs higher. Whereas, in satellite transmission, the message goes at the speed of light to the satellite where it is repeated and sent back to the receiving point on Earth. Thus, the quality is high since the transmission is rebroadcast only one time and does not go through various relay points.

Communication Networks. Networks are commonly used to transmit information from one location to another. With telecommunication networks, it is possible to link telephones, computers, word processors, and various other pieces of electronic equipment so that voice, data, text, and images may be transmitted. The linkage of these machines is made possible through networks—systems for connecting or integrating pieces of equipment for the transmission of information. Each piece of equipment in a network must be able to connect with any other piece of equipment in the network. Networks allow office personnel to send messages electronically across distances.

Local Area Network (LAN). The term local area network describes a privately owned network specially designed to provide communications within a limited geographical area. A local network supports intraoffice, intrabuilding, or intrafacility communications over distances of up to a few miles. The local area network is used as a prime means of tying together various pieces of equipment. For example, an office worker may input a message on a computer and have that message transmitted electronically to a computer located in another part of the building or across town. The office worker at the computer in the same building or across town is able to call up that message and read it without the exchange of a paper document. In addition to tying computers together, LANs also tie word processors, facsimile devices, and reprographics equipment together. Twisted-pair wire cable, coaxial cable, and fiber optic cable are the transmission media in most local networks.

Expanded or Wide Area Network. Although the LAN concept has been confined to the transmission of information over short distances (such as within a building or from one building to another in the same city), the network concept can be expanded to allow information to be sent electronically from city to city and across the nation. Large communication networks make use of transmission media such as cables, microwave towers, and satellite stations. As an example, telephone companies provide business and residential telephone service for voice and data transmission to the general public. Fees for use of the network are paid on a per-call, per-minute, per-mile basis. Public telephone networks are by far the largest category of wide area networks.

Types of Information Transmitted. Three
principal types of information transmitted over communication networks are voice, written messages (text), and images. Voice communications, or telephony, refers to the transmission of speech over a distance. The major transmission equipment for voice is the telephone. The telephone has become the major communication link between people across the street, the city, or the nation.

Another type of information transmitted over communication networks is the written message. The message may be transmitted by teletypewriters, communicating word processors, facsimile equipment, carrier-based message systems (such as computer-based message systems, and other electronic equipment).

The third major type of information transmitted over communication systems is the image. Images transmitted include blueprints, graphs, and pictures. The communications equipment used to transmit images includes videoconferencing equipment and facsimile equipment.

When you classify information transmitted into these three categories (voice, written messages, and images), there is some overlapping. For example, some written messages include images such as graphs and pictures. And some

communications equipment will transmit both written messages and graphs, e.g., facsimile equipment and communicating word processors.

VOICE SYSTEMS

Since the telephone is the major voice communication system in use today, a large part of this chapter will be spent on using the telephone properly and the telephone equipment available. Voice mail will also be discussed briefly in this chapter.

Telephone Procedures. Since Alexander
Graham Bell made his first telephone call to Thomas Watson in 1876, the telephone has become an instrument used extensively in both business and the home. Studies have shown that communicating with others is present in 90 percent of all office jobs; and, much of that communication takes place over the telephone. Since many individuals will have only telephone contact with your company, it is important that you make a good impression on the phone. The image you project can make or lose money for your company.

Your Telephone Personality. No doubt you have used the telephone since you were young. You may be thinking, "Why should I learn to use the telephone? I already know how." However, you may be surprised at the number of people who do not handle the telephone correctly.

What common mistakes are made over the telephone? People sometimes forget that the person on the other end of the line is a human being too. Somehow it is easier to be rude when you cannot see the person. Have you ever called a business office and the telephone rang approximately ten times before someone answered it? Have you ever had someone keep you on "hold" for an extremely long time? Have you ever heard someone answer the phone in a curt, angry tone of voice? The mistakes made on the phone are numerous and inexcusable.

As an office worker, you need to have a pleasant telephone personality. Here are a few suggestions for being more effective on the phone.

Keep a Smile in Your Voice. When you have customers or visitors in your office, a cheerful smile and a cup of coffee or a magazine will keep the in-person callers happy, even when you have to keep them waiting. However, these services cannot be provided over the telephone. Thus, you must rely on your voice and your manner to make the voice-to-voice contact over the telephone as pleasant as the face-to-face contact in the office. The voice that makes the caller feel as if a smile is coming through the receiver is a winner. But how do you develop such a smile in your voice? One way is to smile as you pick up the telephone receiver. If you are smiling, it is much easier to project a smile in your voice. Treat the voice on the other end of the line as you would treat a person who is standing in front of you. Let the individual know that you are concerned. Maintain a caring attitude. Never answer the phone in a voice that is curt or rude. Do not speak in a monotone. Be expressive, just as you would when talking with someone face-to-face. See Illustration 9-6.

Be Natural. Be yourself! Don't adopt an affected tone of voice over the telephone. The person who tries to impress usually appears insincere. Use a vocabulary and a tone of voice that express your best natural self.

Be Considerate. Let the caller know that you want to help. When it is necessary to leave the phone to get information ask, "Will you please wait, or may I call you back?" If the caller decides to wait, then thank the caller for waiting upon returning to the phone. Address the caller by name. It is always nice to hear someone state your name; however, it is particularly enjoyable over the telephone, as it lets the caller know that you recognize a person rather than a voice.

Be Attentive. Listen politely to what the other person says. Don't interrupt. If the caller is unhappy about some situation, allow the caller to explain why. Most of a person's anger is usually vented in telling the story. Therefore, it becomes easier to handle unhappy persons after you have listened to their problems. Use good listening skills. Listen for facts and for feelings. Be patient. Don't evaluate. Try to understand the words that the speaker uses, and act on what the speaker says.

Be Discreet. Carefully explain why your employer cannot answer the telephone. You may say, "Mr. Navarate is away from his desk right now; I expect him back in approximately 30 minutes. May I have him call you when he returns?" Never say, "He's not in yet (at 10 a.m.)"; "He's gone for the day (at 3 p.m.)"; or "He's playing golf (at any time during the day)." A good rule to remember is: *Be helpful, but not specific.*

Illustration 9-6. Keep a Smile in Your Voice

Answering Techniques. Here are some suggestions to help you become more effective when answering the telephone.

Answer Promptly. When the telephone rings, answer it promptly; perhaps on the first or second ring, if possible. If you wait too long to answer the phone, you may lose a valuable caller.

Identify Yourself. If you work in a large company, chances are that the first person to answer the phone will be a receptionist. She or he will probably identify the company. The caller will then ask for a specific person or department. As an office worker in Mr. Navarate's office, you could therefore answer, "Mr. Navarate's office, Joe Lesikar." Other possible ways to answer the phone are: "RJ Computer Corporation" or "Joe Lesikar."

Take Messages Courteously. If you are answering the telephone for someone who is out of the office or for someone who cannot answer at the time, offer assistance. Say, "Mr. Navarate is out of the office. May I take a message or have him call you when he returns?" Then make a note of the message for Mr. Navarate. Be certain that you get the information correct. Repeat the information such as the phone number, any dates and times, etc., to the caller to be sure that you accurately received the message. A sample form for reporting messages is presented in Illustration 9-7.

> TO **Mr. Navarate**
>
> DATE **11/2**   TIME **2 p.m.**
>
> ### WHILE YOU WERE OUT
>
> M **r. Cipriani**
>
> OF **Paint Supply Co.**
>
> PHONE **555-8603**
>
> TELEPHONED ☑   PLEASE CALL ☑
>
> CAME TO SEE YOU ☐   WILL CALL AGAIN ☐
>
> WANTS TO SEE YOU ☐
>
> RETURNED YOUR CALL ☐
>
> MESSAGE _____
>
> _____
>
> _____
>
> _____
>
>   By *Joe Lesikar*

Illustration 9-7. Telephone Message Form

Transfer Calls Carefully. It is frequently necessary to transfer a call to another extension. Before you transfer a call, explain to the caller why you must transfer the call. Make sure the caller is willing to be transferred. For example, you may say, "Mr. Navarate is out, but Jo Fowler can give you the information. May I transfer you to her?" You may also want to give the caller the extension number of the person to whom the caller is being transferred in case there is an equipment malfunction and the transfer does not go through. The caller can then call that number without having to call you again.

Know how to transfer calls properly. You may be able to transfer the call by merely depressing the receiver button and dialing the extension, or you may need to go through an operator who will then transfer the call. In either case, stay with the caller until the transfer is completed.

Ask Questions Tactfully. Care should be used in asking questions, especially when answering telephone calls for others. Ask only necessary questions such as, "May I tell Mr. Navarate who is calling?" or "When Mr. Navarate returns, may I tell him who called?" Never ask, "Who's calling?" Many people are offended by such a blunt question; it may imply that your boss is not available to the caller. If your supervisor is not in or cannot take the call for some reason, ask about the nature of the call so that it can be referred to someone else. For example, you may say, "If you can tell me the nature of your call, perhaps I can help you or refer you to someone else."

Leave Word When You Are Away from Your Telephone. Leave word with the person who answers your telephone while you are gone. Information about where you are going and when you expect to return is a courtesy. Give the person who covers your phone enough information so an uninformed response such as "I don't know" will not be necessary.

Speak Distinctly. Make sure the caller can understand what you say. You can't speak distinctly with gum, candy, or a pencil in your mouth. Nor should you shout. A loud voice sounds gruff and unpleasant over the telephone. It is equally unpleasant to listen to someone who whispers. When you talk over the telephone, you should do the following:

1. Place the receiver firmly against your ear so that a good seal is obtained.

2. Place the center of the mouthpiece about three fourths of an inch from the center of your lips.

3. Speak in a pleasant, normal voice. Watch the speed of your voice; do not talk too fast nor too slow. Speak at a moderate rate. A pleasant voice is friendly, cordial, cheerful, interested, and helpful.

Use Words to Identify Letters. Use words to identify letters in the spelling of names and places when necessary. Some words and letters are difficult to understand over the telephone. The following is a list of words commonly used to designate letters of the alphabet:

A as in *A*lice	*N* as in *N*ellie
B as in *B*ertha	*O* as in *O*cean
C as in *C*harles	*P* as in *P*eter
D as in *D*avid	*Q* as in *Q*ueen
E as in *E*dward	*R* as in *R*obert
F as in *F*rank	*S* as in *S*ugar
G as in *G*eorge	*T* as in *T*homas
H as in *H*enry	*U* as in *U*nion
I as in *I*da	*V* as in *V*ictory
J as in *J*ohn	*W* as in *W*illiam
K as in *K*ing	*X* as in *X* ray
L as in *L*incoln	*Y* as in *Y*oung
M as in *M*ary	*Z* as in *Z*ero

Enunciate Numerals Clearly. Use the following recommended methods of pronunciation for numerals:

Numeral	Sounded As	Formation of Sounds
0	oh	Long *O*
1	wun	Strong *W* and *N*
2	too	Strong *T* and *OO*
3	th-r-ee	A single roll of the *R* and long *EE*
4	fo-er	Long *O* and strong *R*
5	fi-iv	*I* changing from long to short, and strong *V*
6	siks	Strong *S* and *KS*
7	sev-en	Strong *S* and *V* and well-sounded *EN*
8	ate	Long *A* and strong *T*
9	ni-en	Strong *N*, long *I*, and well-sounded *EN*

Close the Conversation Politely. Be sure to close the conversation in a pleasant manner. Say, "Good-bye" or "Good-bye, Mrs. Merrill." As a parting and thoughtful gesture, hang the phone up gently; however, it is a good idea to let the caller hang up first. Be sure to thank the caller if the caller has been helpful in any way.

Helpful Hints for Placing Calls. Whether you are placing a call for your boss or for yourself, here are some helpful hints for making the process smoother.

Be Sure of the Correct Number. If you are not sure of the telephone number, refer to the telephone directory. If the number is not in the directory, check with directory assistance. After checking with directory assistance, make a note of the number for future calls. It is a good idea to keep a list of frequently called numbers at your desk. Such a list can save you time.

Plan Your Call. Take a few moments to plan your call before you make it. Know the purpose of your call and know what you intend to say. Planning calls saves time and money.

Allow Time to Answer. After you have called a number, give the person you are calling at least ten rings to answer. Perhaps you will be saved another call if you give the caller time to answer.

Place Calls Properly for Your Supervisor. It is suggested that supervisors place their own calls in order to save time and to create favorable impressions. However, you may work for someone who does not wish to place calls. If so, identify your supervisor's name before your transfer the call. For example, you may say, "Mr. Navarate of RJ Computer Corporation is calling," and then transfer the phone call to Mr. Navarate.

If your supervisor disappears or makes another call after you place one for him or her, provide some subtle training for your supervisor. It may be that she or he is unaware that such habits are discourteous and irritating to the person being called, implying that the other person's time is not valuable.

Long-Distance Services. Although the majority of telephone calls are local, you may also be asked to handle long-distance calls. You need to be aware of the long-distance services that are available. In placing long-distance calls, it is important to remember time zone differences. Business calls placed too early in the day from the East Coast to the West Coast are not likely to be completed because people on the West Coast may not be at work yet. Also, a person calling from the Pacific Coast to the East Coast in the early afternoon must take into consideration the closing time of offices in the East.

In addition to our national time zones, there are also international time zones. For example, the person who places a call from New York City to London must remember that when it is 11 a.m. standard time in New York City, it is 4 p.m. in London. When it is 11 a.m. in Los Angeles, it is 9 a.m. in Honolulu.

Direct Distance Dialing (DDD). Direct distance dialing is an arrangement whereby it is possible to dial long-distance numbers in other areas directly on a station-to-station basis. The plan divides the United States and Canada into 122 telephone numbering areas, each identified by a three-digit number called an *area code*. Dialed numbers within your code area do not require the use of the area code. In dialing numbers outside your code area, however, the area code must be dialed before the regular number. Prior to dialing the area code, it is necessary to dial "1," which connects the caller with the DDD network. For example, if a person in Cincinnati wishes to call 555-9959 in Chicago, the person first dials 1, then the area code, 312, and then the telephone number, 555-9959.

Area codes are given in the local telephone directory. If the point you wish to call is not shown, dial "Operator" for the area code. If you do not know the number of the person or business you wish to call, long-distance directory information may be used. The procedure for directory assistance is to dial 1, then the area code for the place you wish to call, and then the number 555-1212. Tell the operator the city or town and the name of the person you are calling.

Person-to-Person Calls. The procedure to follow in placing a person-to-person call varies according to the area of the country. You need to consult your local directory for the procedure in your area. However, in most areas, person-to-person calls may be made by dialing "0" plus the area code and the telephone number. When you have completed dialing, the operator will

come on the line and ask for calling information. You then give the operator the name of the person you are calling.

Station-to-Station Calls. A station-to-station call is made when the person calling is willing to talk to anyone who answers. This type of call is faster and cheaper than a person-to-person call. Charges start when the telephone number called is answered, even if the person making the call is unable to speak to whom the caller wishes to talk.

Collect Calls. A call to a distant point may be made collect or reversed charges. When placing such a call, consult your local directory for the procedure. Usually the procedure is the same as in placing a person-to-person call. Dial "0" plus the area code and then the telephone number. The operator then asks for calling information. Give your name, and state that the call is collect. The person answering the call has to accept the charges before conversation may begin.

Calling Card Calls. Calls can be made from any telephone in the United States or Canada to any other city, state, or country with a calling card. To use a calling card, dial "0" plus the area code and the telephone number. The operator will come on the line and ask for your calling card number or you will hear a special tone at which time you will key in your calling card number. You may obtain a calling card for your personal telephone, and many companies give their executives calling cards. The charges are billed to your home or office telephone number.

Wide Area Telecommunications Service (WATS). WATS is a cost-effective way to make long-distance calls. With such a service your company is charged less per call than the normal rate for a long-distance call. There are two types of WATS service available—intrastate and interstate. Intrastate WATS permits calling within a state. Interstate WATS permits calling within a specified band or bands extending outward from the originating state. Bands are the number of divisions or service areas into which the United States is divided.

800 Service. This service permits an individual to call a business toll free. Companies that use this service are listed in the telephone directory with an 800 number. Then the customer making the call is not charged a long-distance fee for the call. Charges to the company with the 800 listing are based upon the number of subscribed service bands, amount of usage, and time at which the usage occurs. For measuring usage charges, the hours of the day and days of the week are divided into rate periods. Lower rates are in effect for the evenings and weekends.

Foreign Exchange Service (FX). With the Foreign Exchange Service, a company can obtain a local number for a plant or subsidiary of the business in a foreign city and arrange for all calls to that number to be billed as local calls. A leased line (one which the business leases from the telephone company) connects the subscriber's telephone to a central office in the foreign exchange area. Since it is a two-way service, FX permits the business subscriber to call any number in the foreign exchange area and people from the foreign exchange area to call the business without a long-distance charge.

Telephone Equipment and Systems. The changes in electronic technology are contributing to numerous changes in telephone systems and telephone equipment. It is anticipated that changes will continue to occur as new advancements are made in electronics. A partial listing of what is available today is given here.

Single-Line Telephone. Single-line telephones are used in homes and small offices. As the name implies, these telephones have only a single line available. These telephones are operated by push buttons or a rotary dial. They are available in table models, wall models, or models with the dial in the handset.

Key System. In telephone jargon, a key is a push-button telephone. A key system includes a group of push-button desk telephones interconnected to allow a group of people to share several outside lines, plus make intercom calls

to each other. The most common key telephone has six buttons, one of which is the hold button. A key telephone is shown in Illustration 9-8. The switching gear for the system is contained in the cabinet which is called the key service unit; the key service unit is shown in Illustration 9-8 also.

Courtesy of AT&T

Illustration 9-8. Key Service Unit

To place an outside call, the caller pushes an unlighted line button and dials the number. To answer an incoming call, the person pushes the flashing button. If it becomes necessary to answer one line while talking on another, the hold button on the telephone is utilized. Here are the correct procedures for placing a call on hold.

1. Ask the person if she or he is willing to hold (the individual may prefer to call back or to have you call back).
2. If the person is willing to be placed on hold, depress the hold key.
3. Answer the call on the incoming line. If the call becomes longer than 30 or 40 seconds, return to the caller on hold. Ask if the caller wants to continue to hold. Don't ever allow a caller to remain on hold for a long period of time without checking with that person.

Large systems can handle up to 21 lines and 52 stations, with adjunct units available if more lines are needed. Larger systems should have an attendant's station, which can be the only telephone that rings for incoming calls. The attendant then uses the intercom line to notify the appropriate party of an incoming call on a particular line.

PBX (Private Branch Exchange) System. A PBX is the general name for the office switchboard and its descendants. The system allows inside telephones to call each other and share a limited number of outside lines. The system can be purchased, leased, or rented from the local telephone company or from any one of a number of other vendors. Although a few manually operated PBXs remain in use today, most are completely automatic. That is, no operator is needed to operate the system. The automatic PBXs are known as PABXs (private automatic branch exchanges); however, the term PBX is used to mean any type of PBX including one that is completely automatic.

The principal difference between a PBX and a key system is that all of a PBX's switching takes place within a central unit or console. Switching is triggered by dialing code numbers instead of pushing buttons. For example, instead of pushing a line button to make an outgoing call, the caller usually will dial 9. Incoming calls go through an attendant unless Direct Inward Dialing is available. Direct Inward Dial (DID) systems allow telephone numbers within a company to be reached by dialing them directly from the outside. A PBX can support far more telephones than a key system while providing similar features. PBX systems are available that permit the integration of local area networks with the PBX. With the integration of the LAN and the PBX, the office is provided with a network capable of handling both voice and written message communications. Voice mail, electronic mail, and numerous other applications can go through an integrated system. A PBX console is shown in Illustration 9-9.

Centrex System. Centrex, or central exchange, is a type of telephone switching system in which incoming calls are dialed direct. The switching equipment is usually located on the telephone company premises, and each tele-

phone served by the system is directly connected to the telephone company's switching center. This arrangement differs from the usual PBX where the switching equipment is installed on the company's premises.

Courtesy of AT&T

Illustration 9-9. PBX Console

Touch-A-Matic® Telephone. The Touch-A-Matic® telephone has an electronic memory that can be programmed with frequently called numbers. Two different memory capacities are available — one that retains 32 numbers and one that retains 16 numbers. As an added feature, the last number manually dialed is automatically retained in the phone's memory. With this service you need not redial if you get a busy signal or if you need to talk to the same person twice in a row. Just push a button and the number is dialed automatically. Also available is a Touch-A-Matic® adjunct unit with the capacity of 32 programmed numbers. This unit can be used in conjunction with another Touch-A-Matic® telephone to expand the memory capacity of your telephone.

Code-A-Phone®. The Code-A-Phone® allows your company to be a 24-hour operation. When your office is closed, the Code-A-Phone® answers calls with a prerecorded message and accepts messages of any length.

Speakerphone. If you need to consult files, take notes, or walk around the room while on the phone, a speakerphone (with a loud speaker attachment) is available. Such a phone also allows a group of people in one office to participate simultaneously in a call.

Reproduced with permission of AT&T Co.

Ford Industries, Inc.

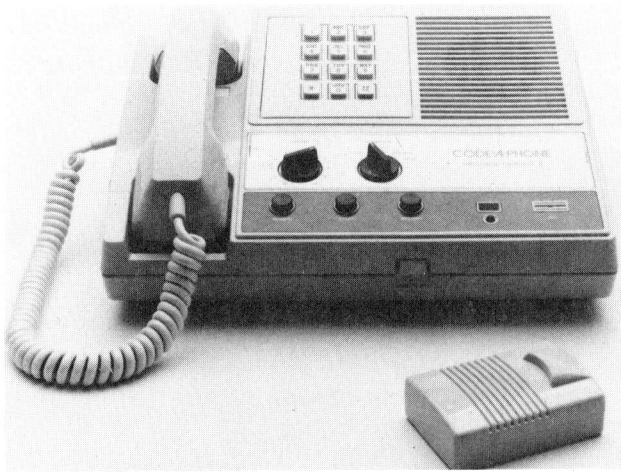

Reproduced with permission of AT&T Co.

Illustration 9-10. Touch-A-Matic® phone, Code-A-Phone®, and a Speakerphone

Portable Paging Device and Portable Conference Phone. Paging devices that can be carried anywhere and clipped to your pocket or belt are available. When someone in the office wants to speak to you, the pager sounds. You then call from the nearest telephone.

Cellular Mobile Telephone. Individuals often need to maintain contact with a central location while moving between different locations. In the past, people used mobile radio telephone systems. However, these systems required powerful transmitters to cover a fairly small distance. For example, one high-powered transmitter could broadcast telephone calls within a 50-mile radius, but only on a limited number of channels. Interference would occur with the adding of new transmitters. Channels soon became overloaded and callers waited long periods for a channel on which to place a call. Phone numbers were also limited; and in some major metropolitan areas, people interested in a mobile telephone had to wait more than a year.

Cellular technology has changed dramatically the mobile telephone industry. With cellular technology, it is possible to have a fully functional telephone in the car, the briefcase, or even a coat pocket. Cellular technology breaks a large service area down into smaller areas called cells. Each cell is served by a low-powered receiver-transmitter. As the mobile caller moves from one cell to another cell, a mobile telephone switching office (MTSO) automatically moves the call from one cell to another cell. The MTSO interfaces with a land based subscriber to complete the mobile calls to fixed locations served by telephone lines. Illustration 9-11 depicts graphically the transactions that occur in cellular technology.

It is anticipated that the use of cellular mobile telephones will grow rapidly in the future for the following reasons: (1) the need to keep in touch with key personnel and clients; (2) the ease of operation; (3) the satisfactory sound quality; and (4) the convenience. As the use of cellular technology becomes widespread, data transmission will be added to the service. It may be possible soon to connect computers through the cellular system. Under development is the capability to access computers and interchange information via data terminals in automobiles.

Franklin H. Blecher. "Advanced Mobile Phone Service." In Land-Mobile Communications Engineering, 1983, p. 297. (© 1980 IEEE)

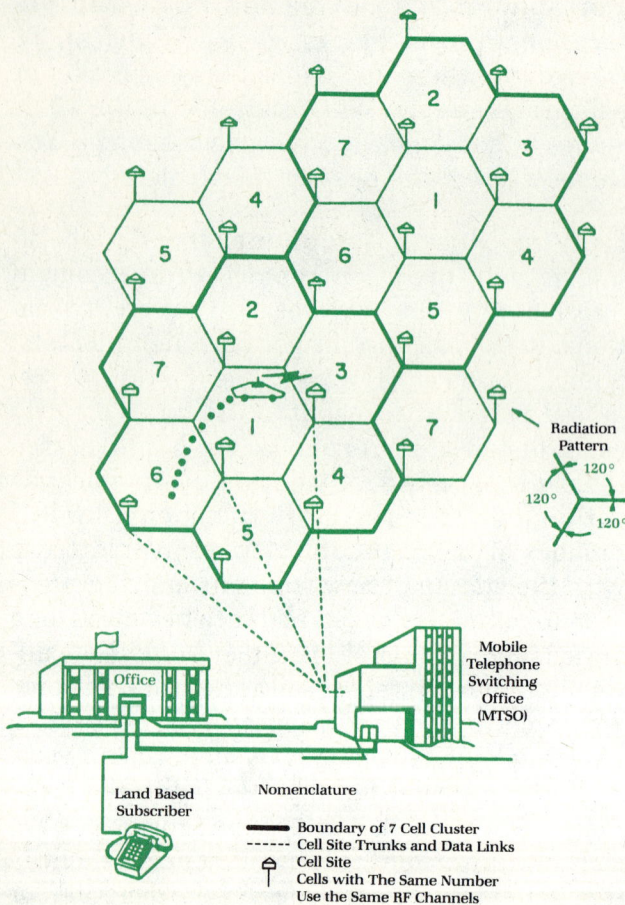

Illustration 9-11. Cellular Technology

Special Equipment for the Handicapped. Various types of equipment and services are available for the handicapped including a volume control telephone, the artificial larynx, a telephone adapter, bells in many frequencies, and so on. If you are handicapped or someone in your company has a physical problem using the telephone, the telephone company has a special consultant who can help. Call your local telephone business office, and they will give you the information that you need.

Special Features of Telephone Systems. Numerous special features are available to telephone users. The following is a description of some of the features you may encounter.

1. *Call forwarding* permits a telephone caller to automatically forward calls to another telephone number.
2. *Call waiting* allows a call to a busy telephone to be held while an audible tone notifies the called party that a call is waiting.
3. *Automatic call back* permits the caller to give instructions to a busy station to call back as soon as the busy station is free.
4. *Speed calling* permits a caller to reach frequently called numbers by using abbreviated telephone codes in place of the conventional telephone number.
5. *Identified ringing* provides distinctive ringing tones for different categories of calls. For example, internal calls may ring one long ring while outside calls ring two short rings close together.
6. *Call holding* allows a user to place a caller on hold while dialing or talking to another person and then return to the caller on hold.
7. *Automatic call stacking* allows calls to arrive at a station that is busy and be automatically answered by a recorded wait message.
8. *Conference calling* allows the caller to talk with several people in different places at the same time by dialing the operator and saying that he or she wishes to make a conference call. It is generally a good idea to arrange for the conference call in advance.
9. *Lockout* is a station control feature that ensures the confidentiality of a call. The lockout feature assures that no one can break into the call while it is in progress.

Cordless Telephone. In the early 1980s the cordless telephone was introduced. These telephones allow a person to communicate over short distances without interconnecting wires. Cordless telephones have a base station and a handset. The base station is a unit with electronic circuits which communicates with the handset. The base station plugs into both the phone jack and an electrical outlet. The handset functions as a portable telephone with a receiver and a transmitter; rechargeable batteries provide power for the handset. The handset may be carried to distances of up to 900 feet and used as a telephone. Each cordless phone uses one of several radio frequencies (electromagnetic waves that change in different time periods) assigned by the FCC (Federal Communications Commission). Many cordless telephones have added features such as phone number memory storage and a function that allows the telephone to act like an intercom.

Voice Mail. Although voice mail or voice messaging, as it is sometimes called, has been around since the mid 1970s, the first systems were costly, large, and possessed limited capability. Today, although voice mail systems are still in their infancy, the systems are more reliable, flexible, easier to use, less costly, and operate through a PBX system. The future is expected to bring an increase in the use of voice mail and a greater integration of voice mail with other electronic systems.

A voice mail system operates essentially as a mailbox for voice messages. A user dials an access number plus a code number unique to the user through the use of keys on a push-button telephone. Once access is granted, the user has two choices — to send messages or receive them. If the user chooses to send a message and the recipient's line is busy, the system will store the message and forward it at a later time. If the user is receiving a message, the time that the message is received can be determined by the recipient. By using a push-button telephone, the recipient can key a special code for access to stored messages. Some systems have message scanning capability enabling the user to determine who called and when they called without listening to the details of each message.

Networking is also becoming a feature of the most up-to-date voice mail systems. Through networking voice messages and text can be transmitted. By entering simple commands at a terminal, a user can review not only incoming voice messages but stored text messages (written) also. The terminal displays the caller's name, length of message, and the time and date it was sent. The user's phone rings and delivers all voice messages that have been received.

Some of the advantages of voice mail are

1. Speeding communications by getting messages through, particularly where there are time-zone differentials. For example, if a user wants to send a message from California at 4 p.m. to another user in New York, the New York office will probably be closed since it is 7 p.m. in New York. The user in California can send the message anyway and have the New York user get it at the beginning of the following workday before the California user has reported to work.

2. Making office workers more productive by eliminating repeated telephone calls where the individual called is not available.
3. Relieving highly qualified secretaries from the tedious, time-consuming task of taking messages.
4. Cutting down on extraneous conversations.
5. Cutting down on internal memorandums.

WRITTEN MESSAGE COMMUNICATION SYSTEMS

In this chapter, information communicated has been divided into three major areas — voice, written, and images. You have just learned about voice communication. The written message today can also be transmitted electronically. Messages can be sent electronically over any transmission media, including twisted-pair wire cables, fiber optic cables, coaxial cables, microwave links, and satellite stations. Messages are transmitted and received in the form of electronic signals that are translated into readable messages by the receiving device, which may be a word processor, a computer, a facsimile device, or any number of other types of equipment. The major systems used in transmitting electronic mail will be discussed in this section. These systems include teletypewriter systems, carrier-based message systems, facsimile devices, communicating word processors, and private computer-based message systems.

Teletypewriters. Teletypewriters are electronically controlled typewriters that send messages over communication lines. Businesses may own their own teletypewriters and transmit messages over public or private telephone lines, or they may use Telex and TWX machines which are owned by Western Union. See Illustration 9-12.

Telex was introduced in 1958 by Western Union, while TWX was first introduced by the Bell System and later purchased by Western Union. Both systems transmit information from one location to another through teletypewriters. These machines comprise a two-way communication network capable of sending and receiving messages around the world in a fast, economical manner. The information is transmitted over telephone lines to the nearest microwave terminal. From that point, the signal is transmitted through the airwaves by a microwave signal to the microwave terminal nearest its destination, where the signal is put back on telephone lines and sent on the Telex/TWX equipment at the receiving point. Teletypewriters can accept messages even when unattended. They turn on automatically when called and answer back automatically with an identification that is different for each subscriber to the service and each location. Telex/TWX messages are less expensive than either a telephone call or a Mailgram®.

Western Union Corporation

Illustration 9-12. Teletypewriter

Carrier-Based Message Systems. Three carrier-based message systems will be discussed here — telegrams, mailgrams, and Easylink. These systems may be fully electronic from the time they are sent to the time they are received or may be supplemented by U.S. Postal Service or messenger delivery.

Telegrams. There are two classes of Western Union telegrams, namely, the regular telegram and the overnight telegram. The regular telegram can be sent any time of the day or night. Western Union guarantees delivery of telegrams to major U.S. cities within 5 hours by messenger or 2½ hours by telephone. The minimum charge is based on 15 words, excluding the

address and signature; an additional charge is made for each additional word.

An overnight telegram can be sent at any time up to midnight for delivery the next morning. The overnight telegram is less expensive than the regular telegram. The minimum charge is based on a 100-word message; an additional charge is made for each word over 100.

In some situations, an overnight telegram is as quick as the regular telegram. For example, assume you work for a company in California. At 4 p.m. PST your supervisor asks you to send a telegram to a New York office. Because of the time difference, the New York office is closed. An overnight telegram and a regular telegram will both be delivered when the New York office opens the next morning. Thus, you would save your company money by sending an overnight telegram.

Mailgrams. The Mailgram® combines Western Union and post office services. Mailgrams® are sent over Western Union communication networks to the post office near the addressee. This service provides a fast and economical way to reach anyone in the continental United States. After the Mailgram® is routed through Western Union to the post office, the message is typed at the post office by high-speed equipment. Then it is inserted into an envelope for delivery the next business day by regular postal carriers. Mailgrams® may be called into Western Union any time during the day or evening. If the message is called in before the end of the business day, it will be delivered the next business day by postal carriers. A Mailgram® costs less than a regular telegram and usually less than a long-distance telephone call.

The Cost of Preparing and Transmitting Telegrams and Mailgrams. Telegrams and Mailgrams® may be typed and delivered to the Western Union office, phoned in, or sent by Telex/TWX. If you are sending a telegram, compose a message that is clear and brief. Avoid unnecessary words and adjectives since you are charged by the number of words. Avoid using abbreviations and contractions that may confuse the reader. If you send a Mailgram®, your communication can be longer since the charge is based on a minimum of 100 words rather than the 15-word minimum of a telegram.

If you telephone the message to Western Union, be certain you have all the necessary information. It is important that you have the correct spelling of names, the correct addresses, and accurate dollar amounts. If your office subscribes to Telex/TWX, the message can be sent through teletypewriters in your office.

Easylink. Easylink is an electronic mail service provided by Western Union. Easylink subscribers can send messages to Telex subscribers and receive Telex messages in their Easylink mailboxes. In addition, Easylink provides overnight and same-day delivery of letter-quality documents through couriers within two hours after receipt of the document at Western Union.

Facsimile Machines.

As you learned in Chapter 6, a facsimile machine, abbreviated FAX, transmits a copy of a document to a location in the same building or to a distant location. There are two basic types of facsimile systems — analog and digital. The oldest of these two types of systems is the analog system; this system is also the slowest, with a typical low-speed system taking from two to six minutes to transmit each page. An analog facsimile device scans an entire document, including blank spaces. Information is scanned line-by-line at a constant speed and transformed into a continuous wave form similar to that of a sound wave. Digital devices are much faster, taking an average of 20 seconds to transmit a page. With a digital system, messages are converted into binary electronic signals as in computers. These systems use special communication networks rather than ordinary telephone lines which are used in analog systems.

The use of the facsimile process should grow in the future, and it has even been projected that by the 1990s facsimile may replace regular mail delivery for most businesses. Prices of facsimile machines have declined in the last few years, and it is anticipated that prices will continue to decline. One of the most significant predictions for the future of facsimile machines is that they will interface with microcomputers and word processors. The facsimile machine could both send information to and receive information from a microcomputer or word processor.

Computer-Based Message Systems.

Computer-based message systems (CBMS) evolved from the capabilities offered by computer-services companies through their time-sharing networks. Computer-services companies had many users accessing the same computer through terminals over their communications networks. These users needed to communicate to facilitate project coordination and control. Computer-based message systems operate on a mailbox principle. The message is delivered via a computer to a terminal. Then, the user must check the mailbox, which is some preassigned location in the computer's memory, in order to receive the message. Each user is assigned an electronic mailbox, and messages are left there until the user makes an inquiry.

One advantage of computer-based message systems is that messages are placed independently. You don't have to know where recipients are to send messages to them. Users can access the electronic mailbox from any terminal located almost anywhere in the world. Many traveling executives carry portable terminals to access their computer-based message systems, and some hotels and motels have terminals available.

Communicating Word Processors.

In Chapter 5 you learned about word processors. Word processors, with the proper hookups, are capable of becoming electronic mail terminals by communicating with each other. Mail can be sent electronically from a word processor at one location to a word processor at a distant location. The communication is received on the recipient's CRT.

Computer Conferencing.

Computer conferencing is person-to-group communication via a computer. Any member of a group can send a message electronically, and it can be read and responded to by others in the group much as if they were assembled around a conference table. However, unlike meetings where everyone is physically present, the group members do not have to assemble at the same time. Instead, a computer stores and forwards the messages to each member when the person turns on the computer and requests the information.

Some of the advantages of computer conferencing include the following:

1. Each person can participate from a different time and place. A message might be read by a conference member in California while the sender is asleep in New York. Computer conferencing relaxes the tight scheduling required for face-to-face meetings or even conference phone calls.
2. There is an automatic written record of all communication. You can record a phone conference or a meeting and transcribe it but to do so takes time and work. In many computer conferencing systems, the host computer can maintain a file of all messages which members can search, save on disk, and print as needed.

There are also some disadvantages to computer conferencing, some of which are as follows:

1. The process takes time to learn. Just as any function on a computer takes time to learn, so does computer conferencing. There are new commands to learn, and different computer conferencing systems have different commands.
2. Good writing skills are essential. Computer conferencing rewards people who write well. Conversely, people who do not express themselves well in writing are at a disadvantage with computer conferencing.

IMAGE SYSTEMS

Image systems communicate exact images such as pictures, blueprints, and graphic displays across distances. Although the type of information transmitted over telecommunication networks has been categorized into voice, written messages, and images in this chapter, that categorization is not an absolute one. Some overlapping exists. For example, there are some written messages which also contain images

(pictures, graphs, and so forth). Some equipment that has already been discussed such as facsimile machines and screens on computers or word processors also transmit images. This section is confined to the transmission of images through videoconferencing and audio-plus-graphics conferencing.

Videoconferencing. Videoconferencing is a system of transmitting audio (sound) and video (pictures) between executives at distant locations thereby eliminating the need for travel. There are two types of videoconferencing—live or continuous motion and freeze frame. With continuous motion, the picture changes 33 times a second to create the impression of a continuously moving picture. With a freeze frame or slow scan, the picture changes only once every few seconds to create a slide show effect. Freeze frame is more economical because it uses conventional telephone lines, while live transmission requires the use of microwave channels.

Videoconferencing may occur with minimal equipment (a screen and a camera at each location) or with numerous pieces of equipment. For example, there might be color TV cameras to transmit pictures of people and graphics, monitors to pick up people images and graphic images, microphones and speakers for audio interaction, and facsimile units for hard-copy transmission of documents. A videoconference is shown in Illustration 9-13.

Photo Courtesy of Satellite Business Systems

Illustration 9-13. Videoconferencing

Audio-Plus-Graphics Conferencing.

Audio conferencing uses voice transmission units to connect two or more conversations. Audio-plus-graphics conferencing involves the transmission of a variety of graphics during an audio conference. The transmission of these graphic materials may be accomplished through the use of facsimile equipment or an electronic blackboard. An *electronic blackboard* is used like any other blackboard; chalk strokes are made on the blackboard and converted to digital signals for transmission over telephone lines. The material placed on an electronic blackboard at the sending location is transmitted to a standard television monitor at the receiving location. The graphics transmitted to the receiving location are displayed on the monitor through the use of one telephone line, while the audio is carried simultaneously on a second telephone line. When copies of the information presented on the blackboard are required, a copier may be connected to the television monitor to provide hard copy. An electronic blackboard is shown in Illustration 9-14.

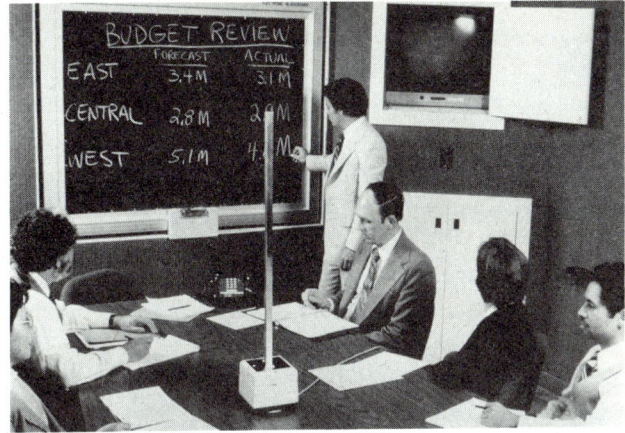

Reproduced with permission of AT&T Co.

Illustration 9-14. Electronic Blackboard

FOR YOUR REVIEW

The following review will help you remember the important points of this chapter.

1. Telecommunications is the process of transmitting information over a distance by electronic impulses.

2. The transmission media used in sending communication from one location to another are twisted-pair wire cables, coaxial cables, fiber optic cables, microwaves, and satellites.

3. Twisted-pair wires have been insulated and twisted into pairs. Twisting minimizes the interference between wires that are packed or bundled into a cable.

4. A coaxial cable consists of a single conductor (usually a small copper wire) surrounded by a plastic insulator and a braided wire sleeve.

5. The fiber optic cable uses a fiber rod that is a nonconductor of electricity made of glass or plastic that conducts or passes light waves. The light signals pass through the rod approximately one and one-half times faster than electronic impulses pass through copper wires.

6. Microwave transmission is land-based transmission in which an electronic signal is transmitted from the sending location through the air to a microwave tower which receives the signal and transmits it to the next microwave tower.

7. Satellite transmission is space-based microwave transmission. An electronic signal is transmitted from the sending location through space to a satellite that orbits some 22,300 miles above our heads. The satellite receives the signal and transmits it to a receiving station on Earth. The satellite functions as a microwave tower in space.

8. Telephones, computers, word processors, and various other pieces of electronic equipment may be linked by networks to transmit voice, data, and images.

9. The term local area network (LAN) describes a configuration of telecommunication facilities designed to provide internal communications within a limited geographical area.

10. Expanded network describes a configuration of communication facilities designed to provide communications over a long distance.

11. A good telephone personality must be developed by an office worker because he/she spends so much time on the phone. On the telephone you need to be natural, considerate, attentive, and discreet.

12. Some important telephone techniques for you to remember are to answer promptly, identify yourself, take messages courteously, transfer calls carefully, ask questions tactfully, leave word when you are away from your telephone, speak distinctly, use words to identify letters, enunciate numerals clearly, and close the conversation politely.

13. Wide Area Telecommunications service (WATS) is a cost-effective way to make long-distance calls for businesses.

14. The 800 Service for businesses permits a business to list an 800 number in the directory, and the customer calling the business is not charged a long-distance fee. The business is charged for the service based on the usage and certain other factors.

15. With Foreign Exchange Service (FX) a company can obtain a local number for a plant or subsidiary of the company in a foreign city and arrange for all calls to that number to be billed as local calls.

16. Single-line telephones and key telephone systems are used in small- to medium-sized businesses where there is no need for a large number of telephones.

17. A PBX is a switching system installed for the exclusive use of one company and is usually located on the premises of the company.

18. Centrex, or central exchange, is a type of telephone switching system in which incoming calls are dialed direct.

19. Mobile telephones now use cellular technology. This technology breaks a large service area down into smaller areas called cells. Each cell is served by a low-powered receiver-transmitter. As the mobile caller moves from one cell to another cell, a mobile telephone switching office (MTSO) automatically moves the call from one cell to another cell.

20. The cordless telephone allows you to communicate via the telephone over distances of up to approximately 900 feet without interconnecting wires.

21. Telephones are equipped with numerous special features some of which are call forwarding, call waiting, automatic call back, speed calling, call holding, automatic call stacking, identified ringing, and conference calling.

22. A voice mail system operates as a mailbox for voice messages. A user dials an access number plus a code number unique to the user through the use of keys on a push-button telephone. Once access is granted, the user can send or receive messages.

23. Teletypewriters are electronically controlled typewriters that send messages over communication lines. Telex and TWX are teletypewriter systems operated by Western Union.

24. Carrier-based message systems use electronic means of transmission plus U.S. Postal Service and messenger delivery. Some examples of carrier-based message systems are telegrams, mailgrams, and Easylink.

25. A facsimile machine (FAX) transmits a copy of a document to a location in the same building or to a distant location. Facsimile machines transmit both written messages and images.

26. Computer-based message systems operate on a mailbox principle. The message is delivered via a computer to a terminal. Then, the user must check the mailbox in the computer's memory in order to receive the message.

27. Word processors, with the proper hookups, can become electronic mail terminals by communicating with each other.

28. Computer conferencing is person-to-group communication via computer. Any member of a group can send a message electronically, and it can be read and responded to by others in the group much as if they were assembled around a conference table.

29. Videoconferencing is a system of transmitting audio and video between executives at distant locations thereby eliminating the need for travel. There are two types of videoconferencing—live or continuous motion and freeze frame.

30. Audio conferencing uses voice transmission units to connect two or more conversations. Audio-plus-graphics conferencing involves the transmission of a variety of graphics during an audio conference.

Antonio Previno started to work for RJ Computer Corporation a week ago as an office worker. His job includes answering the telephone for the five managers in the area. You were asked by Antonio's supervisor to help Antonio learn the company procedures. You explained to Antonio that the telephone should be answered, "Marketing Division, Antonio Previno." Since then, he has answered the telephone technically correct (he says the appropriate words). However, you have noticed several problems with his telephone techniques including the following:

1. When Antonio is extremely busy, he tends to answer the telephone in a rushed, curt manner.
2. You cover Antonio's telephone when he leaves his desk, yet he never tells you where he is going or when he is coming back. He also gives you no information about the managers in the area.

3. You overheard a manager complain because Antonio failed to write the correct telephone number on a telephone message.
4. Antonio does not seem to give callers adequate information. If someone is out of the office, he merely says: "Mr. Bendix is out of the office now."
5. Recently Antonio transferred a call to you; however, he did not tell the caller why she was being transferred. The caller was angry when you answered the telephone.

You think Antonio needs help in understanding proper telephone techniques, but you were only told to help him with company procedures. You think something should be done. Should you talk with your supervisor, with Antonio's supervisor, or with Antonio? Or should you say nothing? Should you suggest a company workshop on telephone techniques? How should the situation be handled?

FOR YOUR UNDERSTANDING

1. Define telecommunications; list and explain four transmission media used.
2. Explain LAN and how it is used.
3. Why is telephone personality important? Give five suggestions for being effective on the telephone.
4. Define and explain FX.
5. Explain cellular technology.
6. How does a cordless telephone operate?
7. List five special features on telephones.
8. How does a voice mail system operate?
9. Define computer conferencing and give two of its advantages.
10. What is an electronic blackboard, and how is it used?

OFFICE APPLICATIONS

On pages 335–339 are office applications that correlate with this chapter.

PART 4

MANAGING INFORMATION

CHAPTER 10

Office Mail

Handling incoming and outgoing mail is tremendously important because the manner in which mail is handled can make or lose money for a company. For example, assume that you allow an order letter to remain on your desk for several days. The customer who is ordering the materials may become upset due to your lack of response and may therefore cancel the order. Such actions, or lack of actions, on your part may result in the loss of a customer for your company, which could ultimately cost thousands of dollars in immediate and prospective sales.

As an office worker, your mail duties usually include getting the incoming mail ready for your employer to review and preparing the outgoing correspondence. These duties require a knowledge of mail classifications as well as mail and shipping services. You also need to apply time-saving steps in preparing the mail for your employer.

GENERAL OBJECTIVES

Your general objectives for this chapter are to

1. Efficiently handle incoming and outgoing mail.
2. Identify classes of mail and determine which class should be used when preparing outgoing mail.
3. Become familiar with special mail services.
4. Define common shipping terms.
5. Identify various shipping services.

INCOMING MAIL

In a large office, the mail probably comes into a central mail room where it is sorted according to the company's departments. A mail room employee then delivers the mail to the individual offices, or the mail is delivered by an electronic cart.

An electronic cart uses a photo-electric guidance system to follow invisible chemical paths painted on carpeting, floor tile, or other surfaces. The cart has separate mail trays for each of the workstations or offices at which the cart automatically stops. The sender of a document places it in the appropriate tray for subsequent pickup by the person to whom it is addressed. That person then removes the document from the cart, and the vehicle continues on its way. With electronic carts, there is no need for employees to leave their desks in order to deliver documents within the same building or to send mail outside the building. An electronic cart is shown in Illustration 10-1.

149

In a small office, the post office may deliver the mail directly to you. Therefore, you may take all outgoing mail directly to the post office.

Courtesy of Bell & Howell Company

Illustration 10-1. Electronic Mail Cart

Sorting Mail. Once you receive the mail in your office or department, you must do a preliminary mail sort. If there are several individuals within the department, sort the mail according to the person addressed. Then place the mail for each individual into separate stacks. When this preliminary sort is completed, sort each person's mail in the following order:

1. *Personal and confidential mail.* Mail that is marked with a personal or confidential notation on the outside of the envelope should not be opened by the office employee. Place this mail to one side so that you do not inadvertently open it.
2. *Mailgrams, special delivery, registered, or certified mail.* This mail is important and should be placed so that the individual to whom it is addressed will see it first.
3. *Regular business mail.* Mail from customers, clients, and suppliers is also considered

important and should be handled promptly.
4. *Interoffice communications.* This mail is generally received in an interoffice envelope that is distinctive in its design and color.
5. *Advertisements and circulars.* This mail is relatively unimportant and can be handled after the other correspondence is answered.
6. *Magazines and catalogs.* These materials should be placed at the bottom of the correspondence stack since they may be read at the executive's convenience.

Opening Mail. Mail may be opened in the mail room or it may be opened in the individual office. If the mail is opened in the mail room, an automatic mail opener such as the one shown in Illustration 10-2 is usually used. Mail opening systems today are extremely efficient, with some systems having the capability of opening as many as 30,000 envelopes an hour. Mail opened in an individual office is usually opened by hand, using an envelope opener. When opening mail, follow these procedures.

1. Have the supplies that you need readily available. These supplies include an envelope opener, a date and time stamp, routing and action slips, a stapler, paper clips, and a pen or pencil.
2. Before opening an envelope, tap the lower edge of the envelope on the desk so that the contents will fall to the bottom and will not be cut when the envelope is opened.
3. Place the envelopes face down with all flaps in the same direction.
4. Open the letters by running them through a mail-opening machine or by using a hand envelope opener.
5. Empty each envelope. Check carefully to see that everything has been removed.
6. Fasten any enclosures to the letter. Attach any small enclosures to the front of the letter. Enclosures larger than the letter should be attached to the back.
7. Mend any torn material with tape.
8. If a personal or confidential letter is opened by mistake, do not remove it from the envelope; mark the front with "Opened by Mistake," add your initials, and reseal the envelope with tape.

9. Stack the envelopes on the desk in the same order as the opened mail in case it is necessary to refer to the envelopes. It is good practice to save all envelopes for at least one day in case they should be needed for reference; then the envelopes may be thrown away.

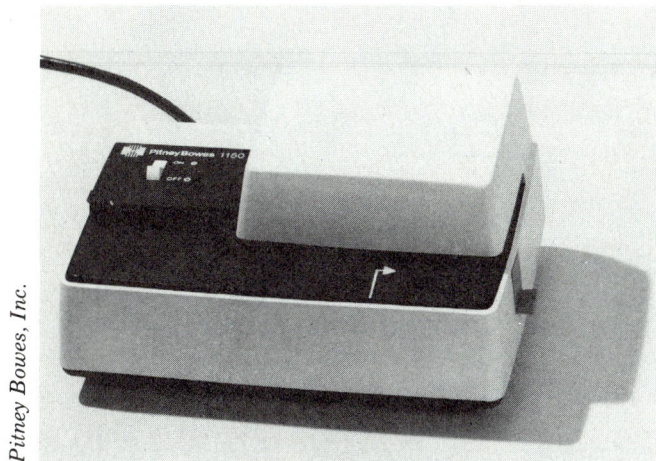

Illustration 10-2. Automatic Mail Opener

Keeping Selected Envelopes. Certain envelopes should *always* be retained. Keep the envelope when the following situations exist:

1. An incorrectly addressed envelope. Your supervisor may want to call attention to this fact when answering the correspondence.
2. A letter with no return address. The envelope will usually have the return address.
3. A letter written on letterhead with a different return address than that written on the envelope. For example, a person may write a letter on a hotel's letterhead and write the business address on the envelope.
4. A letter without a signature. The envelope may contain the writer's name.
5. An envelope that has a postmark which differs significantly from the date on the letter. The letter date may be compared with the postmark date to determine the delay in receiving the letter.
6. A letter specifying an enclosure that is not enclosed. Write "No Enclosure" on the letter and attach the envelope.
7. A letter containing a bid, an offer, or an acceptance of a contract. The postmark date may be needed as legal evidence.

Date and Time Stamping, Reading, Underlining, and Annotating. All correspondence should be date and time stamped. Most companies provide you with some type of date and time stamp. It may be a manual one on which you change the date each morning and rotate the clock face to the appropriate time. Or it may be an automatic date and time stamper.

There are several reasons why it is important to date and time stamp mail. The main reason is that it furnishes a record of when the correspondence was received. For example, a letter may arrive too late to handle the matter mentioned in the letter. Therefore, the stamped date of receipt is recorded confirmation of the day the letter was received and of the resultant inability to take care of the matter. Or the correspondence may be undated. The time stamped on the letter therefore shows *approximately* when the correspondence was written.

After you date and time stamp the correspondence, you should read each piece of material to note the important information. Then reread the correspondence and underline the important words and phrases with a colored pen or pencil. This process enables executives to scan letters for important parts and thus saves them time. However, you must be thrifty in underlining. Underlining too much of the correspondence defeats its purpose — which is to save the executive time in the reading process.

Annotations or explanatory notes assist the executive in answering correspondence. For example, if a check should have been enclosed with a letter and was not, the words "Check Missing" should be annotated in the letter margin. If a bill is received, check the computations; if the computations are wrong, note that on the bill. If a check is enclosed with a letter, examine the check to see that it is made out for the right amount. Annotate any deviations. The purpose of annotating is the same as underlining; it is meant to save the executive time. Whatever you, as an office worker, can do to assist in this important task will be appreciated.

Providing Background Information for the Executive. Many times a piece of correspondence cannot be answered without referring to previous materials. As you read the correspondence, note whether additional materials are needed. If so, pull that information from the file and attach it to the correspondence. On the front of the correspondence, annotate, "See attached letter dated July 18." Again, such a procedure saves time for the executive; and, it is much better to get this information before you are asked to get it. This will enhance your efficiency in the eyes of the executive.

Presenting Mail. After you have completed the preliminary mail sort, and have opened, date and time stamped, underlined, and annotated, you are ready to do a final sort and to place the mail on the executive's desk. It is good practice to place the mail in various folders. Such a practice preserves confidentiality, as other persons walking by the office will not be able to read the mail in the folders. Furthermore, placing the mail in various folders helps the executive know at a glance what mail needs to be handled first. The final sort is one that you will probably want to work out with your employer to be sure that you are doing it in a matter that meets his or her needs. However, here is one suggestion for final sorting. Separate the mail into the following three groups:

1. *Immediate action mail.* This folder includes unopened, personal or confidential letters; Mailgrams, special delivery, registered, or certified mail; and top priority first-class mail.
2. *Regular mail.* This folder includes routine correspondence and interoffice correspondence.
3. *Read-for-information mail.* This folder includes advertisements, circulars, magazines, and catalogs. It is the lowest priority of mail and can be processed at the executive's convenience.

Routing Mail For mail or other matter that should be referred to other departments or to specific individuals, a *referral slip* or a *routing slip* similar to Illustrations 10-3 and 10-4 should be used.

Usually the person who refers or routes materials signs only her or his initials. The blank on the routing slip may be filled in with "letter," "article," "report," etc. If a copying machine is available, copies of letters, memorandums, and similar materials may be made and each person concerned sent a copy rather than circulate a single copy.

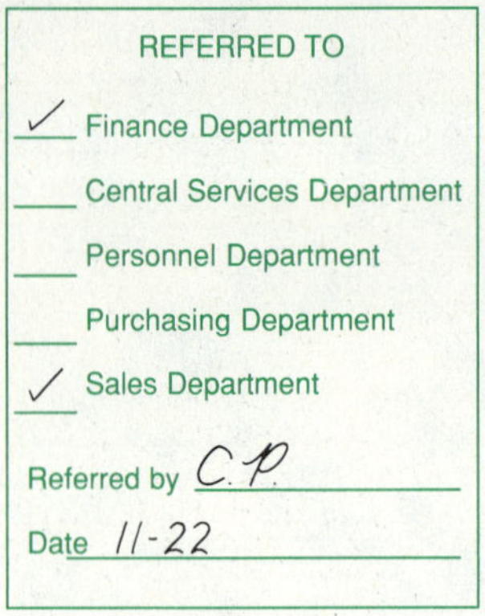
REFERRED TO

✓ Finance Department
___ Central Services Department
___ Personnel Department
___ Purchasing Department
✓ Sales Department

Referred by C.P.
Date 11-22

Illustration 10-3. Referral Slip

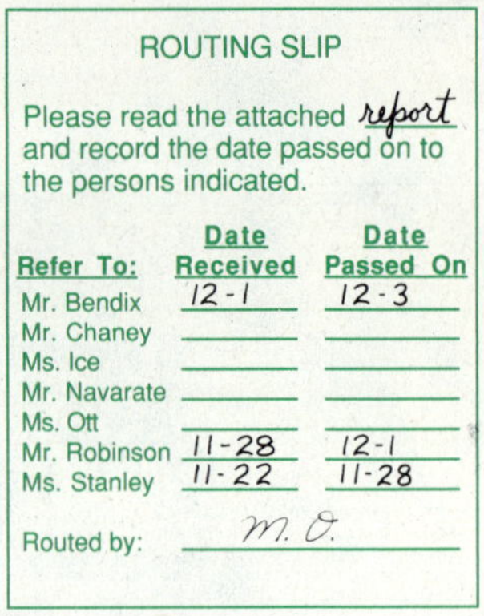
ROUTING SLIP

Please read the attached report and record the date passed on to the persons indicated.

Refer To:	Date Received	Date Passed On
Mr. Bendix	12-1	12-3
Mr. Chaney		
Ms. Ice		
Mr. Navarate		
Ms. Ott		
Mr. Robinson	11-28	12-1
Ms. Stanley	11-22	11-28

Routed by: M.O.

Illustration 10-4. Routing Slip

Keeping a Mail Register. If you receive a large amount of mail or have trouble keeping track of the disposition of mail, you may find it worthwhile to keep a mail register such as the one illustrated in Illustration 10-5. Notice that you record the date and time the mail is received, from whom the mail is sent, the date marked on the correspondence, to whom or to which department the mail is addressed, a description of the type of mail, to whom and when it is referred (i.e., to what department or to which individuals in the ocmpany it is referred), and where it is filed. The column labeled "Separate Mail Received" is used to record the date of receipt of the items that are sent in separate envelopes or packages. Although keeping such a register will require a few minutes of your time each day, it is well worth the time if you have trouble keeping up with the mail.

OUTGOING MAIL

Procedures for handling outgoing mail vary with the size of the business. In large companies, personnel in the mail department handle

MAIL REGISTER

Name *Antonio Previno*

Dates this page *11/10*

| RECEIVED | | FROM | DATED | ADDRESSED TO | | DESCRIPTION | SEP MAIL | REFERRED | | WHERE | FOLLOW |
Date	Time	Name/Address		Dept.	Person	Kind of mail/enc/sep cov	RECEIVED	To	Date	FILED	UP
11/10	9:15 a.m.	F. Gapinsky New York City	11/7		J. Ice	Registered Letter	—	J.I.	11/10		
11/10	9:15 a.m.	Steel Equipment Chicago	11/7	Pur		Expected catalogs file cabinets	11/14	Pur	11/10	Pur	
11/10	9:15 a.m.	G.H. Sims Dallas	11/7		J. Navarate	ACA Banquet tickets					11/16
11/10	9:15 a.m.	L. Cox San Antonio	11/7		M. Ott	Insured package letterheads/forms	—	M.O.	11/10		
11/11	9:30 a.m.	D. Schmidt Peoria			J. Bendix	Confidential - letter	—	J.B.	11/11		
11/11	9:30 a.m.	I.R.S. - local	11/9		J. Bendix	Quarterly taxes - forms enclosed	—	J.B.	11/11		12/2
11/11	9:30 a.m.	Jones, Inc. local	11/9	Sales		Registered letter ordering computer supplies	—	Sales	11/11		
11/11	9:30 a.m.	R. Fugazzi Houston	11/8		P. Jurow	Insured package	—	P.J.	11/11		

Illustration 10-5. Mail Register

most of the work of sending out the mail. However, in a small company, the individual may be totally responsible for getting correspondence ready for mailing.

Preparing Correspondence for Mailing.
Whether you are working in a large or small company, you should follow these procedures before mailing correspondence.

1. Address the envelopes carefully. Check to see that the envelope address and the letter address are identical.
2. Check each letter or memorandum to see that it is signed.
3. See that any special mailing notations are keyed both on the letter and on the envelope.
4. Make sure that all enclosures are included. When an enclosure is smaller than the letter, staple it to the upper left corner of the letter.
5. If enclosures which are too large to be sent

with the letter are sent in a separate large envelope, be sure that the address on the large envelope is also correct. Mark the large envelope with the appropriate class of mail. For example, if the enclosures are to go first class, indicate that on the envelope.
6. Place all interoffice correspondence in appropriate envelopes with the name and department of the addressee listed on the envelope.

If a mail room employee applies postage and seals your mail, neatly stack your correspondence for the employee who picks it up.

Processing Mail. Most large companies have postage meters for processing outgoing mail. Postage meters are electronic, high-volume mailing machines that are capable of processing thousands of envelopes an hour. The envelopes are fed into the machine, and are stacked, sealed, meter-stamped, and counted in one continuous operation. These electronic postage meters also have the capacity to handle special rates, such as registered, certified, return receipt requested, special delivery, and international mail. An electronic postage meter is shown in Illustration 10-6.

up to 70 pounds for mailing. These systems compute and display the correct parcel weight and shipping rate and can be linked to computers to provide accounting departments with shipping charges needed for a customer's invoice. Illustration 10-7 presents an electronic mailing system.

Sealing and Stamping. In a small office, you may be responsible for sealing and stamping your own mail. To seal a number of envelopes quickly, place them in a row on the desk with the flaps facing up. Run a moist sponge across the flaps and press down the flap for each envelope. You can also save time by purchasing stamps in rolls. Place the envelopes to be stamped face up on the desk. Before detaching the stamp from the roll, pass the stamp over a moist sponge, place it on an envelope, and then detach the stamp from the roll. Illustration 10-8 shows a moistener.

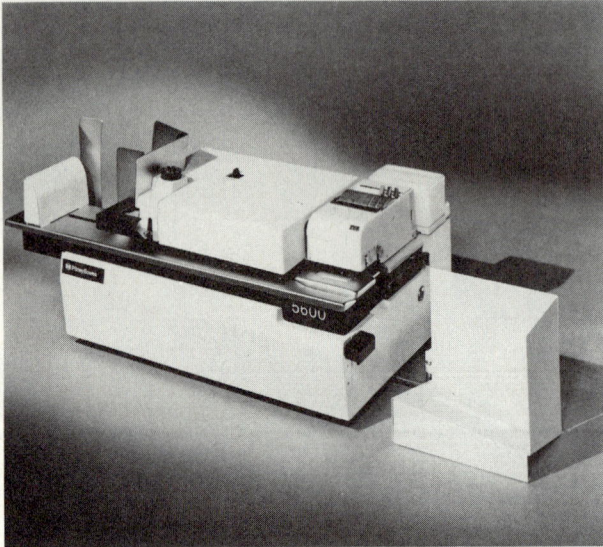

Pitney Bowes, Inc.

Illustration 10-6. Electronic Postage Meter

Electronic parcel processing systems are also available that prepare items which weigh

Using Postal Publications. The *Postal Bulletin* has complete and official postal information. Current information is published weekly in supplement form. Other publications which may assist you with the mailing process

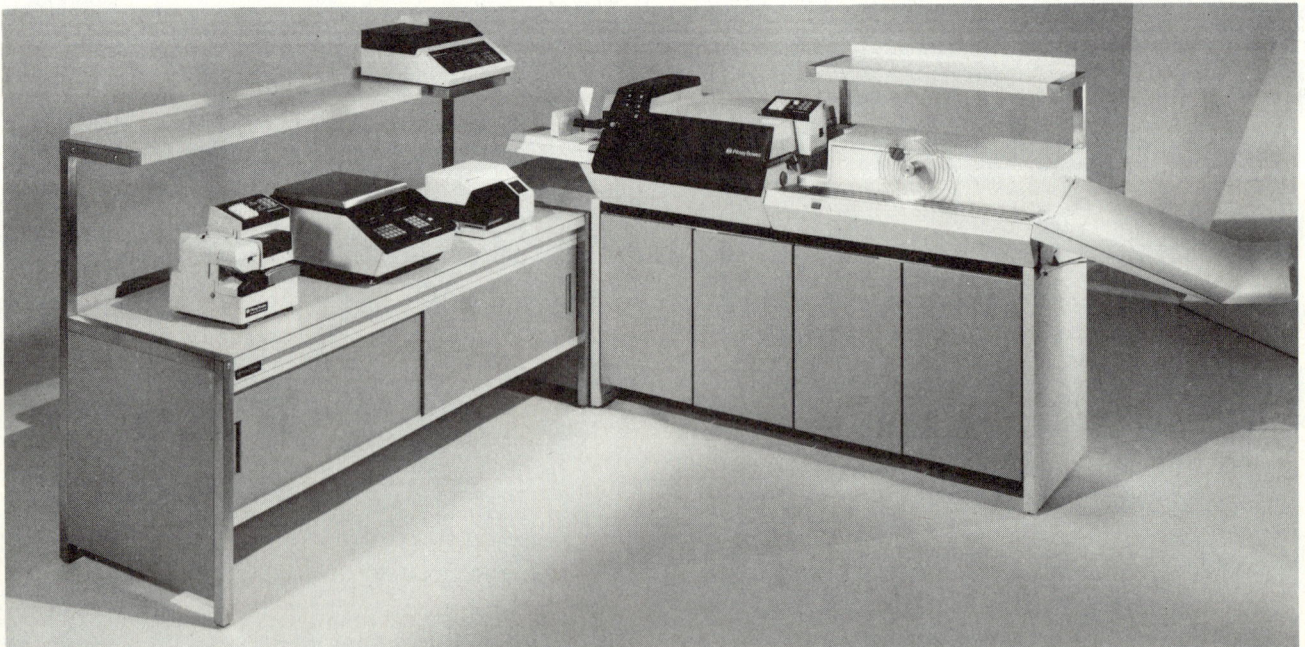

Pitney Bowes, Inc.

Illustration 10-7. Electronic Mailing System

are the *Domestic Mail Manual,* the *International Mail Manual,* and the *National ZIP Code and Post Office Directory.* These publications are available for a fee from the Superintendent of Documents, U.S. Government Printing Office, Washington, D.C. 20402.

Your local post office has brochures on such items as wrapping parcels for mailing, addressing mail, abbreviations for use with the ZIP Code, and your local ZIP Code directory. If you need help in some area of mailing procedures, you should call the customer service number listed under United States Government, U.S. Postal Service, in your telephone directory.

Illustration 10-8. Moistener

Reducing Mailing Costs. Keep an up-to-date mailing list. An up-to-date mailing list eliminates the loss which is caused by sending out incorrectly addressed mail. To keep the list up-to-date, notice must be taken of returned mail, change of address, change of name, etc. Valuable help may be secured from the city directory, the telephone directory, the sales and credit departments of your company, local newspapers, and other sources.

Do not try to guess the weight of the mail. This could be costly for your company. You should carefully weigh the mail on a postal scale.

Place all mail for one individual or for one branch office in the same envelope. If more than one letter is written to an individual in one day, you can save the company money by placing these letters in the same envelope. If mail is sent daily to branch offices, you should hold all the mail for the branches until the end of the day; then, place the mail in one envelope.

Use the correct type of mail service. For example, if mail that can be sent third class is sent first class, the company will pay more postage than is necessary. You should be knowledgeable of the different classes of mail and the special mail services available.

DOMESTIC MAIL CLASSIFICATIONS

Domestic mail includes: (1) matter deposited in the mails for local delivery; (2) matter transmitted from one place to another within the United States; and (3) matter transmitted to, from, or between the possessions of the United States. Domestic mail is divided into four classes.

1. First-class mail
2. Second-class mail
3. Third-class mail
4. Fourth-class mail or parcel post

First-Class Mail. First-class mail consists of letters, post cards, greeting cards, personal notes, checks, and money orders. First-class letters may not be opened for postal inspection. All first-class mail is given the fastest transportation service available. If first-class mail is not letter size, it should be marked "First Class." First-class mail over 12 ounces is called Priority Mail. More details on Priority Mail will be presented under the section on special classes of mail.

Second-Class Mail. Second-class mail is generally used by newspapers and other periodical publishers who meet certain postal requirements. However, the general public can use second-class mail for sending newspapers, magazines, and other periodicals. No handwritten messages can be sent by second-class mail. There is no weight limit for this class of mail. Second-class mail should not be sealed and should be marked "Second Class."

Third-Class Mail.
Third-class mail, sometimes called advertising mail, may be used by anyone, but is used most often by large mailers. Third-class mail includes printed materials and merchandise parcels that weigh less than 16 ounces. Two rate structures are available for this class—a single-piece rate and a bulk rate.

You may have occasion to send printed matter, booklets, and other material by third-class mail with an accompanying letter. This material can sometimes be placed in a large envelope with the letter attached to the outside. The large envelope takes postage at the third-class rate (maximum weight up to, but not including, 16 ounces), and the smaller envelope containing the letter requires postage at the first-class rate. Postage to cover the third-class envelope must be placed on it, and postage to cover the letter must be placed on it. The entire package, however, is treated as third-class mail by the post office. If material sent in an attached envelope weighs 16 ounces or more, the fourth-class rate is used.

If third-class mail consists of merchandise or books, a letter may be enclosed with postage added to the package. There should be an endorsement "Letter Enclosed," below the postage.

Fourth-Class (Parcel Post) Mail.
Fourth-class (parcel post) mail is used for packages that weigh 16 ounces or more. Those packages mailed between larger post offices in the continental United States are limited to 40 pounds and 84 inches in length and girth combined. (Parcels weighing up to 70 pounds and 100 inches in length and girth combined should be sent by Priority Mail.) Parcels up to 70 pounds and 100 inches in length and girth combined can be mailed to and from smaller post offices and from any post office in Hawaii and Alaska. Your local post office has information to assist you on the size and weights that can be mailed to particular locations.

A package should not usually contain a communication other than one that identifies the contents, such as a sales slip or an invoice. However, first-class mail may be sent with a parcel-post package in one of the following ways:

1. Enclosed in the package with the package marked "First-Class Mail Enclosed" below the postage.
2. Enclosed in an envelope and attached to the outside of the package. The address should be on both the parcel and the envelope. The entire package travels as fourth-class mail.

Previously, if a piece of first-class material was attached to a second-, third-, or fourth-class mailing, the Postal Service required postage for both pieces. As a result of a recent ruling, a piece of first-class mail that is incidental (related) to the matter mailed via another class, except nonmerchandise third, does not require the separate, additional postage.

SPECIAL CLASSES OF MAIL

In addition to the four major classes of mail, there are two special classes of mail.

Priority Mail.
Priority Mail is first-class mail that weighs more than 12 ounces. It should be used when fast transportation and expeditious handling are desired. The maximum weight for Priority Mail is 70 pounds; the maximum size is 100 inches in length and girth combined. When using Priority Mail, mark the package or envelope "Priority Mail" in large letters and on all sides.

Express Mail.
Express Mail provides fast service for those who require overnight delivery of letters and packages. Express services can be divided into four types of service.

Express Mail Next Day Service. Express Mail Next Day Service requires that the sender take the shipment to any designated Express Mail post office by 5 p.m. The mail will then be delivered to the addressee by 3 p.m. the next day (weekends and holidays included). Or it can be picked up at a designated post office by the addressee as early as 10 a.m. on the next day that the office is open for regular business. This service comes with a money-back guarantee and shipments are insured (at no extra cost) against loss or damage.

Express Mail Same Day Airport Service. Express Mail Same Day Airport Service includes airport service to and from major airport mail facilities in certain cities. If a sender is interested in using this service, local post office personnel should be consulted as to the availability in that particular city. The sender takes the package to the airport mail facility where it is put on the next available flight to the destination specified. The receiver is then told when the package will be ready for pickup at the destination airport.

Express Mail Custom Designed Service. This service is for businesses with regularly scheduled shipments to or from locations in the country. It is available 24 hours a day, 365 days a year. Options include pickup at the customer's premises for delivery directly to the addressee, mailing from a post office for pickup at the receiving post office, and depositing at an airport mail facility for pickup at the destination.

Express Mail International Service. Businesses with interests abroad can use Express Mail International Service. This service is available in most foreign countries. Since it is not available in all countries, an interested company should check with the local post office for details.

THE ZIP CODE

In Chapter 7 you learned where the ZIP Code is placed on the envelope and how OCR equipment is used in processing mail. Here is a further explanation of use of the five-digit code and the ZIP + 4 code.

In devising the five-digit code, the United States and its possessions were divided into ten geographic areas, each consisting of three or more states or possessions and each given a number between 0 and 9. This number is the first digit of any ZIP Code. See Illustration 10-9.

Because of favorable transportation facilities, key post offices in each area are designated as sectional centers which receive and transmit mail moving between post offices within its section and into or out of the section.

Together, the first three digits of any ZIP Code number stand for a particular sectional center or a metropolitan city. The last two digits of a sectional center ZIP Code number stand for one of the associated post offices served by the sectional center or one of the delivery areas served by the city post office.

For example, in the ZIP Code number 45237, the 4 designates the national area. The 5 designates a subdivision within the region. The 2 designates a sectional center, and the 37 designates a specific post office or delivery area within a multi-ZIP coded city. The ZIP 45237 designates a delivery area in Cincinnati, Ohio. The ZIP Code should be used both for the mailing address and for the return address on all mail.

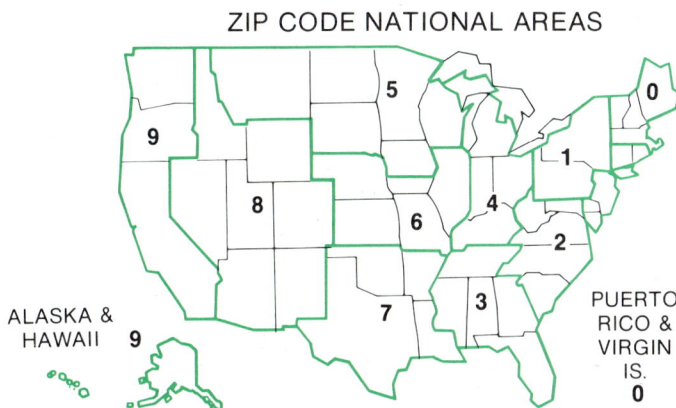

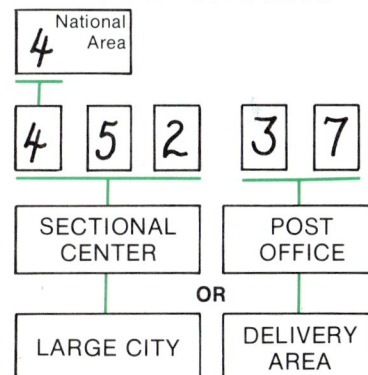

Illustration 10-9. ZIP Code Explanation

The ZIP + 4 code is an expanded ZIP Code designed to improve service to business mailers. National implementation of ZIP + 4 occurred in October, 1983. This nine-digit ZIP further identifies the destination of correspondence and permits even greater mailing productivity. Use of the nine-digit ZIP by business is voluntary; however, many businesses are using it due to its cost cutting features. Presorted first-class letters bearing the ZIP + 4 code receive a one-half cent per piece discount. In addition, there is a three cents per piece discount on mailings of 500 or more pieces. Non-presorted first-class letters with ZIP + 4 codes receive a nine-tenths of a cent discount for 250 or more pieces.

SPECIAL MAIL SERVICES

In addition to the transportation of mail and other matter, the U. S. Postal Service provides a number of other special services.

Registered Mail. Registered mail provides protection and evidence of receipt for first-class and priority mail. When this service is used, the post office guarantees delivery and, in case the mail is lost, becomes responsible to the sender for the declared value of the mail up to $25,000. Registered mail should be sealed. It is most frequently used in sending money and valuable papers such as stocks, bonds, contracts, and bids.

A receipt is always issued to the sender of a registered letter; but for a small additional fee, a return receipt showing the signature of the recipient and the date received will be furnished the sender. For an additional fee, the address where delivered will be shown. The sender may also, upon payment of an additional fee, restrict the delivery of registered mail to the addressee only, or to someone named by the sender in writing. Registered mail service with return receipt requested or demanded is sometimes used in writing credit letters and other letters when the writer wishes to know definitely whether the addressee received the letter.

Whenever letters or packages are sent by registered mail, a record should be kept show-

ing the name and address of the addressee, the contents of the package, its value, and the postage paid. The receipt issued by the post office for each registered piece should be kept with the record. The registry fee is governed by the value of the contents.

Insured Mail. Only third- and fourth-class mail are insurable. The maximum liability of the post office is $500. When a package is insured, a receipt is issued by the post office and the package is stamped *Insured*. This receipt should be kept by the sender as it will be needed if a claim for loss or damage is made. If a package is lost or damaged in the mail, a claim for the amount of the loss may be made at the post office where the package was mailed or received. Simply present the insured mailing receipt and invoice on the damaged parcel or the damaged article itself along with the container or wrapper showing evidence of insurance, postage, and address of sender. If an article valued at more than $500 is to be sent by mail, it can be sent by registered mail and be covered in case of loss. A return receipt is available on parcels insured for $25 or more for an additional fee.

C. O. D. Service. An article which has not been paid for may be sent by mail and the price and the cost of the postage may be collected from the addressee. This is called *collect-on-delivery, cash-on-delivery,* or *C.O.D.* service. C. O. D. service may be used for merchandise sent by parcel post, first class, or third class. However, the merchandise must have been ordered by the addressee. Fees charged for this service include insurance protection against loss or damage. C. O. D. service is not available to foreign countries.

Special Delivery. Special delivery service is available for all classes of mail. It provides delivery during prescribed hours that extend beyond the regular hours of ordinary mail delivery. Special delivery mail is also delivered on Sundays and holidays. This service is available to all customers served by city carriers and to other customers within a one-mile radius of the delivery post office.

The purchase of special delivery does not always mean the article will be delivered by special messenger; special delivery may be delivered by a regular mail carrier. All mail sent by special delivery should be marked prominently with the words "Special Delivery."

Special Handling. Special handling service is available for third- and fourth-class mail only, including insured and C.O.D. mail. It provides for preferential handling in dispatch and transport, but it does not provide for special delivery. A special handling fee must be paid on parcels that require special care. Special handling does not mean special care of fragile items. Anything breakable should be packed with adequate cushioning and marked "Fragile."

Certified Mail. Certified mail provides the sender with a mailing receipt. A record of delivery is maintained at the addressee's post office. It is used for items with little intrinsic value that are sent and handled as ordinary mail. A return receipt, which provides the sender proof of delivery, may be obtained for an additional fee.

Return Receipts. The return receipt gives the sender proof of delivery. It is available on mail that is insured for more than $25, and on certified, registered, and C.O.D. mail. The return receipt identifies who signed for the item and the date it was delivered. For an additional fee, you can get a receipt showing the exact address of delivery.

Postal Money Orders. Money orders are available at all post offices in amounts up to $500. If a money order is lost or stolen, the customer receipt may be presented to the post office, and the money order will be replaced. Copies of paid money orders are available for two years after the date they are paid.

INTERNATIONAL MAIL SERVICE

International mail service is divided into two general categories: postal union mail and parcel post. Postal union articles are further classified as letters, letter-packages, aerogrammes, postcards, printed matter, raised print for the blind, samples of merchandise, small packets, and eight-ounce merchandise packages (Canada only). For more detailed information about rates, classification, and methods of preparing for mailing, consult your local post office or the *International Mail Manual.*

SPECIAL PROBLEMS

There are some special problems in sending mail that you as an office employee may encounter. Some of these special problems are covered here.

Mailing Currency. Currency should generally not be sent through the mail. However, you may find it necessary to mail small amounts of money. If you are mailing coins, you should tape the coins to a small card and insert the card with the letter, or place the card inside a folded plain sheet of paper. Bills should be folded inside the letter. If bills are being sent without a letter, they should be folded inside a plain sheet of paper.

Retrieving Mail. Certainly you should be extremely careful to have all information correct before you mail a piece of correspondence. However, if you discover that you have sent an important piece of mail incorrectly, you may call the post office and ask that the correspondence be held. Then you must go to the post office and fill out the necessary form to retrieve the mail. For identification purposes, you must present an envelope addressed as the incorrectly mailed item. If the correspondence has left the post office, it can still be stopped at the destination post office by calling or telegraphing the post office. You must pay for the telephone call or the telegram.

Incorrectly Addressed Mail. If you receive mail for someone who is unknown at the company where you work, you should mark the mail "Not Known at This Address" and put it in the outgoing mail. If you receive mail for someone who is no longer with the company, but you know the person's new address, merely cross out the old address and write the new address in ink. If you open mail that does not belong to your company, you should write "Opened by Mistake" on the envelope, reseal the envelope with tape, and place it in the outgoing mail.

Changing Addresses. If the company for which you work changes its address, you should notify the local post office of the change. The post office will ask that you fill out a change-of-address card. Mail will then be forwarded to the new address for one year.

Forwarding Mail. First-class mail can be forwarded without charge. On second-, third-, and fourth-class mail, the addressee must pay the postage for having the item forwarded.

Lost Mail. If a piece of correspondence fails to arrive at its destination in a reasonable length of time, you can ask the post office to trace the item. You should report to the post office how the item was mailed—first class, registered, insured, etc. If the lost mail was insured or registered, you may file a claim for reimbursement.

COMMON SHIPPING TERMS AND ABBREVIATIONS

A discussion of transportation facilities and the advantages of each means of transportation will be more interesting and meaningful if the common shipping terms and abbreviations used by transportation companies are understood. The following are the most commonly used terms:

BL. Bill of lading; a printed form giving complete information regarding freight shipments.
Consignor. Person or business sending the shipment; the sender.
Consignee. Person or business to which the shipment is sent; the receiver.
Consignment. The goods being shipped.
Collect. Shipping charges or carrying charges for a shipment are collected from the consignee at the time of delivery.

C.O.D. Collect on delivery; cash on delivery; price of the goods and other costs paid by consignee upon delivery of the goods.
FOB. Free on board; an expression generally used along with the name of a city to designate the point at which charges for transportation originate. For example, if goods are sold in Detroit to be delivered in Cleveland, terms FOB Detroit, the transportation charges from Detroit to Cleveland are to be paid by the consignee. If, however, the goods are sold FOB Cleveland, the transportation charges are to be paid by the consignor. In most businesses, the consignee is expected to pay the transportation charges from the point at which the shipment originated.
LCL. Less-than-carload lot; transportation charges for carload lots are usually less than transportation charges for shipments of less than a carload. LCL shipments, therefore, require more transportation charges per unit than do carload shipments.

BE		*frt*
	Bill of exchange	Freight
CIF		*RR*
	Cost, insurance, and freight	Railroad
cit or ctge		*ry*
	Cartage	Railway
cwt		*shpt*
	Hundredweight— 100 pounds	Shipment
FAS		*via*
		By way of
	Free alongside ship	*WB*
		Waybill

SHIPPING SERVICES

Shipments may be made by air, van, bus, truck, train, or ship. Before you determine the type of service to use, consider the cost, delivery time, and convenience to both the shipper and receiver.

Express Couriers. Express couriers offer the fastest means of transporting shipments by air to all parts of the United States and to most foreign countries. With fleets of aircraft and vans, and highly efficient scheduling, couriers quickly deliver thousands of packages to hundreds of domestic and international destinations. The courier services industry is dominated by these major companies: Airborne, DHL, Emery, Federal Express, Purolator, United Parcel (UPS), and the U.S. Postal Service. Federal Express is the largest of the next-day or overnight services. United Parcel, the U.S. Postal Service, and Federal Express are the three largest second-day delivery services.

Bus Companies. Bus lines offer package express services that provide fast delivery of packages to small towns where there is no airport. Pickup and delivery services are available for an additional charge.

United Parcel Service. United Parcel Service (UPS) is a specialized carrier of packages. If the packages are being transported within a given state, they must weigh 50 pounds or less; and packages that are being transported outside state lines must weigh 70 pounds or less. In both cases, the packages are not to exceed 108 inches in length and girth combined. Packages are insured for a maximum of $100 unless the shipper declares and pays for additional insurance. United Parcel Service provides C.O.D. service and pickup service at the shipper's location if such is desired. "Blue label air" service which is a two-day delivery service is provided in 48 states, Hawaii, some cities in Alaska, and Puerto Rica.

Motor Freight. Motor freight is available for local and long-distance shipments. In recent years, the amount of freight carried by trucks has increased rapidly. Many trucking companies operate coast-to-coast service and have a regular schedule for deliveries at distant points. Most transcontinental trucking companies have connecting services with local trucking lines.

Many trucking companies take advantage of a service called *piggyback* which is offered by the railroads for long-distance hauls. Loaded truck trailers are driven to the railroad station, detached from the trucks, and placed on flatcars provided by the railroad. At the railroad station closest to the point of destination, the trailer is unloaded from the flatcar and driven to its destination. Through this service, areas that do not have railroad lines can be reached.

Railroad Freight. Ordinarily when goods are shipped by railroad freight, they must be delivered by the shipper to a local freight depot and must be called for by the customer at the freight office at the destination. Many railroad companies, however, have instituted store-door delivery whereby shipments are picked up from the shipper by trucks operated by the railroad company and are delivered to the consignee in the same way. This service by the railroad companies has done much to offset the advantages that trucking companies originally had over the railroad companies in transporting freight.

Freight-forwarding companies have been organized to provide a less-than-carload freight service at a special rate. Although some of these forwarding companies are owned and operated by the railroads, others are independently owned. These companies assemble from several consignors less-than-carload shipments going to a certain destination, and in this way they obtain enough freight to receive a carload rate from railroad companies.

Water Freight. Ship transportation is used for transporting goods within the United States as well as to foreign countries. Water freight is considerably cheaper than other methods of transporting goods. River barges in the United States transport such goods as iron ore, coal, and lumber. Freighters carry heavy items overseas; passenger liners carry packaged items.

FOR YOUR REVIEW

The following review will help you remember the important points of this chapter.

1. A preliminary mail sort is done according to departments or individuals receiving the mail.

2. An office worker should open all mail except personal or confidential correspondence.

3. Mail should be date and time stamped, read, underlined, and annotated.

4. A final sort of an individual's mail is placed in folders in the following order:

   a. *Immediate action mail:* personal or confidential correspondence; Mailgrams; special delivery, registered, and important first-class mail.

   b. *Regular mail:* routine correspondence (usually first-class mail) and interoffice correspondence.

   c. *Read-for-information mail:* circulars, advertisements, magazines, and catalogs.

5. A mail register helps you keep an accurate record of mail received.

6. Outgoing mail should be carefully prepared by (1) checking the envelope address against the letter address; (2) checking to see that all correspondence has been signed; (3) checking to see that special mailing notations are keyed on the letter and envelope; (4) determining that any enclosures are included; and (5) properly addressing envelopes for material that must be sent in a separate envelope.

7. Postage meters are used in sealing and stamping mail in large offices.

8. Postal publications that give information concerning different classes and services of mail are available from the Postal Service.

9. To reduce mailing costs

   a. Keep an up-to-date mailing list.

   b. Weigh mail carefully to determine the correct postage needed.

   c. Place all mail for one individual or for one branch office in the same envelope.

   d. Use the correct type of mail service.

10. Domestic mail includes first-, second-, third-, and fourth-class (or parcel post) mail.

    a. First-class mail consists of letters, post cards, greeting cards, personal notes, checks, and money orders. It is sealed and given the fastest transportation service available.

    b. Second-class mail consists of newspapers and periodicals. There is no weight limit for this class of mail. Second-class mail should not be sealed.

    c. Third-class mail includes matter that need not be classed as first class, that cannot be classed as second class, and

that weighs up to, but not including, 16 ounces.

    d. Fourth-class mail (or parcel post) includes merchandise, printed matter, and other matter not included in first-, second-, or third-class mail that weighs 16 ounces or more.

11. Priority Mail and Express Mail are special classes of mail.

    a. Priority Mail is first-class mail that weighs in excess of 12 ounces.

    b. Express Mail provides fast service for customers who require overnight delivery of letters and packages. Express services are divided into four types:

    (1) Express Mail Next Day Service

    (2) Express Mail Same Day Airport Service

    (3) Express Mail Custom Designed Service

    (4) Express Mail International Service

12. The ZIP (Zone Improvement Plan) Code identifies areas within the United States and its possessions for purposes of simplifying the distribution of mail.

13. Some special mail services available are

    a. Registered mail — provides protection and evidence of receipt for first-class and priority mail. The post office guarantees delivery; and if the mail is lost, the post office becomes responsible to the sender for the declared value of the mail for up to $25,000.

    b. Insured mail — only third- and fourth-class mail are insurable. The maximum liability of the post office is $500.

    c. C.O.D. services — an article that has not been paid for by the purchaser may be sent by mail and the item's price and the cost of the postage collected from the addressee. This is called collect-on-delivery or cash-on-delivery service.

    d. Special delivery — mail delivered during prescribed hours that extend beyond the ordinary delivery hours.

    e. Special handling — service available for third- and fourth-class mail only. It provides the quickest handling, dispatch, and transportation available, but does not provide special delivery.

f. Certified mail—a special postal service that provides the sender with proof of delivery or evidence of the mailing of a letter.

g. Return receipt—gives the sender proof of delivery. It identifies who signed for the item and the date it was delivered.

h. Postal money order—money orders in amounts up to $500 are available at post offices.

14. Incorrectly addressed first-class mail may be forwarded without cost. The addressee must pay postage for the forwarding of second-, third-, and fourth-class mail.

15. Packages or freight may be shipped by air, van, bus, truck, train, or ship. Before determining how goods should be shipped, you should consider the cost, speed of delivery, and convenience to the shipper and receiver.

PROFESSIONAL FORUM

Roger Martin is a clerk in the central mail room. He has been with the company for six months. Roger seems like a nice young man who is eager to succeed on his job, but he has made several mistakes. These mistakes were as follows:

1. You had a very important item to mail, and you requested that it be insured for $250. Roger failed to have the package insured.

2. Roger picks up mail from you in the morning and in the afternoon. On several occasions, he has inadvertently left your outgoing mail at other desks in the building.

The employees at these desks have returned the mail to you.

3. On three mornings this week (and on several previous occasions), Roger has missed you on his mail run—he has not picked up your outgoing mail nor brought you the incoming mail.

Each time Roger has made a mistake, you have talked with him about the error. He has been extremely apologetic and has made the excuse that he still has a lot to learn. However, the last time you called a mistake to his attention, he seemed to be quite defensive about the mistake. What should you do now?

FOR YOUR UNDERSTANDING

1. Identify five situations in which incoming mail envelopes should be retained.

2. Explain how underlining and annotating assist the executive.

3. Discuss the advantages of using postage meters instead of manually applying postage.

4. List four procedures that can help reduce mailing costs.

5. Assume that you need to retrieve a piece of mail that has been incorrectly mailed. Can this be done? If so, how?

6. What are the advantages of certified mail and insured mail?

7. Name and describe four commonly used types of shipping services.

OFFICE APPLICATIONS

On pages 341–347 are office applications that correlate with this chapter.

CHAPTER 11

Financial Records

Financial records are an important part of each business organization. Consider a few of the financial records that are essential. You, as an employee, are concerned with getting a paycheck each week, semimonthly, or every month. To insure that you are paid the proper amount, your company must keep detailed records of your earnings, the amount of social security tax withheld, the amount of income tax withheld, and any other deductions for such items as group insurance and retirement plans. Your company must correctly prepare your payroll check, issue numerous other checks, and make bank deposits. Records must also be kept of the amount of money your company receives from its sales and services and the amount of money paid out in expenses. These sales and expenses, along with the total financial picture of the company, must be reported to management and to the owners of the company.

You may not be directly involved in handling the financial transactions of a business, but a knowledge of these transactions will help you to understand the total operations of the business. This chapter provides an overview of some of these transactions.

GENERAL OBJECTIVES

Your general objectives for this chapter are to

1. Write checks.
2. Use appropriate types of endorsements.
3. Make out deposit slips.
4. Reconcile a bank statement.
5. Become familiar with special banking services.
6. Keep a petty cash record.
7. Prepare a balance sheet and an income statement.
8. Recognize the impact of electronic technology on the banking industry.
9. Become familiar with the following payroll taxes: social security tax, income tax, and unemployment tax.
10. Prepare an expense report.
11. Perform mathematical computations on a calculator.

BANKING

The extent to which you will be involved in the company's banking operations usually depends on the size of the company. If you work in a small company, you may write company checks, make bank deposits, and even reconcile bank statements. If you work in a large company, these functions will be handled by the accounting department. Regardless of the size of the company for which you work, it is important that you understand the procedures involved in performing basic banking functions such as writing checks, making deposits, and reconciling bank statements.

Checks Defined. A *check* is an order in writing, signed by the depositor (or other authorized person), directing the bank to pay cash from the depositor's account. The one who orders the bank to pay cash from the account is the *drawer*. The one to whom a check is made payable is the *payee*. The bank is called the *drawee*. Most financial obligations of businesses, as well as of individuals, are paid by checks. Checks provide an easy way to transfer money, and canceled checks serve as receipts. Most businesses use a special type of check called a *voucher* check. This is a check with a detachable portion, or voucher, on which is written the check's purpose. A voucher check is shown in Illustration 11-1.

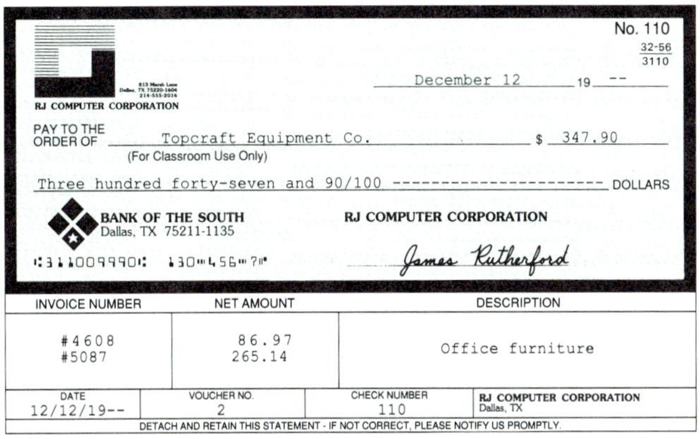
RJ COMPUTER CORPORATION
No. 110
32-56
3110
December 12 19 --
PAY TO THE ORDER OF Topcraft Equipment Co. $ 347.90
(For Classroom Use Only)
Three hundred forty-seven and 90/100 ---------------------- DOLLARS
BANK OF THE SOUTH
Dallas, TX 75211-1135
RJ COMPUTER CORPORATION
James Rutherford

INVOICE NUMBER	NET AMOUNT	DESCRIPTION
#4608 #5087	86.97 265.14	Office furniture

DATE	VOUCHER NO.	CHECK NUMBER	RJ COMPUTER CORPORATION Dallas, TX
12/12/19--	2	110	

DETACH AND RETAIN THIS STATEMENT · IF NOT CORRECT, PLEASE NOTIFY US PROMPTLY.

Illustration 11-1. Voucher Check

Signature Card. When a checking account is opened at a bank, the bank keeps a record of the signatures of persons who are permitted to write checks against that account. A form called a *signature card* is used for this purpose. A signature card for an individual is shown in Illustration 11-2.

When a business opens a checking account, several persons may be authorized to sign checks against the account. In such cases the names of these persons should appear on the signature card. A person who signs checks should always write his or her signature exactly as it appears on the signature card.

Check Writing. In many companies employees' checks are computer originated. For example, payroll information concerning the number of hours per week an employee has worked, the rate of pay, the deductions to be withheld, and so forth, are fed into a computer. The computer then computes the amount to be paid and prints the check. Companies do still prepare some checks manually, however, and you should know the correct procedures for preparing checks. Follow these steps.

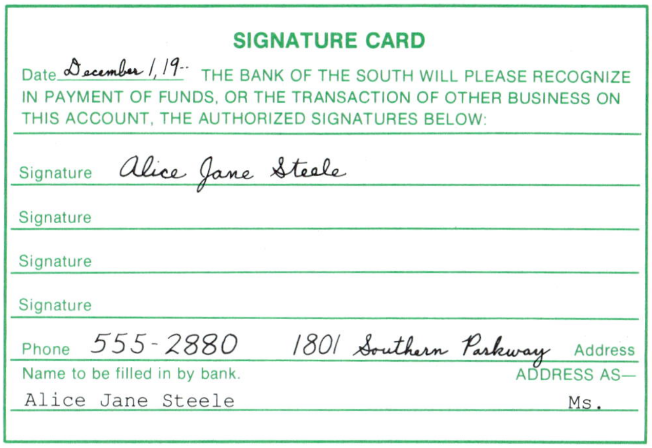
SIGNATURE CARD
Date December 1, 19-- THE BANK OF THE SOUTH WILL PLEASE RECOGNIZE IN PAYMENT OF FUNDS, OR THE TRANSACTION OF OTHER BUSINESS ON THIS ACCOUNT, THE AUTHORIZED SIGNATURES BELOW:
Signature Alice Jane Steele
Signature
Signature
Signature
Phone 555-2880 1801 Southern Parkway Address
Name to be filled in by bank. ADDRESS AS—
Alice Jane Steele Ms.

Illustration 11-2. Signature Card for an Individual

1. The check voucher, stub, or register should be filled out first with the date, amount, and purpose of the check. Most companies use a *voucher check* which has a detachable slip on which the information is recorded. A *check stub* is a short leaf of paper attached to the spine of the checkbook after the check has been detached. A check stub is shown in Illustration 11-3. A *check register* is a separate form for recording the checks that have been written. A check register is shown in Illustration 11-4. Notice that both a check stub and check register contain a blank also for recording any deposits made. The check stub and check register are used more frequently for personal transactions, whereas the voucher check is the principal type of check used for business related transactions.
2. The date should be entered in the space provided on the check.
3. The name of the payee should be written in full and as far as possible to the left in the space provided.

No. 110 $ 347.90	THIS CHECK IS IN FULL PAYMENT OF THE FOLLOWING INVOICES		
Date December 12, 19--	DATE	ITEM	AMOUNT
To Top Craft Equipment	19-- 12-12	4608 5087	347 90
For Invoice #4608 #5087			

	Dollars	Cents
Bal. Bro't For'd.		
Amt. Deposited	7498	00
Total	7498	00
Amt. This Check	347	90
Bal. Car'd For'd	7150	10

TOTAL	347	90
LESS DISCOUNT	—	—
CHECK TOTAL	347	90

No. 110   32-56
                 3110

RJ COMPUTER CORPORATION
813 Marsh Lane
Dallas, TX 75220-1604
214-555-2016

December 12 19 --

PAY TO THE
ORDER OF Top Craft Equipment Co. $ 347.90

Three hundred forty seven 99/100 ——————— Dollars

BANK OF THE SOUTH
Dallas, TX 75211-1135

James Rutherford

⑂311009990⑂   ⑂30⑄456⑄71⑄

Illustration 11-3. Check with Attached Stub

CHECK NO.	DATE	CHECK ISSUED TO	BAL BRG'T FOR'D	7604	74
109	12/11	TO Armstrong Equipment	AMOUNT OF CHECK OR DEPOSIT	106	74
		FOR Invoice #3612	BALANCE	7498	00
110	12/12	TO Top Craft Equipment Co.	AMOUNT OF CHECK OR DEPOSIT	347	90
		FOR Invoice #4608 #5087	BALANCE	7150	10

Illustration 11-4. Separate Check Register

4. The amount of the check must be written twice. It is first written in figures after the dollar sign. The figures should be placed as close as possible to the printed dollar sign so that no additional figures can be inserted. The amount of the check is then written on the following line with words for the dollar amount and figures for the cents. Express cents in fractions of 100. The words should be started as far as possible to the left. If the written amount does not fill the entire space, draw a line through the excess space.

5. If you are writing a check for less than $1, circle the amount written in figures; write *Only* before the spelled-out amount.

6. Erasures or changes should be avoided in writing checks. If a mistake is made, write *Void* across the face of the check and the check voucher, stub, or register.

Check Depositing. In addition to writing checks, you may frequently be required to make deposits to the personal account of your supervisor or to the account of the business. To make bank deposits correctly, you should know about endorsements and deposit slips.

Endorsements. Before a check can be deposited, it must be endorsed. An *endorsement* is a written signature by the holder of a check, note, or other negotiable instrument for the purpose of transferring ownership. The endorsement is usually written on the back of the instrument. A rubber stamp may be used instead of a personally written signature if the check or other negotiable instrument is to be deposited only and not transferred to someone else. The following types of endorsements are the most common and are shown in Illustration 11-5.

1. Blank Endorsement. A *blank endorsement* requires only the signature of the payee or the present holder of the negotiable instrument. A blank endorsement makes the check payable to *any holder*. Therefore, if the check is endorsed in this manner, it should not be sent through the mail because if it is lost, anyone who finds it can turn it into cash.

2. Full Endorsement. A *full endorsement* transfers ownership of a negotiable instrument to a *definite person* or *firm* to whose order the instrument is made payable. The name of the person to whom or to whose order the instrument is payable is written above the signature of the holder.

3. Restrictive Endorsement. A *restrictive endorsement* transfers the ownership of a negotiable instrument for a *specific purpose*. For example, if a person has several checks to deposit at a time when it is not convenient to go to a bank, the checks can be endorsed with a restrictive endorsement so that they are not cashed for any other reason.

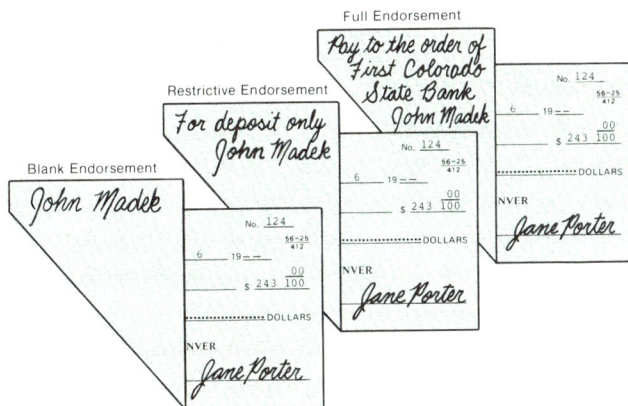

Illustration 11-5. Blank, Restrictive, and Full Endorsements

The Deposit Slip. Banks supply special blank forms known as *deposit slips* that usually provide space to record the following information:

1. The account number and the name of the individual or the business to whose account the deposit is to be credited. If this information is not preprinted, you must record it.

2. The date on which the deposit is made.

3. A list of the currency and coins to be deposited.

4. A list of the checks or other items to be deposited.

5. The American Bankers Association (ABA) transit number.

6. The total of the deposit.

Checks may also be listed on the deposit slip according to the name of the bank (if the bank is local) or the city in which the bank is located (if the check is drawn on an out-of-town bank). This plan is used in filling out the deposit slip shown in Illustration 11-6. Other banks prefer that the American Bankers Association (ABA) transit numbers be used in listing checks. In Illustration 11-6, checks are listed by ABA transit numbers. The ABA number is usually printed in the upper right portion of the bank check. In Illustration 11-1, the numbers 32-56 indicate the ABA transit number that has been assigned to that bank. The number 3110, appearing below the line, is a Federal Reserve number that is used by banks in sorting checks; this Federal Reserve number is not used in listing the checks on a deposit slip. Each depositor should ask the bank which method is preferred and then use that method.

Checks and deposit slips are processed electronically. In order to aid in this electronic processing, the bank's transit number and the depositor's account number are preprinted in magnetic ink characters in a uniform position at the bottom left of Illustration 11-1. When a check or deposit slip is received at the bank, the amount, the date, and other information are recorded in magnetic ink. Optical Character Recognition (OCR) equipment sorts the checks and deposit slips and posts them to the depositor's account.

After the checks and money to be deposited have been verified by the bank teller, a receipt is returned to the depositor. The receipt becomes a part of the depositor's accounting records.

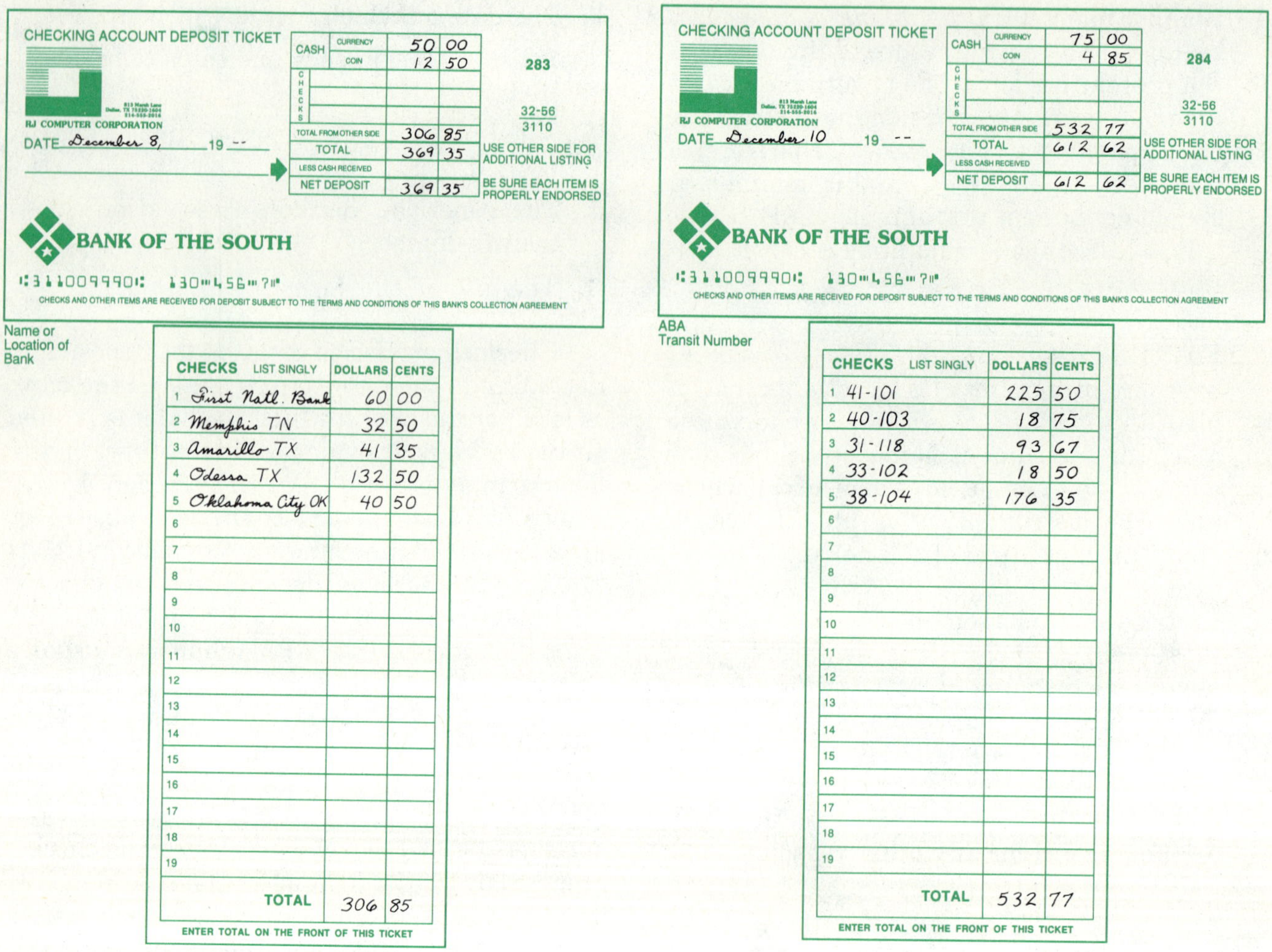

Illustration 11-6. Deposit Slips

Checking Account Plans. Many banks and savings and loan institutions offer interest-bearing checking accounts. Interest is paid on the average daily balance of the account. Most of these banks and savings and loan institutions have also established a certain minimum balance that must be maintained to avoid a service charge on the account. If the minimum balance within a month's period of time falls below the amount set, you are charged a maintenance fee and possibly a charge for each check that is written. If the balance does not fall below the minimum balance established, you pay no service charge. Consider these two examples of interest-bearing checking accounts.

Example 1: Your average daily balance for one month is $400; the bank has set a minimum balance of $500. You are paid 5¼ percent interest on the $400 or $1.75. An explanation of the computation of the $1.75 is explained below.[1] Since your balance falls below the $500 minimum, you are charged a $2.00 maintenance fee plus 15 cents for each check written. You have written 20 checks during the month. You are charged $3.00 for the checks written plus the $2.00 maintenance fee, making a total charge of

---

[1]The formula for computing ordinary interest is: Principal × Rate × Time = Interest. The principal in Example 1 is $400. The rate is 5¼ percent, and the time is 30 days (one month). Therefore, the calculation is

$$\$400 \times 5.25\% \times \frac{30}{360} = \$1.75.$$

(In computing ordinary interest, 360 days are considered as the numbers of days per year; when computing exact interest, 365 days are used.)

$5.00. Your account, therefore, has a net loss rather than a net gain because your charge ($5.00) is greater than your interest earned ($1.75). Your account is actually charged $3.25 (the difference between $5.00 and $1.75).

Example 2: Your average daily balance for one month is $1,000; the bank has set a minimum balance of $500. You are paid 5¼ percent interest on the $1,000 or $4.37. There is no service charge since you maintained the minimum balance. Therefore, the net gain in your account is $4.37.

The Bank Statement Reconciliation.

Periodically, usually monthly, the bank prepares a bank statement for each depositor. The statement shows the amounts deposited and withdrawn, any bank service charges, any interest, and the account's balance for the month. The depositor should verify the statement's balance by checking it against the balance shown on the last check stub or shown on other accounting records. Proving the accuracy of the bank statement and the check stub statement is called *reconciling the bank statement.*

Reconciling the bank statement involves closely comparing the bank statement with the company records of deposits and withdrawals. In addition, bank service charges and any other special fees must be taken into consideration, although these charges usually are not known until the bank statement is received.

Follow these procedures in reconciling the bank statement:

1. Look at the check stubs to see that all check amounts have been deducted from the preceding balances and that all deposit amounts have been entered and added to the balances.
2. Sort in numerical order the canceled checks that have been returned by the bank. Usually a statement is accompanied by the checks that have been paid by the bank.[2]

3. If checks are returned by your bank, verify each check with the corresponding check stub. Place a check mark on the stub.
4. On a separate sheet of paper, list the numbers and the amounts of the checks that are outstanding. An *outstanding check* is an issued check that has not yet been cashed by the bank nor deducted from the depositor's account. Total the outstanding checks.
5. Add the total unlisted deposits to the bank balance.
6. Add to the checkbook balance any interest earned on the checking account.
7. Deduct the total amount of the outstanding checks from the balance shown on the bank statement.
8. Deduct from the checkbook balance any service charges or special fees. If there are any charges, they will be shown as separate deductions on the bank statement. The checkbook balance and the balance on the bank statement should now agree.
9. If the reconciliation does not balance after a careful verification, the discrepancy should be brought to the attention of the bank. However, errors are seldom traced to faulty bookkeeping by the bank.

The following computation shows how the balance on the bank statement in Illustration 11-7 is reconciled with the company's checkbook balance of $9,418.25.

Bank balance, June 1		$9,563.83
Less checks outstanding:		
No. 790	$62.50	
No. 792	19.10	
No. 808	24.60	
Total checks outstanding		$ 106.20
Correct bank balance		$9,457.63
Checkbook balance, June 1 . . .		$9,418.25
Add: interest earned		39.38
Correct checkbook balance . . .		$9,457.63

Stop-Payment Orders.

It is sometimes necessary to stop payment on a check if the check has been incorrectly written, lost, or stolen. You may stop payment if the check has not cleared the bank on which it was drawn. A charge is usually made for this service. The procedure for

---

[2]Some banks use *check truncation* (also referred to as *check retention* or *check safekeeping*). With this process, the bank keeps your checks rather than returning them to you. You get a monthly statement listing the number and amount of each check that has been cashed. You may get a copy of a check you need (sometimes a fee is charged for this service) or you may get a special checkbook in which you automatically make copies of each check that you write.

```
       BANK OF THE SOUTH
       Dallas, TX 75211-1135

       Checking Account Statement          ACCT.  130-456-7
                                           DATE   6/1/--
                                           PAGE   1

       RJ Computer Corporation
       813 Marsh Lane
       Dallas, TX 75220-1604
```

BALANCE FORWARD	NO. OF CHECKS	TOTAL CHECK AMOUNT	NO. OF DEP.	TOTAL DEPOSIT AMOUNT	INTEREST	SERVICE CHARGE	BALANCE THIS STATEMENT
7,429 55	19	54,330 07	5	56,424 97	39 38		9,563 83

CHECKS AND OTHER DEBITS				DEPOSITS AND OTHER CREDITS	DATE	BALANCE
787	2,350.67				5/01	5,078.88
788	670.50			10,520.60	5/03	14,928.98
789	7,545.67	791	1,967.83		5/05	5,415.48
793	1,100.00				5/08	4,315.48
794	100.00			12,670.09	5/10	16,885.57
795	8,250.43	796	4,586.20		5/12	4,048.94
797	675.58				5/15	3,373.36
798	1,560.23			12,955.70	5/17	14,768.83
799	7,850.99	800	1,000.00		5/19	5,917.84
801	1,256.79			11,697.82	5/22	16,358.87
802	7,573.25	803	1,362.99		5/24	7,422.63
804	2,000.00				5/27	5,422.63
805	510.33			8,580.76	5/29	13,493.06
806	2,828.75	807	1,139.86		5/31	9,563.83
				39.38INT		

```
PLEASE EXAMINE AT ONCE.                                    KEYS TO SYMBOLS
IF NO ERRORS ARE REPORTED           AD - AUTOMATIC DEPOSIT        DM - DEBIT MEMO
WITHIN 10 DAYS, THE ACCOUNT WILL    AP - AUTOMATIC PAYMENT        EC - ERROR CORRECTED
BE CONSIDERED CORRECT.              AR - AUTOMATIC REVERSAL       INT - INTEREST
PLEASE ADVISE US                    CB - CHARGE BACK              OD - OVERDRAWN
IN WRITING OF ANY CHANGE            CC - CERTIFIED CHECK          RC - RETURN CHECK CHG
IN YOUR ADDRESS.                    CM - CREDIT MEMO              RT - RETURN ITEM
                                    CO - CHARGE OFF               SC - SERVICE CHARGE
```

Illustration 11-7. Bank Statement

stopping payment on a check differs with the individual bank. You may be able to initiate the stop-payment action by telephone. However, most banks require that you come into the bank and fill out a form as confirmation of the stop-payment action.

SPECIAL BANK SERVICES

In addition to understanding the proper procedures for writing checks and making deposits, you should have a knowledge of the methods of transmitting money other than by regular checks. There are times when personal checks or business checks are not acceptable for payment.

Cashier's Check. A check issued by a bank and drawn on the bank's own funds is called a *cashier's check*. You may purchase a cashier's check from a bank by giving the bank cash or your own personal check. In addition, you must pay a small service charge to cover the cost of issuing the check. Since a cashier's check is

drawn on the bank's funds, it is a guaranteed form of payment. If you do not have credit established and the amount of your purchase is large, a business may request a cashier's check in payment of goods or services.

Bank Draft. Most banks deposit part of their funds in other banks, and a bank may draw upon its funds that have been deposited elsewhere. The check that a bank uses to draw on its deposit in another bank is known as a *bank draft*. The bank draft is frequently used as another form of payment when a personal or a company check is not acceptable and when an individual or a company wishes to send money to an individual or a business in another locality.

Bank Money Order. A *bank money order* is usually sold to people who wish to send money through the mail. It can normally be cashed at any other bank both in the United States and abroad. It is negotiable and can be transferred by endorsement. The amount of a single bank money order differs depending on the bank from which you buy the money order. The maximum amount of a single money order may be $100 at some banks and $500 at other banks. However, any number of money orders may be issued to the same person to be sent to the same payee.

Traveler's Check. The American Express Company and most banks and travel agencies issue a special form of check called a *traveler's check,* which makes it possible for a person to pay for expenses when traveling. Traveler's checks are sold in various denominations. A small fee is charged, depending upon the amount purchased. When the checks are purchased, they must be signed by the one who is to use them. When they are cashed, they must be countersigned by the purchaser in the presence of the one who cashes the check.

Safe-Deposit Box. Most banks have large vaults that contain small boxes known as *safe-deposit boxes*. These boxes are available for the convenience of persons and businesses that wish to store articles of value or important business papers for safekeeping. There is a rental charge for the use of these boxes.

The bank has strict rules about access to safe-deposit boxes. At the time a safe-deposit box is rented, the renter must register her or his signature. The renter is then given a key. Two keys are required to open a safe-deposit box: the renter's and a duplicate kept by the vault supervisor. If more than one person is authorized to have access to the box, each must register his or her signature. Each time the box is used, the person's name must be registered and the time in and the time out recorded.

Your employer may want you to have access to the safe-deposit box in order to deposit or to obtain important papers or securities. Any information that you may have about the contents of the employer's safe-deposit box should be held in strict confidence. Whenever any items are removed from the box, you should leave in the box a list of the items taken.

ELECTRONIC BANKING

Electronics is revolutionizing the banking industry. Electronic fund transfers (EFTs) allow customers to obtain money, to transfer funds from one account to another, to deposit money, and to pay bills without the use of checks or services of a bank teller. Simply stated, EFTs use computer and electronic technology as a substitute for checks and other paper forms of banking. Although banking experts agree that the paper check will still be with us in the year 2000, an increase in EFTs is expected because of cost savings for the bank and increased convenience for the customer. The services listed below utilize electronic fund transfers.

Automated Teller Machine. Automated teller machines (ATMs) allow customers to obtain cash, to deposit cash, to transfer money from a checking account to a savings account, and to borrow money without writing a check or going to a bank. See Illustration 11-8. Shopping malls and supermarkets are popular locations for ATMs.

To use an ATM, you insert a magnetically encoded plastic card (similar to a credit card) into an electronic terminal and you enter your own confidential personal identification number (PIN). Thus, you may withdraw cash, make deposits, or transfer funds between accounts. The terminal is connected to a computer at some other location. The bank that is served by the computer may be across the street or it may be miles away.

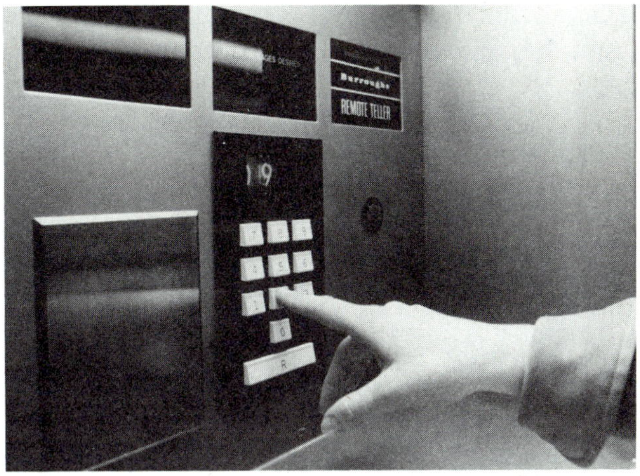

Illustration 11-8. Automated Teller

Direct Payroll Depositing. Some companies directly deposit an employee's wages. The employee's net pay is withdrawn from the company's bank account and is deposited directly into the employee's bank account. Use of direct payroll depositing eliminates the writing of paychecks, relieves the employee of the inconvenience of going to the bank, and decreases the possible loss or theft of paychecks. In some areas of the country, the federal government deposits social security payments directly into the recipients' bank accounts rather than issuing social security checks.

Automatic Bill Payment. In some areas of the country it is also possible to automatically pay utility bills, mortgage payments, and insurance premiums. The utility company forwards the monthly bill to the customer's bank, the bank subtracts the amount of the utility bill from the customer's bank balance, and then the customer receives a copy of the paid utility bill for his or her records.

Point-of-Sale Transfer. Point-of-sale (POS) systems allow the electronic transfer of money from a purchaser's bank account to a store's bank account. For example, a cashier or salesperson can pass a customer's bank issued card, which is called a debit card, through a reader attached to a POS terminal that functions as a cash register. The amount of the purchase is entered on the keyboard; the customer punches in his or her personal identification number. The amount of the bill is instantly deducted from the customer's checking account and added to the store's account.

Transferring funds at the moment of purchase is a compelling reason for merchants to install point-of-sale systems. Funds available to a merchant at the moment of purchase accelerate the merchant's cash flow and reduce the number of bad checks and fraudulent credit card charges, both of which are costly to banks and merchants.

Pay-by-Phone Systems. From the comfort of your home or the convenience of your office, pay-by-phone systems permit you to telephone your bank (or other financial institution) and instruct it to pay certain bills or to transfer funds between accounts. You can also learn your checking, savings, and credit balances through the use of such systems. There are three things you need in order to use the system:

1. Access to a Touch-Tone telephone.
2. Your EFT card number.
3. Your password or personal identification number (PIN).

ACCOUNTING RECORDS

As an office support employee you are not expected to have an extensive knowledge of accounting, but you should be familiar with some accounting records. Possibly you will be expected to keep simple records, such as petty cash accounts, and to type certain financial statements.

Petty Cash Record. In every office there are minor bills which are paid in cash. For example, emergency office supplies or a small quantity of

postage stamps may be needed. In order to provide for such expenses, a fund called a *petty cash fund* is set up. An office worker or a secretary is generally in charge of this fund. The fund is usually small—$50 to $100. A check is written for the initial amount of the fund, and the office worker or secretary keeps the money. Each time a payment is made from the petty cash fund, a voucher or a receipt, similar to the one shown in Illustration 11-9, is prepared.

Illustration 11-9. Petty Cash Voucher

When the money in the petty cash fund gets low, the fund must be replenished. The following steps are standard procedure in replenishing a petty cash fund:

1. Total the amount spent according to the vouchers and any other receipts.
2. Count the cash on hand.
3. Add the cash amount to the total amount spent. The answer should equal the original amount of the fund.
4. Prepare or request a check for replenishing the fund. The amount of the check will equal the expenditures. Usually the check or check request must be supported by the vouchers and receipts.
5. Cash the check and add the money to the petty cash fund.

Balance Sheet. The balance sheet shows the condition of the business on a certain date—how much it owns and how much it owes. In order to interpret a balance sheet, you must have an understanding of the major sections. Notice the balance sheet that is shown in Illustration 11-10. It contains three main sections—assets, liabilities, and owner's equity.

The assets of a business are the properties or economic resources owned by the business. There are two major classifications of assets — current assets and plant and equipment. Current assets consist of cash and assets that are reasonably expected to be turned into cash or be sold or consumed within a short period, usually one year. Notice in Illustration 11-10 that merchandise inventory is listed under current assets. This inventory will be sold during the course of the business operations.

Plant and equipment assets are relatively long-lived assets that are held for use in the production or sale of other assets or services. Notice in Illustration 11-10 that land and buildings are listed under plant and equipment.

Another asset category that may be included on the balance sheet is long-term investments. Stocks, bonds, and promissory notes that will be held for more than one year appear under this classification.

```
                        GRIFFITH CORPORATION
                           Balance Sheet
                         December 31, 19--


                              Assets

        Current Assets
          Cash                                      $ 22,240
          Accounts Receivable          $ 41,500
            Less Allowance for Bad Debts   2,500      39,000
          Merchandise Inventory                     105,725
          Supplies                                    4,000
          Prepaid Insurance                           2,900
            Total Current Assets                              $173,865
        Plant and Equipment
          Office Equipment             $ 18,000
            Less Accumulated Depreciation  8,100   $  9,900
          Factory Equipment            $276,000
            Less Accumulated Depreciation 163,500   112,500
          Buildings                    $125,000
            Less Accumulated Depreciation  20,000   105,000
          Land                                       35,000
            Total Plant and Equipment                        $262,400
        Total Assets                                         $436,265


                            Liabilities

        Current Liabilities
          Accounts Payable                          $ 38,600
          Estimated Income Tax Payable                15,100
          Salaries and Wages Payable                   1,965
          Interest Payable                             1,250
            Total Current Liabilities               $ 56,915
        Long-Term Liabilities
          Mortgage Payable                          $ 50,000
          Notes Payable, Due December 31, 2000        22,500
            Total Long-Term Liabilities               72,500
        Total Liabilities                                    $129,415


                          Owner's Equity

        Common Stock                                $150,000
        Retained Earnings                            156,850
          Total Owner's Equity                               306,850

        Total Liabilities and Owner's Equity                 $436,265
```

Illustration 11-10. Balance Sheet

Liabilities are the debts of the business. Current liabilities are debts that must be paid within a year. Long-term liabilities are debts that are not due and payable for a comparatively long period, usually more than one year. Common long-term liability items are mortgages payable, bonds payable, and notes payable.

The owner's equity or capital section of the balance sheet shows the interest of the owner or owners of a business in its assets. From this section you can tell if the business is owned by one person, a partnership, or a corporation. Notice on the illustration that common stock and retained earnings are listed under the owner's equity section. This business is a corporation. The investment of the stockholders (owner's equity) is shown in the common stock. The amount of past earnings that have not been distributed to the owners is shown in the retained earnings.

If the business were operating as a partnership, the owner's equity section of the balance sheet might appear as follows:

H. H. Edwards, Capital	$ 58,000
J. R. Herrera, Capital	100,000
S. R. McCurdy, Capital	25,000
Total Capital	$183,000

Income Statement. Another financial statement that reflects the financial picture of the business is the income statement. The income statement covers the activities of a business for a certain period of time. It shows the total amount of money earned and the total amount of the expenses involved in earning the money. Illustration 11-11 gives a typical income statement. This income statement covers one year. Notice the heading indicates the period of time covered.

GRIFFITH CORPORATION
Income Statement
For Year Ended December 31, 19--

Sales			$415,100
Cost of Goods Sold			
Merchandise Inventory, January 1		$ 38,500	
Purchases		294,675	
Merchandise Available for Sale		$333,175	
Less Inventory, December 31		51,000	
Cost of Goods Sold			282,175
Gross Profit on Sales			$132,925
Operating Expenses			
Selling Expenses			
Sales Salaries and Commissions	$28,575		
Advertising Expense	19,300		
Miscellaneous Selling Expense	2,500		
Total Selling Expenses		$ 50,375	
General Expenses			
Officers' Salaries	$23,060		
Office Salaries	8,300		
Depreciation, Office Equipment	1,800		
Insurance	2,050		
Utilities	2,790		
Total General Expenses		38,000	
Total Operating Expenses			88,375
Net Income from Operations			$ 44,550
Other Expenses			
Interest Expense			5,000
Net Income before Estimated Income Tax			$ 39,550
Estimated Income Tax			15,100
Net Income after Income Tax			$ 24,450

Illustration 11-11. Income Statement

The first section of the income statement is the income section. This section shows the total amount of sales the company has made and the cost of the merchandise that was sold. The difference between these two items is the gross profit on sales. If there were no other expenses in connection with the sales, the gross profit would be the amount of net income earned by the business. However, additional expenses are incurred in the operation of a business. For example, the employees must be paid and insurance and utilities must be paid. Notice under operating expenses, these costs are itemized. The total amount of operating expenses is deducted from the gross profit on sales to arrive at the net income from operations. Any other income or expenses are computed and the net income is obtained.

Preparing Financial Statements. If you are asked to prepare financial statements, you should follow the form previously used in the organization. Since financial statements involve figures, you must be particularly cautious when preparing them. The statements must be carefully proofread. It is a good idea for you to get someone else to read the copy aloud to you while you check from the original material. It is also a good idea to check the calculations on a calculator.

PAYROLL RECORDS

An understanding of the payroll records and reports that are required by law is essential— not only for the person who works in the payroll department but for every individual who receives a paycheck. If you work in the payroll department, you must be familiar with these records and reports in order to perform your job. If you receive a paycheck, you need to be familiar with the payroll laws in order to understand the deductions that will be taken from your gross earnings each pay period. The laws and acts that relate to payroll are the Federal Insurance Contribution Act (social security), the Fair Labor Standards Act, income tax laws, and federal and state unemployment compensation acts.

Federal Income Tax. Most employers are required to withhold for federal income tax purposes amounts that are determined by a formula or tax tables. Amounts vary depending on the salary and the number of tax exemptions claimed by the employee. Each employee must fill out a copy of Form W-4, which shows the number of exemptions. A Form W-4 is shown in Illustration 11-12. The amount of income taxes withheld by employers is paid quarterly or

--------------------- Cut here and give the certificate to your employer. Keep the top portion for your records. ---------------------

Form **W-4A** Department of the Treasury Internal Revenue Service	**Employee's Withholding Allowance Certificate** ▶ For Privacy Act and Paperwork Reduction Act Notice, see reverse.	OMB No. 1545-0010 **1987**

1 Type or print your full name *Amelia Lee Alvarez*	2 Your social security number *123-45-6789*

Home address (number and street or rural route) *1311 Conflans Avenue*	3 Marital Status	☒ Single ☐ Married ☐ Married, but withhold at higher Single rate
City or town, state, and ZIP code *Dallas, TX 75211-1135*		**Note:** If married, but legally separated, or spouse is a nonresident alien, check the Single box.

4 Total number of allowances you are claiming (from line G above, or from the Worksheets on back if they apply) . . .	4	*1*
5 Additional amount, if any, you want deducted from each pay	5	$

6 I claim exemption from withholding because (check boxes below that apply):
a   ☐ Last year I did not owe any Federal income tax and had a right to a full refund of **ALL** income tax withheld, **AND**
b   ☐ This year I do not expect to owe any Federal income tax and expect to have a right to a full refund of **ALL** income tax withheld. If both a and b apply, enter the year effective and "EXEMPT" here . . . . ▶   Year 19
c   Are you a full-time student? . . . . ☐Yes ☐No

Under penalties of perjury, I certify that I am entitled to the number of withholding allowances claimed on this certificate or, if claiming exemption from withholding, that I am entitled to claim the exempt status.
Employee's signature ▶ *Amelia Lee Alvarez*   Date ▶ *January 5* , 1987

7 Employer's name and address (Employer: Complete 7, 8, and 9 only if sending to IRS)	8 Office code	9 Employer identification number

Illustration 11-12. W-4 Form

monthly to the District Director of Internal Revenue when the FICA (Federal Insurance Contribution Act) taxes are paid.

Federal Insurance Contribution Act (Social Security).

Social security provides income upon retirement, benefits for survivors in the event of the employee's death, and hospital and medical insurance (Medicare) for persons 65 years of age or older. In order to pay for the benefits which you collect upon retirement, both you and your employer contribute an equal amount of money each pay period to the federal government. The government accumulates the money in an account and pays you the benefits when you retire or pays benefits to your survivors in the event of your death.

Unemployment Compensation Tax.

This tax provides some relief to those who become unemployed as a result of economic forces outside their control. To finance the program, all employers covered by the law are subject to a federal and state tax. The state employment rate and the wage base subject to the tax vary from state to state. Provision is made for employers with a favorable record of employment to pay a low rate; employers who have an unfavorable record of employment pay a high rate. However, the federal tax is uniformly calculated at a rate of .8 percent on a base of $7,000 for all employers.

Fair Labor Standards Act.

The Fair Labor Standards Act of 1938, better known as the Wages and Hours Law, requires that businesses engaged in interstate commerce keep a record of hours worked and pay a minimum hourly wage. In addition, the law requires that certain employees be paid at a rate of at least 50 percent greater than the regular hourly rate for all time worked in excess of 40 hours during a workweek. Persons in administrative or executive positions are not governed by the law, however. While the Wages and Hours Law does not require any reports of a business showing hours worked, examiners may inspect the business records to determine whether the employer is meeting the requirements of the law.

Other Deductions.

There are many other deductions that may be made from wages. Com-

mon examples are local or state income taxes, union dues, charitable contributions, savings bonds, group insurance, and hospitalization. An example of a payroll check with a list of deductions is shown in Illustration 11-13.

					No. 324

RJ COMPUTER CORPORATION

32-56
3110

February 15   19 --

PAY TO THE ORDER OF   Amelia L. Alvarez $ 395.85

(For Classroom Use Only)

Three hundred ninety-five and 85/100------------------------ DOLLARS

BANK OF THE SOUTH
Dallas, TX 75211-1135

RJ COMPUTER CORPORATION

James Rutherford

⑆311009990⑆ ⑆130⑆456⑆⑆7⑆

STATEMENT OF EMPLOYEE EARNINGS AND PAYROLL DEDUCTIONS

RJ COMPUTER CORPORATION

PERIOD ENDING	HOURS	EARNINGS REGULAR	OVERTIME	TOTAL EARNINGS	FEDERAL INCOME TAX	FICA TAX	HOSP. INS	OTHER	TOTAL DEDUC- TIONS	NET PAY
2/15/--	90 1/2	484.00	20.63	504.63	61.50	30.28	12.00	5.00	108.78	395.85
YEAR-TO-DATE TOTALS		1408.00	20.63	1428.63	169.30	85.72	36.00	15.00	306.02	1122.61

Illustration 11-13. Payroll Check

The amount of money that you and your employer pay is based on a percent of your salary. This percent has risen steadily for the last several years. The base on which the tax is levied has also increased. Table 11-1 gives these rates for a five-year period. The base means the total amount of your salary that is used in figuring the FICA tax. For example, assume you made $50,000 in 1986. The base for 1986 was $42,000; you would not pay the tax on $8,000 (the difference between $50,000 and $42,000). Now assume that you made $30,000 in 1986. You would pay the tax on the total ($30,000) since you made less than the base figure of $42,000 (1986).

Table 11-1. FICA Tax Rate for 1986–1990

FICA Tax Rates

Year	Employer	Employee	Base
1986	7.15 percent	7.15 percent	$42,000
1987	7.15 percent	7.15 percent	43,800
1988	7.51 percent	7.51 percent	*
1989	7.51 percent	7.51 percent	*
1990	7.65 percent	7.65 percent	*

*Automatic cost-of-living adjustment
**1988–1990 percentages are projected figures.

All employees who work in occupations covered by the provisions of the Social Security Act must have an account number. To obtain an account number, you must file an application with your local social security office. You will receive a card stamped with your account number. If you lose your card, you may apply for a duplicate.

EXPENSE REPORTS

With the amount of travel that most executives do today, the office worker needs to frequently prepare expense reports. Companies reimburse the executive for expenses in two ways. Some companies provide the executive in advance with money for travel. Other companies do not reimburse the executive until after the trip is completed. In either case, the executive must submit details of the trip expenditures on an expense report form.

As an office worker, your responsibility is to prepare the expense report. Most companies require that receipts be submitted for such items as air fare, hotel bills, registrations, and car rentals. Usually no receipts are required for meals, tips, and taxi fares. However, some companies limit the amount of money that can be charged for meals. Mileage for use of personal automobile is usually reimbursed at the rate established by the Internal Revenue Service. When you prepare the expense report, you should check to see that all necessary receipts are attached, that the correct amounts are given on the expense report, that the form is filled out properly, and that the total amounts are computed correctly. See Illustration 11-14.

ENTER ONLY ONE AMOUNT PER LINE, PER DAY.

RJ Computer Corporation							WEEKLY EXPENSE REPORT		
NAME Jack Navarate	SAVE NO	ENDING SPEEDOMETER	CHANGED DRIVER'S LISCENSE NO					TR NO S	
WEEK ENDING	SATURDAY November 19	SUNDAY	MONDAY	TUESDAY	WEDNESDAY	THURSDAY	FRIDAY	SATURDAY	TOTALS
PERSONAL MOTEL OR HOTEL	Bent Tree Inn								
CITY Chicago									
STATE Illinois									
ROOM CHARGE (ATTACH RECEIPT)	11	70 00	70 00						140 00
BREAKFAST		5 00	4 00	5 25					
LUNCH		8 25	8 50	8 75					
DINNER		12 00	15 00	13 00					
TOTAL MEALS →	12	25 25	27 50	27 00					79 75
OTHER PERSONAL	13								
COMPANY OWNED AUTOMOBILE GAS-OIL	14								
OTHER OPERATING (INCLUDE PARKING TOLLS, TAXES, AND FEES)	15	8 00	6 00						14 00
PARTS AND REPAIRS	16								
MISCELLANEOUS (EXPLAIN · ATTACH RECEIPT IF OVER $25.00) ENTERTAINMENT	17								
OTHER TRANSPORTATION (AIR FARE, CAR RENTAL)	18	362 71							362 71
MISC. OTHER (EXPLAIN · ATTACH RECEIPT IF OVER $25.00)	19								
TOTAL FOR DAY		465 96	103 50	27 00					WEEK'S EXPENSES 596 46
EXPLANATION OF ENTERTAINMENT AND MISCELLANEOUS							INCREASE MY ADVANCE	21	
							DECREASE MY ADVANCE	22	
							ISSUE CHECK	23	596 46
						PLEASE SIGN	*Jack Navarate*		

Illustration 11-14. Expense Report Form

The following review will help you remember the important points of this chapter.

1. A check is an order in writing which directs the bank to pay cash from the depositor's account.

2. A voucher check is a check with a detachable portion on which is written the purpose of the check.

3. When writing a check, the check stub should be filled out first. Then the amount should be written twice on the check. The figures should be placed as close as possible to the printed dollar sign so that no additional figures can be inserted. When writing the amount of the check in words, the words should be started as far to the left as possible in the space provided. No erasures or changes should be made on the check.

4. When a checking account is opened at a bank, the bank keeps a record of the signatures of persons who are permitted to write checks on the account. This record is called a signature card.

5. A blank endorsement requires only the signature of the payee.

6. A full endorsement transfers ownership to a definite person or firm to whose order the instrument is made payable.

7. A restrictive endorsement transfers the ownership of a negotiable instrument for a specific purpose.

8. Checks may be listed on a deposit slip by the name of the bank (if the bank is local), by the city (if the bank is out of town), or by the ABA transit number on the check.

9. Magnetic ink characters are preprinted on checks and deposit slips to aid in the electronic processing of these documents.

10. Many banks and savings and loan insitutions offer interest-bearing checking accounts. Interest is paid on the average daily balance of the account.

11. Balancing a bank statement with a checkbook balance is called reconciling the bank statement.

12. Payment may be stopped on a check if it has not yet cleared the bank on which it was drawn.

13. A cashier's check can be purchased by giving the bank cash or a personal check for the amount of money desired plus a small charge for the service. A cashier's check is drawn on the bank's own funds.

14. The check that a bank uses to draw on its deposits in another bank is known as a bank draft.

15. A bank money order is usually sold to people who wish to send money through the mail.

16. Traveler's checks may be used all over the world. They allow a person to pay for traveling expenses without carrying large sums of cash.

17. Safe-deposit boxes are available at banks for the convenience of persons and businesses that wish to store articles of value or important papers for safekeeping.

18. Electronic technology has revolutionized the banking industry, and it is projected that additional electronic advances in the future will continue to influence banking. Electronic banking has made possible the automatic transfer of funds without the use of checks or other paper documents traditionally needed to complete a financial transaction.

19. To provide for small office expenses, a petty cash fund is set up. This fund usually contains about $50 to $100.

20. Financial statements prepared by a business include a balance sheet and an income statement.

21. The balance sheet shows how much a business owns and how much it owes.

22. An income statement gives the net income of a company for a particular period of time.

23. Payroll deductions from an employee's paycheck include federal income tax, social security, state income taxes, union dues, insurance, charitable contributions, savings bonds, and hospitalization.

24. The Fair Labor Standards Act requires that businesses engaged in interstate commerce keep a record of hours worked and pay a minimum hourly wage.

25. The office worker is responsible for gathering the information, checking receipts, and preparing the expense accounts of executives.

PROFESSIONAL FORUM

Martin Klug, one of the employees in the payroll department, has been ill for a week. You have been asked to help with the work of that department during his absence. During this time, you have seen the payroll records for several of the executives who work for RJ Computer Corporation.

On your coffee break, one of your best friends, Monica Helms, asks you if you have discovered what any of the executives make. You tell her that you have. She then asks you to tell her what one of the top executives makes. You have been a friend of Monica's for a long time, and you trust her. You definitely feel that if you give Monica the information she will not repeat it to anyone else in the firm. What should you do? Should you give Monica the salary information?

FOR YOUR UNDERSTANDING

1. Explain the procedures for reconciling a bank statement.
2. List and explain three types of special services that a bank offers.
3. How has electronic technology affected the banking industry?
4. Distinguish between a balance sheet and an income statement.
5. Identify two payroll deductions.
6. What are the office worker's responsibilities in regard to expense accounts?
7. Explain the advantages of a restrictive check endorsement.
8. Explain POS transfers.

OFFICE APPLICATIONS

On pages 349–367 are office applications that correlate with this chapter.

CHAPTER 12

Records Management

Vast amounts of information are generated daily in offices today. The information appears in various forms—as paper documents (letters and reports), microfilm or microfiche, or even electronic mail. Regardless of what form the information takes, it is essential that a system be established to store and retrieve the information when necessary. A common complaint of the business executive is, "Although the information volume has increased significantly in the past few years, our office efficiency has decreased. It is difficult and sometimes impossible to find essential information when needed." Studies have shown that the cost of finding one piece of information which has been misplaced is between $80 to $120.

As an office worker, it is essential that you understand the importance of records management and be able to apply effective records management procedures in the office. In this chapter you will learn the alphabetic filing rules, classification systems, and the basic filing procedures. You will also become familiar with micrographics and computerized filing systems.

GENERAL OBJECTIVES

Your general objectives for this chapter are to

1. Understand the nature of records and records systems.

2. Become familiar with careers available in records management.

3. Identify and use the basic classification systems.

4. Learn and apply the basic alphabetic filing rules.

5. Become familiar with filing methods.

6. Become familiar with supplies and equipment used in records management.

7. Become familiar with micrographics and automated filing methods.

RECORDS DEFINED

A *record* is any type of recorded information whether that information be recorded in letter form, book form, report form, as a photograph, as a blueprint, or as a map. Records contain information about an organization—its functions, policies, procedures, decisions, and operations. The record that we traditionally expect in the office is in paper form. And, although for a number of years the concept of "the paperless society" has been possible from a technical standpoint, paper documents continue to be one of the major forms for accumulating information. However, records also can take the form of microfilm or microfiche, a hard disk, or a floppy diskette. Whatever the form, any recorded information constitutes a record.

In order for a records system to function there must be information, equipment, money, and people. Information is generated by many sources and may appear, as mentioned earlier, on a piece of paper or on a magnetic form. Equipment in a records system includes all of the hardware used in processing the records. Money provides the resources for planning and operating the system. People include the necessary personnel to get the right record to the right person at the lowest cost.

RECORDS MANAGEMENT CAREERS

Records management is the systematic control of records from the creation of the record to its final disposition. If you work in a small office, you may have the total responsibility for preparing the correspondence and carrying it through the records management cycle from distribution to storage, retrieval, and final disposition. If you work in a large office, there may be a centralized records management department which files records, determines retention schedules, makes decisions on equipment, and disposes of records. Your responsibilities for records management in such a company will probably be limited to your immediate office needs—creating, storing, and retrieving information.

In large companies with records management departments, it is possible to pursue a full-time records management career. You might begin as a records center clerk and advance to a position such as records manager. Four records management positions are described here. If you are interested in pursuing a career in records management, you might review the literature provided by the Association of Records Managers and Administrators, Inc. (ARMA).

Records Clerk. The duties of a records clerk include sorting, indexing, filing, and retrieving records. The records clerk also searches and investigates information in files. The records clerk must possess mechanical aptitude, be able to analyze data for answers to questions, and relate well to people.

Records Analyst. The records analyst inventories records to determine type and volume, develops classification systems and procedures to be used in storing records, and evaluates and recommends equipment and layout for active records. The records analyst must relate well to people and have analytical skills.

Records Supervisor. The records supervisor maintains records systems and procedures, develops efficient and economical methods of records maintenance, and selects and supervises staff. The records supervisor must work effectively with all levels of personnel and have good organizational and supervisory skills.

Micrographics Supervisor. The micrographics supervisor operates a micrographics program. (Micrographics is a term which refers to the procedures for creating, using, and storing records on film). He or she works closely with records analysts and other corporate members in the development of micrographics applications and trains micrographics technicians. The micrographics supervisor must have good organizational and analytical skills and must be able to translate micrographics system specifications into work procedures.

CLASSIFICATION SYSTEMS

Records managers do not always agree on the classification systems of records. Some managers categorize the systems into two—alphabetic and numeric. Other managers add a third method called the alphanumeric and others add subject, geographic, and chronologic. In this chapter, three classification systems will be used: (1) alphabetic with name, subject, and geographic order; (2) numeric; and (3) chronologic.

Alphabetic Classification. The alphabetic classification uses letters of the alphabet to determine the order in which the names of people and companies are filed. The ARMA (Association of Records Managers and Administrators) rules are used in this text; these rules are presented in Appendix H. There are three primary types of ordering within an alphabetic classification system: (1) by name, (2) by subject, and (3) by geographic location.

Name Ordering. When name ordering is used, records are filed by the names of people, organizations, agencies, and businesses. This classification is one of the most commonly used and is found in one form or other in almost every office. With name ordering, the name of the company, the person, or the organization addressed determines the filing order of outgoing correspondence. The name of the company, the individual, or the organization writing the letter determines the filing order of incoming correspondence. A name ordering file is shown in Illustration 12-1. Correspondence is filed according to the ARMA alphabetic filing rules.

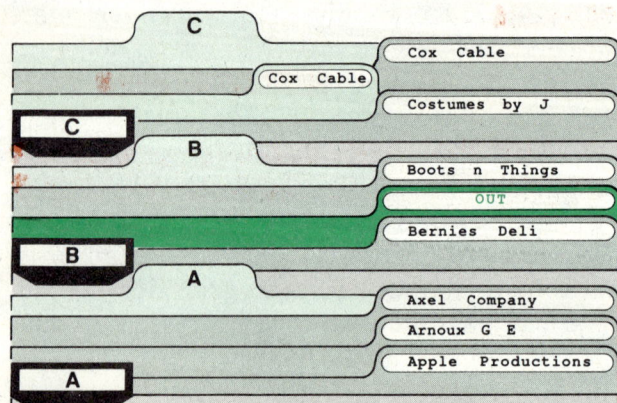

Illustration 12-1. Alphabetic Name Arrangement

Alphabetic name ordering has the following advantages:

1. It is a direct system. There is no need to refer to anything except the file itself to find the name.
2. The dictionary order of arrangement is simple to understand.
3. Misfiling is easily checked by alphabetic sequence.
4. It is less costly to operate than other filing methods.

5. Only one sorting is required.
6. Papers relating to one correspondent are filed in the same location.

Some disadvantages of the alphabetic name classification are as follows:

1. Misfiling may result when rules are not followed.
2. Similarly spelled names may cause confusion when filed under the alphabetic method.
3. Related records may be filed in more than one place.
4. Expansion may create problems, especially if the expansion takes place in one section of the file where there is no room remaining in that particular section for the insertion of more guides and folders.
5. Excessive cross-referencing can congest the files.
6. Confidentiality of the files cannot be maintained since the file folders bearing names are instantly seen by anyone who happens to glance at a folder.

Subject Ordering. With subject order, correspondence is filed according to the subject of the material. Although subject order is useful and necessary in certain situations, it is the most difficult and costly method of classification to maintain. Each paper must be read completely to determine the subject. And it is a difficult order to control since one person may read a piece of correspondence and determine that the subject is one thing, and another person may read it and decide that the subject is something entirely different. For example, one person classifying records concerning personnel grievances may determine that the subject is "grievances," while another person may determine that the subject is "personnel—grievances."

A necessary part of a subject file is an index. The index is a list of all subjects under which a piece of correspondence may be filed. Without an index, it is almost impossible for the subject filing method to function satisfactorily. The list should be kept up to date as new subjects are added and old ones eliminated. When new subjects are added, the index provides guidance to avoid the duplication of subjects. The index may be kept on standard sheets of paper and filed in a notebook or on index cards and filed in a card file box. A subject list kept on sheets of paper provides an easier way to see at a glance which subjects exist in the file than does a card index. When subjects are added to the list, however, the sheets must be reworked and updated. With a card index, a card indicating the new subject is simply inserted in the index. A subject index is shown in Illustration 12-2.

```
              SUBJECT INDEX

        Accounting
           Budget
           Financial Statements
           Invoices

        Advertising
           Agencies
           Newspaper
           Radio
           Television

        Committees
           Staff Development
           United Way

        Personnel
           Developmental Leave
           Grievances
           Salaries
           Vacations
```

Illustration 12-2. Subject Index

The alphabetic subject order has the following advantages:

1. Correspondence about one subject is grouped together.
2. The system can be expanded easily by adding subdivisions.

Some disadvantages of the subject order are as follows:

1. It is difficult to classify records by subject.
2. Liberal cross-referencing is necessary since one piece of correspondence may contain several subjects.
3. The system does not satisfactorily provide for miscellaneous records.
4. It is necessary to keep an index of subject headings contained in the file.
5. It is the most expensive method to maintain since it requires very experienced file clerks.

6. Preparation of materials for the subject file takes longer than any of the other methods, since each piece of correspondence must be thoroughly and carefully read.

Geographic Ordering. Geographic ordering is a file arrangement in which related records are grouped by place or location. The main divisions may be states, counties, cities, sales territories, etc. The breakdown into geographic divisions and subdivisions must, of course, fit the type of business, its organization, and its need for specific kinds of information. Geographic files are particularly appropriate for sales records filed by location. For example, the guides used may indicate the state of the sales. The folders may then be arranged by the city or town within the state and finally alphabetically by individuals or companies within the city. If there are several folders for one particular city, special guides may be inserted to show an alphabetic breakdown within the city. Geographic ordering is shown in Illustration 12-3.

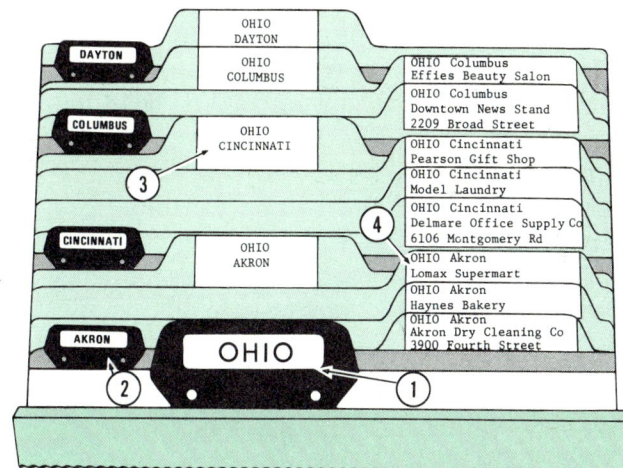

Illustration 12-3. Geographic Arrangement

The advantages of geographic ordering are as follows:

1. It provides for grouping of records by location.
2. The volume of correspondence within any given geographic area can be seen by glancing at the files.
3. It allows for direct filing if the location is known.

The disadvantages of geographic ordering are as follows:

1. Multiple sorting increases the possibility of error and is time-consuming.
2. The complex arrangement of guides and folders makes filing more difficult.
3. Reference to the card file is necessary if the location is not known.
4. It takes longer to set up than does the alphabetic name ordering method.

Numeric Classification. With the numeric classification of filing, guides and folders are assigned numbers and are arranged in numeric sequence. A numeric system has four parts (1) an accession book, (2) an alphabetic card index, (3) the main numeric file, and (4) a miscellaneous alphabetic file.

The alphabetic card index file is first consulted to determine the number assigned to the client or company. If it is a new client or company (one with which the office has not previously done business), the accession book must be consulted for the next available number. A page from an accession book is shown in Illustration 12-4. Once the number has been determined or assigned, the correspondence is placed in the appropriate number file. If there is little correspondence with a particular client or company, it may not be necessary to set up a separate file. In such a case, the correspondence is placed in the miscellaneous alphabetic file. A numeric classification system is shown in Illustration 12-5.

Number	Name	Page 105
		Date
504	Travel World	3/16/--
505	M E Baker	3/16/--
506	Browning Supply Co	3/17/--
507	Jan Chinook	3/17/--
508		

Illustration 12-4. Accession Book

The numeric classification system has the following advantages:

1. Expansion is unlimited.

2. It is confidential; a card file must be consulted before files on important papers can be located.
3. Once an index card is prepared and a number is assigned to a piece of correspondence, filing by number is quicker than filing alphabetically.
4. Misfiled folders are easily located because numbers out of place are easier to locate than misfiled alphabetic records.
5. All cross-references appear in the card file and do not congest the file folders or drawers.
6. A complete list of the names and addresses of correspondents is instantly available from the alphabetic card file.
7. In an office using the numeric classification system, orders, invoices, ledger accounts, and correspondence of one customer all bear the same number, making reference to them easy.

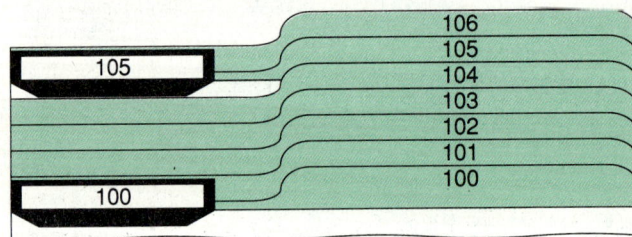

Illustration 12-5. Numeric Classification

Some disadvantages of the numeric classification system include the following:

1. It is an indirect method. The card file must be consulted before a paper can be filed.
2. More equipment is necessary; therefore, the cost is higher.
3. Numbers may be transposed without being detected.
4. Since two classifications of filing are involved—alphabetic name ordering and numeric—the disadvantages of the name ordering classification are also disadvantages of the numeric classification.
5. If the card file and the accession book are not kept carefully, one correspondent's papers might be assigned several numbers and filed in several folders.

6. As the numbers used become larger, it is harder to remember them and misfiling can easily result.

Numeric Classification Variations.
There are several variations of the basic numeric classification. Three of these variations are described here—terminal digit filing, middle digit filing, and skip numbering.

Terminal Digit Filing. Terminal digit filing is one variation of the straight numeric classification. In straight numeric filing, as the files increase, the numbers assigned become higher. However, when the numbers become several digits long, it becomes difficult to file papers. Terminal digit filing, which is designed to remedy this difficulty, is done by final digits. For example, assume you have a legal file for Case 389023. The last, or terminal, digits (23) would identify the drawer number. The second pair of digits (90) would indicate the number of the file guide, and the first two digits (38) would be the number of the file folder in the drawer.

In a large organization where numeric filing is used extensively, research shows that terminal digit filing saves up to 40 percent of the filing costs by assuring a uniform work load among office workers, better employee relations, fewer misfiled papers, and unlimited expansion. Terminal digit filing is shown in Illustration 12-6.

Middle Digit Filing. Another variation of the straight numeric classification is middle digit filing, which is similar to terminal digit filing with the exception that the two middle digits identify the drawer. The first two digits identify the guide number in the drawer; the final two digits identify the folder.

Skip Numbering. A third variation of the numeric classification is skip numbering. When expansion in a file is anticipated and an alphabetic sequence is desired in the permanent file as well as in the card file, the numbers assigned to names may be spaced quite far apart. For example, an alphabetic group of names may be assigned numbers with skips of 100 or more between the letters. All names beginning with

A may be assigned 100 sequence numbers; all names beginning with B may be assigned 200 sequence numbers; all names beginning with C may be assigned 300 sequence numbers, and so forth.

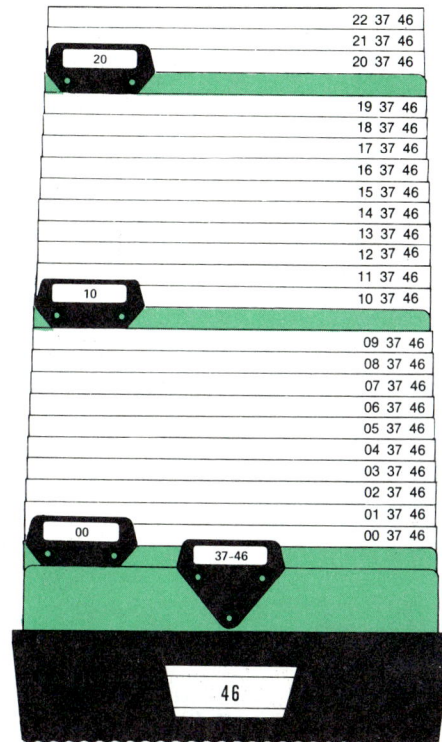

Illustration 12-6. Terminal Digit Filing

Chronologic Classification.
A chronologic classification system is an arrangement in which records are stored in date order. Chronologic arrangements have basic applications (1) as tickler files, (2) as transaction files, (3) as a supplement to another classification system, and (4) within individual files.

The term "tickler file" comes from the fact that the file is used to "tickle" your memory and remind you to take certain actions. For example, when something must be taken care of on a certain date, a card is prepared with the necessary information and placed in date or chronologic order. The file is checked each morning to see what must be done that day. The basic arrangement of a tickler file consists of a series of 12 guides with the names of the months printed on the tabs and 31 guides with the number 1 through 31 representing each day of the month printed on the tabs. The tickler file is generally kept on the office worker's desk. A tickler file is shown in Illustration 12-7.

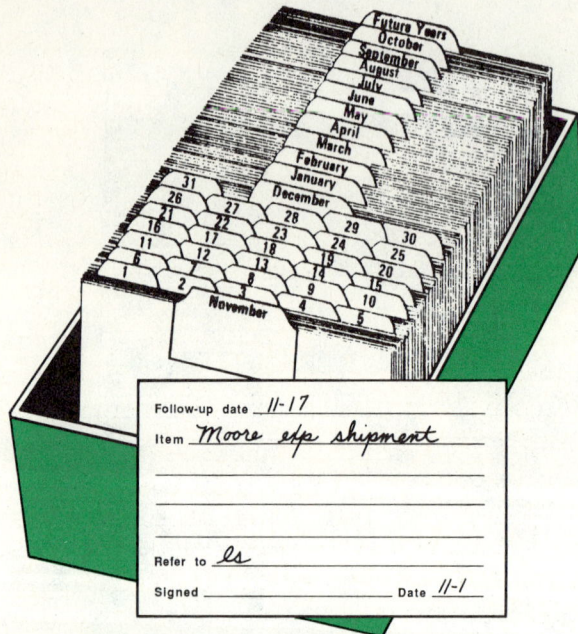

Illustration 12-7. Tickler File

Transaction files organize records by date. This file is appropriate for documenting transactions that occur on a day-to-day basis such as sales records, shipping records, and so forth. A chronologic file may also be used as a supplement to an alphabetic classification system. For example, you may keep a chronologic index with a subject ordering system. The index would contain the dates of the correspondence along with the name of the individual or company and the subject under which the correspondence is filed. Such a system allows you to find correspondence with limited information. Assume your employer asks you to locate a piece of correspondence addressed to Leroy Hampton, dated January 11. With a subject ordering system, it would be difficult to locate the correspondence given this information. By maintaining a chronologic index, you can quickly find the correspondence requested. A chronologic index is shown in Illustration 12-8.

The chronologic principle is followed with all filing classifications as papers are placed within folders. The top of each paper is at the left of the folder, and the paper with the most recent date is on top so that anyone who opens a folder can see immediately the latest piece of correspondence.

MANUAL FILING METHODS

Manual filing refers to the process of storing and retrieving records without the aid of mechanical or automated devices. When you place a letter in a folder and file it in a four-drawer file cabinet, you are using manual filing methods.

Select the Correct Classification. You have learned the basic classifications of filing correspondence and the advantages and disadvantages of each classification. If you are setting up a new filing system in an office, you should be familiar with these methods and be able to recommend the system most appropriate for the needs of the company. If you are working with already established files, you may be able to recommend a more efficient filing classification based on your knowledge.

Obtain the Correct Equipment and Supplies. Various types of filing equipment are available. Although you may have little to do with the selection of filing equipment, you should keep current about the technology so that you can recommend the latest equipment if given the opportunity.

In addition to filing equipment, you need to obtain the right supplies; i.e., guides, folders, labels, sorters, and miscellaneous items. As an office worker, you will usually be responsible for ordering these supplies; thus, you need to know what is available. You will learn more about equipment and supplies later in this chapter.

Prepare and File the Materials. Before records can be stored in a folder, they must be prepared for filing. Records must be inspected, indexed, coded, cross-referenced (if necessary), sorted, and filed. These steps are explained here.

Date	Name of Company or Individual	Subject Filed Under
1-11-88	Leroy Hampton	Advertising--Radio
2-10-88	Jonathan R Clark	Accounting--Budget
3-20-88	Patricia Irwin	Personnel--Grievance

Illustration 12-8. Chronologic Index

Inspect. Incoming correspondence must never be filed until its contents have been read by your employer. Therefore, before filing any incoming correspondence, be certain to inspect the correspondence for a release mark. This mark may be the executive's initials, a file stamp and the office worker's initials, a code or check mark, or some other agreed upon designation. Outgoing correspondence does not need a release mark since the original copy has been written by your employer or you. However, do not file the copy until the original has been signed, since changes may need to be made.

Index. The process of determining where a piece of correspondence is to be filed is called indexing. In alphabetic name ordering, indexing means determining the name that is to be used. On incoming correspondence, the most likely name to use is in the letterhead. On outgoing correspondence, the most likely name to use is in the address.

In alphabetic subject ordering, indexing means determining the most important subject discussed in the correspondence. If there are two subjects, the correspondence should be filed under one subject and cross-referenced under the other. In alphabetic geographic ordering, the location to be used must be determined. When using the numeric classification, the name and number to be used must be determined.

Code. Coding is the marking of the correspondence by the name, subject, location, or number that was determined in the process of indexing. The correspondence may be marked by underlining, circling, or checking. Coding is important since it saves time in the refiling process.

When a paper has been removed from the files and must be refiled, the office workers does not have to reread the correspondence.

Cross-Reference. For correspondence that can be filed under more than one name, a cross-reference sheet or card should be prepared and filed. For example, if a company that you have been doing business with changes its name from Heun and Miller Corporation to Carvell, Heun, and Miller Corporation, you will want to cross-reference the correspondence under Heun and Miller Corporation, at least until everyone in the office is aware that the name has been changed. Without cross-referencing, material from this company could be misplaced. A cross-reference card and a cross-reference sheet are presented in Illustration 12-9.

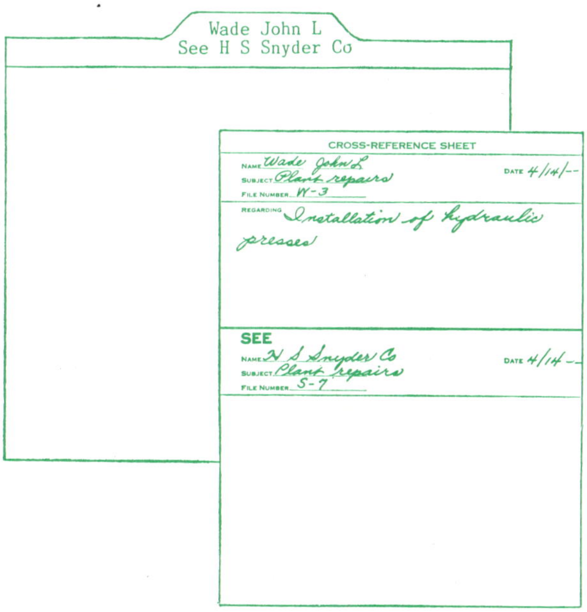

Illustration 12-9. Cross-Reference Card and Cross-Reference Sheet

Sort. Sorting is the arrangement of materials in the order in which they are to be filed. In sorting by hand, the materials should first be sorted into a few groups, then into the final arrangement. For example, when sorting materials alphabetically, they might be arranged into groups of A to C; D to H; I to M; N to S; and T to Z. Then each group would be sorted according to the alphabetic letters A, B, C, etc. The guide on each flap of a sorter can carry any filing designation desired. A sorter is shown in Illustration 12-10.

Illustration 12-10. Sorter

Prepare Labels. Consistency should be observed when preparing file labels. Some suggestions to follow are:

1. Start the caption three spaces from the left edge of the label.
2. Capitalize the entire key unit; capitalize only the first letter of the second, third, and any subsequent units.
3. Spell out all abbreviations.
4. Use the same style of labels on all folders. For example, if you decide to use labels with color strips, be consistent. If you decide to use colored labels, be consistent.

Files. The caption on the file folder should first be checked to be sure that it is the right one. Then the folder should be lifted part way out of the file drawer so that papers may be inserted

without wrinkling or crumpling. Place the top of the sheet face forward at the left edge of the file folder. If you have more than one paper for a folder, the most recent date is placed on top. In other words, the papers are filed chronologically within the folder. Small-sized items should be taped to a regular size sheet of paper or filed side-by-side so the folder will not bulge at one end. Large-sized items should be neatly folded. Material to be filed should always be placed *behind* the guides. When papers need to be fastened together, a stapler may be used. No more than 50 sheets should be placed in a single folder.

Retrieve the Materials. Once records have been filed, the next step is to be able to find them quickly and efficiently. The manual retrieval of records involves the office worker pulling the necessary materials from a file. However, many times material is needed for a period of time by someone in another department or office. If this is the case, some type of requisition, charge-out, and follow-up methods are necessary.

Requisition Forms. A requisition form may be filled out identifying the material borrowed, the name and location of the borrower, the date appearing on the material, the date borrowed, and the date to be returned to the files. This form is usually prepared in duplicate, with one copy kept in a tickler file and the other copy inserted in an out guide or folder. A requisition form is shown in Illustration 12-11.

Illustration 12-11. Requisition Form

Out Guide, Out Folder, and Out Card. The out guide is usually a pressboard guide with the word OUT printed on the tab. This guide is used to replace a folder which has been removed from the files. When an entire folder is taken from the files, papers for a particular correspondent cannot be filed until the folder has been returned. By using an out folder, materials accumulated for a particular correspondent can be filed while the mail folder is being used. An out card is used to replace a single piece of correspondence within a folder. An out folder and out card are shown in Illustration 12-12.

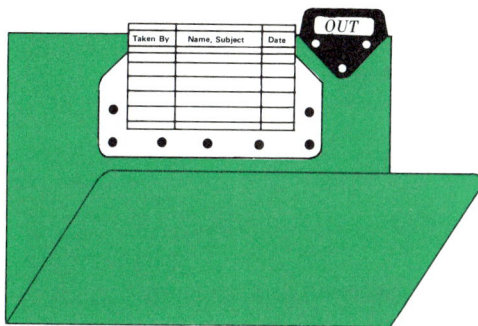

Illustration 12-12. Out Folder and Out Card

Follow-Up Procedures. Once material has been taken from the files, it is important that it be returned within a reasonable time. Follow-up records must be maintained in case materials are not returned when they should be. You learned earlier that a requisition form may be prepared in duplicate, one copy being placed in the out guide, the other in the tickler file. Such a system provides a quick and efficient method of tracking materials that have not been returned. If requisition forms are not used, then a slip of paper or card may be prepared with the necessary information and placed in the tickler file.

Misplaced Records. Although you may be very careful in your filing, papers do occasionally get misplaced. When they do, here are some tips to help you find the paper.

1. Look in the folder immediately in front of and immediately behind the correct folder.
2. Look between folders.
3. Check to see if the paper has slipped to the bottom of the file drawer.
4. Look in the miscellaneous folder.
5. Look for the second, third, or succeeding units of a name rather than for the key unit.
6. Check for misfiling due to misread letters; for example, C for G; K for H; and so forth.
7. Check for alternative spellings of words; for example, McDonald or MacDonald.
8. Look for a double letter instead of a single one.
9. Check for the transposition of numbers.
10. Look in a related subject file.
11. Look in the sorter.
12. Look on the executive's desk.

Transfer and Store the Materials. Not only is efficiency important when you file and find correspondence used in day-to-day business operations, but it is important to know the following: (1) how long to keep papers, (2) when to destroy papers, and (3) when to transfer papers to inactive files. Good records management means that unnecessary papers are destroyed and important papers are retained in an appropriately accessible manner. For example, personnel files that are to be kept indefinitely may be microfilmed to save space. Certain legal papers may require that they be kept in their hard-copy form. Other papers of limited importance may be destroyed.

Retention Categories. As an office worker, you usually will not decide how long to keep important papers. The legal counsel for a company is generally consulted as to the length of time that important documents should be retained. If your company is large, it may have identified a retention schedule for various types of papers. If your company does not have a records-retention schedule, you should check with your supervisor before making any decisions about how papers should be stored, transferred, and destroyed. To understand more about the way papers are classified, consider the following categories.

Vital Records. Vital records cannot be replaced and should never be destroyed. Vital records are essential to the effective and continued operation of the organization. Examples of vital records are corporate charters, property records, stock ledgers, and tax records. These records are generally stored in fireproof cabinets or in a safe.

Important Records. Important records such as inventory records, product designs, and financial records are necessary to the continuation of the business and are replaceable only with a considerable expenditure of time and money.

Useful Records. Useful records such as information on personnel, internal reports, and certain correspondence from outside companies are replaceable; but their loss may involve delay or inconvenience to the firm. Each particular business must determine which records it considers useful to its ongoing operation.

Nonessential Records. Certain records may be destroyed after their purpose has been fulfilled. Examples of nonessential records are interoffice memorandums, announcements, and general correspondence requiring no follow-up. Records that are to be destroyed may be burned or shredded if they are of a confidential nature. If they are not confidential, they may be sold to paper purchasers or donated to charitable organizations for recycling.

Retention Schedules. Retention schedules differ depending on the nature of the business; however, Table 12-1 presents an example of one retention schedule.

Transfer and Storage. Infrequently used records should be transferred to the inactive files and stored in inexpensive equipment. Two basic methods of transferring materials are the perpetual and the periodic transfer.

Table 12-1.

Records Retention Schedule

Records to Be Kept Permanently	Records to Be Kept for Two Years	Records to Be Destroyed After Approximately Six Months
Property Records	Financial Statements	General Correspondence
Tax Records	Accounts Receivable Records	Routine Incoming and Outgoing Correspondence on Completed Business
Licenses Issued to Company	Budgets	
Stockholder Records	Inventories	
Minutes of Board of Directors Meetings	Credit Files	
	Operating Reports	
	Deposit Records	

Perpetual Transfer. With the perpetual method, materials are continuously transferred from the active to the inactive files. This type of transfer system works well in offices where jobs are completed by units. For example, when a lawyer finishes a case, the file is complete and probably will not be needed again. Therefore, it can be transferred to the inactive files. Perpetual transfer does not work well where the business correspondence is on a continuous basis.

Periodic Transfer. The periodic transfer method is more satisfactory for most businesses. When using the periodic transfer method, records may be transferred periodically on a one-period, two-period, or maximum-minimum basis. In the one-period method, all correspondence is moved from the active files to the inactive files at least once a year. This system is easy to control, but frequent trips to the inactive files are usually necessary to refer to materials that are only a few months old.

With the two-period method, an inactive file and an active file are maintained side-by-side. During certain predetermined periods, materials from the inactive files are transferred to the records storage center or destroyed, and materials from the active files are transferred to the inactive drawers.

The maximum-minimum method of transfer is possibly the most useful method. Maximum and minimum refer to the age of the records at the time of transfer. For example, active materials (six months old or less, or whatever age is determined as active by the business) are kept in active files. Older materials (all materials for the year preceding the last six months) are transferred to the inactive files in a storage center. If the transfer date is determined to be June 30, all materials dated in the preceding year are transferred on June 30. Thus, transferred material varies in age at the time of transfer from 6 months (minimum age) to 18 months (maximum age).

Storage Equipment. Efforts should be made to keep the expense of storage center equipment to a minimum. Usually materials are transferred to the storage center in inexpensive cardboard file boxes, and inexpensive shelving is used to hold these boxes. Color-coded cardboard boxes are available for ease in finding materials which have been transferred to a storage center.

Disposal Control. Records that no longer have any use should be destroyed. Destroying records may simply mean dropping them into the wastebasket. However, important records should not be destroyed in this manner. Here are several suggestions for destroying important records.

1. Use a shredder which cuts the paper into confetti-like strips.
2. Use a baler which compacts the records into bundles for easy handling.
3. Deliver the papers to a recycling plant.

FILING SUPPLIES AND EQUIPMENT

Conventional filing supplies include such items as file folders, file guides, labels, tabs, and other miscellaneous materials. Basic storage equipment consists of manual files. These files are available in several styles, sizes, and shapes.

Filing Supplies. The most commonly used filing supplies are file folders, file guides, index cards, cross-reference sheets, out guides, gummed labels, transparent gummed tape, thumbers (rubber finger guards), colored pencils, and fasteners (preferably wire staples).

File Folders. A file folder is a container for correspondence or other materials; the manila folder is the most commonly used. The filing designation is typed on a gummed label that is attached to the tab (projection) at the top of the back part of the folder. Manila folders are made with tabs of various widths, such as straight cut, one-half cut, one-third cut, and one-fifth cut.

In addition to the manila folder, suspension folders are available. These folders are sometimes called *hanging folders* since they hang on metal rods that are attached to the sides of a file cabinet drawer. Separate cellophane tabs are available for these folders. These tabs may be placed in any position (first, second, third, etc.) in the pre-cut slots in the folder. Labels are typed and inserted in the tabs.

File Guides. A guide is usually made of heavy pressboard and is used to separate the file drawer into various sections. Each guide has a tab on which is printed a name, a number, or a letter representing a section of the file drawer in accordance with the filing plan. For example, the letter *A*, or the number 100, or the subject Sales Statistics may appear on the tab.

Guides with hollow tabs in which labels are inserted are also available. The filing notation is typed on a colored label which is inserted into the tab. The use of color can expedite the filing process by calling attention to a section, a subject, a frequently used name, or a particular folder position in the file drawer. Suspension folders with file guides are shown in Illustration 12-13.

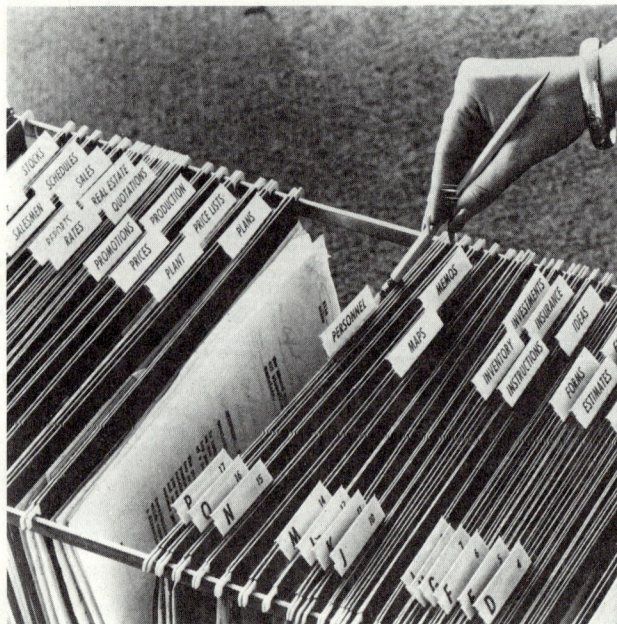

Esselte Pendaflex Corporation

Illustration 12-13. Suspension Folder With File Guides

File Folder Labels. File folder labels may be purchased in sheets or in continuous strips and in various sizes and colors. Just as color guides can be used to make the filing process more efficient, so can colored labels be used on file folders. In addition to speeding up the filing process, color can also make the process more accurate. Folders with colored labels may be located and replaced with greater ease and accuracy.

Metal Tabs. Metal tabs (tabs that are slipped over the edge of a folder) can be used to indicate different kinds of information, different subjects, etc. For example, in a sales manager's office, a blue metal tab on the monthly sales record might indicate that a particular salesperson is ahead of her or his quota; a red metal tab might indicate that the salesperson has fallen dangerously below his or her quota. In a credit department, an account that is 30 days past due might be indicated by a yellow tab, an account that is 60 days past due by a blue tab, and an account that is 90 days past due (and to which no additional credit should be extended) may be indicated by a red tab.

Filing Equipment. Numerous types of filing equipment are available. A few commonly used types of equipment are presented here.

Vertical Files. Vertical files, the most often used type of filing equipment, are available in one- to six-drawer units. They may be obtained in standard letter size or in legal size and in various colors. One standard-size file drawer holds from 4,500 to 5,000 pieces of filed material.

Lateral Files. The drawer of a lateral file rolls out sideways thereby exposing the entire contents of the drawer. Less aisle space is needed for a lateral file than for a vertical file since the depth of the lateral drawer is less than its width. A vertical file and a lateral file are shown in Illustration 12-14.

Open-Shelf Files. With open-shelf filing, folders are placed vertically on open shelves and no drawers are involved. More material may be accommodated per square foot of floor space since open-shelf files can extend all the way to the ceiling. Because of the openness of the files, they may not appear as neat as vertical files. See Illustration 12-15.

Mobile Files. The purpose of the mobile file is to bring the file unit to the operations area rather than forcing the employee to go to the file. Most mobile files are small single units which have rollers and can be easily pushed like carts. A mobile file is shown in Illustration 12-16 on page 194.

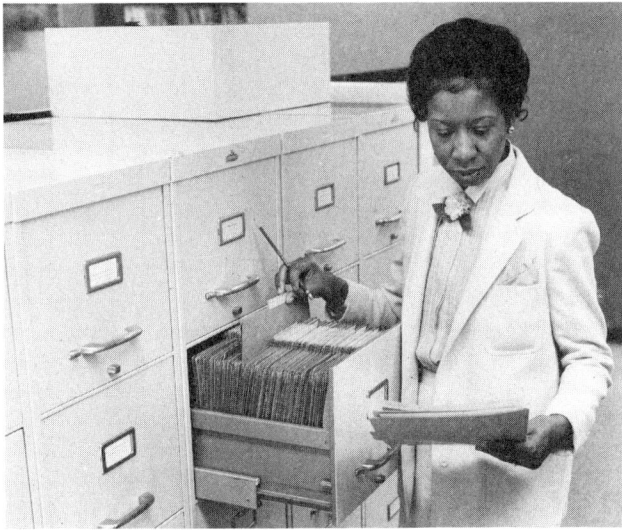

Illustration 12-14. Vertical File and Lateral File

Illustration 12-15. Open-Shelf File

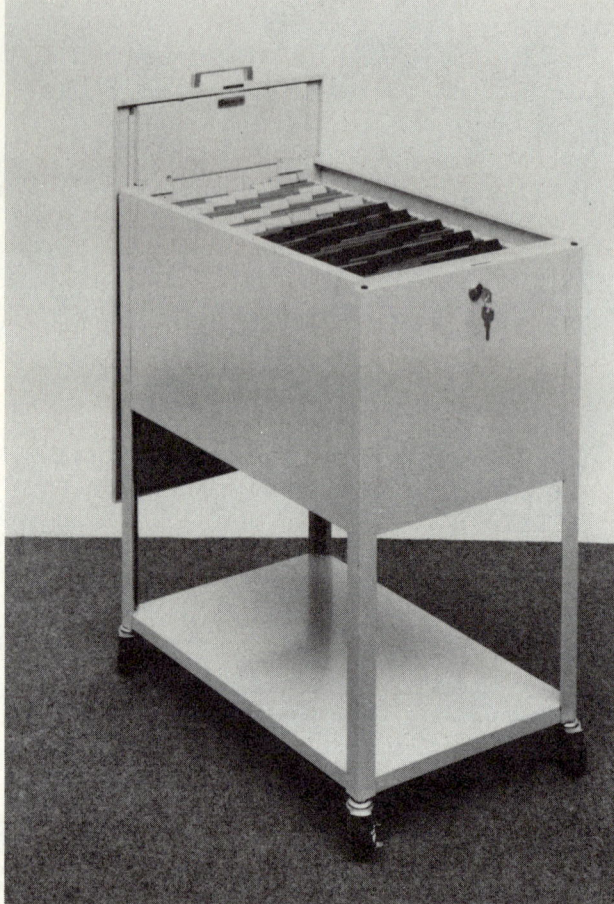

Borroughs Division of Lear Siegler, Inc.

Illustration 12-16. Mobile File

√ **Visible-Card Files.** Many types of visible-card files are used in business offices. The cards may be arranged in a tray as shown in Illustration 12-17 in the form of a book, or on a revolving wheel.

The cards are so arranged that one card overlaps another with the upper or lower edge of each card visible. A name, or some other designation, is visible on each card. An entire card can be examined by lifting the cards that overlap it. Visible cards may be easily removed from the trays for insertion into a machine, or manual recording may be accomplished without their removal. Visible-card files are very popular for personnel, sales, credit, accounting, purchases, and other departmental records that require quick reference for information and for record-making purposes.

Horizontal Files. Horizontal files are most commonly found in engineering or architec-

tural offices where maps and blueprints are filed. A horizontal file is much larger than a vertical file and allows large materials to lie flat.

Octavue-Postindex

Illustration 12-17. Visible-Card File

MECHANIZED (SEMI-AUTOMATED) FILING METHODS

The manual equipment presented previously is the least expensive and least complex filing equipment available. Mechanized equipment involves the use of machines and is relatively expensive. Therefore, careful consideration should be given to the needs of the business before determining that a mechanized system should be installed. Two types of mechanized equipment are presented here—movable-aisle systems and motorized shelf files.

Movable-aisle systems consist of modular units of regular files mounted on tracks constructed in the floor. Wheels or rails permit the individual units to be moved apart for access. Illustration 12-18 depicts a movable-aisle system.

With a motorized file system, an index register contains the file numbers of all folders within the system. The office worker depresses

Illustration 12-18. Movable-Aisle System

the file number needed on the keyboard of the file console. The shelf where the file is stored then rotates to a position in front of the operator. A motorized file is shown in Illustration 12-19.

Illustration 12-19. Motorized File

MICROGRAPHICS

With the advent of the computer, it is possible for companies to produce more and more records in less time than has been possible in the past. The growth of these records requires an increase in storage capacity. Records managers are using micrographics for reducing paper records to a very small size (microforms) and for saving storage space. Micrographics refers to the technology by which information can be reduced to a microform, stored conveniently, and then easily retrieved for reference and use. Microforms are available in several different formats. Two of the most common types are presented here—microfilm and microfiche.

Microfilm is a roll containing a series of frames or images much like a movie film. Paper records are photographed on film and the size of the document is reduced. Microfilm may be stored on reels or in cartridges, cassettes, or jackets. *Microfiche* is a sheet of film containing a series of images arranged in rows and columns on a card. Although it is available in several sizes, the 6-by-4-inch microfiche is considered the standard size sheet. Microfilm and microfiche are shown in Illustration 12-20.

To read a microform, you must place it in a projector called a reader or viewer. A microfilm cassette reader is shown in Illustration 12-21.

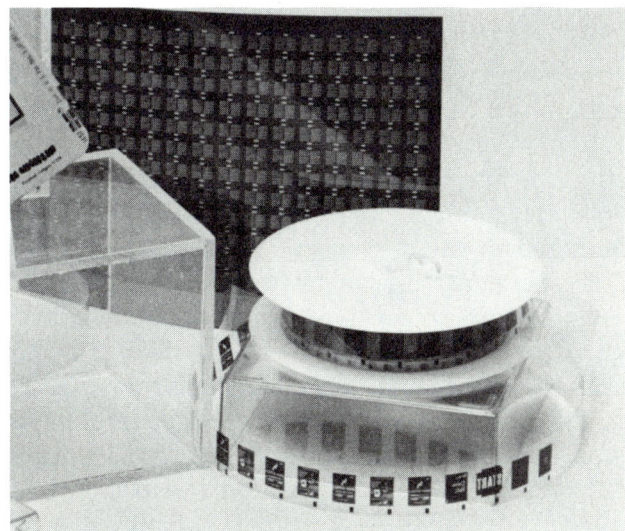

Illustration 12-20. Microforms

Delco Associates, Inc.

Illustration 12-21. Microfilm Cassette Reader

AUTOMATED FILING SYSTEMS

The increase in the number of records being produced today, along with the need for quick retrieval of these records, has resulted in automated filing systems being used more and more. And, it is anticipated that automated filing systems in the form of computers and computers combined with micrographics will be a direction of the future.

Computer Storage. Information may be captured and stored internally through keystrokes, through optical character recognition, or through computer input microfilm (CIM), which will be discussed later in this chapter. When information is stored internally, it is stored in the computer's memory. For example, with electronic mail, a piece of correspondence is stored in the memory of the computer. That correspondence is transmitted from the sender's computer to the receiver's computer and called up on the VDT. No paper copy is made unless the receiver wants one, and the correspondence is not transferred to external storage unless the receiver wants to keep it in that form. The correspondence is merely held in the computer's memory or "file box" until called for by the receiver and erased from the "file box" after it has been read.

However, most information that is stored temporarily in the computer's memory is transferred to some type of external media — usually a tape or a disk. Optical disks and laser technology are used in some document storage systems today, and it is expected that the use of optical disks will continue, perhaps even becoming an alternative to traditional microfilm systems. A system can store up to 60,000 letter-size documents on one optical disk. The equivalent of 83 four-drawer file cabinets can be stored in a space no larger than a breadbox. Documents can be filed in six seconds and retrieved in three seconds.

Indexing information on magnetic media is accomplished by using key words from the stored information. The index may be maintained on a disk or other magnetic form and can be viewed on a VDT. Once the file name has been determined through the index, the file number or key words are entered on the keyboard, and the information may be printed or viewed on the screen.

Consider this example of a budget file being maintained on disk. When the budget of a company is prepared, it is entered on the computer and transferred to a disk. When the budget needs to be reviewed, the disk is placed on the computer, the file name of the budget is called up, and the budget appears on the screen. When changes need to be made, these changes are made directly by keystroking and then transferred to the disk.

Another example of a computerized filing system is the maintenance of flight reservations. Airline personnel input information concerning flight numbers and dates. A record of how many people are on the flight and the space available is maintained on the file at all times. If a customer cancels a flight, this information is also fed into the files.

Computer and Micrographics Integration. The combination of micrographics and the computer has made the storage and retrieval of microforms a speedy, inexpensive, and efficient process. Two types of integration are presented here — computer output microfilm and computer input microfilm.

Computer Output Microfilm (COM). It is possible to produce or output a large amount of paper documents in a short period of time with the computer, but the storage of these paper documents is expensive. With COM, no paper documents are produced; instead, documents are produced on microfilm or microfiche. Once information is fed into the computer and stored on magnetic tape, needed documents can be translated into readable form and shown on a VDT. A microfilm camera photographs the displayed information and reduces it to micro-form size for later viewing on a microform reader or viewer.

Computer Input Microfilm (CIM). Computer input microfilm is the reverse of COM. Data on microfilm are converted into computer readable data for use in the computer. A CIM device simply converts information on microfilm into a form that the computer can read. With CIM, it becomes possible to use microfilm rather than magnetic tapes or disks as the long-term retention medium for data. Storage on microfilm is less expensive than storage on a tape or disk.

Computer Aided Retrieval (CAR). CAR systems are designed to solve two common problems encountered in records systems — the high expense and the difficulty of finding documents filed manually. Here is how CAR works. Documents are indexed by the entry of such data as the date, author, and subject into a computer. In retrieving documents, the user may request all documents written on a particular date, by a particular person, or dealing with a specific subject. The computer then gives the user a report of the number of items requested. The user has the option to narrow, broaden, or otherwise alter the search.

CAR can be operated on-line or off-line. With on-line CAR, the retrieval is connected to the computer. Several levels of assistance may be given to the operator, depending upon the computer program. With minimum computer assistance, the operator keys in information and the computer responds by displaying the roll of film that should be inserted. The operator then inserts the film, and the computer advances the film until it finds the information requested. With maximum assistance, the operator keys in the search information and the record image is displayed on the screen without further operator intervention.

Off-line CAR has indexing and retrieval as separate functions. Using the computer terminal, the operator keys in information to begin the search for the record. The location of the record is then displayed on the VDT, and the operator is responsible for finding the record.

Records Management Software. With the increased use of microcomputers in offices today and the projection that this use will continue to increase, numerous software packages have been developed and are continuing to be developed for records management. These software packages include records retention maintenance, request processing, vital records control, indexing (including keyword retrieval on primary, secondary, and tertiary classifications), automated destruction, record security procedures, space management, and printing of labels and tabs.

FOR YOUR REVIEW

The following review will help you remember the important points of this chapter.

1. Records management is the systematic control of records from the creation of the record to its final disposition.
2. Four types of positions available in records management are a records clerk, a records analyst, a records supervisor, and a micrographics supervisor.
3. The main classification systems are as follows: alphabetic classification by name, subject, and geographic location; numeric classification; and chronologic classification.

4. A numeric classification system has four parts: (1) an accession book, (2) an alphabetic card index, (3) the main numeric file, and (4) a miscellaneous alphabetic file.

5. Three variations of the numeric classification system are terminal digit filing, middle digit filing, and skip numbering.

6. Chronologic classification systems have four basic applications: (1) as tickler files, (2) as transaction files, (3) as a supplement to another classification system, and (4) within individual files.

7. Efficient filing is built upon an understanding of the basic filing rules. See Appendix H for a review of these rules.

8. When filing manually, the following steps should be taken:
   a. Inspect
   b. Index
   c. Code
   d. Cross-reference
   e. Sort
   f. Prepare labels
   g. File

9. When removing materials from the file, an out guide, out folder, or out card should be placed in the file from which the material is taken.

10. Follow-up records, in the form of a card placed in a tickler file, must be maintained in case materials are not returned at the appropriate time.

11. When papers are misplaced, several steps should be followed when looking for them; e.g., look in the folder immediately in front of and immediately behind the correct folder; look between folders; check to see if the paper has slipped to the bottom of the file drawer; and look on the executive's desk.

12. Managing records includes determining how long to keep the records as well as storing, transferring, and destroying records.

13. Records can be divided into four categories for retention purposes—vital records, important records, useful records, and nonessential records.

14. Retention schedules that indicate how long particular records are to be kept should be established by a business.

15. Records may be transferred through two basic methods—the perpetual method or the periodic transfer method. With the perpetual transfer, materials are continuously transferred from active to inactive files. With the periodic transfer method, records may be transferred on a one-period, two-period, or maximum-minimum basis.

16. Transferred records should be stored in inexpensive cardboard files.

17. Records that no longer have any use should be destroyed through shredding, baling, or delivering to a recycling plant.

18. Some manual filing supplies include file folders, file guides, file folder labels, and metal tabs.

19. Manual filing equipment includes vertical files, lateral files, open-shelf files, mobile files, visible-card files, and horizontal files.

20. Mechanized filing equipment, which is more expensive than manual equipment, includes movable-aisle systems and motorized shelf files.

21. Micrographics refers to the technology by which information can be reduced to a microform, stored conveniently, and then easily retrieved for reference and use.

22. Microforms are available in several different formats, with the most common formats being microfilm and microfiche. Microfilm is a roll containing a series of frames or images much like a movie film. Microfiche is a sheet of film containing a series of images arranged in rows and columns on a card.

23. Automated filing systems are being used more and more today. These systems utilize mainframe computers, microcomputers, and micrographics.

24. When a computer is used in filing, information is usually stored on some type of external media; i.e., tapes and disks. Optical disks and lasers are some of the newer technological advances in records management.

25. The combination of micrographics and the computer has made the storage and retrieval of microforms a speedy, inexpensive, and efficient process.

26. Computer output microfilm, computer input microfilm, and computer aided retrieval are all types of integration of micrographics and the computer. Computer output microfilm

uses the computer to aid in producing and reading microfilm. With computer input microfilm, information is read from microfilm into the computer, manipulated by the computer in some way if needed, and printed out or converted back to microfilm.

27. With computer aided retrieval (CAR), the computer is used to quickly retrieve documents filed on microfilm. CAR can be on-line or off-line. With on-line CAR, the retrieval is connected to the computer. According to the computer program, the operator may receive minimum or maximum assistance. With minimum assistance, the operator must go through several steps before the record is displayed. With maximum assistance, the operator keys in the search information and the record is displayed on the screen. Off-line CAR has indexing and retrieval as separate functions. The operator keys in the search information and then is responsible for finding the record.

28. Numerous records management software packages are now available for use on the microcomputer.

PROFESSIONAL FORUM

Your office job includes preparing statistical reports and filing. You work hard and fast to get out the reports as soon as possible. Your supervisor, Ms. Hardwick, is quite pleased with your work. She has told you that you get out the reports quicker than anyone else who has had the job. After you complete the reports, your work load is much lighter; and you are not quite as busy for about a week.

Another officer worker, Lisa Williams, never seems to get her work done. She does not like to file, so she puts off her filing for as long as possible. Several times when you have not been too busy she has made remarks to you indicating that she feels you should help her with her work. A few weeks ago, you did help her. You filed for three days and got all of her filing done. Since then she has not done any of her filing. You feel that if she would work harder, she could get her work done. You do not like her "little remarks" to you insinuating that you do nothing while she is busy. The tension is building between the two of you. You want to have a good working relationship with her. How should you handle the situation?

FOR YOUR UNDERSTANDING

1. Explain why records management is important.
2. List and describe the three filing classification systems. 181
3. Explain how abbreviations in personal and business names are treated in filing.
4. What does "inspect" mean in relation to filing, and why is it important to inspect a document before filing? 187

5. List and explain the four retention categories. 190
6. Define micrographics. 195
7. Describe two ways in which the computer and micrographics are integrated in records management. 197
8. Define computer aided retrieval. 197

OFFICE APPLICATIONS

On pages 368–375 are office applications that correlate with this chapter.

PART 5

SECURING THE RIGHT JOB

CHAPTER 13

Job Search

How do I go about finding the job I want? If this question is not an important one to you at present. it will become increasingly important as you finish your schooling and look for a job. The steps that you take in applying for a job, the job interview, and the follow-up of that interview are all areas in which you must plan carefully.

The job interview is a time when you must sell the interviewer on your abilities. What skills do you have that will be beneficial for the business? What personal traits do you have that will help the business? Remember, there are probably several other people applying for the same job. You may have excellent skills and work well with people; but unless you can *convince the interviewer* that your skills are good and that you are the right person for the job, you will not be hired. This chapter, then, is important to you in that it will help you to develop skills needed to apply for a job.

GENERAL OBJECTIVES

Your general objectives for this chapter are to

1. Consider the type of company where you would like to work.
2. Learn where to get information concerning job opportunities.

3. Write a letter of application.
4. Prepare a resumé.
5. Learn how to conduct yourself on a job interview.
6. Fill out an application form.
7. Write a follow-up letter.

DECIDING ON THE TYPE AND SIZE OF COMPANY

Before applying for a job, you should have some idea of the type of company in which you are interested. Would you like to work for a manufacturing industry, a service industry, a government agency, or an educational institution? What are your career goals? Do you plan to work for one year, five years, or twenty years? Would you like to move up in the company? All these questions are important considerations for you. If you plan to stay with the company for a number of years and would like to move up in the company, you should look for a company in which you would have opportunities for promotion. You would want to work for a company that is growing and has a good profit picture. Would you like to work in a small office or a large office? What are advantages and disadvantages of each?

The Small Office. The small office usually provides a more relaxed, family atmosphere. Because of the limited number of employees, the people usually know each other well. And, as an office employee in a small company, you will have a wide variety of duties. For example, your duties may include handling the mail, filing, preparing correspondence and reports, keeping a small set of books, answering the telephone, and receiving visitors. Since the company has fewer employees, the personnel policies of a small office are usually more general than those of a large office. This may mean that you have more freedom. You may be allowed to take a longer lunch hour or an occasional day off when the work load permits.

However, the small office has two possible disadvantages. The amount of money you can make may be limited. Also, you are usually restricted as to promotional opportunities. There simply may be no place to promote you no matter how qualified you are.

The Large Office. In a large office, your job will probably be more specialized. There are mail clerks to handle the processing and delivering of mail, switchboard operators to route calls, receptionists to receive visitors, file clerks to handle the bulk of the company's filing, etc. You may consider this specialization an advantage or disadvantage depending on your own personal goals.

A large office can provide more promotional opportunities simply because of the number of jobs available and the turnover of the people in these jobs. However, you must consider that along with the number of promotional opportunities available there is also more competition for each job. Your salary may be more in a large office due to the company making a greater percentage of profit, and large offices usually have more benefits than small offices. These benefits include such things as retirement plans, stock option plans, sick leave days, vacation policies, and hospitalization and life insurance plans.

FINDING JOB INFORMATION

One of the first things to do is to get all the information you can about job opportunities in your community or wherever you would like to work. These suggestions are helpful in getting the needed information:

1. Register and cooperate with your college placement department.
2. Talk with your friends and relatives.
3. Make personal visits to companies where you would like to work.
4. Read the want ads in newspapers.
5. Visit state employment agencies.
6. Contact private employment agencies.
7. Watch for civil service announcements.

Go to Your Placement Office. Many colleges maintain placement departments for the purpose of placing their graduates in positions. Your school may not have enough employment calls from employers to provide positions for all students, but on the whole, you will find that the officials of your school are well informed about employment opportunities in the community and are glad to help you obtain a position. They know the employers who are willing to take beginners, and they also know your qualifications and abilities.

You will undoubtedly have an opportunity to discuss the matter of employment with the placement director of your school some weeks before you graduate. You should seek his or her advice and help. The placement director will try to place you in a position where you will have the best opportunity for success.

Most schools take pride in their graduates, for a school is often judged by them and their success. Your school has spent much time and money maintaining contacts with business firms in the surrounding territory, showing them that the school is in a position to furnish competent office help, both with and without experience. This does not mean, however, that the school must take full responsibility for getting you a job. You, too, should be exploring all the other available sources of information concerning job opportunities.

Check With Your Friends and Relatives. When you are about ready to graduate and go to work, talk with your friends and relatives. You may learn of many employment opportunities through them since many vacancies in desirable positions never reach an employment agency or the classified advertisements in the newspapers. Many business vacancies are filled within the organization by friends of those already employed. Remember, though, that some firms will not employ relatives of employees. It is well for you to inquire whether such a policy might keep you from obtaining employment in an organization where you would like to work.

Visit Companies. If you are particularly interested in obtaining a position with a certain company or in a particular type of business, the *direct canvass* (sometimes called *cold canvass*) is often the most successful procedure. This is particularly true if you have a great deal of ability, an abundance of enthusiasm, and a gift for selling yourself. An employer may be so impressed with your qualifications and personality that you will be offered a job even though there is no actual vacancy. You are not asking a favor or begging for a job if you are capable. You expect to earn your salary and to be an asset to the company.

The difficulty of obtaining a job in this way is that you may find it impossible to obtain an interview with the person who is actually in charge of employment. Secretaries or receptionists are often directed to say "No" to anyone who calls in this manner. If possible, find out who is in charge of employment before you go to the firm so that you can ask for that person specifically. This can usually be done by telephone beforehand, without revealing your identity, by asking who is in charge of hiring people for office jobs.

Another way of canvassing a number of firms is to send out letters of inquiry or letters of application. A large number of companies can be contacted in this way, of course, but your letter must be superior. If you receive favorable answers, you will then find it much easier to secure an interview.

Read the Want Ads in Newspapers. This source of employment information can be helpful if you live where the community newspapers are large enough to carry classified ads. In most large cities, and in some smaller ones,

employers use advertisements to attract applicants. Some typical want ads are shown in Illustration 13-1.

GENERAL OFFICE
Stock brokerage firm needs responsible individual who is detail oriented and has a strong math aptitude. General office experience preferred. Keyboarding skills of 50 to 60 wpm needed. If interested, call Ms. Burtness for an appointment at 555-9350.

RECEPTIONIST
Downtown law firm seeks receptionist. Duties include phone, payroll, and insurance. Good benefits. Call 555-3861.

SECRETARY
The Dallas News is seeking a skilled secretary to become part of our exciting business. Interested candidates should have knowledge of computer systems and microcomputer-based word processing. Keyboarding skills must be a minimum of 60 wpm. Excellent oral and written communications skills required. If qualified, apply in person at *The Dallas News*, Houston and Main, Personnel Office, First Floor.

Illustration 13-1. Want Ads

Employment agencies also use want ads to advertise the positions they are trying to fill. While you are following personal leads, direct canvassing, and perhaps visiting employment agencies, watch the classified ads in the newspaper. These ads give an excellent review of the types of positions that are open at any time and sometimes provide information about the salaries offered and the qualifications required.

Register With State Employment Agencies. Most states operate employment agencies in connection with state unemployment compensation laws. An unemployed person who has worked previously can register with these offices and be referred to available jobs. If no jobs are available that match the person's qualifications, the person is eligible for unemployment compensation. A person who has never worked before can also register and be referred to jobs that are available. When registering with one of these agencies, ask to talk to the employment interviewer who is assigned to handle the kinds of jobs for which you are qualified.

Visit Private Employment Agencies.
There are many excellent private employment agencies that can help you get a position. Your college placement director or your business friends can name some of the reputable agencies in your community. You may also find them listed in the Yellow Pages of the local telephone directory. If you are seeking the services of private employment agencies, you should be interested mainly in those agencies that specialize in filling office vacancies.

These agencies charge a fee for finding a position. In many of the agencies, the fee is paid by the employer. However, in some of the agencies the employee must pay the fee. This fee is usually based on a certain percentage of the employee's salary for a given period of time.

Check for Civil Service Openings. Many people are employed by the city, state, and federal governments. Most of these jobs come under civil service and are secured on the basis of competitive examinations. Information about city and state civil service jobs may be obtained from state employment agencies and by calling the Office of Personnel Management, United States Government.

WRITING A LETTER OF APPLICATION

The letter of application is often the key to securing an interesting and challenging position that will give you economic security. As such, this letter may be one of the most important letters you will write. It is basically a sales letter because it tries to sell your services, skills, knowledge, and abilities. Prepare your letter thoughtfully, and rehearse what you plan to say as though you were making a sales presentation. The appearance, format, arrangement, and contents of the letter are extremely important in making a good impression and in ultimately obtaining your objective — an interview.

The Goals of a Letter of Application.
There are three basic goals of a letter of application. They are as follows:

Arouse Interest. You want to gain the interest of the potential employer without being cute or dull. Consider the following examples of poor beginnings:

> I can do it! I can have those letters flying from the word processor; I can make your company more productive.

> This letter is in reply to your ad which appeared in the *News*. I am interested in the job you have to offer.

The first example is too cute, and the writer used too many "I's." The second example is overused and dull. Instead, provide the employer with a brief statement of your qualifications. Let the reader know you are interested in the company and what you can do for the company, but don't oversell. Consider the following examples:

> The position you have advertised sounds both challenging and interesting. After finishing an Associate of Arts Degree in Office Occupations and working part time as an office employee while going to school, I believe I have the skills necessary to fill the job.

> Your employment announcement calls for an office worker who is interested in learning and has good office skills. My training at Cedar Ridge College for the last two years has provided me with these skills.

In both cases you let the prospective employer know that you are interested in performing for the company. You also let the person know briefly what skills you have.

Describe Your Abilities. The next paragraph of the letter should describe in more detail the abilities you have and should call attention to your enclosed *resumé* (also called a *data sheet* or *vita*).

> In May of this year, I will graduate from Cedar Ridge College. During my two years of school, I have taken courses in word processing, office machines, shorthand, keyboarding, and office procedures. My keyboarding skill is 70 words a minute and my shorthand skill is 100 words a minute. My resumé, which is enclosed, gives more details concerning my education and experience.

Request an Interview. Remember, the purpose of the letter is to get an interview. Therefore, you should ask for that interview, and you should ask directly. Here is an example.

> Please give me an opportunity to discuss my qualifications with you. My telephone number is 555-2041.

Letter-Writing Techniques. Here are some additional techniques which will assist you as you write your letter of application.

1. The letter should look impressive. It must be neat. It must be an originally prepared letter. Never use a copy—even a well-produced copy is unacceptable. Prepare your letter on a good grade of 8½" × 11" bond paper. Read the letter carefully for any spelling or grammatical errors. The letter must be free from strikeovers, smudges, messy corrections, wrinkles, or tears.
2. Keep the letter short. Put the details in the resume. Remember, the letter should attract the reader's eye and call attention to the resume.
3. Address the letter to a specific person. Never address an application letter "To Whom It May Concern." If you do not have a name, take the time to find out. Call the company and ask. Or ask the school placement office, your friend, or whoever told you about the job.
4. Use an acceptable letter style. Stay with a traditional letter style such as a block or modified block style. This is not the time to try one of the lesser used styles such as the simplified one. Some people are not familiar with this style and may assume it is incorrect. If you need to review letter styles, see pages 104–105.
5. Use the "you" approach. The "you" approach means that the writing is done from the reader's point of view. You want to discuss what you can do for the company, but from the perspective of what the company needs. Let the reader know that you understand the requirements of the position and that you have the qualifications and willingness necessary to do a good job for the company.
6. Be honest. Tell the reader what you can do, but do not exaggerate. After all, if you get the job, you will be expected to do what you said you could do. The letter of application is no time to be boastful.

A sample letter of application is shown in Illustration 13-2 on page 209.

PREPARING A RESUMÉ

The resumé is intended to relieve the application letter of many details regarding your qualifications. It provides a summary of your education and experience. Just as the letter of application is a sales letter, so the resumé is a piece of sales literature. It represents a very important product—YOU.

To a certain degree, a resumé reflects what is important in the changing business world. Thus, what is included in a resumé changes from time to time. Prior to the anti-discrimination legislation of the 1960s and 1970s, almost all data sheets had a section labeled "Personal Data." This section included such things as age, marital status, number of children, height, weight, and hobbies. Our laws now state that it is illegal to discriminate on the basis of age, race, sex, etc. Therefore, most authorities recommend that personal items be left off the resumé. What the prospective employer needs to know is whether you have the qualifications for the job. However, although employers are limited by law on what they can ask you to provide, you can submit any data you wish on a resumé. If you feel that some of your personal characteristics will assist you in getting the job, list them. You should analyze the job situation carefully and determine what is best for you in a given situation.

The Sections of a Resumé. As you have just learned, sections of a resumé may vary. There is no perfect model. Each individual needs to develop his or her own resumé. However, there are certain parts which are common to most resumés. These parts are presented here.

Career Objective. This section lets the reader know what your present and long-range career goals are.

> Career Objective: To achieve a position as a word processing operator in a law firm, with a long-range goal of being a word processing manager.

Education. In this section you should begin with your most recent education—list the school you attended last and the degree obtained (if applicable). Then list your other education in reverse chronological order. If you graduated many years ago, it is usually not necessary to list your high school. However, if you are a recent high school graduate, you should list it. It is wise to list the courses or programs that you have taken which would be helpful to you in getting the position.

Work Experience. Just as you list your most recent education first, you should also list your most recent work experience first and then work backwards. List the company where you worked, the dates of employment, and your duties. You may want to reverse the order of education and experience on your resumé. For example, if you have had excellent experience that directly relates to the job for which you are applying, you probably would want to list that first. Remember, the resumé is a sales piece. You want to call attention to your best selling features first.

Extracurricular Activities, Memberships, and Honors. If you have participated in special activities, maintained memberships in professional organizations, or achieved honors, you may wish to list these. Such activities illustrate that you have many interests and leadership qualities. Employers are usually impressed with such characteristics, which may provide you with an added advantage as you are compared to other people who also are applying.

References. Listing references is vital, since the prospective employer must verify your qualifications. Three references are considered a minimum number; four references are considered a maximum number. The most effective references are previous employers, followed by references from your instructors. Personal references are considered to be less acceptable. However, if you have limited work experience and a weak educational background, you may list one personal reference.

It is important that you choose your references carefully. Attempt to select those individuals who know your qualifications well and will take the time and trouble to respond to a

reference request. Before you list a person as a reference, it is essential that you obtain permission from that person.

Resumé Format. There is no set format to be used. Use a format that is clear, concise, and fits your needs. Just as the application letter is to be free from spelling and grammatical errors, so must the resumé. It should be prepared on a good grade of 8½″ × 11″ bond paper, with no strikeovers, smudges, or poor corrections. If you are a college student, a one-page resumé is usually adequate. However, if you have extensive work experience, your resumé may need to be two or even three pages long. Remember, the rule is to present the necessary information as concisely as possible. No prospective employer wants to read through five or six pages of material presented in a wordy manner. A sample resumé showing one acceptable form is presented in Illustration 13-3 on page 209.

PREPARING FOR THE INTERVIEW

The interview will not be an ordeal if you adequately prepare for it. Knowledge of what to do and what to say will help eliminate a great deal of nervousness. If you use some of the techniques described in this chapter, your poise and assurance will greatly improve. Remember that you are striving to sell certain skills and knowledge which are needed in an office.

After reading your letter of application and studying your resumé, the employer usually sets up an interview. In an interview, an employer wants to appraise your appearance, personality, temperament, physical characteristics, manners, and other traits — things that cannot be put on an application. He or she wants to find out firsthand if you are friendly, cheerful, and sincere. The interview is a "sizing-up" process — an opportunity to get acquainted, both on the prospective employer's part and on yours. So, although it may be a new experience for you, approach it with confidence.

AMELIA ALVAREZ
1311 Conflans Avenue
Dallas, TX 75211-1135
555-2041

CAREER OBJECTIVE

To achieve a position as a word processing operator in a large company, with a long-range goal of being an office manager.

EDUCATION

Cedar Ridge College, Dallas, Texas, September 1986 to May 1988, Associate of Arts Degree in Office Occupations.

Courses Studied: word processing, keyboarding, office machines, business math, accounting, business communications, and management.

Oakpark High School, Dallas, Texas, September 1983 to May 1986.

Courses Studied: bookkeeping, office practice, and keyboarding.

WORK EXPERIENCE

Student assistant in the Business Division of Cedar Ridge College, September 1987 to May 1988. Responsibilities included producing tests, duplicating materials, and filing.

Receptionist, Memorial Medical Center, 110 Grace Street, Dallas, TX, June 1987 to August 1987. Responsibilities included preparing correspondence, filing, bookkeeping, and answering the phone.

EXTRACURRICULAR ACTIVITIES, MEMBERSHIPS, AND HONORS

Vice-President of Phi Kappa Theta
Dean's list
President of Phi Beta Lambda

REFERENCES

Ms. Mary Lee Patterson, Cedar Ridge College, 4789 Keist, Dallas, TX 75202-1133.

Dr. Morris Adams, Cedar Ridge College, 4789 Keist, Dallas, TX 75202-1133.

Dr. J. L. Phillips, Memorial Medical Center, 110 Grace, Dallas, TX 75211-1135.

Illustration 13-3. Resumé

1311 Conflans Avenue
Dallas, TX 75211-1135
May 10, 19--

Ms. Marjorie Ott
RJ Computer Corporation
813 Marsh Lane
Dallas, TX 75220-1604

Dear Ms. Ott

Your employment announcement for a word processing operator specifies an individual with good keyboarding and English skills and one who is willing to learn. My two years training in office occupations at Cedar Ridge College plus my one year of work experience have provided me with good skills and experiences. I am eager to get started in such a position and am willing to work hard.

During the last two years, I have completed an Associate of Arts Degree in Office Occupations from Cedar Ridge College. I studied word processing, keyboarding, office practices, and accounting. I can keyboard at 70 words a minute and operate word processing equipment. Prior to beginning college, I worked for one year in the office of Memorial Medical Center. While there, I acted as a receptionist and did some keyboarding and filing. The enclosed resume gives further details concerning my qualifications and experience.

May I have the opportunity to discuss my qualifications with you? You can reach me by telephoning 555-2041 between 9 a.m. and 4 p.m.

Sincerely

Amelia Alvarez

Amelia Alvarez

Enclosure

Illustration 13-2. Letter of Application

Check Your Personal Appearance. First impressions are *important*. Many people feel that appearance counts for 75 to 90 percent in an interview. You may know all the answers and be able to do the work accurately and efficiently, but you must also win the approval of your interviewer.

Dress in a businesslike way. Avoid extremes in clothing, makeup, and hairstyles. In other words, don't overdress or underdress. Attention to dress and personal grooming will give you confidence.

Think About the Questions That You May Be Asked. It is a good idea to give some thought to questions that the interviewer may ask and to how you should respond. Such preparation will help your poise and confidence when you approach the interview.

You may be asked questions about your skills in keyboarding and word processing, grades in bookkeeping or accounting, and questions about your mastery of office machines. Be sure that you know the answers to these questions. Other questions that you may be asked include ones such as, "Why do you want to work for this company?" and "What salary do you expect?" Appropriate responses to these and other questions are presented in the next section.

Speak in a firm, clear voice; give direct answers. A hesitant, evasive answer immediately leaves doubt in the interviewer's mind. Practice going through an interview, phrasing your answers to possible questions. Such preparation will help your poise and confidence when you approach the interview.

Take With You What You May Need. In preparing for an interview, plan to take with you certain things that you may need. You should always have a pen, a small notebook, and a pocket dictionary if you are applying for an office position. List in the notebook the information needed if you are asked to fill out an application. If you are required to take tests, the person testing you will usually provide the needed materials. Some companies require a transcript of your grades. Take one with you or arrange to have one mailed if requested. Be early so that you will not feel hurried.

Be Prepared to Take Tests. Today it is legally required that employment tests directly relate to the qualifications of the job. Directly related tests for the prospective office worker may include word processing, shorthand, transcription, spelling, English, math, and other similar tests which determine your abilities to handle the office position. Be prepared to demonstrate your abilities at the interview. Don't panic when the word *test* is mentioned. Be confident of your abilities and maintain a calm, relaxed manner.

STARTING THE INTERVIEW

When you arrive for the interview, your first contact will usually be the receptionist who plays an important role in an organization. Make it a point to be friendly. You may say, "Good morning, I am Amelia Alvarez. I have an appointment to see Ms. Ott at 10:30." The receptionist may then ask you to be seated for a few minutes. While you are waiting, try not to show any signs of nervousness. Usually there are magazines available to read while waiting. If one is available, it will help take your mind off the interview. When Ms. Ott is ready to see you, the receptionist may go with you to the office and introduce you. Or the receptionist may give the directions to the office, and you will have to introduce yourself. If you have to introduce yourself, an appropriate greeting is, "Good morning, Ms. Ott. I am Amelia Alvarez. I am here to see you about the word processing position." If the individual has no nameplate on the office door or on the desk, you might ask when you enter the office, "Are you Ms. Ott?" Then, when you find the proper person, proceed with the introduction.

"Please Be Seated." You are now in the presence of the person who will interview you. Stand quietly until you are asked to be seated. When you are seated, look directly at the interviewer and wait for the interviewer to begin the conversation. See Illustration 13-4. This is not the time to give attention to your personal appearance. Be responsive to all questions, but do

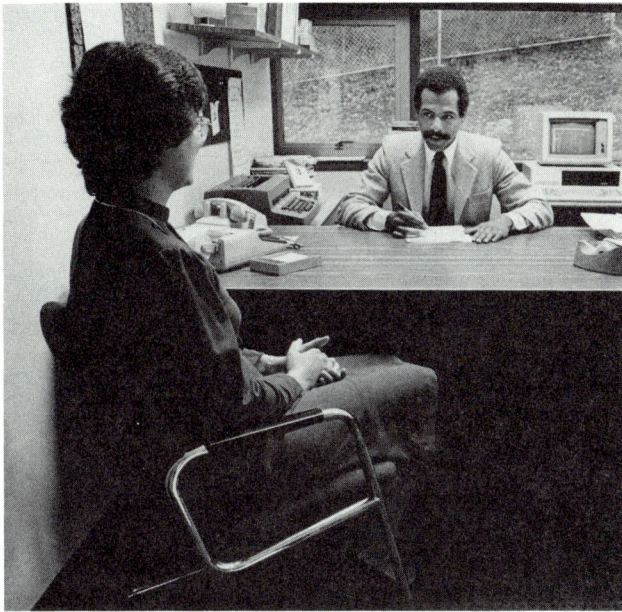

Illustration 13-4. Applying for a Job

not be a yes-and-no person. Answer with a complete sentence — several, if necessary. Speak up and tell the little extra things that you can do, but don't talk too much about your abilities. When you have answered all the questions about your skills and knowledge, the first part of the interview is over. By this time, you should have gained considerable confidence in your ability to answer the interviewer's questions.

"Why Do You Wish to Work for This Company?" This will likely be a difficult question for you to answer, unless you happen to be applying for a position in a business that especially interests you or one about which you are well informed. The interviewer is, of course, interested in determining whether you are the kind of person who will fit into the organization and whether you will make a loyal and willing worker. Your answer to this question will be guided somewhat by the situation and the conversation at the moment, but try to have a good answer ready. You can say that you have a high regard for the company and would like an opportunity to work for it.

"What Salary Do You Expect to Receive?" Persons who are experienced in hiring office workers know that applicants are inter-

ested in the starting salary. The question of salary, therefore, is usually mentioned without the applicant raising the question. If you are asked whether you would be willing to begin working at a specific salary level, be prepared to give an answer. If you feel that the starting salary is below the average for that particular type of work, you may reply that you had hoped to start at a slightly higher salary, but that you are primarily interested in an opportunity to show what you can do and take advantage of chances for promotion. This is a tactful way of giving the employer an opportunity to offer you more salary or at least to assure you of a rather definite promotion, provided you do well on the job. Many large companies have well-defined salary limits for beginning workers, with promotions based on length of service and the ability to produce quality work.

"Where Have You Worked Previously?" If you are asked this question, describe the experience that is most closely related to the job for which you are applying. The employer is interested in knowing what type of experience you have had that will help you handle this job. Do not take up the employer's time by giving a long list of previous employment that is unrelated to the position for which you are applying.

If you have limited work experience, don't let such a question bother you. Before the interview determine the strengths in your background. Speak confidently of those strengths. For example, you might say, "While I haven't been paid for working, I have studied courses that cover most routine work which is done in an office. I feel that I can do the work for you, Ms. Ott, for I am a willing worker."

"What Skills Do You Have That Will Help You Do This Job?" Obviously the interviewer is interested in the skills that you have. This is no time to brag. State the facts. Tell the interviewer what you are capable of doing. Talk about the skills that directly relate to the prospective job. For example, if the position for which you are interviewing is a word processing operator, talk about your keyboarding, English, and spelling skills. Tell the interviewer your straight-copy keyboarding speed and how many words or lines a minute you can produce from recorded correspondence. Tell the interviewer that you are a good English student and can apply the rules of grammar, punctuation, and spelling when producing written correspondence.

"Now, Do You Have Any Questions?"

After the interviewer has completed asking questions, you may be given a chance to ask a few. Here is your opportunity to ask questions pertaining to the job if you are interested in it. You may inquire just what the duties of the job are if they have not been discussed. You may also wish to discuss working hours and other matters that are of importance to you.

If the interviewer feels that you have the qualifications for the position, you will probably be given an application form to fill out if you have not already done so.

ENDING THE INTERVIEW

An initial interview probably will not last more than a few minutes. Listen carefully and observe the interviewer's actions so that you will sense when the interview is over. Leave at once, not by slow degrees. Rise from your chair, thank the interviewer, and leave. See Illustration 13-5. If you have not been offered the job, perhaps you can find out whether you are being favorably considered by asking whether the college placement office will be notified when a decision has been reached. You might also offer to come back for another interview if that is desired. Thank the receptionist as you leave.

Do not be discouraged if you do not get an immediately favorable decision. There may be others who are also applying for the position. Business is interested in getting the best people it can, which is all the more reason why you should master the skills needed for the job and the ability to prepare yourself for the interview.

DON'TS FOR THE INTERVIEW

So far, suggestions have been made about things to do, the positive side of the interview.

Illustration 13-5. Thanking the Interviewer

Here are some don'ts:

1. Don't use nervous gestures and movements, such as fidgeting, tugging at your clothes, stroking your chin, and showing other evidences of being ill at ease.
2. Don't put personal belongings or your hands on the interviewer's desk.
3. Don't argue. You are not undergoing the interview to prove a point.
4. Don't interrupt. Let the interviewer complete all questions or statements before you speak.
5. Don't ask too many questions. Ask important questions only. If questions like When do I get my first raise? When will I be promoted? When do I get a vacation? How long is the coffee break? are of primary importance to you, then the company may not be interested in your services.
6. Don't tell jokes. Let the interviewer do that, if he or she wishes.
7. Don't comment on the furnishings of the interviewer's office. There may be a temptation to say something complimentary about a photograph or a painting, but don't.

8. Don't brag. If the company hires you, you may have to live up to your boasts.

9. Don't criticize. If you are hired, you will have ample time and opportunity to make constructive suggestions for improvement.

10. Don't smoke. If the interviewer asks you if you smoke, say yes if you do smoke, but that you prefer not to at the moment; say no if you do not smoke.

11. Don't chew gum. You do not look your best with a mouthful of gum.

FILLING OUT THE APPLICA- TION FORM

Early in your experience of applying for a position, you will have occasion to fill out application forms for employment. You may do this either before or after being interviewed. On page 214 appears an application form similar to those found in many business offices today. In some businesses, all applicants fill out a form, while other firms ask only those who are seriously being considered for a position to fill out one. Likewise, some businesses request that applicants print or type the information requested on the form. Others require the applicant to handwrite the form so that the personnel department may have a sample of how well or how poorly the person writes. Use your best handwriting in filling out an application form and use a pen. Fill in all blanks. If you have no response, write "none" or "not applicable," or draw a wavy line in the appropriate space. In addition to the information given on the application form, you may wish to attach a resumé (see page 209) if this item did not accompany your letter of application.

When filling out forms in an office, avoid asking unnecessary questions, the answers to which you should already know. Read each question carefully before answering it. From your manner in filling out the form, you will be judged as to how well you will undertake any given task and how well you can follow written directions.

Be careful not to spoil the form so that you do not have to ask for another one. Be sure to answer all questions truthfully. Some firms may discharge you after months of faithful and satisfactory service if they find out that you were untruthful in answering questions asked during the interview or in filling out the application form. It is better to leave questions unanswered than to be untruthful. Be particularly careful with your spelling because it is even more important than good handwriting.

Usually the information requested on an application form can be divided into the following parts.

Name. Usually your full name is desired. Write your name very clearly—especially your last name—so that it can be read easily. Some application forms request that the name be printed, although printing may not be required on the rest of the form.

Address and Telephone Number. Use an address at which you can be reached easily. Many times a student whose home is some distance from the city where he or she is seeking employment has, for the sake of convenience, a temporary address. If such is the case, the temporary address should be used on the application form. If the address used is the home or office of a friend, this fact should be indicated. It is also important that you make arrangements so that you can be reached by telephone if you do not have one at your residence.

Social Security Number. All employees must have a social security number. If you do not have a number, you should apply for one on an Application for a Social Security Number Card form which is available at any Social Security office or Internal Revenue Service office. Beginning with the 1987 tax year, all individuals five years of age or older must have a social security number if the individuals are being claimed as an exemption for income tax purposes.

The Social Security office will send you a card with your number on it. You should always carry your card with you since the number is used as one of the primary identification numbers. For example, colleges require students to provide their social security numbers, the Military Service requires social security numbers, and banks require social security numbers

RJ COMPUTER CORPORATION

813 Marsh Lane
Dallas, TX 75220-1604
214-555-2016

Name: Alvarez (LAST) Amelia (FIRST) Lee (MIDDLE) Social Security Number: 123-45-6789
Present Address: 1311 (NO) ConFlans (STREET) Dallas (CITY) TX (STATE) 75211-1135 (ZIP) Tel. No 555-2041

U.S. Citizen? Yes
Have you ever been convicted of a crime? No   If yes, describe in full:
Have you ever been employed by RJ Computer Corporation? No   When?
Have you ever had or do you now have a worker's compensation claim pending for an injury while working for any employer? No
If yes, give date and nature of accident
List relatives working for RJ Computer Corporation: None
List acquaintances now employed for RJ Computer Corporation: None

Person to be notified in case of emergency: Helen Alvarez (NAME) (RELATIONSHIP)
Home Address: 1311 ConFlans, Dallas TX 75211-1135   Tel. No 555-2041
Business Address: 201 Main Street, Dallas TX 75201-1130   Tel. No 555-3042

SCHOOL	NAME & ADDRESS OF SCHOOL	COURSE OF STUDY	DATES ATTENDED	CIRCLE LAST YEAR COMPLETED	DID YOU GRADUATE?	DIPLOMA, DEGREE, OR CERTIFICATE
High	Oakpark High School Dallas, TX	Business	Sept. 1983 May 1986	1 2 3 ④	☒ Yes ☐ No	Diploma
College	Cedar Ridge College Dallas TX	Office Occupations	Sept. 1986 May 1988	1 ② 3 4	☒ Yes ☐ No	Associate of Arts Degree
Other (Specify)				1 2 3 4	☐ Yes ☐ No	

EMPLOYMENT RECORD

Present or Last Employment:

Name of Firm	Type of Business	Your Dept. Manager	Your Job Title	Salary
Cedar Ridge College	College	Dr. Morris Adams	Student Assistant	$450/job

Address: 4789 First, Dallas TX   Phone 555-4710   Date Started: Sept. 1987   Date Left: May 1988   Reason for Leaving: Graduated

Previous Employment:

Name of Firm	Type of Business	Your Dept. Manager	Your Job Title	Salary
Memorial Medical Center	Hospital	Dr. J.L. Phillips	Receptionist	$1,000/mo

Address: 110 Brace, Dallas TX   Phone 555-8011   Date Started: June 1987   Date Left: Aug. 1987   Reason for Leaving: To attend college

Previous Employment:

Name of Firm	Type of Business	Your Dept. Manager	Your Job Title	Salary

Address   Phone   Date Started   Date Left   Reason for Leaving

List Other Employers:

U.S. Military Experience: Branch of Service None   Date Entered
Do you have a valid Drivers License? Yes   Type Operator   Was it ever suspended? No
Have you ever been bonded? No

REFERENCES (not former employers or relatives)

NAME AND OCCUPATION	ADDRESS	PHONE NUMBER
Ms. Mary Lee Patterson	Cedar Ridge College 4789 First, Dallas TX 75202-1133	555-2311
Dr. Morris Adams	Cedar Ridge College 4789 First, Dallas TX 75202-1133	555-4710
Dr. J.L. Phillips	Memorial Medical Center 110 Brace, Dallas TX 75211-1135	555-8011

I hereby authorize any former employer or any other person given as reference to answer any and all questions that may be asked concerning me. The facts set forth in my application for employment are true and correct. I understand that any false statements on this application shall be considered sufficient course for dismissal. RJ Computer Corporation is an equal opportunity employer.

Applicant's Signature: Amelia Lee Alvarez

INTERVIEW EVALUATION

Applicant Leave This Area Blank

Illustration 13-6. Application for Employment

when opening accounts. It is a good idea to have a second copy of your card maintained in a separate file in case you lose your card. However, if all records of your social security number are lost or destroyed, you may obtain another card by filing a form with the Social Security office, indicating where and about when you first applied for your number.

Education. Give complete information regarding the schools you have attended, including grade school if that is requested. Most companies are interested in knowing whether you plan to continue your education by attending evening college or registering for other special training courses that may be offered in the community. If you showed any unusual talent in any of your subjects in school or received any special recognition for outstanding work, mention it under "General Comments," if space is provided, or on your resumé if no space is provided on the application form.

Type of Work Desired. Many application forms provide space for you to indicate the type of work in which you are most interested. If you are primarily interested in secretarial or general office work, indicate that. If, however, you also like other types of office work, mention them. As a beginner, you may not get just what you want, but you may have a chance to start some other type of work and later be transferred to the type of job you want or for which you feel you are especially trained.

Work Experience. List all work experiences that you have had, giving the most recent experience first. Be sure that you have accurate dates of all your previous employment. If you have limited full-time experience but you have worked part time, include this work record also. Employers are usually interested in your total work experience background.

References. Be prepared to list the full name, business position, address, and telephone number of three or four people — not relatives — who will vouch for you. These people should know you well and should be able to speak about your qualifications for the position.

Before applying for a job, it is a good idea to write down the reference information so that you do not appear unprepared or disorganized when you are asked to fill out the application form.

FOLLOWING UP THE INTERVIEW

Comparatively few jobs are filled as a result of the first interview. The choice will usually be narrowed down to a few applicants, and then the final selection will be made. The *follow-up,* therefore, is of great importance. Follow up your interview promptly with a letter thanking the employer for the interview and reviewing points of special interest. If you were told to send in the application form, the letter in Illustration 13-7 is typical of one that might be sent.

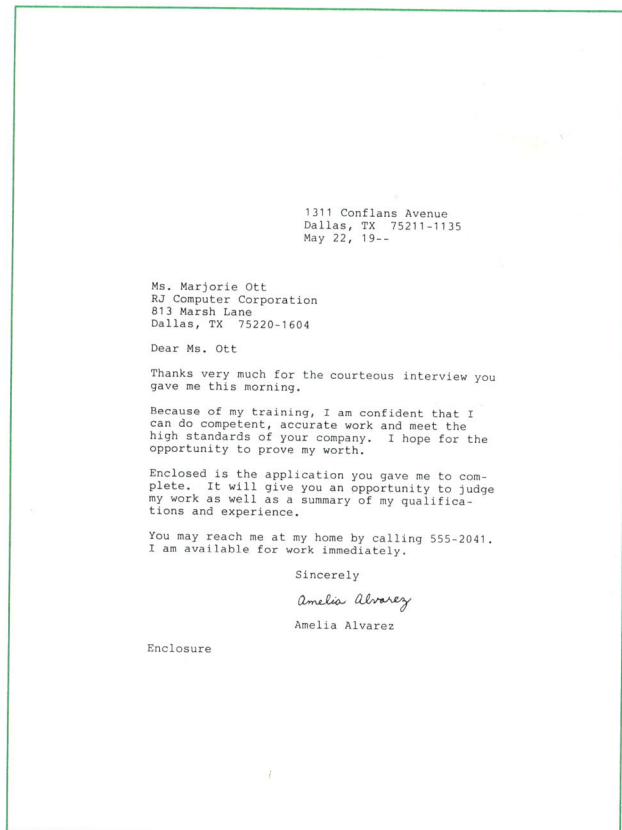

1311 Conflans Avenue
Dallas, TX 75211-1135
May 22, 19--

Ms. Marjorie Ott
RJ Computer Corporation
813 Marsh Lane
Dallas, TX 75220-1604

Dear Ms. Ott

Thanks very much for the courteous interview you gave me this morning.

Because of my training, I am confident that I can do competent, accurate work and meet the high standards of your company. I hope for the opportunity to prove my worth.

Enclosed is the application you gave me to complete. It will give you an opportunity to judge my work as well as a summary of my qualifications and experience.

You may reach me at my home by calling 555-2041. I am available for work immediately.

Sincerely

Amelia Alvarez

Amelia Alvarez

Enclosure

Illustration 13-7. Follow-up Letter

A second follow-up letter may be advisable a week or two after the first one. You should not annoy the employer unnecessarily; but if no action is taken in regard to the application within a reasonable time, a very short letter is not out of place. The second letter should merely remind the employer of your having filed a letter of application and should express willingness to return for another interview.

Of course, it is possible that, after the interview, you may decide not to accept the position. In such a case you should promptly write a courteous letter in which you express your appreciation for having been considered an applicant and explain why you do not wish to accept the position. Although you decide not to take the position now, you may at a later date wish to be reconsidered. At that time, the employer will appreciate the courtesy and thoughtfulness you have shown.

FOR YOUR REVIEW

The following review will help you remember the important points of this chapter.

1. Decide on the type and size of company for which you wish to work before applying for a job.
2. Job information is available through
   a. The placement office at school
   b. Friends and relatives
   c. Direct canvass of companies
   d. Want ads in newspapers
   e. State employment agencies
   f. Private employment agencies
   g. Civil service announcements
3. The goals of a letter of application are to
   a. Arouse interest
   b. Describe your abilities
   c. Request an interview
4. Points to remember in writing the letter of application are as follows:
   a. The letter should look impressive.
   b. The letter should be short.
   c. It should be addressed to a specific person.
   d. An acceptable letter style should be used.
   e. The "you" approach should be used.
   f. The writer should be honest.
5. Common parts of the résumé are
   a. Career objective
   b. Education
   c. Experience
   d. Extracurricular activities, memberships, and honors
   e. References
6. Some of the questions that you should be prepared to answer during the job interview are as follows:
   a. Why do you wish to work for this company?
   b. Where have you worked previously?
   c. What skills do you have that will help you do this job?
   d. What salary do you expect to receive?
   e. Do you have any questions you would like to ask?

7. There are several things which you should not do in an interview. Here are a few.
   a. Don't use nervous gestures.
   b. Don't interrupt.
   c. Don't tell jokes.
   d. Don't brag.
   e. Don't criticize.
   f. Don't chew gum.

8. It is important to fill out an application form correctly and completely. The general information requested on an application form includes
   a. Your name, address, telephone number, and social security number.
   b. Your education.
   c. Your work experience.
   d. References.

9. You should write a follow-up letter after the interview which
   a. Thanks the interviewer for seeing you.
   b. Reviews your strong points.
   c. Lets the reader know you are interested in the job.

PROFESSIONAL FORUM

Jerry Matthews has just finished a one-year office education course in college. He has done well in school. He is proficient on a word processor and a computer. His math and English skills are good, and he works well with people. He has applied at five different companies for an office job, but he has been turned down for all of the jobs. Jerry knows he has the skills necessary to handle the jobs, and he does not understand why he has not been hired. Here is what happened on his last job interview.

Jerry was ten minutes late for the interview. He left home in time to get to the office, but he had trouble finding a parking place. When he went in, he told the receptionist that he was sorry that he was late but that he couldn't find a parking place. Jerry was uptight over being ten minutes late, so he decided to have a cigarette while waiting for the interviewer. The first question that the interviewer asked him was, "Tell me a little about yourself." Jerry thought he did a thorough job with the question. He spent ten minutes telling the interviewer many of the details of his life. Jerry's hair is long, and because of nervousness, he frequently pushed his hair behind his ears. When the interviewer asked him if he had worked before, he said that he had only had summer jobs. He told the interviewer that he had been on four interviews previously, and he felt that the interviewers were unfair when they did not offer him the job.

What mistakes did Jerry make?

FOR YOUR UNDERSTANDING

1. What types of information should be included in a letter of application?
2. What steps should you take in preparing for an interview?
3. How should you answer the following questions:
   a. What salary do you expect to receive?
   b. What skills do you have that will help you in doing this job?
   c. Why do you want to work for this company?
4. How should a resumé be prepared?
5. Explain how to fill out an application form.
6. What is the purpose of a follow-up letter after an interview? What information should this letter contain?

OFFICE APPLICATIONS

On pages 377–380 are office applications that correlate with this chapter.

CHAPTER 14

Job Knowledge

The interviewer has just said to you, "We want you to work for us." The job sounds challenging, and you are ready to use the skills and knowledge that you have so carefully developed over the last few years. However, if you are to be the best employee that you can be, there are certain things you must know. You need answers to immediate questions such as "When do I begin working?" "What are the working hours?" and "What should I wear to work?" And, as you begin working, you need to understand the company policies and procedures. You must be familiar with the formal policies such as vacation days allowed and sick leave allowances. You should also become familiar with the informal policies such as telephone practices and bringing food and drink to your desk. The purpose of this chapter is to call attention to specific items which you should know.

GENERAL OBJECTIVES

Your general objectives for this chapter are to

1. Learn what information you should know before you report for work.
2. Understand the importance of learning about the history and organization of the company.

3. Discover the importance of being familiar with company policies — both formal and informal.
4. Become acquainted with evaluation procedures.

WHAT YOU NEED TO KNOW BEFORE REPORTING FOR WORK

After you have been told the job is yours, you need to understand the following details:

1. When do I begin working?
2. To whom should I report?
3. What are the working hours?
4. What should I wear?

When Do I Begin Working? You may be employed to start working immediately, the next day, the next Monday, or at the beginning of the next pay period. Many businesses that pay salaries at the end of the week may prefer new employees to begin work on Monday. Others that pay on the fifteenth and on the last day of the month may prefer to have new employees begin on the sixteenth or on the first day of the month.

218

To Whom Should I Report? If you are offered a job during the interview and accept it, the person who employs you will usually tell you immediately to whom you are to report. You may be asked to report to the employment manager, the personnel director, the receptionist, the head of the department where you are to work, or to some executive. In any event, obtain the name of the person, including his or her office number and address.

What Are the Working Hours? Before beginning your first day on the job, you should know the starting time, the time and length of the lunch break, and the closing time. You will also want to know whether any overtime is expected of you and if so, what the practice is for paying overtime. Since Saturday work may also be included in your workweek, you will want to find out about that.

Arrive at work on time, no matter how early your office opens. Nothing is quite so embarrassing to a new employee as to be late and have to make excuses. Employees are expected to be at their desks ready for work at the start of the business day. If you find it necessary to do some last-minute grooming after you reach the office, make a point of arriving a few minutes early in order to begin work on time.

You may be working in an office where the entire office closes during lunch, or you may be asked to alternate lunch breaks with other employees so that someone is in the office at all times. Be sure not to infringe on another person's time.

When you were in school, you may have had study or recreation periods. On the job, however, things are different. You start work in the morning, and, except for lunch and perhaps short rest periods, you are not finished until the close of the business day. If you do not feel like working, you just don't take the afternoon off. To many beginners, the pressure of the business office is a great strain during the first few weeks. It is absolutely necessary, therefore, for you to watch your health and get plenty of rest during the first few weeks.

What Should I Wear? Get up early enough to dress and to attend to your personal grooming

without being hurried. If you don't allow yourself sufficient time, you may feel hurried all day and not be at your best. It is important on this first day that you make a good impression on your fellow workers. Dress in business clothes and pay special attention to your hair, face, teeth, and hands. If you are likely to be standing or walking very much during the day, wear comfortable shoes. Follow a middle-of-the-road approach in dress for that first day. Do not wear something that is flashy. You want to direct attention to you as a person — not to what you are wearing. But, on the other hand, do not wear something that is drab and dull. Wear something that is comfortable and that you know looks good on you.

WHAT DO YOU NEED TO KNOW ABOUT THE COMPANY?

To feel a part of your company, it is important that you become familiar with its organization and history. Discover how your department and supervisor fit within the company structure. Learn the names of the company's officers, how long the company has been in business, and whether or not it is growing. As you begin work, keep your eyes and ears open to find out all that you can. The more knowledgeable you are about the company, the better an employee you can be.

Organization. Companies are organized in various ways depending on whether they are large or small. A very small company may have one owner or perhaps two people who jointly own and operate the company. Large companies have more complex organizational structures. The officers of a large company usually consist of a president, one or more vice-presidents, a secretary, and a treasurer. Each of these individuals may have a staff who works for them. In addition to these officers, there can be various department managers. The kinds of departments vary depending on the organization's needs, but some typical departments found in both large and small businesses are production, purchasing, marketing, research, accounting, and sales. Each department will be organized to accomplish the necessary objectives and to operate efficiently.

You need to know about the organization of your company because it will help you understand how you, your supervisor, and your department fit into the total organization. It will help you know about the reporting structure of the company. For example, you should know which of the employees report to your supervisor and to whom your supervisor reports.

Even if your supervisor does not report to the top administration, you will want to learn the names of the administrators quickly.

Where do you find such organizational information? Most large companies have some type of organization chart. If you are not given one, ask for one. A simple organization chart of a manufacturing company is shown in Illustration 14–1. Notice that there is a chairperson of the board, a president, a vice-president of personnel, a vice-president of sales, a vice-president of manufacturing, a secretary-treasurer, and two plant managers.

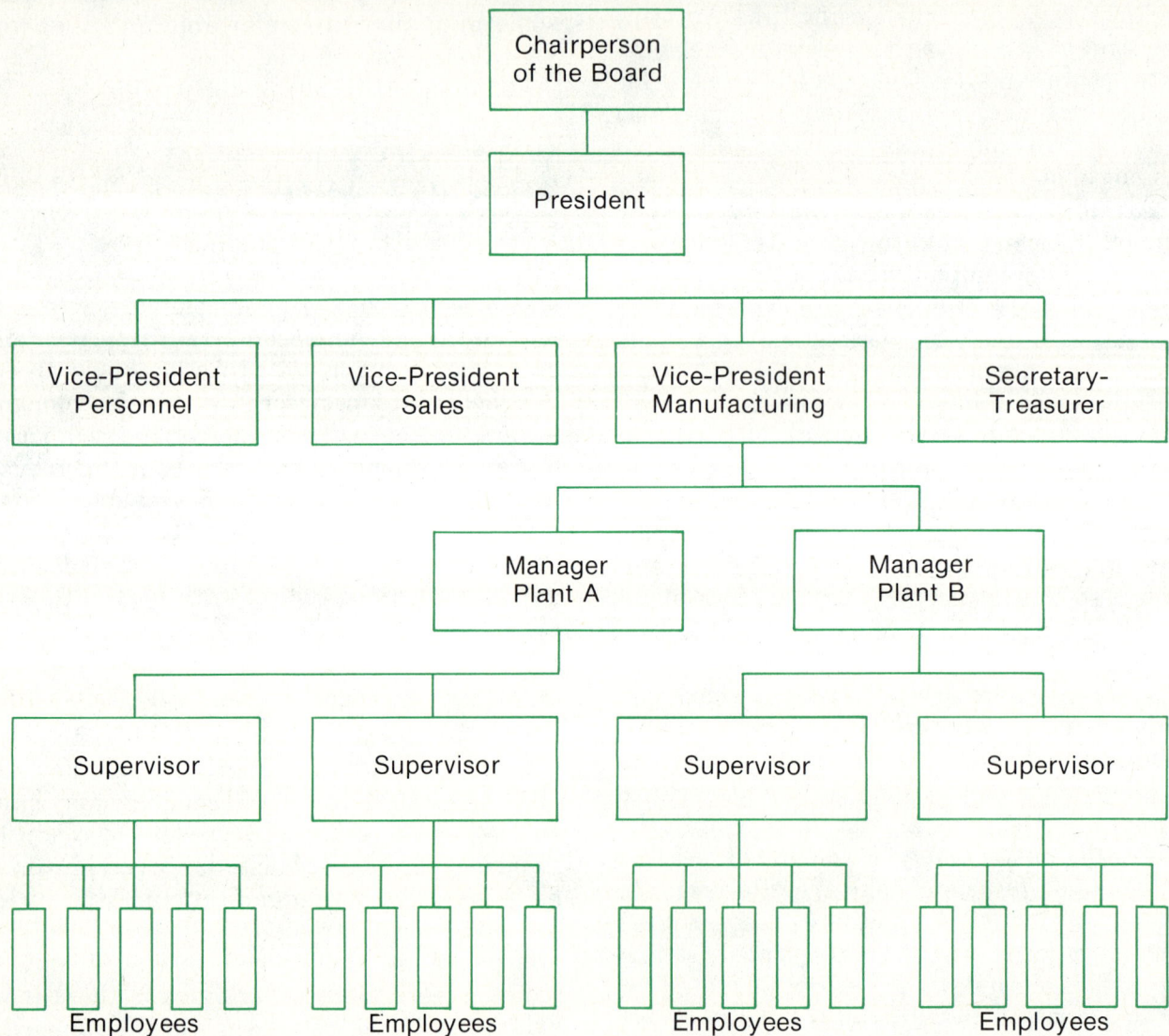

Illustration 14-1. Organization Chart of a Manufacturing Company (Details of the organizational structure for the personnel department, the sales department, and the secretary-treasurer's office have been eliminated.)

History. The company's history is also important to you since it gives you more knowledge of the company. A history of the company is usually presented at the beginning of the publication called an annual report. If your company publishes an annual report, read the reports from the last two or three years. Information such as how long the company has been in business, what the sales of the company are, what types of products the company manufactures, and the subsidiaries or branches of the company can help you understand more about the place where you work.

The main purpose of an annual report is to reflect the financial position of the company. An earnings statement and a statement of financial position are presented in the report. You can use these reports to determine whether sales or profits are up or down as compared with the previous year.

Another source of information about the company's history is a company periodical. If your company publishes one, read it carefully. However, if your company does not publish such information, ask your employer or one of your co-workers to tell you something about the company's history.

Formal Policies. Formal company policies are usually spelled out in a "policies and procedures manual." This booklet will include information about working hours, pay raises, evaluation procedures, vacation periods, sick leave, insurance benefits, retirement benefits, termination policies, etc. The booklet is usually quite detailed, and you will need to read it carefully as shown in Illustration 14–2. The following questions are usually answered by referring to the "policies and procedures manual."

When and How is My Salary Paid? In most offices, salaries are paid weekly, semimonthly, or monthly. If salaries are paid weekly, your beginning salary may be quoted on a weekly basis.

Most businesses pay salaries by check. If you do not have a savings or checking account where you can deposit or cash your check, the company may provide you with an identification card to facilitate your cashing the check

at the bank on which it is drawn. Be careful not to let other employees see your check or the amount of money if paid in cash. This is a personal matter and should be kept to yourself. If there are any mistakes in the amount received, the matter should be taken up immediately with your supervisor or the head of the payroll department.

Illustration 14-2. Know Your Benefits

What Deductions Are Made from My Salary? Most employers are required by law to deduct a certain amount for social security taxes and for federal income taxes, depending upon the employee's earnings. In addition, there may be deductions for group insurance, hospitalization, pensions, union dues, company savings plans, and for the purchase of government savings bonds and stock in the company. In verifying the amount you receive each payday, sometimes called *take-home pay,* you must know what deductions are made from your salary. Usually these deductions are explained in the company manual. If not, find out from your immediate superior. When you receive your salary, your check or pay envelope will have a stub or a receipt showing the amounts of the deductions.

What Is the Vacation Policy? Most companies have rather well-defined policies on vacations for their employees. For example, employees who have been working for the company for six months may be entitled to one week of vacation with pay; those who have been working for the company for a year or longer may be entitled to two weeks of vacation with pay. Some companies provide additional days of vacation based on the length of service. Union agreements with the company may determine the length of vacation.

In most businesses, vacations may be taken during a certain period which may cover several months during the summer or during some other part of the year. Some business concerns encourage their employees to take vacations during the winter, especially if business is relatively slack during the winter months. Usually when a vacation schedule is being arranged, those employees with the longest service with the company are given preference in selecting vacation periods.

Am I Allowed Any Sick Leave? Policies of companies differ regarding payment of salaries when employees are absent because of illness. In some companies, employees are not paid for any time taken off from work, except for vacations. Other companies have more liberal policies regarding sick leave. For example, after an employee has been working a year or more, he or she may be entitled to a certain number of days of sick leave with pay.

Under no circumstances, however, should employees feel that they are entitled to take days of sick leave if they are not actually ill enough to be away from work. Some companies attempt to overcome the tendency for employees to take sick leave by providing a bonus of several days' vacation to those who have not used up their allowance for sick leave during the year. Ordinarily, when employees are absent because of illness or for any other reason, they are expected to notify their supervisor, department head, or some other executive so that the work done by them can be taken care of by others.

Does the Company Have Group Insurance and Hospitalization Plans? Many companies have set up plans whereby an employee can obtain life insurance and hospitalization care after being with the company a certain length of time. In fact, some companies require all employees to enroll for such protection as soon as they become qualified for it. Usually the company pays part of the cost of such protection, and the employee pays part, with cost to the employee being deducted from her or his salary.

Does the Company Offer a Retirement Plan? When you first begin your job, retirement may seem so far off that you are not interested in such benefits. However, it is to your advantage to know what these benefits are. Most companies offer some type of retirement plan. Some companies contribute monthly to a retirement plan for every employee, and you are not required to contribute any money. Other companies contribute a certain percentage to a retirement fund, and the remaining percentage is deducted from your check. If you leave the company before retirement, you usually are eligible to get a portion of these monies returned to you — some companies will refund the total amount in the retirement fund. If retirement benefits are not explained to you, check with the personnel manager or payroll department of your company. They can give you the needed information.

How Will I Be Evaluated? If you apply your skills and knowledge, opportunities for advancement will be available. In most companies, as well as in civil service and government positions, a periodic checkup is made of all employees to determine which ones are working up to capacity and which ones are worthy of promotion. Normally, as a beginner, you will be rated at the end of the first three-month period, the first six-month period, the first year, and then at least once a year thereafter.

You will be observed and checked informally by the supervisor or department head rather constantly, but the formal evaluation of your work may be done by means of a *merit rating blank*. On the merit rating blank or checklist, certain performance and personality factors of the employee are rated by the supervisor and perhaps others in order to give a fair and accurate picture of the employee. This rating is usually followed by a conference as an opportunity to improve your work and yourself. See Illustration 14–3.

After you learn what items are on the merit rating checklist, you should make a personal checklist and check or rate yourself from time to time. If your company does not have such a merit rating list, it is desirable to check yourself anyway. A checklist similar to those used to rate office workers is shown on page 386. You will observe that many of the traits listed are based on qualities that you will be developing throughout this course.

Illustration 14-3. Being Evaluated

Informal Policies. Informal policies are those policies that are not written down but which are observed by the employees. You need to be particularly sensitive to these policies. An important rule to follow when you are new to a job is: Observe carefully what the other employees are doing. You may not be told what the informal policies are, and your only means of finding out may be by observation. Or some kind person may take you aside and tell you the informal policies of the company. However,

whether you are told of these policies or not, you should be aware that they exist. The following are some of the questions that you may have in regard to informal policies.

Will I Be Allowed Time for Refreshments or Rest? Practices of business differ in regard to this question. In some offices, especially in large offices with departments that are closely supervised, employees are expected to be at their desks all the time, except during definite break periods that may be permitted. In other offices, however, employees are on their own and are expected to use judgment in the amount of time they are away from their desks. See Illustration 14-4.

Illustration 14-4. Taking a Break

Many offices have vending machines that dispense candy, soft drinks, and coffee so that employees may have access to refreshments during working hours without leaving the premises. In other situations, you may be permitted to leave the office for refreshments.

Some offices have conducted studies to show that a few minutes of relaxation increase the efficiency of an employee who has worked continuously for some time. The coffee break is common practice in many offices, but be sure to find out what the regulations are in your office. If your office provides facilities for refreshment or allows you time away from your desk, do not take advantage of your employer by spending 15 or 20 minutes away from your desk several times each day while you eat or drink. If your office has definite break periods, be back at your desk and ready to resume work when your break is over. Remember that two 15-minute breaks each day add up to 150 minutes for a five-day week, or a total of over three weeks during a year, based on a 40-hour workweek.

Will I Be Allowed to Bring Food or Drinks to My Desk? Some offices do not object to your bringing food or drinks to your desk. You may have had a busy morning or afternoon, and it may have been impossible for you to get away from your desk for a break. However, some offices object to this practice. It can be a particularly bad practice if you are a receptionist. A customer who sees you eating or drinking at your desk is likely to get the impression that the office is not too efficiently run. You appear to be so involved in your needs that you cannot handle the affairs of the business. If you are a receptionist, it is a good idea to avoid eating or drinking at your desk entirely. However, if you have a job in which you do not come in contact with people outside of the business, it may be acceptable. Watch what is done in your company and obey the informal policies.

Will I Be Permitted to Smoke? As a result of research studies, people today are more aware than ever before about the health problems that may be caused by smoking. Some people, even if they do not smoke, feel that it is offensive and even harmful to their own health to be around

people who are smoking. Many offices do not have a policy regarding smoking. Employees are allowed to smoke if they wish. Other offices do not permit employees to smoke at their desks but have designated smoking areas. Regardless of how smoking is handled in your company, you should be aware of and sensitive to the needs of the people with whom you work.

May I Use the Telephone? Find out what the company policy is regarding the use of the telephone for personal calls. If such use is forbidden, observe the regulation implicitly. Even if personal calls are permitted, it is best not to make such calls during office hours. Discourage your friends from calling you. The new employee who spends part of the day talking on the telephone with outside friends is wasting time and will become unpopular with other employees.

What If I Have Questions? Obviously there are times when you must ask questions; that is okay. It is better to ask a question about something than to do the job incorrectly. However, remember that you can learn a great deal by observing. Thus, before you ask someone a question, ask yourself: (1) Can I find the answer to my question through observation? (2) Can I find the answer by checking the files or by reading company information? If either answer is yes, do not ask your question. However, if you can't find the answer, then ask your supervisor or your co-workers. During the first few days you are on the job, it is best to accumulate your questions by making notes and to then ask your supervisor at an appropriate time. Determine when your supervisor is least busy and then ask your questions. Do not interrupt her or him at a rushed time of day.

FOR YOUR REVIEW

The following review will help you remember the important points of this chapter.

1. Before you report to work, you should have answers to the following questions:
   a. When do I begin working?
   b. To whom should I report?
   c. What are the working hours?
   d. What should I wear?

2. You should become familiar with the organization of the company — how the company

is set up and the name of the person or persons to whom you and your supervisor report.

3.   You should become familiar with the history of the company. This history is usually published in booklet format.

4.   After you begin work, you should become familiar with both the formal and informal company policies.

   a. Formal policies are spelled out in a "policies and procedures manual."

Examples of policies usually written are

(1) Salary information

(2) Vacation policies

(3) Sick leave policies

(4) Group insurance and hospitalization

   b. Informal policies are those policies that are not written down but which are observed by the employees. Informal policies are usually concerned with such things as

(1) Taking coffee breaks

(2) Eating in the office

(3) Smoking in the office

(4) Using the telephone

5.   You will be evaluated informally on your job. This informal evaluation is conducted as your supervisor observes and checks your work.

6.   You also will be evaluated formally on your job. This formal evaluation is sometimes conducted by means of a rating blank.

PROFESSIONAL FORUM

Ralph Fuller has been employed as a bookkeeper with Wright Electric Company for only three days. On his first day, he was given a policies and procedures manual which he reviewed carefully. However, such things as coffee breaks, eating at one's desk, and talking on the telephone were not mentioned in the manual. Ralph knows that most companies allow their employees to take coffee breaks. The first two days that he worked were so busy that he did not take a morning or afternoon break. None of the other employees asked him to go with them, and he did not even notice if they were on a break. On the third day, he was still extremely busy. However, he decided to go to the coffee shop and bring back a cup of coffee to drink at his desk. As he was drinking the coffee, he suddenly realized that he had not seen any other employees drinking coffee at their desks. However, no one told Ralph that he should not do so.

During this three-day period, two of his best friends called. They were eager to see how he liked his new job. Ralph hated to tell them that they could not call him at work since he did not know the company policy on personal phone calls. He kept his conversation short. However, he is not sure as to how to handle the situation if they call again. What should Ralph do about the coffee situation and the telephone situation?

FOR YOUR UNDERSTANDING

1.   Distinguish between formal and informal company policies.

2.   Discuss three formal policies that are important to you as an employee.

3.   List and explain two informal policies that are important for you to understand.

4.   What information is presented in an organization chart?

5.   How are employees usually evaluated?

6.   Why is it important to know about the history of the company?

OFFICE APPLICATIONS

On pages 381–386 are office applications that correlate with this chapter.

CHAPTER 15

Job Success

All of us want to be successful at what we do; and since we spend such a large amount of our lives in a work situation, it is extremely important to be successful on the job. Throughout your study of this text, you learned about the importance of office skills such as keyboarding, word processing, records management, letter writing, and handling the mail. And, as you have completed the learning activities of each chapter, you have become more proficient in these areas. You have also learned about the importance of human relations and listening skills in the office. This chapter focuses on applying human relations skills in practical ways in the office.

You may find yourself in a work situation where you are unhappy and feel that you are not being successful. If such a situation occurs, it is time for you to ask yourself some hard questions about your goals in life. Or, you may be in a situation where you are fired from a job for some reason. This chapter helps you to understand how to deal with both situations.

Successful office work also requires good organizational and time management skills in order to handle the numerous details and paperwork involved. This chapter will help you to improve your skills in these areas also.

GENERAL OBJECTIVES

Your general objectives for this chapter are to

1. Apply human relations concepts that enable you to work more effectively with people inside and outside the company.
2. Become knowledgeable of how to successfully leave a position.
3. Demonstrate the ability to organize your work by analyzing your time, placing priorities, and organizing materials and supplies.

WORKING WITH OTHER EMPLOYEES

If you develop certain fundamental principles of getting along with others, your career in the business world will be much more pleasant and your opportunities for advancement will increase. The following are a few suggestions that will help you:

1. Do not give orders to others unless you have the authority. Bossy persons are usually disliked.
2. Do not pass the buck. Accept the responsibility of tasks assigned to you.

3. Do not override another person's authority.

4. Respect people for their good qualities, even though they may have faults. Try to find something good in everyone.

5. Never make another person feel defeated. Admit that others' ideas have merit before advancing your own.

6. Be a good loser but do not develop a defeatist attitude when your own ideas are not accepted as being the best. If you are wrong, admit it.

7. Do not pretend to know all the answers, to be an authority on all subjects, or to try to impress others with your knowledge.

8. Do not attempt to settle all arguments. Such a person is seldom liked by others.

9. Do not rely on verbal orders. Put them in writing.

10. Never give a harsh or impatient answer. Before giving a blunt reply, think it over.

11. Be cheerful, even though things do not go your way.

12. Do not hold a grudge against anyone. Practice forgiveness.

13. If you cannot say something pleasant, don't say anything. Do not be a gossip, a bearer of bad news, or a rumor spreader.

14. Never make a promise that you cannot keep.

15. Do not be overly solicitous. It may seem insincere to the other person.

16. Express appreciation with a pleasant "Thank you" when an associate has helped you.

17. Be considerate of others, as you would want others to be of you.

18. Learn to listen without interruption, particularly if instructions are being given.

19. Pay special attention to your attire, grooming, and manner.

20. Try, at all times, to improve your work organization and efficiency.

Selecting Your Office Friends.

You probably have had many close friends while attending school, and you have had the time to spend with them socially. In business you should also have friends, but they need not be as intimate as your social friends.

If you have a quarrel with any of your outside friends, you can refrain from seeing them. If, however, you quarrel with close business friends, you cannot very well ignore them when you work side-by-side all day. Do not be too hasty, therefore, in picking your office friends when you take a new position.

It is up to you to get along with co-workers even though this may mean overlooking their undesirable traits. If you have difficulty in getting along with certain workers in the office, those persons may be an obstacle to you in getting work done and in carrying out the wishes of your employer. As an employee, you have a responsibility to observe the proper rules of conduct and to gain the respect and cooperation of other employees.

Developing Social Friendships.

Most businesses do not object if employees develop personal friendships with other employees, provided the friendships do not cause unfavorable comment, or interfere with work. Care must be exercised, however, to avoid affiliating yourself with an office clique. In some offices, such groups spend considerable time together outside the office and then take company time to discuss social gatherings and other events engaged in by the group. It is advisable not to get mixed up in such groups.

Office cliques frequently cause rivalry among different groups, and such rivalry eventually causes hard feelings among employees. Many times personal opposition among certain groups carries over into the conduct of the everyday work of the office. Employees in one group may take every opportunity to criticize work done by another person. If you are involved in situations of this kind, the reactions will be harmful to you as well as to your employer.

An employee should not take the initiative in trying to promote friendship with a superior. This situation would be especially noticed by other employees and would probably earn you the title of "apple polisher." If you are a secretary to an executive, however, it is essential for you to be on a friendly basis with other executives in the company and their secretaries. These semipersonal but businesslike friendships make it easier for you to receive the cooperation of other executives.

Although you must realize the importance of a friendly attitude toward all employees in your office, you need not meet them on the same moral or social level. You need not partake in the same social activities or have the same outside interests and activities that other employees have. On the other hand, you should not have a superior attitude toward other employees even though you may come from a family that is more prominent socially and financially.

You must learn to distinguish between genuine friendliness and nosiness. The person who says "Good morning" or "How are you today?" may be exhibiting a naturally friendly attitude toward a co-worker. Take these greetings as such. If, however, you are in possession of confidential information, you must guard against those who seem to pry, using friendship as a lever to get information to which they are not entitled.

The office grapevine may be the means of spreading gossip or unfounded rumors. Although office gossip may be without malicious intent, frequently it causes hard feelings or actual personal damage. Avoid it; do not pass it on to others. Often, too, the grapevine may be used by officials to gauge the reaction of employees toward a new policy or other kinds of changes contemplated in the office. In this sense, it acts as a trial balloon. In such cases, you must make up your own mind without undue discussion with fellow employees and without attempting to influence them.

Learning Names. Learning the names of your immediate associates and supervisors requires little effort. However, learning the names of people in other departments and the names of customers requires considerable effort. See Illustration 15–1. There are several techniques that can help you learn names quickly.

One technique is to use the name immediately after you have been introduced. For example, you may say, "I'm looking forward to working with you, Mrs. Greenspan." Another useful technique is to develop a card file of the company personnel and frequent customers. Many customers may have business cards that you can tape onto index cards and keep in a file. For customers without business cards, as well

as for personnel within your company, you can write the name, address, phone number, and any other pertinent information on index cards and maintain them in a file. Take a few minutes each week to look through your card file and to mentally associate the names with the faces. You will soon find that names come easily for you.

Another successful technique is word association. Many memory experts suggest this method. It requires that you take the individual's name or a portion of the name and mentally associate a word or phrase with it. For example, if a man has a last name of Ivy, you might mentally think of the ivy plant. This mental image will trigger recall of the person's name the next time you meet him. You should also make an effort to learn people's telephone voices because people like to be recognized. A response such as, "How are you doing today, Mr. Edwards?" after an individual says "Hello" starts the telephone conversation on a warm and friendly note.

Illustration 15-1. Learning Names

Cooperating With Others. You may have the feeling that when your particular job, or part of a job, is finished, you need not worry about helping anyone else. Remember, however, that you are an employee of the company and that the efforts you put forth further the interests of the company as a whole and of each employee. The time may come when you have more work than you can do and will want some other employee to help you. Keep this in mind when you have finished your work and find others with more to do than they can finish. Do not, however, assume an egotistical attitude that you know everything there is to know about the business and can do anyone's work. If you help someone else, do not make that person feel obligated to you. You should merely offer your help in the spirit of cooperation and with a desire to further the interests of the entire business. See Illustration 15-2.

Illustration 15-2. Working Together

One way to make enemies in the office is to borrow working materials habitually from other employees. If, on occasion, you must borrow working materials, be sure that they are returned promptly.

Making Requests of Others. You may frequently have the responsibility of passing on instructions or orders to others. Extreme care should be exercised in keeping within the bounds of authority. Do not take it upon yourself to give orders unless you are properly authorized to do so. Always be diplomatic. For

example, if you are working for a superior who asks you to pass on certain orders to other executives and department heads about a meeting, do not say, "Will you please come to a meeting at nine o'clock in the morning?" You should say, "Mr. Chaney is calling a meeting for nine o'clock in the morning in his office. Will you be there?"

Observing Office Hours. In most offices, the working hours are arranged so that they will be fair to both the employer and the employee. The smooth operation of an office depends to a large degree upon strict observance of these hours by all persons concerned. You may be employed in an office where there is a tendency on the part of the employees who have completed their work to spend their time taking care of personal affairs. Avoid following such a procedure. It can hardly be considered ethical for an employee to spend time writing personal letters or receiving and making personal telephone calls during working hours.

Get to work in sufficient time in order to begin work *on time*. A work process in which you participate, or for which you are responsible, may be held up by your tardiness. There is no surer way to call unfavorable attention to yourself than by getting to work late.

In most offices, all employees, regardless of ranking, are considered to be on the same level so far as keeping busy is concerned. Each employee should feel a responsibility to keep busy. If one person in an office takes privileges out of the ordinary, other employees feel that they are entitled to the same privileges. Such practices cannot be permitted if a business is to operate efficiently and if there is to be harmony among all employees.

Accepting Responsibilities. If you are one of several workers of equal rank, you may sometimes feel that you are being imposed upon to do more work than is required of others or to work overtime more often than other employees. This procedure may be one way the employer has of finding out whether you are capable of turning out more work or are willing to accept more responsibilities.

Certain office tasks are your responsibility. They go with the job you are being paid to do. The fact that on occasion you may not be able to finish is no excuse for passing the buck. You may need to study your job more carefully and reorganize your work habits for greater efficiency.

Experience on many types of jobs will better qualify you for positions of authority and responsibility. If you are placed in a position where you supervise other employees, your judgment and ability will be more highly respected by them if they know that you have done the type of work they are doing. On the other hand, experience in many different types of jobs may lead you to think of certain work as routine or unimportant. You may be inclined to belittle an employee who has difficulty in grasping certain routines. Be encouraging and helpful rather than superior. One of the best ways to get those working under your supervision to develop the proper spirit in their work is to make them feel that the job they are doing is vitally important to the success of the business, no matter how minor the job may be.

Displaying Flexibility.
Flexibility is defined as "capable of being bent; pliable." In today's office, flexibility means that and even more. You learned in Chapter 1 that the business world is rapidly changing. If you are to deal with this change, you must be flexible. You must be willing to operate new machines and to learn new ways of doing a job.

You must also be flexible in your relations with other employees. You may work with someone who does not do a job in the manner that you think it should be done. But, unless you are the supervisor, you cannot tell the employee how to do the job. You must learn to accept the fact that a task can be done in different ways and still be accomplished. You must be willing to adjust your thinking and work habits to fit the organizational needs.

Respecting Privacy.
You have no right to pry into other office employees' private affairs or to offer unsolicited advice or comments about their appearance, attitudes, or job performance.

Bad feelings can quickly arise between employees if one is insistent on trying to delve into the private affairs of another. None of us would want someone else to ask questions or make comments concerning our personal lives. The golden rule is an excellent rule to follow in the office. "Treating others as you would have others treat you" is a quality to be admired and respected.

Being Empathetic.
The dictionary defines empathy as "an understanding so intimate that the feelings, thoughts, and motives of one are readily comprehended by another." In your relations with co-workers, it is important that you use empathy. We must walk a mile in someone else's shoes before we can know that person's problems. A co-worker may have had a particularly trying morning — everything went wrong from the moment that person stepped out of bed. Thus, that co-worker may arrive at the office in an irritable mood. It happens to all of us. Your responsibility, therefore, is to display empathy by putting yourself in his or her shoes. See Illustration 15–3. Remember the times when everything has gone wrong for you. Understand and accept the person's behavior.

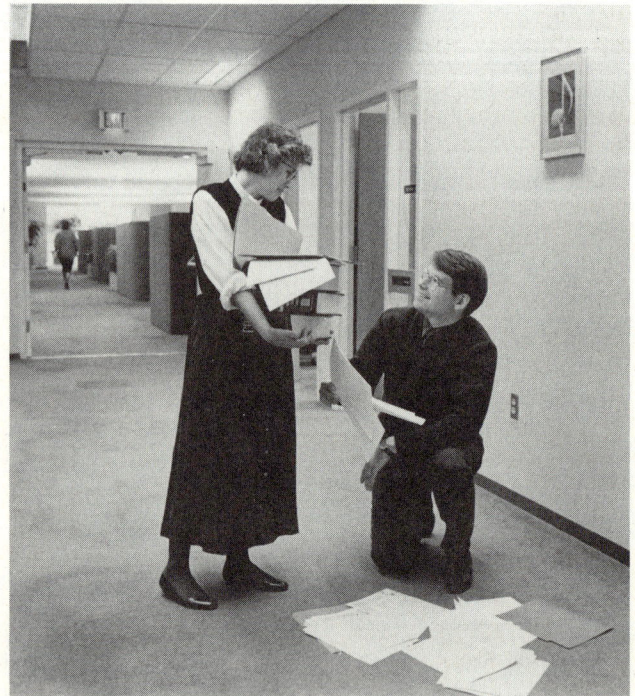

Illustration 15-3. Being Empathetic

WORKING WITH CUSTOMERS AND SALESPEOPLE

Most of what has been said about working with other employees also applies to working with customers and salespeople. Although there are occasions when a combination of business and social interests works out satisfactorily, it is generally agreed that employees who get along best are those who keep their business and personal interests entirely separate.

Relationships with customers should always be on the highest personal and professional level. Every employee is a representative of the firm and plays an important part in its public relations. You help or hinder your employer in many ways: the way you answer the telephone or write a letter; the way you reply to an inquiry; the way you receive callers; and the way you dress and handle yourself.

Entertaining Customers and Salespeople. You may have occasion, from time to time, to help entertain customers and salespeople who are in town. For example, some customer who wants to see some of the sights of the city may ask your employer for an escort. If you are selected for this purpose, keep the situation purely on a professional basis.

Accepting Gifts. A salesperson who has worked with your employer and to whom you have been helpful may send you a gift as an expression of appreciation. You may also receive small remembrances from your own business or from department heads for whom you have done a special favor. Accept such gifts purely as an expression of appreciation for business services that you have rendered. As a matter of ethics, however, be on guard in accepting special favors or gifts.

Displaying Social Tact. There are times when work in the office is such that some employees must work overtime in order to keep the work up-to-date. If you are a female employee and have dinner with one of the male employees, you should not expect him to pay for your meal. You should take it as a matter of fact that you will pay for it yourself, even though the man may offer to pay. If the man insists on paying for your meal, however, do not argue with him. Likewise, if a man has dinner with one or more of the women employees who are working overtime, the man need not pay for their meals. Remember, this is an age of equality. Thus, women are just as capable of paying for their own meals as men are.

In nearly every business there are times when groups of employees get together in the office for a party or celebration. Many offices have informal get-togethers preceding the Christmas holidays. Ordinarily refreshments are served, and frequently gifts are exchanged. It is not considered good taste to buy expensive gifts for your fellow employees or for your employer. Office employees participate in the planning and preparation of the party. Its success depends upon the cooperation of everyone; therefore, you should do your share of accepting willingly and cheerfully whatever job is assigned to you. Your conduct at the party should always be such that you do not embarrass yourself, your employer, or your fellow employees.

Making Introductions. Learn to make introductions with poise and ease. The general rule for making introductions is that the person due the most consideration is named first; that is, others are introduced to that person. In a business situation, the person usually named first is the one in the higher position. For example, if Mr. Allen, the president of another company, visits your manager, you would say, "Mr. Allen, this is Mr. Navarate." If the visitor already knows your manager's name, it is possible to merely state the visitor's name. You may say, "This is Mr. Allen of Bache Equipment."

If an executive is introducing an office employee to a client, the client is named first. A young person is introduced to an older person. The adage that a man is always introduced to a woman is no longer invariable. For example, a 16-year-old girl may be introduced to a 40-year-old man; and, a woman may be introduced to a man of the same age who is more important (i.e., in offices held or in achievements). However, the traditional rule is in force when a man and woman of approximately the same age and status are introduced: The man is introduced to the woman. For example, you might handle the introduction by saying, "Melissa Bender, this is Don Ingleman." Notice in this situation that no titles are used. With the informality of life today it is not always necessary to use Mr., Mrs., Miss, or Ms. However, you would use a title such as "Doctor" or "Governor" when introducing such individuals.

Traditionally the woman has remained seated when introduced to someone, unless that person is much older or very prominent. But today, everyone rises when being introduced. There is no reason why a woman should remain seated when being introduced. Furthermore, it has been traditional for a man to wait until a woman extends her hand before he extends his. However, this practice is also changing. Whether you are a man or a woman, extend your hand. Whoever gets there first will then extend his or her hand first. Always remove your glove before shaking hands. The exceptions to this rule are when your hands are full of things and you therefore cannot physically remove the glove, or when you are outside and it is cold. Your handshake should be firm, but not bone-crushing or too long-lasting. Two or three seconds is long enough to hold someone's hand. Along with a firm handshake, there should be a smile and a warm tone of voice.

LEAVING A JOB

No matter how good a job you have or how successful you feel on the job there are days when most of us think, "I'm walking out right now, and never coming back." Just know that those feelings are normal, but never act hastely on such feelings. Remember that you have put much time, energy, and money into your education for a particular job; you have probably spent many hours in actually finding the job, and you have invested months or years in the job and the company. It is always wise to consider carefully before making a decision to leave a job. Here are some ways to logically analyze the directions you should take if you continue to

feel over an extended period of time that you are in the wrong job.

Analyze the Reasons. Why are you unhappy with your job? Sit down in a quiet place away from the office and analyze why you are unhappy. What has occurred to cause your unhappiness? Are you having trouble getting along with one of your co-workers? Are you having trouble getting along with your employer? If the answer to either of these questions is "yes," ask yourself why you are having difficulty. Is it something you have done? Is it something the other person has done? Try to avoid the answer that it is a personality difficulty. That answer is too general. What is the personality trait that is contributing to the problem? Can you identify and isolate the trait or traits? Is there some way that you can improve the situation? It may be as simple as going to the other person and talking through the problem. Or, it may be necessary for you to take a good look at yourself and how you are behaving. You may need to change some of the ways you are reacting to the individual.

Is it a money problem? Are you not making enough money to support yourself in the manner in which you like to live? Is there a chance to make more money at a later point with the company, or are you making as much as you can? Have you been passed over for a promotion that you feel you deserve? Money and promotion problems are usually linked together, since most of the time increases in salary come with promotions. If after analyzing the situation you discover that the problem is really salary or promotion, ask yourself what you can do about it. Are you performing at your top level? Are you continuing to learn on the job so that you are ready for that next step? Are you an enthusiastic worker? Do you get along with others? The purpose of this questioning phase is to determine if there are problems with you that you are willing to correct.

Is the problem one of boredom? Are you in a job that is not challenging to you? If the answer is "yes," ask yourself why it is not challenging. Are you looking for new opportunities to grow on the job? Can you make the job more than it is by seeking out new ways to perform the job or additional responsibilities that you might take on? Again, ask yourself the difficult questions. If the way you are handling the job is contributing to the boredom, then set about to change the way you deal with the job.

Determine Your Goals. Once you have spent time analyzing your reasons for unhappiness and you are still certain that you want to leave the job, then spend some time looking at your goals. Part of the reason for your unhappiness now may be that you did not spend enough time before accepting your present job in determining what your long term career goals are. Ask yourself where you want to be in your career in the next two years, five years, and ten years. What type of company can provide the opportunities you need? Before you leave your present position, spend time reading job ads to determine what is available in your geographic location. Or, if you are willing to change locations, spend some time determining what other locations have to offer. Be certain that you are being realistic about your abilities and what is available in the marketplace.

If your long-term career goals demand more education than you presently have to get the type of job you want, spend some time determining how you might get the additional education you need. You might be able to take night classes at a local college or business school while holding your present job. If your career goals suggest an entirely new career, determine if you are willing to spend the time and money required to get the additional schooling and experiences necessary to succeed in that career. Also, determine the job opportunities available in that career. Is it a field where many jobs are presently available and the future growth is good, or is it a field with a limited number of opportunities?

Once you have determined your career goals, consider what strengths you have to fulfill these goals. Also, consider your weaknesses. For example, if your career goal is to be an accountant but you don't enjoy working with figures for long periods of time, then it would be wise to reconsider your goals. It is important that you be realistic with yourself about your interests and abilities.

Special Problems of Being Laid Off. You may not have chosen to leave a job because of your unhappiness, but you may have been laid off. That lay off may have been due to a financial situation with the company where jobs are being discontinued, or it may have been due to your inability to do the job in the manner expected by your employer. Whatever the reason, it is difficult to be laid off. Know that your feelings of rejection and insecurity are normal. It will take a period of time for you to feel okay about the situation. However, even if you are laid off because of inability to do the job well, do not consider yourself a failure. Obviously, you have not been able to do this particular job to the satisfaction of your employer but that does not mean that you are a failure. You have failed at one job; that does not mean that you will fail at all jobs. When you have been laid off, it is time to take a hard look at who you are and what you can do. If a lay off results from your inability to do the job, try to be as objective about your performance as possible. Listen to what your employer tells you about your performance. What can you learn for the future? What steps do you need to take to see that you do not find yourself in the same situation again? Where do you need to improve? Talk with your spouse, your friends, or your closest advisers. Have open and frank dialogue with them. They may be able to give you some points for improvement that your employer has not done. You will also be able to talk through your anger with your family or friends. It is certainly not a good idea to become angry at work and lash out at your employer. However, it is also normal to feel anger; and you can express that anger to family or friends.

Before you begin looking for another job, spend time analyzing your career goals and evaluating yourself. It is not a good idea to take a new job too quickly. Give yourself enough time to release your anger, to evaluate your strengths and weaknesses, and to consider your career goals.

The Exit Interview. Whether you are leaving a job on your own or you are being laid off, most companies do an exit interview. A sample exit interview form is shown in Illustration 15–4. This exit interview is usually done by an impartial party, not your immediate supervisor. A staff member in the personnel office many times is the one to do the exit interview. This interview is not a time to "get even," to make derogatory remarks about your supervisor, or to unduly criticize the company. Keep in mind the old adage about not "burning your bridges." If you are leaving of your own volition, you may wish to return some day. Regardless of the reasons for leaving, you will probably need a reference from the company. It is time to state your reasons for leaving as objectively as possible. Be honest but not vindictive. State your reasons for leaving concisely and clearly. For example, if you are leaving for a job with greater opportunities for growth, you can say, "To accept a position with greater responsibilities." Being honest does not mean that you give all details. For example, you may have had serious problems with some of your co-workers and that is one reason for your leaving. However, just as the exit interview is not a place to criticize your employer, it is also not a place to criticize your fellow employees.

ORGANIZING YOUR WORK

As an office worker, you will have much detailed work to do. If you are to effectively master this detailed work, you must be able to organize your work, which really means organizing your time. To do this, you must be aware of the types of jobs you do and how often they occur. One of your first steps then is to analyze your job.

Analyzing Your Job. Are you aware of how you spend your time? For example, how much time do you spend keyboarding, making out reports, handling mail, taking calls, and filing? If you have no idea how much time you spend in these areas, it is a good idea to find out. You might chart your activities for one or two weeks. An example of a chart is presented in Illustration 15–5. Notice that you determine the activities of your job and then record the time you spend in these activities over a period of time. Obviously the number of hours or minutes you spend in each activity will vary from day to day or week to week, but it will be approximately the same over a period of time.

ACTIVITY LOG								
Day and Date	Handling Mail	Typing	Telephone	Filing	Duplicating	Record Keeping Activities	Miscellaneous	Total Hours
Mon. 2-25	1	4	1	1	0	0	1	8
Tues. 2-26	1:30	3:30	2	30 min.	30 min.	0	0	8
Wed. 2-27	1	5	1	1	0	0	0	8
Thurs. 2-28	1	2	2:30	1	30 min.	1	0	8
Fri. 2-29	1:15	4:30	30 min.	45 min.	0	30 min.	30 min.	8
TOTALS	5:45	19	7	4:15	1	1:30	1:30	40

Illustration 15-5. Activity Log

EXIT INTERVIEW/TERMINATION FORM

TO BE COMPLETED BY SUPERVISOR:

NAME: _____ _____ _____   Soc. Sec. No.: _____
        Last   First   M.

ELIGIBLE FOR REHIRE _____ Yes _____ No

JOB TITLE _____

COMMENTS _____

FULL TIME
HIRE DATE _____   TERMINATION DATE _____
                              (LAST DAY WORKED)

REASON FOR TERMINATION _____
_____
_____

TO BE COMPLETED BY INTERVIEWER:

Areas of concern discussed during the exit Interview should be determined below by the Interviewer.

IF INVOLUNTARY, CHECK BELOW:

_____ PERFORMANCE   _____ MISCONDUCT

PROPERTY CLEARANCE FORM INITIATED _____
                                   Supv. Initials/Date

_____
Immediate Supervisor

SUBJECT AREA	Satis-factory	Unsatis-factory	No Opinion	Comments
1. Work load/ Responsibilities				
2. Working Conditions				
3. Satisfaction Received from Work				
4. Attention to Employee Ideas				
5. Supervision				
6. Employee Benefits				
7. Advancement Opportunities				
8. Other				

INTERVIEWER'S CHECKLIST

_____ Property Clearance Form Completed
_____ Termination Notification Form Completed
_____ Benefits Discussed
_____ Retirement Funds Discussed
_____ Leave Balance _____ Day(s) Discussed

_____ _____
Interviewer   Date

_____ _____
Employee   Date

Post Employment Plans _____   _____ Not Interviewed   _____ Explain

Additional Comments _____

Illustration 15-4. Exit Interview Form

Once you have this information, what do you do with it? You analyze it critically to see if there are areas in which you can operate more efficiently. Assume that you are spending one hour a day in processing mail. Is there some way you can decrease this time? For example, are you turning all the envelopes face down and doing all the opening at once rather than individually? This point may seem minor to you, but it is the efficient handling of minor details that allows you the time needed to handle major tasks.

In addition to looking at the time you spend on each activity, you also need to analyze areas in which you are consistently behind. For example, you may find that filing is a task that you consistently put off. This can be a serious error since up-to-date files are a must. If this is happening to you, resolve to eliminate this problem area. Set aside a period of the day when you know that the office is relatively quiet, and do your filing then. If you are unable to get all the material filed in one day, be sure that you have the material sorted in a folder on your desk so you can easily find a piece of correspondence if needed.

Placing Priorities.

One of the areas in which you should be skillful is deciding in what order to do your work. Which jobs are the most important? Which job must you handle first? Establishing priorities is not easy; you must exercise good judgment. Assume a customer calls with a problem. You are extremely busy typing a report, and you tell the customer you will have someone call her or him later. You may have lost valuable dollars for your company because you exercised poor judgment by not handling the problem immediately.

In addition to using good judgment, you need to be aware of deadlines. Assume several people give you jobs to do, and all of them ask that the work be done as quickly as possible. If the work seems to be of equal importance, you may not know which to do first. If you are not given a deadline on a job, find out when the job is needed. In establishing priorities, remember:

1. Use good judgment in deciding what should be handled first; think through situations carefully.

2. Ask for a deadline on work you are given.

Planning Your Daily Schedule.

Before you leave the office for the day, you should plan your schedule for the next day. In planning your schedule, priorities are important. Do you have an important unfinished job that must be finished the next morning? Check your calendar and the tickler file to see if there are items to be handled the following day. (See Chapter 12 for setting up a tickler file.)

When you report to work in the morning, check the schedule that you have made for yourself the previous afternoon, and get organized for the day's activities. Do you have all the needed supplies? Do you have all the necessary information to prepare the reports, etc.? If you will first get yourself organized, the day will go more smoothly, and you will save yourself the time and frustration of continually having to stop and get needed supplies or information.

Do you have routine work to do each day? If so, make the routine work a habit by setting aside a certain period of time each day to do it. Handling the work in this manner takes away the tension that generally builds when you continually postpone a job that must eventually be done.

Planning Your Weekly Schedule.

In addition to planning your daily activities, you should carefully plan your weekly activities. Schedule routine activities at the best possible time. For example, if you need to order supplies weekly, determine a time to do so—probably when your work load is relatively slow. It can be extremely frustrating and take twice as long to order supplies when you have numerous interruptions. If you do not use many supplies, you may determine that it is less time-consuming to order your supplies monthly rather than weekly.

You also need to consolidate certain jobs into time blocks each week, or every two weeks, or even every month. If your office has light correspondence, you may choose to file correspondence weekly rather than daily. Again, you should decide on a time when you will have relatively few interruptions.

In determining your slack periods, it may

help to draw a diagram of weekly routine work. Then, set aside time for special work. For example, you may block off 9:00 a.m. to 12:00 M. on Monday for special work and 1:00 p.m. to 3:00 p.m. on Monday for routine work. Obviously you cannot predict all the work you will have in a week, but depicting it in diagram form can help you determine your slack times.

Organizing Materials and Supplies. Your desk should be organized so you can get your work done as efficiently as possible. All materials which are not in use should be kept off your desk. Have you ever noticed an office worker who seems to spend half the time searching for a pencil or pen which inevitably turns up under all the clutter on the desk? Most of us can be more productive in an organized situation than in a disorganized one. Notice the desk in Illustration 15–6. It is neat with every item in its particular place.

Illustration 15-6. Office Desk

Photo Courtesy of Westinghouse Furniture Systems

Your desk drawers should also be organized. The organization will depend upon your particular work requirements; however, there are a few general suggestions that can be made. The center drawer might hold the supplies which you use frequently—paper clips, rubber bands, telephone pads, pencils, pens, etc. The top drawer might hold your stationery and forms. This drawer is usually equipped with sloping partitions which allow you to separate the paper and forms into various divisions. Notice how the center drawer and top drawer are arranged in Illustration 15–7. The middle drawer might be used for your work in progress, and the bottom drawer might be used for your personal articles.

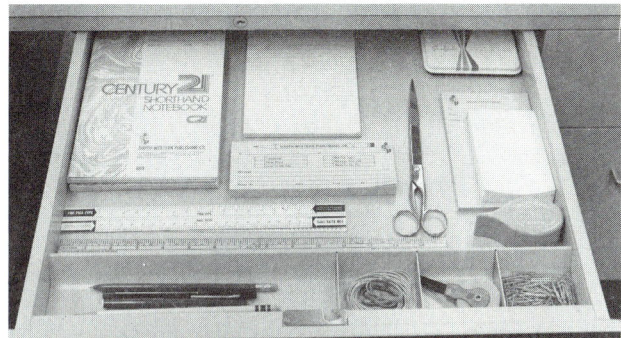

Illustration 15-7. Center and Top Desk Drawers

If you order materials for your department and keep them in a supply cabinet, see that order is maintained there also. Nothing is quite so upsetting as hunting for supplies in a disorganized supply cabinet. The supply cabinet should be organized with groups of supplies in one place. For example, letterhead, onionskin, bond paper, carbon paper, and envelopes should be in one area. Frequently used supplies should be placed on the most accessible shelves. To help keep the supplies in place, you can type small labels for each item and attach the labels to the shelf where the items are stored. Periodically

you should check the supply cabinet to see which supplies should be ordered. Reorganize the supplies, if necessary.

FOR YOUR REVIEW

The following review will help you remember the important points of this chapter.

1. In order to succeed on the job, you need to be able to work well with other employees.
   a. Carefully select your office friends.
   b. Avoid becoming part of an office clique.
   c. Do not take the initiative in promoting friendship with a superior.
   d. Be friendly, but not nosy.
   e. Do not participate in office gossip.
   f. Learn the names of your associates quickly.
   g. Cooperate with other employees in getting a job done.
   h. Observe office hours.
   i. Accept responsibilities.
   j. Display flexibility.
   k. Respect privacy.
   l. Be empathetic.
2. You must be able to work well with customers and salespeople.
   a. Relationships with customers and salespeople should be on a professional level.
   b. You may accept gifts from customers or salespersons as an expression of appreciation for business services, but you should be on guard in accepting special favors or gifts.

3. Before leaving a job, spend time analyzing the reasons why you want to leave. Ask yourself questions such as, "Why am I unhappy?" "Is there something I am doing that is causing my unhappiness?" "Is it a money problem?" "Is it because I have not been promoted?" "Is the problem one of boredom?"
4. After determining the reasons that you want to leave, spend time determining what your career goals are and how you may accomplish those goals.
5. If you are laid off from a job, do not consider yourself a failure. Listen to what your employer has to say about the reasons that you are being laid off. Then, determine ways that you may not make the same mistakes twice. Before looking for another job, spend time analyzing your career goals.
6. During the exit interview, be honest about your reasons for leaving. However, do not be extremely critical or vindictive. State your reasons for leaving in a clear and concise manner; be as objective as possible.
7. Work organization includes analyzing your job, placing priorities, planning your daily schedule, and organizing materials and supplies.

PROFESSIONAL FORUM

Ruthie Nagai has worked one month for RJ Computer Corporation. She wants to do a good job, and she works hard. However, she has trouble producing enough work. She is continually behind, and other office employees have to help her do her work. Ruthie asks you, "Can you help me? I never get as much work done as

everyone else does. I really want to do a good job. I am trying, but I am always behind. How can I improve?"

You have noticed that Ruthie is extremely disorganized. Her desk is always cluttered with papers. After arriving at work, she wastes an hour before she settles down to do any work.

Then, when she does get started, she stops many times to get information that is necessary for the job she is doing. What suggestions would you make to Ruthie to improve her productivity?

FOR YOUR UNDERSTANDING

1. Explain why just understanding human relations is not sufficient in an office situation.
2. How do office friendships and outside friendships differ?
3. What harm can office cliques cause?
4. Discuss three techniques for learning names quickly.
5. Define empathy, and explain how you would apply it in an office environment.
6. Whose name would you first mention in making the following introductions:

   a.   man and woman
   b.   young person and older person
   c.   client and office employee
7. What steps should you take when you are considering leaving a job?
8. How should you respond in an exit interview?
9. Why is it important to organize your work in the office?
10. How would you analyze the time you spend on various office jobs?

OFFICE APPLICATIONS

On pages 387–389 are office applications that correlate with this chapter.

Subject and Verb Agreement

This section presents a review of some of the basic rules concerning subject-verb agreement.

1. When the subject consists of two singular nouns and/or pronouns connected by *or, either...or, neither...nor,* or *not only...but also,* a singular verb is required.

   Jane or *Bob has* the letter.
   Either *Ruth* or *Marge plans* to attend.
   Not only a *book* but also *paper is* needed.

2. When the subject consists of two plural nouns and/or pronouns connected by *or, either...or, neither...nor,* or *not only...but also,* a plural verb is required.

   Neither the *secretaries* nor the *typists have* access to that information.

3. When the subject is made up of both singular and plural nouns and/or pronouns connected by *or, either...or, neither...nor,* or *not only...but also,* the verb agrees with the last noun or pronoun mentioned before the verb.

   Either *Ms. Rogers* or the *assistants have* access to that information.
   Neither the *men* nor *Jo is* working.

4. Disregard intervening phrases and clauses when establishing agreement between subject and verb.

   One of the men *wants* to go to the convention.

5. The words *each, every, either, neither, one,* and *another* are singular. When they are used as subjects or as adjectives modifying subjects, a singular verb is required.

   Each person *is* deserving of the award.
   Neither boy *rides* the bicycle well.

6. The following pronouns are always singular and require a singular verb:

anybody	everybody	nobody	somebody
anyone	everyone	nothing	something
anything	everything	no one	someone

   Everyone plans to attend the meeting.
   Anyone is welcome at the concert.

7. *Both, few, many, others,* and *several* are always plural. When they are used as subjects or adjectives modifying subjects, a plural verb is required.

   Several members *were* asked to make presentations.
   Both women *are* going to apply.

8. *All, none, any, some, more,* and *most* may be singular or plural, depending on the noun to which they refer.

   Some of the supplies *are* missing.
   Some of that paper *is* needed.

9. A collective noun is a word that is singular in form but represents a group of persons or things. For example, the following words are collective nouns: committee, company, department, public, class, board. These rules determine the form of the verb to be used with a collective noun.
   a. When the members of a group are thought of as one unit, the verb should be singular.

   The *committee has* voted unanimously to begin the study.

   b. When members of the group are thought of as separate units, the verb should be plural.

   The *board are* not in agreement on the decision that should be made.

10. *The number* has a singular meaning and requires a singular verb; a *number* has a plural meaning and requires a plural verb.

    A *number* of people *are* planning to attend.
    The number of requests *is* surprising.

Pronouns

Common rules concerning pronoun usage are presented in this section.

1. A pronoun agrees with its antecedent (the word for which the pronoun stands) in number, gender, and person.

   Roger wants to know if *his* book is at your house.

2. A plural pronoun is used when the antecedent consists of two nouns joined by *and*.

Mary and *Tomie* are bringing *their* stereo.

3. A singular pronoun is used when the antecedent consists of two singular nouns joined by *or* or *nor*.

A plural pronoun is used when the antecedent consists of two plural nouns joined by *or* or *nor*.

Neither *Elizabeth* nor *Johann* wants to do *her* part.
Either the *men* or the *women* will do *their* share.

4. Do not confuse certain possessive pronouns with contractions that sound alike.

its (possessive)	it's (it is)
their (possessive)	they're (they are)
theirs (possessive)	there's (there is)
your (possessive)	you're (you are)
whose (possessive)	who's (who is)

As a test for the use of a possessive pronoun or a contraction, try to substitute *it is, they are, it has, there has, there is,* or *you are*. Use the corresponding possessive form if the substitution does not make sense.

Your wording is correct.
You're wording that sentence incorrectly.
Whose book is it?
Who's the owner of this typewriter?

5. Use *who* and *that* when referring to persons.

He is the *boy who* does well in keyboarding.
She is the type of *person that* we like to employ.

6. Use *which* and *that* when referring to places, objects, and animals.

The card *that I* sent you was mailed last week.
The fox, *which* is very sly, caught the skunk.

APPENDIX B
PUNCTUATION AND CAPITALIZATION

Punctuation

Correct punctuation is based on certain accepted rules and principles rather than on the whims of the writer. Punctuation is also important if the reader is to interpret correctly the writer's thoughts. The summary of rules given in this appendix will be helpful in using correct punctuation.

The Period

The period indicates a full stop and is used

1. At the end of a complete declarative or imperative sentence.
2. After abbreviations and after a single or double initial that represents a word.

acct.	etc.	Ph.D.
U.S.	viz.	p.m.
N.E.	i.e.	pp.

However, some abbreviations that are made up of several initial letters do not require periods.

FDIC (Federal Deposit Insurance Corporation)
FEPC (Fair Employment Practices Committee)
AAA (American Automobile Association)
YWCA (Young Women's Christian Association)

3. Between dollars and cents. A period and cipher are not required when an amount in even dollars is expressed in figures.

$42.65 $1.47 $25

4. To indicate a decimal.

3.5 bushels   12.65 percent   6.25 feet

The Comma

The comma indicates a partial stop and is used

1. To separate coordinate clauses that are connected by conjunctions, such as *and, but, or, for, neither, nor,* unless the clauses are short and closely connected.

We have a supply on hand, but I think we should order an additional quantity.
She had to work late, for the auditors were examining the books.

2. To set off a subordinate clause that precedes the main clause.

Assuming that there will be no changes, I suggest that you proceed with your instructions.

3. After an introductory phrase containing a verb form.

To finish his work, he remained at the office after hours.
After planning the program, she proceeded to put it into effect.

If an introductory phrase does not contain a verb, it usually is not followed by a comma.

After much deliberation the plan was revoked.
Because of the vacation period we have been extremely busy.

4. To set off a nonrestrictive clause.

Our group, which had never lost a debate, won the grand prize.

5. To set off a nonrestrictive phrase.

The beacon, rising proudly toward the sky, guided the pilots safely home.

6. To separate from the rest of the sentence a word or a group of words that breaks the continuity of a sentence.

The secretary, even though his work was completed, was always willing to help others.

7. To separate parenthetical expressions from the rest of the sentence.

We have, as you know, two persons who can handle the reorganization.

8. To set off names used in direct address or to set off explanatory phrases or clauses.

I think you, Mr. Bennett, will agree with the statement.
Ms. Linda Tom, our vice-president, will be in your city soon.

9. To separate from the rest of the sentence expressions that, without punctuation, might be interpreted incorrectly.

Misleading: Ever since we have filed our reports monthly.
Better: Ever since, we have filed our reports monthly.

10. To separate words or groups of words when they are used in a series of three or more.

Most executives agree that dependability, trustworthiness, ambition, and judgment are required of their office workers.
Again I emphasize that factory organization, correlation of sales and production, and a good office organization are all necessary for maximum results.

11. To set off short quotations from the rest of the sentence.

He said, "I shall be there."
"The committees have agreed," he said, "to work together on the project."

12. To separate the name of a city from the name of a state.

Our southern branch is located in Atlanta, Georgia.

13. To separate abbreviations of titles from the name.

William R. Warner, Jr.   Ramona Sanchez, Ph.D.

The Semicolon

The semicolon should be used in the following instances:

1. Between independent groups or clauses that are long or that contain parts that are separated by commas.

He was outstanding in his knowledge of typing, shorthand, spelling, and related subjects; but he was lacking in many desirable personal qualities.

2. Between the members of a compound sentence when the conjunction is omitted.

Many executives would rather dictate to a machine than to a secretary; the machine won't talk back.

3. To precede expressions such as *namely* or *viz., for example* or *e.g., that is* or *i.e.,* when used to introduce a clause.

We selected the machine for two reasons; namely, because it is as reasonable in price as any other and because it does better work than others.
There are several reasons for changing the routine of handling mail; i.e., to reduce postage, to conserve time, and to place responsibility.

4. In a series of well-defined units when special emphasis is desired.

Emphatic: The prudent secretary considers the future; he or she makes sure that all the requirements are obtained, and he or she uses his or her talents to attain successfully the desired goal.

Less emphatic: The prudent secretary considers the future, makes sure that all the requirements are obtained, and uses his or her talents to attain successfully the desired goal.

The Colon

The colon is recommended in the following instances:

1. After the salutation in a business letter except when open punctuation is used.

Ladies and Gentlemen: Dear Ms. Carroll:

2. Following introductory expressions, such as *the following, thus, as follows,* and other expressions that precede enumerations.

Please send the following by parcel post:
Officers were elected as follows: president, _____ ; vice-president, _____ ; secretary-treasurer, _____ .

3. To separate hours and minutes when indicating time.

2:10 p.m.   4:45 p.m.   12:15 a.m.

4. To introduce a long quotation.

The agreement read: "We the undersigned hereby agree...."

5. To separate two independent groups having no connecting words between them and in which the second group explains or expands the statement in the first group.

We selected the machine for one reason: in competitive tests it surpassed all other machines.

The Question Mark (Interrogation Point)

The question mark should be used in the following instances:

1. After each direct question.

When do you expect to arrive in Philadelphia?

An exception to the foregoing rule is a sentence that is phrased in the form of a question, merely as a matter of courtesy, when it is actually a request.

Will you please send us an up-to-date statement of our account.

2. After each question in a series of questions within one sentence.

What is your opinion of the IBM word processor? the Xerox? the CPT?

The Exclamation Point

The exclamation point is ordinarily used after words or groups of words that express command, strong feeling, emotion, or an exclamation.

> Don't waste office supplies!
> It can't be done!
> Stop!

The Dash

The dash is used in the following instances:

1. To indicate an omission of letters or figures.

> Dear Mr. —
> Date the letter July 16, 19 — .

2. Sometimes in letters, especially sales letters, to cause a definite stop in reading the letter. Usually the dash is used in such cases for increased emphasis. One must be careful, however, not to overdo the use of the dash.

> This book is not a revision of an old book — it is a brand new book.

3. To separate parenthetical expressions when unusual emphasis is desired on the parenthetical expression.

> These sales arguments — and every one of them is important — should result in getting the order.

The Apostrophe

The apostrophe should be used

1. To indicate possession.

> The boy's coat; the ladies' dresses; the girl's book.

   a. To form the possessive singular, add *'s* to the noun.

> man's work   bird's wing   hostess's plans

An exception to this rule is made when the word following the possessive begins with an *s* sound.

> for goodness' sake   for conscience' sakes

   b. To form the possessive of a plural noun ending in a *s* or *z* sound, add only the apostrophe (') to the plural noun.

> workers' rights   hostesses' duties

   c. If the plural noun does not end in *s* or *z* sound, add *'s* to the plural noun.

> women's clothes   alumni's donations

   d. Proper names that end in an *s* sound form the possessive singular by adding *'s*.

> Williams's house   Fox's automobile

   e. Proper names ending in *s* form the possessive plural by adding the apostrophe (') only.

> The Walters' property faces the Jones' swimming pool.

2. To indicate the omission of a letter or letters in a contraction.

> it's (it is), you're (you are), we'll (we shall)

3. To indicate the plurals of letters, figures, words, and abbreviations.

> Don't forget to dot your i's and cross your t's.
> I can add easily by 2's and 4's, but I have difficulty with 6's and 8's.
> More direct letters can be written by using shorter sentences and by omitting and's and but's.
> Two of the speakers were Ph.D.'s.

Quotation Marks

Certain basic rules should be followed in using quotation marks. These rules are as follows:

1. When a quotation mark is used with a comma or a period, the comma or period should be placed inside the quotation mark.

> She said, "I plan to complete my program in college before seeking a position."

2. When a quotation mark is used with a semicolon or a colon, the semicolon or colon should be placed outside the quotation mark.

> The treasurer said, "I plan to go by train"; others in the group stated that they would go by plane.

3. When more than one paragraph of quoted material is used, quotation marks should appear at the beginning of each paragraph and at the end of the last paragraph.

> " _____
> _____
> _____
> " _____
> _____
> _____ "

4. Quotation marks are used in the following instances:

a. Before and after direct quotations.

The author states, "Too frequent use of certain words weakens the appeal."

b. To indicate a quotation within a quotation, use single quotation marks.

The author states, "Too frequent use of 'very' and 'most' weakens the appeal."

c. To indicate the title of a published article.

Have you read the article, "Automation in the Office"?
He asked, "Have you read 'Automation in the Office'?"

Omission Marks or Ellipses

Ellipses marks (... or ***) are frequently used to denote the omission of letters or words in quoted material. If the material omitted ends in a period, four omission marks are used (....). If the material omitted is elsewhere in the quoted material, three omission marks are used (...).

He quoted the proverb, "A soft answer turneth away wrath: but...."
She quoted Plato, "Nothing is more unworthy of a wise man...than to have allowed more time for trifling and useless things than they deserved."

Parentheses

Although parentheses are frequently used as a catch-all in writing, they are correctly used in the following instances:

1. When amounts expressed in words are followed by figures.

He agreed to pay twenty-five dollars ($25) as soon as possible.

2. Around words that are used as parenthetical expressions.

Our letter costs (excluding paper and postage) are much too high for this type of business.

3. To indicate technical references.

Sodium chloride (NaCl) is the chemical name for common table salt.

4. When enumerations are included in narrative form.

The reasons for his resignation were three: (1) advanced age, (2) failing health, (3) a desire to travel.

Capitalization

In this section are summarized the rules for capitalization that will be convenient for reference purposes.

Common Usage

The following are examples of the most common usage of capitalization:

1. The first word of every sentence should be capitalized.
2. The first word of a complete direct quotation should be capitalized.
3. The first word of a salutation and all nouns used in the salutation should be capitalized.
4. The first word in a complimentary close should be capitalized.

Outline Form

Capitalize the first word in each section of an outline form.

First Word After a Colon

Capitalize the first word after a colon only when the colon introduces a complete passage or sentence having independent meaning.

In conclusion I wish to say: "The survey shows that...."

If the material following a colon is dependent on the preceding clause, the first word after the colon is not capitalized.

I present the following three reasons for changing: the volume of business does not justify the expense; we are short of people; the product is decreasing in popularity.

Names

1. Capitalize the names of associations, buildings, churches, hotels, streets, organizations, and clubs.

The Business Club, Merchandise Mart, Central Christian Church, Peabody Hotel, Seventh Avenue, Administrative Management Society, Chicago Chamber of Commerce

2. All proper names should be capitalized.

Great Britain, John G. Hammitt, Mexico

3. Capitalize names that are derived from proper names.

American, Chinese

246

Do not, however, capitalize words that are derived from proper nouns and that have developed a special meaning.

pasteurized milk, china dishes, morocco leather

4. Capitalize special names for regions and localities.

North Central states, the Far East, the East Side, the Hoosier State

Do not, however, capitalize adjectives derived from such names or localities that are used as directional parts of states and countries.

far eastern lands, the southern United States, southern Illinois

5. Capitalize names of government boards, agencies, bureaus, departments, and commissions.

Civil Service Commission, Social Security Board, Bureau of Navigation.

6. Capitalize names of the deity, the Bible, holy days, and religious denominations.

God, Easter, Yom Kippur, Genesis, Church of Christ

7. Capitalize the names of holidays.

Memorial Day, Labor Day

8. Capitalize words used before numbers and numerals, with the exception of the common word, such as page, line, and verse.

The reservation is Lower 6, Car 27.
He found the material in Part 3 of Chapter X.

Titles Used in Business and Professions

The following are rules for capitalizing titles in business and professions.

1. Any title that signifies rank, honor, and respect, and that immediately precedes an individual's name should be capitalized.

She asked President Harry G. Sanders to preside.
He was attended by Dr. Howard Richards.

2. Academic degrees should be capitalized when they precede or follow an individual name.

Mrs. Constance R. Collins, Ph.D., was invited to direct the program.
Fred R. Bowling, Master of Arts

3. Capitalize titles of high-ranking government officers when the title is used in place of the proper name in referring to a specific person.

Our Senator invited us to visit him in Washington.
The President will return to Washington soon.

4. Capitalize military and naval titles signifying rank.

Captain Meyers, Lieutenant White, Lieutenant Commander Murphy

1. Spell out numbers 1 through 10; use figures for numbers above 10.

   We ordered *ten* coats and *four* dresses.
   About *60* letters were keyed.

2. If there are numbers above and below ten in correspondence, be consistent — either spell out all numbers or place all numbers in figures. If most of the numbers are below 10, put them in words. If most are above 10, express them all in figures.

   Please order *12* memo pads, *2* reams of paper, and *11* boxes of envelopes.

3. Numbers in the millions or higher may be expressed in the following manner in order to aid comprehension.

   3 billion (rather than 3,000,000,000)

4. Always spell out a number that begins a sentence.

   Five hundred books were ordered.

5. If the numbers are large, rearrange the wording of the sentence so that the number is not the first word of the sentence.

   We had a good year in 1976.
   Not: Nineteen hundred and seventy-six was a good year.

6. Spell out indefinite numbers and amounts.

   A *few hundred* voters

7. Spell out all ordinals (first, second, third, etc.) that can be expressed in words.

   The store's *twenty-fifth* anniversary was held this week.

8. When adjacent numbers are written in words or written in figures, use a comma to separate them.

   On Car 33, 450 cartons are being shipped.

9. House or building numbers are written in figures. However, when the number one ap-pears by itself, it is spelled out. Numbers one through ten in street names are spelled out; numbers above ten are written in figures. When figures are used for both the house number and the street name, use a hyphen that is preceded and followed by a space.

101 Building	2301 Fifth Avenue
One Main Place	122 - 33d Street

10. Ages are usually spelled out except when the age is stated exactly in years, months, and days. When ages are presented in tabular form, they are written in figures.

    She is eighteen years old.
    He is 2 years, 10 months, and 18 days old.

Name	*Age*
Jones, Edward	19
King, Ruth	21

11. Use figures to express dates written in normal month-day-year order. Do not use "th," "nd," or "rd" following the date.

    May 8, 1987
    Not: May 8th, 1987

12. Fractions should be spelled out unless they are part of mixed numbers. Use a hyphen to separate the numerator and denominator of fractions written in words when the fraction is used as an adjective.

    three-fourths inch
    5 5/6

13. In legal documents, numbers may be written in both words and figures.

    One Hundred Thirty-Four and 30/100 Dollars ($134.30)

14. Amounts of money are usually expressed in figures. Indefinite money amounts are written in words.

    $100
    $3.27
    several hundred dollars

15. Express percentages in figures; spell out the word percent.

> 10 percent

16. To form the plural of figures, add s.

Technological advances will increase in the 1980s.

17. In times of day, use figures with a.m. and p.m.; spell out numbers with the word o'clock. In formal usage, all times are spelled out.

> 9 a.m.
> 10 p.m.
> eight o'clock in the evening

This section presents a review of fractions, decimals, and percentages.

Fractions $\dfrac{2\ \text{Numerator}}{3\ \text{Denominator}}$

1. To add or subtract two or more fractions
   a. Find the lowest common denominator.
   b. Express each fraction as an equivalent fraction, having the lowest common denominator as the denominator for each fraction.
   c. Add or subtract the resulting fractions.
   d. Reduce to lowest terms if necessary.

   Example:

   $$\frac{1}{2} + \frac{2}{16} + \frac{5}{12}$$

The lowest common denominator of 2, 16, and 12 is 48.

$$\frac{1}{2} = \frac{24}{48}$$

$$\frac{2}{16} = \frac{6}{48}$$

$$\frac{5}{12} = \frac{20}{48}$$

$$\frac{24}{48} + \frac{6}{48} + \frac{20}{48} = \frac{50}{48} = 1\frac{1}{24}$$

2. To multiply fractions
   a. Multiply the numerators.
   b. Multiply the denominators.
   c. Reduce to lowest terms if necessary.

   $$\frac{2}{15} \times \frac{3}{7} = \frac{6}{105} = \frac{2}{35}$$

3. To divide fractions
   a. Invert the second fraction.
   b. Multiply (according to the multiplication rule).

   $$\frac{2}{3} \div \frac{3}{4} = \frac{2}{3} \times \frac{4}{3} = \frac{8}{9}$$

Decimals

1. To convert a fraction to a decimal, divide the numerator by the denominator.

$$\frac{2}{5} = .4 \text{ because:} \qquad 5\overline{)2.0} \;\; .4$$

$$\frac{13}{20} = \quad 20\overline{)13.00} \;\; .65$$
$$\underline{12.0}$$
$$100$$
$$\underline{100}$$
$$0$$

Note: Add to the dividend as many zeros as necessary to complete the division process.

2. To convert a decimal to a fraction
   a. Delete the decimal point and use the resulting number as the numerator.
   b. Count the number of places the decimal point would have to be moved in the given decimal to get it just to the right of the units digit in the numerator. (For example, in 21.410 it will be 3 places.)
   c. The denominator will be a 1 followed by as many zeros as places counted in Step 2b.

For example, to convert .414 to a fraction, use 414 as the numerator.
The decimal point has to be moved three places to the right.
The denominator will be 1 followed by three zeros.

$$.414 = \frac{414}{1000}$$

3. To add and subtract decimals
   a. Place the decimal points of the numbers to be added or subtracted in a vertical column before performing the addition or subtraction.

For example, to add 0.5, 2.30, 30.495 and 0.05, first write the numbers in a column; then add.

0.5		0.500
2.30		2.300
30.495		30.495
0.05	or as	0.050
33.345		33.345

   b. Follow the same procedure in subtraction. Place the decimal points of the numbers to be subtracted in a vertical column. Each amount must have the same number of decimal places, so it may be necessary to add zeros before performing the subtraction.

For example, to subtract 1.9 from 2.871, add two zeros at the end of the 1.9 as follows:

$$\begin{array}{r} 2.871 \\ -1.900 \\ \hline .971 \end{array}$$

4. To multiply decimals
   a. Multiply in the same manner as for whole numbers except the decimal point must be placed correctly in the answer.
   b. Count the number of digits to the right of the decimal point in the multiplicand and in the multiplier; then count the same number of places from right to left in the product and insert the decimal point.

Example:

$$\begin{array}{rl} \$5.20 & \text{2 decimal places} \\ \times .35 & \text{2 decimal places} \\ \hline 2600 & \\ 1560 & \\ \hline \$1.8200 & \text{2 + 2 = 4 decimal places} \end{array}$$

   c. In some cases it is necessary to add zeros in the product to obtain the required number of decimal places.

Example: .00031 × 3.21

$$\begin{array}{rl} 3.21 & \text{2 decimal places} \\ \times .00031 & \text{5 decimal places} \\ \hline 321 & \\ 963 & \\ \hline .0009951 & \text{5 + 2 = 7 decimal places} \end{array}$$

5. To divide decimals
   a. Change the divisor to a whole number by moving the decimal point in the divisor to the right until the divisor becomes a whole number.
   b. Move the decimal point in the dividend the same number of places.
   c. Place the decimal point in the quotient directly above the new decimal point in the dividend.

Example: Divide 23.56 by 1.5

$$\begin{array}{r} 1\,5.706 \\ 1.5\,\overline{)\,23.5\ 600} \\ \underline{15} \\ 85 \\ \underline{75} \\ 106 \\ \underline{105} \\ 10 \\ \underline{0} \\ 100 \\ \underline{90} \\ 10 \end{array}$$

Percent

1. To change a percent to a fraction, drop the percent sign, place the number over 100, and reduce the fraction to lowest terms. If the numerator results in a decimal, multiply numerator and denominator by an appropriate power of 10 to clear the decimal.

$$4\% = \frac{4}{100} = \frac{1}{25}$$

$$5.5\% = \frac{5.5}{100} = \frac{55}{1000} = \frac{11}{200}$$

2. To change a percent to a decimal, move the decimal point two places to the left and drop the percent sign.

$$12\% = .12$$
$$3\% = .03$$

3. To find a certain percent of a number, convert the percent to a decimal and multiply by the number.

Example: 34% of 500

$$\begin{array}{r} 500 \\ \times .34 \\ \hline 2000 \\ 1500 \\ \hline 170.00 = 170 \end{array}$$

4. To calculate the percent of increase or decrease
   a. Determine the amount of increase or the amount of decrease.
   b. Divide the amount of increase or the amount of decrease by the reference amount.
   c. Then multiply the result by 100 percent.

Percent of increase $= \dfrac{\text{Amount of increase}}{\text{Reference amount}} \times 100\%$

Percent of decrease $= \dfrac{\text{Amount of decrease}}{\text{Reference amount}} \times 100\%$

Example: Joan typed 30 letters on Wednesday and 40 letters on Thursday. Calculate the percent of increase in her letter production on Thursday as compared to Wednesday.

$$40 - 30 = 10 \text{ (Amount of increase)}$$

$$\frac{10}{30} \times 100\% = .333 \times 100\% = 33.3\%$$

5. To calculate reference values or amounts

   a. Compute the percent of original value or amount by adding 100 percent plus the percent of increase.

b. Convert the percent of original value or amount to a decimal by dividing the result from the above by 100 percent.

c. Divide the original value or amount by the result from (b).

Example: Joan keyed 40 letters on Thursday. This was a 33.3 percent increase over her Wednesday letter production. Calculate the number of letters Joan prepared on Wednesday.

$$100\% + 33.3\% = 133.3\%$$

$$\frac{133.3\%}{100\%} = 1.333$$

$$\frac{40}{1.333} = 30$$

STATIONERY, SECOND SHEETS, AND CARBON PACKS

Selection of Stationery, Second Sheets, and Carbon Paper

Types of Paper. Paper may be manufactured from rag fibers or sulphite (wood pulp). The higher the rag content or cotton content, the better the quality of paper. Paper containing 100 percent cotton content is the best paper manufactured. Cotton content ranges from 25 percent to 100 percent. Letterhead stationery is usually placed on paper containing from 50 to 100 percent cotton content.

Weight of Paper. Paper for office use comes in weights which range from 7 pounds to 32 pounds. The number of pounds is determined by the weight of a ream of paper which consists of 500 sheets 17 × 22 inches. Two thousand sheets of 8½-inch × 11-inch paper are cut from one ream. The weight of the paper is printed on the box or package. For example, if the label on the end of the ream reads "Sub 20," that particular ream is 20-pound paper. The most common weights of paper for office use are 16-, 20-, and 24-pound weights. Letterhead is usually on paper of from 20 to 24 pounds. Interoffice memorandums are usually on paper from 13 to 20 pounds.

Watermark. The watermark is the content information that is imprinted in the paper. It contains the brand of the paper and the percentage of cotton fiber in the paper. Paper also has a right and wrong side which you can determine by the watermark. The right side shows a readable watermark.

Second Sheets. The paper used to make a carbon copy is called a second sheet or onionskin. It is lightweight paper so that the copies will take up little filing space and may be mailed at low cost. It comes in 8 to 13 pound weights, with 9 pounds being the most frequently used weight. Second sheets are available in several colors—white, yellow, blue, pink—since some offices like to use a color coding system in routing copies. For example, the blue copy may be routed to the accounting department, the yellow copy to the receiving department, etc.

Second sheets are manufactured in cockle, smooth, or glazed finishes. When you need to make a large number of copies with high quality results, you should select a smooth finish. Glazed second sheets should be used when you are only concerned with making a maximum number of copies. Cockle finish onionskin makes a pretty carbon copy in that it resists smearing; however, fewer copies can be made on cockle finish than on smooth or glazed finishes since the cockle finish cushions the striking blow of the type bar or element.

Carbon Paper. With the advent of copying machines, fewer carbon copies are made now than were made in the past. However, your responsibilities as an office worker involve selecting and using the most economical method of making copies. And, if you are making only a few copies, a carbon copy is usually the most economical method.

When preparing letters and other business reports that require multiple carbon copies, you should be able to assemble a carbon pack quickly and efficiently. Although there are several methods of assembling carbon packs, two of the most commonly used techniques are described on page 254.

The selection of proper carbon paper for office work is very important. Although carbon paper is sometimes purchased on the basis of its low price, the selection of a good grade will prove to be economical.

Various weights and qualities of carbon paper can be obtained. The standard weight carbon paper is easier to handle than the lightweight, but is not as good as the lightweight when making numerous copies of typewritten material. The durability of carbon paper depends upon its finish which may be soft, medium soft, medium, medium hard, or hard.

The type size and the hardness of the platen

ASSEMBLING CARBON PACKS

METHOD A

1. Place a sheet of paper for a carbon copy (second sheet) on the desk; on top of that sheet place a sheet of carbon paper, carbonized side down. For each extra copy desired, add one set (a second sheet and a carbon). Place a letterhead or a plain sheet of heavier paper on top of the pack for the original copy.
2. Turn the pack around so the second sheets and the glossy sides of the carbon sheets face you.
3. Tap the sheets gently on the desk to straighten the pack. To keep the sheets straight when feeding:
   a. Place the pack in the fold of an envelope or in the fold of a plain sheet of paper.
   b. After the pack is inserted in the typewriter, remove the envelope or paper fold.
4. Insert the pack by holding it firmly in one hand while turning the platen slowly with the other. To insert the carbon pack into the typewriter easily:
   a. Release the paper-release lever.
   b. Feed the pack around the platen until the sheets appear at the front.
   c. Reset the paper-release lever.

METHOD B

1. Arrange an original and second sheets for insertion into the typewriter.
2. Turn the platen until the sheets are gripped slightly by the feed rolls; then lay all but the last sheet over the top of the machine.
3. Place the carbon sheets between the sheets of paper with the carbonized surface toward you. Flip each sheet back as you add each carbon.
4. Roll the pack into typing position. To avoid wrinkling, release and reset the paper-release lever after the rollers behind the platen have grasped the carbon pack.
5. Remove the carbon sheets after the typing is completed. As the carbon sheets do not extend to the top edge of the paper, it is easy to remove all the sheets at one time by pulling them out as you hold the left top edge of the paper.

Assembling a carbon pack   *Inserting the carbon pack*
METHOD A

Assembling a carbon pack in a typewriter   *Removing the carbon sheets*
METHOD B

affect the choice of the carbon paper finish. If a typewriter has a soft platen and pica or larger type, a soft finish carbon paper should be used. When a typewriter has a hard platen and elite or smaller type, a hard finish carbon paper is preferable. Medium finish is used for all situations not covered above

The carbon paper weight is determined by the number of copies that are being made. The number of copies with the weight necessary are:

Number of Copies to Be Made	Weight of Carbon Paper to Use
Nine or More Copies	Light
Five to Eight Copies	Medium
One to Four Copies	Standard

Carbon paper should be kept in a box or a folder so that it will lie flat and will not become wrinkled or curled at the edges. A wrinkle in a piece of carbon paper will cause "trees" or smudges to appear on the carbon copies. Carbon paper with "carbon free" corners or bottom edges will prevent smudging the fingers when removing the carbon.

When it becomes difficult to read the carbon copy, the used carbon paper should be discarded. Usually a sheet of carbon paper should not be used more than ten times. Remember, however, that if the entire sheet is not used, the ends should be alternated each time the paper is used.

"One-time carbon" is a lightweight carbon paper that usually comes as part of an assembly of business forms, such as invoices and sales orders. It is inexpensive, and its use saves the keyboard operator's time in assembling the forms and carbon paper. As its name implies, it is normally used only once.

Copying film is a solvent ink-coating carbon. This film permits itself to re-ink, and gives you three to five times the wear of conventional carbon paper.

NCR (no carbon required) paper eliminates the use of carbon paper and may be used for a wide variety of business forms. The initials "NCR" also stand for the NCR Corporation, which developed the no-carbon paper and which gives forms' manufacturers permission to make the paper and to use it in multiple copy forms.

APPENDIX F

PROOFREADING

PROOFREADER'S MARKS

Symbol	Meaning	Marked Copy	Corrected Copy
Cap or ≡	Capitalize	dallas, texas	Dallas, Texas
∧	Insert	two people (or three)	two or three people
ℓ	Delete	the man and woman	the man
⊏	Move to left	human relations	human relations
#	Add space	follow these	follow these
/ lc	Lowercase letter	in the Fall of 1983	in the fall of 1983
⌒	Close up space	sum mer	summer
tr or ∼	Transpose	When is it	When it is
⊐	Move to right	skills for living	skills for living
⌄	Insert apostrophe	Macs book	Mac's book
⌄⌄	Insert quotation marks	She said, No.	She said, "No."
⊔	Move down	fallen	fallen
⊓	Move up	straight	straight
¶	Paragraph	¶ The first and third page	The first and third page
No new ¶	No new paragraph	No new ¶ The first and third page	The first and third page
sp	Spell out	Dr.	Doctor
Stet or	Let it stand; ignore correction	most efficient worker	most efficient worker
___	Underline or italics	Business World	Business World
⊙	Insert period	the last word	the last word.

Proofreading Suggestions

1. Concentrate as you proofread. Read slowly; this is not the time for speed-reading.

2. Proofread the copy twice — once reading from left to right and once reading backwards (from right to left).

3. Make the dictionary a friend. Look up the spelling of any words that you are unsure are spelled correctly.

4. Watch closely for omissions of *ed* or *s* at the end of words.

5. Pay attention to dates. Do not assume that they are correct. Check the dates against a calendar to be sure that a Thursday is actually on May 13, for example. Be specifically careful of the year during the months of January and February. It is difficult for us to adjust to a new year for a while.

6. If punctuation causes you difficulties, check these marks after you have completed all other proofreading. Be careful not to omit a closing parenthesis or quotation mark.

7. Be consistent in the use of commas. If you are unsure of whether or not a comma should be used, check the comma rules in Appendix B.

8. Be consistent in the use of capital letters. Check Appendix B for the rules if you are unsure.

Care of Your Typewriter

To insure the best performance and the longest life from your typewriter, you should take good care of your machine. This care includes properly using the machine and properly cleaning its keys.

Instruction Booklets. Typewriter manufacturers furnish instruction booklets with each typewriter purchased. This booklet provides detailed instructions on how to operate and care for your machine. It gives information on special features of the machine such as the dual-pitch mechanism, the half-space back space key, the element, and the page-end indicator. It also provides instructions on changing the ribbon, using correction tape, and cleaning the typewriter. It will be to your advantage to thoroughly read this instruction booklet.

Cleaning. The element or type bars on your typewriter should be kept clean. If they are not regularly cleaned, the keys will become clogged with ink, and your typewritten product will look messy. Various methods may be used to clean your keys; several are listed below.

Liquid Type Cleaners. Liquid type cleaners may be used successfully on type-bar or element machines. On a type-bar machine, the liquid cleaner is applied directly to the type bars. Care should be taken to only apply the necessary amount of fluid. If too much fluid is applied, the fluid drips into the machine, sometimes causing problems such as type bars sticking or reacting sluggishly.

To clean an element, remove it from the machine, hold the element in one hand, and apply the liquid cleaner with the other hand. Any excess liquid can be removed by blotting with a paper towel.

Plastic Type Cleaners. Plastic cleaners consist of a puttylike substance that pulls the dirt from the keys. These putty cleaners may be used successfully on type-bar or element machines. To clean the element with a putty type cleaner, the element must be removed from the machine. Rotate the element with one hand while applying the cleaner with the other hand.

Paper Type Cleaners. A paper cleaner is a sheet of paper with an adhesive substance. This sheet is rolled into the machine, the machine is set on stencil, and the typist types the keys clean. A paper towel may also be used fairly successfully in this manner since the towel is absorbent.

Brushes. Most typewriter manufacturers provide a set of brushes for cleaning their machines. A short, stiff bristle brush is usually provided to brush ink buildup from the type bars or elements.

Professional Cleaning. In addition to the cleaning that you do on your typewriter, it is wise to have the typewriter professionally cleaned every few years. The professional cleaner can disassemble the machine and thoroughly clean the various parts. The frequency of having your typewriter professionally cleaned depends on the amount of use of the machine. You might need to have it cleaned once every three or four years. Or, if your typewriter is used extensively, you might have it cleaned every one or two years.

Error Correction

Although one should strive for perfection in typing, it is humanly impossible to type for a great length of time without making an error. Many typewriters have a self-correcting mechanism which allows the typist to make a good correction with minimal effort. However, you should be familiar with basic correction devices and techniques, and be able to use them well.

Self-Correcting Ribbon. Many typewriters are manufactured with self-correcting ribbons. When you make an error, you back space to the point where the error was made by using a special error correction key. You then restrike the incorrect character to delete it from the paper, and then type the correct character. In the process, the self-correcting ribbon on the typewriter "lifts off" the incorrect character. The self-correcting ribbon must be replaced after it is used once.

Eraser. You can get a good correction by using an eraser if you erase properly. A very effective eraser is the stick type which may be a hard or soft eraser. The hard eraser or the more abrasive eraser is usually gray or white in color. This type of eraser should be used when erasing on an original. When erasing, you should use a soft, circular motion in order to avoid making a hole in the paper. If you are using a ribbon that is extremely dark, it is helpful to take the plastic type cleaner and place in on the letter to pull off the excess ink before you begin to erase. A soft eraser is used on carbon copies. If either eraser becomes dirty, you should clean it on scratch paper, on sandpaper, or on an emery board. A dirty eraser will smear the copy.

Eraser Shield. An eraser shield, a metal or celluloid device with small slits of different sizes, is convenient in assisting the typist to make an erasure without interfering with the correct portion of the copy. The eraser shield is held in place with one hand while the erasure is made with the other hand. If you do not have an eraser shield, use special care not to blur or smudge the letters adjacent to the erasure. If you do blur them, lightly strike over them again.

Liquid Correction. Liquid correction fluid allows you to brush over the error and thus conceal it. The liquid is made in various colors (e.g., white, blue, yellow) so if you are using a colored original or colored second sheets, the liquid shade will match the paper color. If you are making a liquid correction in a situation where you plan to send out the original, you must correct carefully so you do not achieve a "painted on" look. Lightly brush over the incorrect letter or letters, being careful not to brush

outside the outlines of the letters. Apply the liquid sparingly. When it dries, type the correct letter or letters.

If you are using liquid correction fluid on copy that is to be reproduced on a copy machine or on an offset press, you need not be as careful in applying the fluid. The liquid correction fluid does not show up on the copies run; only the type shows. Thus, you can quickly "paint" over an errror.

Correction Paper. A special paper coated with a chalklike chemical can also be used to correct errors. The coated side is placed over the error. Back space to locate the error, place the coated side of the correction paper over the error, and retype the erroneous letter. By doing so, the letter is coated with the white substance. Remove the correction paper and then back space and type the correct letter. Correction paper also comes in colors so that you may match the paper on which you are typing. This paper is best used in interoffice correspondence or on something for which you are not too concerned about the appearance of the copy since the coating may rub off. If the coating does rub off, the correction looks like a strikeover.

Typewriting Techniques and Shortcuts

There are many typewriting techniques and shortcuts that can save you time. You make yourself a more valuable employee if you are familiar with these procedures.

Small Cards and Labels. On some typewriters it is difficult to type cards and labels because they slip in the carriage feed; and it is almost impossible to type at the bottom of the card or label. For most typewriters, special devices may be obtained for use in typing cards and labels. Any typist can, however, prepare special devices that will help in typing cards and labels.

Pleat Sheet

1. Crease a narrow pleat across the middle of a sheet of 8½- by 11-inch paper to form a pocket into which the card or label can be inserted. Tape the sides of the pocket.

2. Insert the pleated sheet into the machine until the pleat comes into the writing position.

3. Place the card or label in the pleat and turn the platen backwards.

4. Remove the card or label after typing it, leaving the pleated sheet in the machine so that the next card or label can be fed in the same manner as the first.

Card Holder. You may also use a card holder. Cut a slit in the paper a little shorter than the width of the label or card to be typed. Insert the label or card in the slit portion and then feed the paper into the machine. Illustration G-1 shows the way the pleat sheet and the card holder should look.

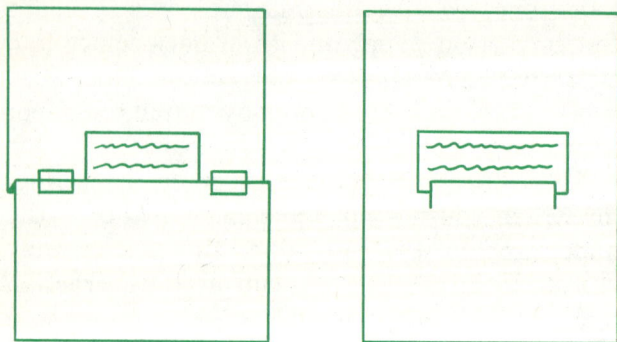

Illustration G-1. Pleat Sheet and Card Holder

Bottom-Line Typing. As you type close to the bottom of a sheet of paper, there is a tendency for the paper to begin to slip. This slippage can be controlled through a simple technique. As you begin to get close to the bottom of the page, insert a sheet of paper between the back of the original sheet and the platen. This extra sheet provides greater tension on the platen and keeps the original sheet from slipping.

Chain-Feeding of Cards and Envelopes. When a number of cards are to be typed or a number of envelopes addressed, considerable time can be saved by chain-feeding. There are two basic methods of chain-feeding—the back-feeding method and the front-feeding method. To chain-feed by the back-feeding method, follow the procedures on page 261. To chain-feed by the front-feeding method, follow the procedures on page 261.

Horizontal and Vertical Ruling. The most common way of drawing horizontal lines on the typewriter is by using the underscore key. However, on a type-bar machine you also may rule by placing a pencil or pen in the notch in the card holder. Hold the pencil or pen steady, and move the carriage to the right or left. On an element machine, follow the same procedure except use the tab key to go to the right and the back space key to go to the left.

Vertical lines may be typed with the underscore key by taking the paper out of the machine and placing it back in the machine sideways. Or, you may draw vertical lines with a pencil or pen. Again, place the pencil or pen in the notch in the card holder. Pull the "line finder" or "ratchet release" forward on the machine to disengage the spacing mechanism. Hold the pencil or pen steady and turn the platen either up or down.

Characters Not on the Typewriter Keyboard. Certain characters may not be on your typewriter keyboard, and it will be necessary for you to construct them. Listed below are the instructions for several characters that you may need to construct.

1. Degree Symbol (°). Use the small letter o to type the degree symbol. After striking a figure, turn the platen back slightly and strike the small letter o.

2. Division Sign (÷). The division sign is made by typing the colon, back spacing, and typing the hyphen.

3. Equal Sign (=). The hyphen is used twice in making the equal sign. The equal sign is made by striking the hyphen, back spacing, turning the platen slightly forward, and re-striking the hyphen.

4. Exclamation Point (!). The exclamation point is made by typing the apostrophe and the period. The proper procedure for making the exclamation point is to strike the period, back space, and then strike the apostrophe.

5. Feet or Minutes ('). The apostrophe on the keyboard may be used as a symbol for feet or for minutes.

6. Fractions (⅝). If fraction keys are included on your keyboard (such as ½ and ¼), it is best to use them. However, when it is necessary to type fractions that are not on the keyboard, use the regular keyboard numbers with a diagonal mark between them.

Following a whole number, there is no space before a fraction typed with a fraction key, but

CHAIN-FEEDING OF CARDS AND ENVELOPES

Back Feeding Cards and Envelopes

1. At the left side of the typewriter, stack the cards or envelopes face up with the bottom edges toward you.

2. Insert the first card or envelope to the proper typing position. Insert a second card or envelope behind the platen in the "feed" position.

3. After you have addressed the first card or envelope, twirl it out of the machine with your right hand. With the left hand, feed another card or envelope into the "feed" position.

4. As each card or envelope is twirled out of the machine, the next card or envelope will move up into typewriting position. Chain-feeding is thus carried on by inserting a new envelope into feed position each time the addressed envelope is removed.

Front Feeding Cards and Envelopes

1. Stack the cards or envelopes at the left side of the typewriter, face down, with envelope flaps toward you.

2. After the first card or envelope has been addressed, roll it back toward you until about a half inch shows above the alignment scale.

3. The next card or envelope should be inserted from the front, placing it between the first card or envelope and the platen.

4. To remove the first card or envelope and to position the second one, turn the platen back. Chain-feeding is thus carried on by feeding all cards or envelopes from the front of the platen.

Back feeding envelopes

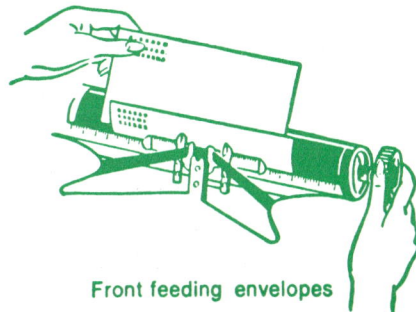

Front feeding envelopes

there is a space between a whole number and a fraction constructed with a diagonal mark. Examples are 54⅞ and 54½.

Do not mix constructed fractions with keyboard fractions. For example, if the two fractions referred to above were used in the same letter, they should be typed as 54⅞ and 54½.

7. Inches or Seconds ("). The keyboard quotation mark may be used as a symbol for inches or for seconds.

8. Multiplication Sign (×). Type the small letter x with a space before and after it to note multiplication. The space may be omitted in crowded tabulation work or in specifications.

9. Plus Sign (/). Type the diagonal mark, back space, and type the hyphen to construct a plus sign.

10. Pounds (#). After a number, the # symbol is used to indicate pounds.

Multiple Copy Control. The multiple copy control adjusts the position of the platen to allow for various thicknesses of typing material. Copy controls usually have about five positions. For normal typing requirements, the control should be at the first position or "A" position. As you increase the number of copies being typed, move the copy control to a higher position.

Impression Control. The impression control enables you to adjust the striking force of the element or type bars. For most typing jobs, you should set the impression control at the midpoint level. If you have multiple copies in your machine, it will be necessary to move the control to a higher number. Check your typewriter instruction booklet for the procedure to use on your machine.

Top-Bound Reports. Reports which are bound at the top can be corrected without unstapling or unbinding the report. To do so, feed a blank sheet of paper into the machine until the paper shows about a two-inch top margin. Insert the bottom of the sheet to be corrected behind the top edge of the blank paper and in front of the platen. Roll the platen back to the line to be corrected, position the paper for the correction, and type it.

Positioning for Corrections. If an error is discovered after a page has been removed from the typewriter, it is necessary to reposition the page

carefully. To do so, use the paper release lever to move the page sideways and the variable line spacer to roll it up and down. Each typewriter will vary as to the relationship of the typing line to the aligning scale. You should learn your machine. Know the exact distance between the bottom of the typed line and the aligning scale. Check the accuracy of the alignment by setting the ribbon control on stencil position. Try typing over one of the characters. If no further adjustments are necessary, return the ribbon control to normal position (ribbon position).

Here is an additional tip on positioning your paper for corrections.

1. Place a transparent second sheet over the typewriter page. Roll the two sheets into the typewriter and position the page correctly.
2. Test your positioning by typing over a letter near the erased one. Continue this process until the copy is in exact position.
3. Roll the sheets forward a couple of inches. Fold back the thin second sheet and tear it off. Roll the page into position and type the correction.

Squeezing Letters. If a letter is omitted at the end of a word but is not noticed until the line or the entire page has been typed, a single omitted letter can be inserted without retyping the line or the page.

On a type-bar electric machine, move the carriage to the space following the last letter in the word. Hold down the carriage release, and move the carriage backward a half space with your hand. Hold the carriage in this position with one hand, and type in the letter with the other hand.

Since there is no carriage on an element machine, the squeezing procedure is different. Place the center line on the card holder on the space after the omission. With the right hand, press against the projection on the right side of the element until the center line moves back about a half space or use the half-space mechanism. Hold the element in position and strike the letter. If you have several letters to squeeze, continue with this same procedure for each letter. The following sentence shows that the letter "t" should be squeezed in on the word "that."

He knew all tha there was to know
about the new procedure.

The corrected sentence should appear as follows:

He knew all thatthere was to know
about the new procedure.

Spreading Letters. To spread letters on a type-bar electric machine, position the carriage as if you were going to type the first letter of the incorrect word in its regular position. Then, hold down on the carriage release and position the carriage a half space forward from this point. Hold the carriage with one hand and strike the correct letter with the other hand. Continue in this same manner until all the letters are typed.

Just as squeezing is a different process on an element machine so is spreading a different process. Assume that you are going to spread one letter into the space occupied by two letters. Space over until the center line on the card holder is directly underneath the space of the second letter that you have erased. Use the half-space mechanism on many element machines or push and hold the projection on the right of the element until the center line on the card holder is in the center of the space where the first two letters were erased. Type the letter to be inserted. If you have additional letters to spread, continue in this same manner. In the following sentence "had" has been spread into the space occupied by "have."

The students had completed their
tasks.

WAS

The students have completed their
tasks.

Guide Sheets. When you are typing a project that includes a number of pages, it will be to your advantage to prepare a guide sheet. This sheet should help you in judging top and bottom margins. To assist you in knowing when you are getting close to the bottom margin (particularly if you are typing footnotes on the page), it is helpful to have an indication of how many lines remain on your page. You can make your own guide by numbering a page in the right margin from 1 to 33 and from 33 to 1. A sample guide sheet is shown in Illustration G-2. When typing the project, the guide sheet is placed behind your original so that the guide sheet numbers extend to the right of the original. The original and the guide sheet are inserted together. If you are making carbon copies, the carbon and second sheets are placed in back of the original and guide sheet.

cation of how many lines re-	19
	20
your page. You can make your	21
	22
de by numbering a page in the	23
	24
argin from 1 to 33 and from	25
	26
When typing the project,	27
	28
de sheet is placed behind	29
	30
ginal so that the guide sheet	31
	32
extend to the right of the	33
	33
The original and the guide	32
	31
re inserted together. If you	30

Illustration G-2. Guide Sheet

The foundation of efficient filing is an understanding of the basic alphabetic filing rules and an ability to apply these rules. Fourteen filing rules are presented here along with illustrative examples.

Rule 1: Order of Indexing Units

A. Personal names

A personal name is indexed in this manner.
(1) The surname (last name) is the key unit.
(2) The given name or initial is the second unit.
(3) The middle name or initial is the third unit.
(4) Unusual or obscure names (frequently foreign names) are indexed in the same manner. If it is not possible to determine the surname in such a name, consider the last name as the surname. Cross-reference unusual or obscure names using the first name written as the key unit.

Examples of Rule 1A

	Index Order of Units in Names		
Names	**Key Unit**	**Unit 2**	**Unit 3**
Albert C. Edmond	Edmond	Albert	C
Harold J. Edmond	Edmond	Harold	J
Harold James Edmond	Edmond	Harold	James

*All punctuation is omitted when indexing personal and business names. See Rule 3.

B. Business Names

Business names are filed as written using letterheads or trademarks as guides. Business names containing personal names are indexed as written. Newspapers and periodicals are indexed as written. For newspapers and periodicals having identical names that do not include the city name, consider the city name as the last indexing unit. If necessary, the state name may follow the city name.

Examples of Rule 1B

	Index Order of Units in Names			
Names	**Key Unit**	**Unit 2**	**Unit 3**	**Unit 4**
Carl T. Garland Motors	Carl	T	Garland	Motors
Garland Camera Shop	Garland	Camera	Shop	
Garland Daily News	Garland	Daily	News	
Times Herald (Garland)	Times	Herald	Garland	
Times Herald (Houston)	Times	Herald	Houston	

Rule 2: Minor Words in Business Names

Each complete English word in a business name is considered a separate indexing unit. Prepositions, conjunctions, symbols such as &, $, #, @, %, and articles are included and considered as spelled in full — and, dollar, number, at, percent. The only exception is the word "the" used as the first word of a business name. The is considered as the last indexing unit.

Examples of Rule 2

| | Index Order of Units in Names | | | |
Names	Key Unit	Unit 2	Unit 3	Unit 4
At Home Laundry	At	Home	Laundry	
Champion & Ford Electric	Champion	and	Ford	Electric
The Champion Day School	Champion	Day	School	The

Rule 3: Punctuation and Possessives

All punctuation is disregarded when indexing personal and business names. Commas, periods, hyphens, and apostrophes are disregarded, and names are indexed as written.

Examples of Rule 3

| | Index Order of Units in Names | | |
Names	Key Unit	Unit 2	Unit 3
Charlie's Hair Shop	Charlies	Hair	Shop
Charlies' Pawn Shop	Charlies	Pawn	Shop
Town-East Jewelry	Town East	Jewelry	
Town-North Cleaners	Town North	Cleaners	

Rule 4: Single Letters and Abbreviations

A. **Personal Names.**   Initials in personal names are considered as separate indexing units. Abbreviations of personal names (Wm., Jas., Thos.) and brief personal names or nicknames (Liz, Bill) are indexed as they are written.
B. **Business Names.**   Single letters and abbreviations in business names are indexed as written. If there is a space between single letters, index each letter as a separate unit. An acronym (a word formed from the first, or first few, letters of several words), however, is indexed as one unit regardless of punctuation or spacing (AMA, YMCA, Y.W.C.A.). Radio and television station call letters are indexed as one word. Cross reference spelled-out names to their acronyms if necessary. For example: American Management Association SEE AMA.

Examples of Rule 4

| | Index Order of Units in Names | | | |
Names	Key Unit	Unit 2	Unit 3	Unit 4
J. V. Hildebrand	Hildebrand	J	V	
Jas. W. Hildebrand	Hildebrand	Jas	W	
Wm. R. Hildebrand	Hildebrand	Wm	R	

J K of Texas	J	K	of	Texas
JKS Appliances	JKS	Appliances		
KRLD Television Station	KRLD	Television	Station	
U.S.A. Motors	USA	Motors		

Rule 5: Titles

A. Personal Names. A personal title (Miss, Mr., Mrs., and Ms.) is considered as the last indexing unit when it appears. If a seniority title is required for identification, it is considered as the last indexing unit in abbreviated form, with numeric titles (II, III, etc.) filed before alphabetic titles (Jr. and Sr.). When professional titles (D.D.S., M.D. Dr., Mayor) are required for identification, they are considered as the last units and filed alphabetically as written. Royal and religious titles followed by either a given name or a surname only (Father Leo) are indexed and filed as written. When all units of identical names, including titles, have been compared and there are no differences, filing order is determined by the addresses.

Examples of Rule 5A

	Index Order of Units in Names			
Names	**Key Unit**	**Unit 2**	**Unit 3**	**Unit 4**
Father James	Father	James		
S. R. Harrold II	Harrold	S	R	II
S. R. Harrold III	Harrold	S	R	III
S. R. Harrold, Jr.	Harrold	S	R	Jr
S. R. Harrold, Sr.	Harrold	S	R	Sr
Frederick Johns, M. D.	Johns	Frederick	MD	
Ms. Helen Johns	Johns	Helen	Ms	

B. Business Names. Titles in business names are filed as written.

Examples of Rule 5B

	Index Order of Units in Names			
Names	**Key Unit**	**Unit 2**	**Unit 3**	**Unit 4**
Doctors' Hospital	Doctors	Hospital		
Dr. Pepper Bottling Co.	Dr	Pepper	Bottling	Co

Rule 6: Married Women

A married woman's name is filed as she writes it. It is indexed according to Rule 1. If more than one form of a name is known, the alternate name may be cross-referenced. A married woman's name in a business name is indexed as written and follows Rules 1B and 5B.

Examples of Rule 6

Index Order of Units in Names

Names	Key Unit	Unit 2	Unit 3	Unit 4
Mrs. Wood's Cookies	Mrs	Woods	Cookies	
Mrs. Joan Carr Tillman (Mrs. Robert Tillman)	Tillman	Joan	Carr	Mrs
Mrs. Robert M. Underwood	Underwood	Robert	M	Mrs

Rule 7: Articles and Particles

An article or a particle in a business or personal name is combined with the part of the name following it to form a single indexing unit. The indexing order is not affected by a space between a prefix and the rest of the name; the space is disregarded when indexing. Examples of articles and particles are Da, El, La, Mac, Mc, Saint, St., Ste., San, Van, Von der.

Examples of Rule 7

Index Order of Units in Names

Names	Key Unit	Unit 2	Unit 3	Unit 4
Paul Alan LaFaver	LaFaver	Paul	Alan	
MacDugal's Meat Market	MacDugals	Meat	Market	
McDouglas & Edwards Automotive	McDouglas	and	Edwards	Automotive
Mary Lou St.Marie	St Marie	Mary	Lou	

Rule 8: Identical Names

When personal names and names of businesses, institutions, and organizations are identical, filing order is determined by the addresses. Cities are considered first, followed by states or provinces, street names, and house numbers or building numbers in that order.

When the first units of street names are written as figures, the names are considered in ascending numeric order and placed together before alphabetic street names. Street names with compass directions are considered as written. Numbers after compass directions are considered before alphabetic names (East 8th, East Main, SE Eighth, Southeast Eighth, etc.)

House and building numbers, written as figures, are considered in ascending numeric order and placed together before spelled-out building names. If a street address and a building name are included in an address disregard the building name. ZIP Codes are not considered in determining filing order.

Seniority titles are indexed according to Rule 5 and are considered before addresses.

Examples of Rule 8

Index Order of Units in Names

Names	Key Unit	Unit 2	Unit 3	Address
Elizabeth F. Bowman Dallas, Texas	Bowman	Elizabeth	F	Dallas

Elizabeth F. Bowman San Diego, California	Bowman	Elizabeth	F	San Diego
Brother's Pizza 1120 14 Street Dallas, Texas	Brothers	Pizza		1120–14
Brother's Pizza 512 25 Street Dallas, Texas	Brothers	Pizza		512–25
Brother's Pizza 8010 Apple Avenue Dallas, Texas	Brothers	Pizza		8010 Apple
Brown Computers 200 Forrest Building	Brown	Computers		200 Forrest
Brown Computers 500 Forrest Building	Brown	Computers		500 Forrest
Brown Computers Five Hundred Building	Brown	Computers		Five Hundred Building

Rule 9: Numbers in Business Names

Numbers spelled out in a business name are considered as written and filed alphabetically. Numbers written in digit form are considered as one unit. Names with numbers as the first unit written in digit form are filed in ascending order before alphabetic names. Arabic numerals (2, 3) are filed before Roman numerals (II, III). Names with inclusive numbers (33–37) are arranged by the lowest number only (33). Names with numbers appearing in other than the first position (Pier 36 Cafe) are filed alphabetically within the appropriate section and immediately before a similar name without a number. In indexing numbers written in digit form which contain nd, rd, st, and th, ignore the letter endings and consider only the digits.

Examples of Rule 9

	Index Order of Units in Names			
Names	**Key Unit**	**Unit 2**	**Unit 3**	**Unit 4**
4–Cent Copy Center	4	Cent	Copy	Center
4th Street Garage	4	Street	Garage	
400–410 Daniels Court	400	Daniels	Court	
Four Seasons Health Spa	Four	Seasons	Health	Spa
Highway 30 Cafe	Highway	30	Cafe	
Highway Service Station	Highway	Service	Station	

Rule 10: Organizations and Institutions

Banks and other financial institutions, clubs, colleges, hospitals, hotels, lodges, motels, museums, religious institutions, schools, unions, universities, and other organizations and institutions are indexed and filed according to the names written on their letterheads. "The" used as the first word in these names is considered the last filing unit.

Examples of Rule 10

	Index Order of Units in Names			
Names	**Key Unit**	**Unit 2**	**Unit 3**	**Unit 4**
Bank of DeSoto	Bank	of	DeSoto	
Dallas Savings and Loan	Dallas	Savings	and	Loan
First United Christian Church	First	United	Christian	Church
Horace Mann Elementary School	Horace	Mann	Elementary	School
Hotel Piedmont	Hotel	Piedmont		
Texas State Teachers Association	Texas	State	Teachers	Association
University of Texas	University	of	Texas	

Rule 11: Separated Single Words

When a single word is separated into two or more parts in a business name, the parts are considered separate indexing units. If a name contains two compass directions separated by a space (South East Car Rental), each compass direction is a separate indexing unit. If a name contains two compass directions written as one word or as a hyphenated word, then it is considered a single indexing unit (southeast and south-east).

Examples of Rule 11

	Index Order of Units in Names			
Names	**Key Unit**	**Unit 2**	**Unit 3**	**Unit 4**
Air Port Travel Services	Air	Port	Travel	Services
Airport Car Rental	Airport	Car	Rental	
South East Bookstore	South	East	Bookstore	
Southeast Dry Cleaners	Southeast	Dry	Cleaners	

Rule 12: Hyphenated Names

Hyphenated personal names are considered as one indexing unit and the hyphen is ignored (Jones-Bennett is a single indexing unit). Hyphenated business and place names and coined business names are considered as one indexing unit and the hyphen is ignored.

Examples of Rule 12

	Index Order of Units in Names			
Names	**Key Unit**	**Unit 2**	**Unit 3**	**Unit 4**
Mid America Lumber Company	Mid	America	Lumber	Company
Mid States Truck Leasing	Mid	States	Truck	Leasing
Joann Miles-Palmer	MilesPalmer	Joann		
Jo-Ann Patterson	Patterson	JoAnn		
Saf-T-Glove Company	SafTGlove	Company		

Rule 13: Compound Names

Compound personal names when separated by a space are considered as separate indexing units. (Although St. John is a compound name, St. is a prefix and follows Rule 7 which considers it a single indexing unit.) Compound business or place names with spaces between the parts of the name follow Rule 11, and the parts are considered separated units.

Examples of Rule 13

	Index Order of Units in Names			
Names	Key Unit	Unit 2	Unit 3	Unit 4
Mary Ann Edwards	Edwards	Mary	Ann	
Maryann Edwards	Edwards	Maryann		
New Jersey Electronics	New	Jersey	Electronics	
New York Lighting Company	New	York	Lighting	Company

Rule 14: Government Names

The name of a federal government agency is indexed by the name of the government unit (United States Government) followed by the most distinctive name of the office, bureau, department, etc., as written. The words "Office of," "Department of," "Bureau of," and so forth are considered as separate indexing units if they are part of the title. If "of" is not a part of the name as written, it is not considered an indexing unit.

The names of state, province, county, parish, city, and town political divisions are indexed by their distinctive names. The words "State of," "County of," and "City of" are considered separate indexing units if they are part of the title.

With foreign government names, the distinctive English name is the first indexing unit. This name is followed by the balance of the formal name of the government. Branches, departments, and divisions follow in order by their distinctive names.

Examples of Rule 14

Names	Index Form of Names
Department of Commerce State of Alabama Montgomery, Alabama	Alabama State of Commerce Department of Montgomery Alabama
Leon County Department of Public Welfare Tallahassee, Florida	Leon County Public Welfare Department of Tallahassee Florida
Management Divisions Agricultural Research Service U.S. Department of Agriculture	United States Government Agriculture Department of Agriculture Research Service Management Divisions
Operations Division Department of the Secretary of State Dominion of Canada Ottawa, Canada	Canada Dominion of State Secretary of Department of Operations Division Ottawa Canada

270

first
Read ½

Union
United Dairy
United States Ag Dep
US Play Card

YOUR COMPANY

Throughout this course, you are to assume that you work for RJ Computer Corporation; the company sells microcomputers, computer software, and supplies. The address and telephone number is 813 Marsh Lane, Dallas, Texas, 75220-1604, (214) 555-2016.

HISTORY

RJ Computer Corporation began operation four years ago. The president and owner of the corporation is James Rutherford, and the vice president is Patricia Jurow. At its inception, there were four other employees in addition to Mr. Rutherford. Over the past four years, the company sales have increased significantly, with sales this past year of $3 million. It is projected that sales will continue to increase this year, with the anticipated sales figure at $3,200,000. The number of employees has also increased. In addition to the president and vice president, there are three managers — a sales manager, purchasing manager, and finance manager. There are also forty-five additional support personnel for a total of fifty employees in the corporation.

YOUR DUTIES

You work as a general office support employee in the Purchasing Department. Your immediate supervisor is Jack Navarate, the manager of the Purchasing Department. Your duties include preparing memorandums, letters, reports, requisitions, answering the phone, filing, managing records, and receptionist duties for the department. In the Office Applications which are presented in this text, you will learn how to perfect your skills in performing these duties.

CHAPTER 1
THE CHANGING BUSINESS WORLD

OFFICE APPLICATIONS

Office Application 1-1   (Objective 1)

In this chapter you learned that the business world of today is different from the business world of yesterday. Read three articles in business periodicals concerning the following topics:

1. Equipment used in the office today
2. Skills required in the office today

Some of the periodicals that you may wish to use are (1) *The Secretary,* (2) *Modern Office Procedures,* (3) *The Office,* (4) *Business Week,* and (5) *Office Administration and Automation.* On a 5″×3″ card, report the article in the following manner:

1. List the source at the top of the card.
2. Write a short summary of the article.
3. Write a short paragraph of what you learned from the article.

Office Application 1-2   (Objective 2)

You learned in this chapter that change is an important part of the business world. Do one of the following activities:

1. Read two articles from a business periodical on changes that are taking place in the business office today. Report your findings in an oral report to the class.
2. Interview two office employees on the changes that have occurred in their offices in the last two years. Give your findings to your class in an oral report.

Office Application 1-3   (Objective 2)

Choose one of your class members to work with you on this project. Ask each other these questions.

1. Is your first reaction "no" when you are asked to change a procedure you are used to doing a certain way? *No*
2. Do certain kinds of change make you anxious or afraid? If so, what types of changes cause these reactions? *Maybe, Relocate!*
3. When it is clear that change must take place, do you try to hinder it or help it? *Mostly help.*
4. Do you have any ideas about how to implement change? *Yes*
5. What is the value of change? *Opportunties to be creative & flexible*
6. What do creativity and flexibility have to do with change? *It implementing prepare yourself that changes are inevitable*

After each of you has answered these questions, think through one change that has happened to each of you in the last year. How did you react to this change? Each of you is to write a separate summary of the change that occurred to you and how you handled the change. Turn in your paper to your instructor.

Office Application 1-4   (Objective 3)

Peruse the Sunday paper for various types of office positions that are available. Locate at least ten different positions. Note what skills are needed in each position, the experience required, and the salary available, if given. Write a short summary on your findings; turn in your paper to your instructor.

Office Application 1-5 (Objective 4)

If you are to be successful in the office, competencies are needed in English, spelling, math, and human relations. To discover how competent you are in these areas, complete the exercises on pages 275–281.

Office Application 1-6 (Objective 4)

After your instructor has graded your exercises in Office Application 1-5, the two of you should evaluate those areas where you need to improve and then you should determine what steps you can take to improve those areas. Write a paper that indicates your improvement steps. Give the original to your instructor; keep a copy for your files. As you complete each improvement step, check it off on your copy. At the end of the course, your instructor will want to look at your completed activities.

ENGLISH COMPETENCY

Subject and Verb Agreement

Directions: Circle the subject; underscore the correct verb.

1. A number of us who attended the meeting (want, wants) to know more about the plans for the Dallas business show.

2. The sales staff (seem, seems) to feel that such conferences should be held four times a year.

3. The pilot and co-pilot of the plane (isn't, aren't) flying today.

4. The City Council (entertain, entertains) differing views on the matter.

5. Banks that (give, gives) that type of service (don't, doesn't) get much business.

Choosing the Right Word

Directions: Underscore the correct word in each sentence.

6. The auditor is (confident, confidant) that profits this year will (accede, exceed) those of last year.

7. Active competition (between, among) the many companies in the industry has (already, all ready) resulted in price decreases.

8. Mr. Dunlop, our legal (council, counsel, consul), will present our case before the judges.

9. As Mr. Edwards became more (adopt, adapt, adept) in his work, he won many (complements, compliments) from his superiors.

10. Whenever a person (accedes, exceeds) the limits of good taste, I become angry.

Commas

Directions: Insert commas where they are needed in the following sentences.

11. Will you tell us, Ms. Land, whether this price includes the case?

12. Among the operations that call for both typing and calculating is the
    preparation of purchase orders invoices payroll forms etc.

13. Miss Hunt is a thoughtful conscientious worker.

14. I shall be glad to have Ellen Edwards one of my associates confer with you.

15. This new plan furthermore will call for changes.

The Semicolon and Colon

Directions: Insert colons or semicolons in the following sentences.

16. It is not work that kills people it is inactivity.

17. People used to think that advertising was mere publicity it was successful,
    so they believed, only if it gained attention.

18. There has been a large demand for this item within recent weeks
    consequently, there will be a slight delay in filling the order.

19. In his talk the man said "Appearance counts greatly when a person is to be
    chosen from among a number of people, because appearance affects the
    attitude of the person doing the choosing."

20. Please address all packages in the following manner Mr. Herbert Taylor,
    3302 Main Street, Baltimore, MD 21206-5555.

The Quotation Mark and the Dash

Directions: Place quotation marks or a dash in the following sentences.

21. Mr. Matares writes, These flowers are not suitable for that purpose.

22. Show the prospect how the use of this machine will save him money,
    said Helena.

23. There is a good deal of hokum in many political speeches.

24. In this week's issue of Forbes, there is an article entitled Rising
    Interest Rates.

25. The courses listed on pages 29 and 30 namely, Accounting II, Business
    Law, and Organizational Behavior are required.

276

The Question Mark and the Exclamation Point

Directions: Place a question mark or exclamation point in the following sentences.

26. Will you be able to come on December 24?

27. "How can that statement be reconciled with the report?" asked a member of the committee.

28. Was it Mr. Marks who stated, "These are the dates of the convention"?

29. Stop littering!

30. "What a fine piece of work you have done!" exclaimed Mrs. Kinoshita.

Punctuation

Word Division

Directions: Assume that each of the following words falls at the end of a typewritten line. Indicate whether the word has been divided correctly by checking the "correct" or "incorrect" column. If the word has been divided incorrectly, write how it should be divided in the "correction" column.

	Correct	Incorrect	Correction
31. stre-ngth		✓	
32. a-bove		✓	
33. remit-tance	✓		
34. ben-efit		✓	
35. would-n't			
36. self-control-led			
37. Dr. James Jones			
38. 3,-006			
39. bookk-eeping			
40. connec-tion			

Capitals

Directions: Capitalize the necessary words in the following sentences.

41. This is a monroe calculator.

42. Pattern no. 82B is the one I want.

43. The ouachita river runs through Arkansas.

44. The supreme court is in session.

45. sincerely yours

Numbers

Directions: Cross out all numbers that are written incorrectly; write them correctly.

46. I have an appointment on December 1st.

47. These coats sell for $56.50, $67, and $79.75, respectively.

48. The sales tax on the purchase is 8 cents.

49. He lives at 1 Madison Avenue.

50. 25 people are expected this evening.

SPELLING COMPETENCY

Directions: Indicate whether the following words are spelled properly by checking "correct" or "incorrect" in the columns provided. If the word is spelled incorrectly, write the correct spelling in the "correction" column.

		Correct	Incorrect	Correction
1.	accomodate	_____	_____	_____
2.	advantagous	_____	_____	_____

3. controled	_____	*controlled*	*controlled*
4. disapoint	_____	*disappoint*	*disappoint*
5. embarass	_____	*embrar*	_____
6. familiar	✓	_____	_____
7. fourty	_____	*fourth*	_____
8. grammer	_____	_____	*grammer*
9. indespensable	_____	_____	_____
10. lisense	_____	_____	*license*
11. managment	_____	✓	*managment*
12. nickle	_____	_____	*nickel*
13. ninty	_____	*ninety*	*ninety*
14. ocassion	_____	✓	*occassion*
15. occurred	✓	_____	_____
16. paralel	_____	✓	*paralle*
17. permissable	_____	✓	_____
18. priviledge	_____	✓	*priviledge*
19. questionaire	_____	✓	*questionaire*
20. seperate	_____	✓	*separate*

HUMAN RELATIONS COMPETENCY

Directions: Evaluate yourself on each of the following statements by checking the columns labeled "often," "sometimes," or "never." After you evaluate yourself, ask a friend to evaluate you also.

	Self-Evaluation			Friend's Evaluation		
	Often	Sometimes	Never	Often	Sometimes	Never
1. I accept other people.	____	____	____	____	____	____
2. I respect other people's opinions.	____	____	____	____	____	____

	Self-Evaluation			Friend's Evaluation		
	Often	Sometimes	Never	Often	Sometimes	Never
3. I admit I am wrong when I make an error.	____	____	____	____	____	____
4. I do what I say I will do.	____	____	____	____	____	____
5. I get the facts in a situation before making a decision.	____	____	____	____	____	____
6. I am willing to help others.	____	____	____	____	____	____
7. I do not indulge in gossip.	____	____	____	____	____	____
8. I treat everyone with the same respect.	____	____	____	____	____	____
9. I openly express my views.	____	____	____	____	____	____
10. I am sensitive to what others feel.	____	____	____	____	____	____
11. I say "please," "thank you," and "you are welcome" often.	____	____	____	____	____	____
12. I am alert to the nonverbal behavior of others.	____	____	____	____	____	____
13. I listen to what others say.	____	____	____	____	____	____
14. I trust others.	____	____	____	____	____	____
15. I make sure I understand what the other person is saying before I respond.	____	____	____	____	____	____
16. I consider other people's experiences and backgrounds.	____	____	____	____	____	____
17. I judge other people.	____	____	____	____	____	____
18. I categorize people.	____	____	____	____	____	____
19. I become upset when my ideas are questioned.	____	____	____	____	____	____
20. I criticize other people.	____	____	____	____	____	____

MATH COMPETENCY

DIRECTIONS: Work the following problems on a separate sheet of paper. Record your answers in the answer blanks provided.

1. The profits from a company must be split evenly among 12 partners. The profits amount to $245,456 for the year. What is each partner's share?

_____

2. The XYZ Department Store had $545 in the cash register by noon. At the time of opening that morning, there was $150 in the cash register, with $12 of that money being sales tax. How much had the store sold by noon?

_____

3. The Irving Police Department bought eight cars at a cost of $8,746 each. The department also bought three vans at a cost of $10,110 each. What was the department's total expenditure? _____

4. June Dyer was offered a job that paid $30.50 a day for eight hours. She would like to take the job, but she is not sure if it pays more than the $3.75 per hour which she presently makes. What would be the rate of pay per hour on the new job? _____

5. Jack Rogers worked 11.5 hours at a rate of $4.25 per hour. How much did he earn? _____

6. Mr. LaFaver paid $22,500 for a piece of land at the rate of $2,000 per acre. How many acres did he buy? _____

7. Mrs. Wilmer had 123 customers on Monday. On Tuesday, she had an increase of 46 customers. What percentage increase did she enjoy?

_____

8. A company bought a building priced at $30,000 and made a down payment of 25 percent. How large of a loan will the company need?

_____

CHAPTER 2

RELATIONSHIPS

OFFICE APPLICATIONS

Office Application 2-1 (Objective 1)

In this chapter you learned the importance of understanding yourself. This activity will help you to think more about who you are and what you value.

1. At the top of a sheet of paper, write: "At present, I am a person who...."
2. At the top of another sheet, write: "I want to become the kind of person who...."

Complete the sentences by writing eight to ten statements about who you are now and who you want to become. After you finish your statements, discuss them with your classmates. Each person should talk about who she or he is and who she or he wants to become. Give this project serious thought and openly share your feelings with your classmates.

Office Application 2-2 (Objective 2)

Read the following case to analyze what basic needs are not being met. Answer the questions on a separate sheet of paper.

Kathleen Green has worked for Towle Manufacturing Company for five years. She is a public information assistant who issues press releases on new company products and information concerning employees. Kathleen has enjoyed the work because it required use of her creative talents. Recently, however, Kathleen has been depressed; and yesterday she called in sick. Today she told her associate that her sickness was only a mild headache. She also stated that as soon as she called the office to report her sickness, her head-

ache disappeared. Here are some events that have happened to Kathleen in the last month:

   a. She asked for a full-time assistant since her work load became extremely heavy; her request was turned down.
   b. At the last marketing committee meeting, Kathleen suggested a new ad campaign for a product; her plan was rejected.
   c. Kathleen asked to attend a conference on marketing strategies. Her boss said that the idea was good, but things were currently too busy at the office for Kathleen to miss work. The boss assured her there would be other conferences that she could attend.

1. Are some of Kathleen's needs not being satisfied? If so, what are they?
2. If situations continue at the office as they have during the last month, do you think Kathleen will have more health problems? If so, why?
3. What action would you suggest that Kathleen take?

Office Application 2-3 (Objective 2)

Answer the following questions in relation to what you learned in Chapter 2.

Situation 1

You are working for George Jones. Mr. Jones gives you a report to prepare at 4:45 p.m.

Your working hours are from 8 a.m. to 5 p.m. He explains to you that the job is extremely important, that top management is waiting on the report, and that the executives are having a meeting at 6 p.m. to discuss it. The delay in getting the report to you was unavoidable. Mr. Jones asks that you stay and key the report. You know it will take you approximately 45 minutes to finish it. You have a dinner date at 5:30 p.m. If you stay to key the report, you cannot possibly make the dinner date. Explain the company's needs and your needs in this situation. Are the two needs compatible or opposing?

Situation 2

You are working for Ms. Clarice Smith. Your usual coffee break time is 10 a.m. Ms. Smith has made it very clear in the past that she expects you to take your coffee break at 10 a.m. and at no other time. However, several times during the last month she has rushed to you at 9:55 a.m. with some work that needs to be done immediately. She has never explained why these assignments are so urgent. She merely instructs you to do the work. On each occasion you have done the work and missed your coffee break. This morning, Ms. Smith again rushes in with something that is a rush job at 9:55 a.m. Explain your needs and the company needs in this situation. Are the two needs compatible or opposing?

Situation 3

You are working as a typist for Pedro Diaz. You feel that you are doing a good job, and Mr. Diaz has told you many times that he is happy with your work. However, you have been with the company for two years and you have not received a raise in pay. You know that other typists who have been with the company a shorter period of time have received raises. How would this affect your attitude toward your work, your supervisor, and the company? What should be done about this situation?

Office Application 2-4   (Objective 3)

Judith Milling is a department manager for First Word Processing. She has a problem with two employees. Here is the situation.

David Wilkerson and Fusako Goro are word processing operators in the center that Judith Milling manages. Fusako has been having some personal problems. She has come in late twice during the last month. Each time David has made a remark (that the entire office heard) about Fusako coming in late. Fusako did not respond to his remarks. Last week, Fusako called in sick but that evening David saw Fusako at the grocery store. The next morning (again while the entire office listened) David said, "It's a shame you were sick yesterday; but you weren't so sick last night, were you?" Fusako informed him that it was none of his business. Today, Fusako was ten minutes late coming back from lunch. When she came in David remarked, "I wish I were the office pet." Fusako yelled, "Get off my back, will you? You aren't my boss!"

Judith thinks that Fusako will soon solve her personal problems; and since she has been a good employee, Judith thinks Fusako deserves another chance. However, Judith is very concerned about David's actions. David's work production has been good; however, Judith has never talked with him about his obvious lack of human relations skills. Now she is wondering if she has made a mistake, since the entire office is being disrupted.

1. Explain the communication problem between Fusako and David.
2. Describe the communication problem between Judith and David.
3. Should Judith talk to David about his behavior? If so, what should she say?

OFFICE APPLICATIONS

Office Application 3-1 (Objectives 1 and 2)

Maintain a five-day log of the time you spend reading, writing, speaking, and listening. You won't be accurate to the minute, but make a concentrated effort to record the amount of time spent on each activity. At the end of the five-day period, total your time spent on each activity. How much time did you spend listening? Analyze your ineffective behaviors. What listening barriers did you use? Use the form on page 288.

Office Application 3-2 (Objective 3)

Compare two lecture classes you attend this week with regard to the following: (1) the techniques you use in listening; (2) the listening barriers you encounter; and (3) how successful you are in listening in each class. Use the two forms on page 289 to record your answers for each lecture. Identify the class under the class column. Under the next two columns, list your effective listening techniques and listening barriers. Rate your listening behavior in the last column as either *successful* or *unsuccessful*.

Office Application 3-3 (Objective 3)

Your instructor will read an article to you. Apply the effective listening behaviors you learned in this chapter. Try to remember the article's main points. Do not take notes. Your instructor will ask you some questions at the conclusion of the article. Answer these questions in writing. Your instructor will then lead the class in a discussion of the correct answers to discover if any listening barriers occurred.

Office Application 3-4 (Objective 3)

Read the following case and then answer the questions below.

Ruth Squires is a computer programmer at a local bank. One evening, after spending two hours working overtime on a program, Ruth decided to go to Swann's Department Store to return a blouse she had bought. The blouse did not fit properly. She had to wait approximately 15 minutes before she could get anyone to help her. When she finally did get a salesperson, here is what happened from Ruth's frame of reference.

"I told the clerk I wished to return the blouse, since it didn't fit. She examined the blouse; and then, in what sounded to me to be a very accusing voice, told me that I could not return the blouse because I had worn it. I told her that I hadn't worn it; I had only tried it on. At this point she practically accused me of lying and said that there was makeup on the blouse, so obviously I had worn it. By this time, other people waiting for service were listening to our conversation. I was embarrassed, but I again assured her that I had not worn the blouse. Then I examined the blouse for any makeup stains. I could find none, and I told her so. She completely lost control and said that people like me caused the department store to lose money, since we were always trying to cheat. My face was red, but I tried to keep my composure. I told her I wanted to see the manager; she told me that wouldn't do any good. But I stood my ground and insisted on seeing the manager."

What listening barriers did the clerk use? What listening barriers did Ruth use? How should Ruth and the salesperson have handled the situation to avoid such a confrontation?

Office Application 3-5 (Objectives 3 and 4)

Now that you have studied the material in this chapter, rate yourself again on the Listening Test presented on page 32. Determine the areas in which you need to improve. Write a plan of action for yourself, identifying how you plan to improve in each area. Discuss your plan for suggestions and possible modifications with your instructor.

LISTENING TIME LOG

	Reading Time	Writing Time	Speaking Time	Listening Time	Ineffective Listening Habits
First Day	_____	_____	_____	_____	_____
Second Day	_____	_____	_____	_____	_____
Third Day	_____	_____	_____	_____	_____
Fourth Day	_____	_____	_____	_____	_____
Fifth Day	_____	_____	_____	_____	_____
Totals	=========	=========	=========	=========	=========

LISTENING ANALYSIS OF CLASS LECTURES

Class	Effective Listening Techniques	Listening Barriers	Listening Rating

Class	Effective Listening Techniques	Listening Barriers	Listening Rating

OFFICE APPLICATIONS

Office Application 4-1 (Objective 1)

Using at least two reference sources, do library research on the history of the computer. Present your research in written form to your instructor; include the reference sources that you used.

Office Application 4-2 (Objective 2)

The following terms are used in data processing. On a separate sheet of paper, define each term. You will need to do some research to discover the meaning of these terms. Usually textbooks written on data processing contain a glossary of terms. Check your library for publications.

1. Binary code
2. Bytes and bits
3. GIGO
4. RAM
5. ROM
6. On-line
7. Off-line
8. CAD/CAM
9. Debugging
10. User-friendly

Office Application 4-3 (Objective 3)

In order to become more familiar with computer systems, do one of the following:

1. Visit the computer center of your school. Determine the type of equipment used. Write a short report describing the equipment available.
2. Visit a retail computer store in your city or town. Prepare a brief report on the equipment available in the store.

Office Application 4-4 (Objective 4)

In each of the following situations describe the type of computer equipment you would recommend as the most effective for the situation. Explain the reasons for your choices.

Situation 1

A large company with branch offices in five cities desires to send communications quickly and efficiently between its home office and its branches. The company wants to computerize all possible operations—inventory, accounting, payroll, manufacturing processes, and so forth.

Situation 2

An accountant who recently started her own business in her home wants to keep her records in a manner that will be both fast and accurate. She presently has six sets of books which she keeps; she anticipates obtaining approximately four more sets in the immediate future.

Situation 3

Laura Wouk started a small photography business in her home five years ago. The business has grown considerably since its beginnings, and last year she rented an office building. She now has two partners and does approximately $600,000 of business each year. She is interested in getting her accounting functions on a computer. She feels that the business will continue to grow and that the need for computer-generated information will expand in the future.

Office Application 4-5 (Objective 5)

In order to become familiar with computer languages, do one of the following:

1. Interview a computer programmer or manager in a local business. Ask the individual what computer languages are used in the company. Write a short report on your findings.
2. Do library research on two languages which are currently in use. Write a short report on your findings, listing your reference sources.

Office Application 4-6 (Objective 6)

Using computer periodicals such as *Personal Computing, Byte,* or *PC Week,* research the projected future directions of the computer in both business offices and homes. Write your findings in a short report, giving your reference sources.

CHAPTER 5

OFFICE APPLICATIONS

Office Application 5-1 (Objective 1)

In the first section of this chapter, there is some information on the development of word processing. Using this information as a foundation, conduct library research on the development of word processing. Review at least two references; write a report of your findings, listing the reference sources that you used. If you have word processing equipment available, use this equipment in preparing your report.

Office Application 5-2 (Objective 2)

Read the following case and then answer the questions below.

You work as a consultant for a management firm. You recently received a call from a law firm that is interested in using word processing equipment. Here is the situation at the law firm.

The law firm is a relatively small one, with five lawyers, two secretaries, and one receptionist. The two secretaries take all the dictation and do all the correspondence for the five lawyers. The receptionist answers the phone, greets callers, keeps a limited set of books, and orders supplies. The correspondence for the two secretaries is quite heavy; sometimes they request the help of the receptionist in taking dictation and preparing correspondence. Dictation equipment is not used in the office. Both secretaries often spend an entire morning taking dictation in the office of one of the attorneys. The lawyers handle divorce cases, wills, and other civil matters. An attitudinal problem has developed in the office. Both secretaries feel they are overworked. Bad feelings have developed between the receptionist and the secretaries. The receptionist does not feel the need to help the secretaries; however, the secretaries feel that the receptionist can help them. The attorneys do not feel the work load is heavy enough to hire another secretary, but they are willing to invest in equipment that would allow them to get the work done faster and more efficiently.

1. What problems exist in the law firm at the present?
2. Should another employee be hired?
3. How could the work assignments be simplified?
4. Would you suggest that word processing equipment be purchased? If so, what equipment would you suggest?
5. What are the advantages of using word processing equipment?

Office Application 5-3 (Objective 3)

Analyze the following case and answer the questions below.

Miller, Malevan, and Morris is a 25-member law firm in Dallas. The firm specializes in tax, real estate, and corporate law. The office staff consists of an office manager, bookkeeper, receptionist/telephone operator, and ten secretaries. Secretaries work for two or three attorneys and use electronic typewriters.

The attorneys expect perfect quality correspondence and frequently revise their originals—sometimes as many as three times. They dictate to the secretaries, but often there are interruptions during the dictation. Many times the secretaries are asked to stay after 5 o'clock to take dictation. Quick turnaround times are the rule rather than the exception in the office.

1. What problems do you see in the way this firm is handling its work?
2. What would you suggest be done to handle these problems?

Office Application 5-4 (Objective 4)

To become familiar with the latest word processing equipment, do one of the following:

1. Visit a store that sells word processing equipment and software; ask for a demonstration of the equipment and software, getting any brochures that may be available explaining the equipment and software. Present your findings in an oral report to the class.
2. Do library research on the latest equipment available in the word processing area. Periodicals which you might find helpful are *The Office, Modern Office Technology, Office Administration and Automation,* and *Words.* Using five-inch by three-inch cards, record your findings. Place your source at the top of each card.

Office Application 5-5 (Objective 5)

To understand more about centralized and decentralized structures in word processing,

visit a business in your area that uses word processing equipment; or if your school uses word processing in the administrative areas, talk with school personnel. Determine the following:

1. Is a centralized, decentralized, or centralized/decentralized structure used?
2. What are the advantages and disadvantages of the structure (as seen by the business or school)?

Write your findings in a report. You may wish to include an illustration (such as the ones presented in your text) showing the type of structure used.

Office Application 5-6 (Objective 6)

To determine the career opportunities in word processing, do the following:

1. Check the classified ads in the Sunday newspaper for a period of three weeks to determine the opportunities available and the skills necessary for word processing operators.
2. Write your findings in report form, giving the name of the newspaper and the date the listings appeared.

Office Application 5-7 (Objectives 6 and 7)

Newspapers and periodicals carry numerous articles on new developments in word processing technology. Review five recent articles covering information on new developments and future directions in word processing. Write your findings in a short report. List your reference sources.

OFFICE APPLICATIONS

Office Application 6–1 (Objective 1)

Your employer asks you to make copies of the following correspondence. In each situation, list the type of process you would use and the reasons for choosing that particular process. Keyboard your answers on plain paper.

1. Copy of a drawing; three copies are needed immediately.
2. One hundred copies of an advertisement; the advertisement contains line drawings and a photograph.
3. Sales letter announcing a new product to be sent to 2,000 customers.
4. Two copies of an incoming letter.
5. Ten copies of an interoffice memorandum.
6. Company policy manual to be revised; 500 copies are needed.
7. A drawing to be sent from a company branch in Dallas to another company branch in Oklahoma City.

Office Application 6–2 (Objectives 1 and 2)

Select one of the following assignments:

1. Visit a reprographics distributor in your area; learn about the different types of reprographics equipment sold. Obtain brochures (if available) of the equipment. Write a report of your findings. Make two copies of your report, using a photocopy machine.
2. Visit the print shop of a large business. Determine the following:
   a. What types of equipment are used?
   b. What are the job requirements for personnel employed in the print shop?
   c. Are there copy machines at decentralized locations in the business? If so, what types of machines are used? What are the special features on these machines?
   d. Does the company have plans for the purchase of additional reprographics equipment in the future? If so, what type of equipment do they plan to purchase?

Write your findings in a report; make two copies of your report on a photocopying machine.

Office Application 6–3 (Objective 3)

Research the copyright law. Write a paper on the legality of (1) making 25 copies of a chapter from a textbook; (2) making 10 copies of a piece of music; (3) making one copy of the personnel file of an office worker to give to a friend who is in another company and is interested in employing the person; and (4) making one copy of an article in a periodical for use in a report.

Office Application 6–4 (Objective 4)

Research the future directions of reprographics by reviewing articles in three recent periodicals. You might want to use such periodicals as *The Office, Administrative Management,* and *Words.* Write your findings in a report, giving your reference sources. Make two copies of your report on a copying machine.

OFFICE APPLICATIONS

Office Application 7-1   (Objective 1)

Rewrite the following sentences and apply the effective letter-writing techniques that you learned in this chapter.

1. Your kind letter of October 8 was received today.
2. I wish to thank you for your recent order.
3. As per my letter of November 5, the typewriter is unsatisfactory.
4. Please send us the information at your earliest convenience.
5. The repair costs on the photocopier were less than usual.
6. Thank you in advance for responding to my request.
7. A preponderance of businesspersons were consulted on this esoteric matter.
8. People's propensity to consume goods is insatiable.
9. You will receive the merchandise without any more delay.
10. You will not be sorry if you buy one of our new seat belts.

Office Application 7-2   (Objectives 1 and 3)

Rewrite the following letter beginnings so that they will be effective.

1. I received your order today and wanted to thank you for it.
2. Enclosed please find my check in the amount of $510.36 in payment for your Order 34560.
3. I regret to inform you that the seat belts you ordered are no longer being manufactured.
4. This check affirms my intent to subscribe to your weekly investment publication, *Financial News*.
5. I hope you will send us your subscription renewal today.

Office Application 7-3   (Objective 2)

Assume that you have been asked to order 10 reams of paper, 5 boxes of envelopes, 48 bottles of correction fluid, and 1 dozen typewriter ribbons. Plan the order letter and prepare the outline. If additional information is needed, state what that information is.

Office Application 7-4   (Objective 5)

Identify the numbered parts of the business letter on page 300.

Office Application 7-5   (Objectives 2 and 3)

RJ Computer Corporation has been asked to contribute $10,000 to the local YWCA to help build a new gym.

Plan and write a paragraph which says "yes" to the above situation. Plan and write a paragraph which says "no" to the above situation. Decide which paragraph would be better written deductively and which paragraph would be better written inductively.

Office Application 7-6   (Objectives 3, 5, 6, and 7)

Write a letter for each of the following situations.

1. Order the following materials:
   100 ¼" black multistrike printer ribbons, part No. Nesco 9934 B @ $1.75 ea.

20 copy holders, 9″ × 12″ H, plastic, part No. Nesco 3297B @ $10.95 ea.

20 six outlet power strips with surge, spike, and noise suppression, 6', 3 wire power cord, 15 amp circuit breaker, part No. Nesco 4421C @ $83.00 ea.

50 boxes paper, 1 part 15# green bar, 3,000 sheets per box, perforated edges, 9½″ × 11″, part No. Nesco 7866A @ $26.43 ea.

Order these materials from Hughes Corporation, 3125 Dallas Avenue, Duncanville, TX 75116-1846. They are to be sent by a delivery service to reach you no later than November 15. They are to be billed to RJ Computer Corporation's account.

2. Mr. Rutherford, the president of RJ Computer Corporation, owns a warehouse building in Greensboro, North Carolina. He has advertised the sale of the building in a Greensboro paper and has asked your employer, Jack Navarate, to respond to the requests for information. The ad reads as follows:

Warehouse building on five acres of land, outskirts of Greensboro, North Carolina, 10,000 square feet, $800,000.

Answer the following request for information from Alan Higgins, 104 West Kemp Road, Greensboro, NC 27410-3476:

I am interested in the warehouse you have advertised in the paper, but I have a few questions. Can I purchase the building without buying all five acres? If so, how much will the building cost? Are you willing to finance the purchase? If so, how much interest will you charge? When can I see the building?

Here are your plans for responding to this request. You will sell the building and a half acre of land without selling the remaining 4½ acres. The building and the land on which the building stands will cost $600,000. You are willing to finance the purchase at an interest rate of 10 percent. Higgins can see the building any afternoon between 2 and 5 p.m.

Mr. Navarate will sign the first letter ordering supplies, and Mr. Rutherford will sign the second letter. Mr. Navarate prefers block letter style with open punctuation;

Mr. Rutherford prefers modified block letter style with mixed punctuation. Make a file copy of both letters. Use the letterheads provided on pages 301–303 and key the appropriate address on the back of the letter in the space provided. Fold the letters using the appropriate method.

Office Application 7-7 (Objectives 3, 4, 5, 6, and 7)

Write a letter for each of the following situations.

1. On October 5, Miss Regina Parsons of Douglas Enterprises, 7891 Loop 12, Houston, TX 77002-9425, ordered the following material from your company. RJ Computer Corporation is unable to supply the CRT turntable in simulated walnut finish; it is available in simulated pecan finish. RJ Computer is able to supply the other items listed.

1 300-1200 BAUD modem, full-duplex, auto-dial, RS-232 interface, part No. NB-6330-2X @ $385.00

2 CRT turntable, simulated walnut finish, 360° rotation, 22″ W×16″ D×4″ H, part No. NB-6621-X @ $54.59 ea.

2 Computer equipment locking device, 3 mounting plates, 2½' vinyl-coated steel cable, 2 keys with lock, part No. NB-4728-C @ $24.30 ea.

Your employer, Mr. Navarate, is out of the office. Joan Ice, Assistant Purchasing Manager, will sign the letter; she prefers the AMS simplified letter style. Make a file copy of the letter. Use the letterhead provided on page 305 and key the appropriate address on the back of the letterhead in the space provided. Fold the letter, using the appropriate method.

2. You have been asked by Mr. Mike Rowse, Temporary Office Workers, 3986 East Commerce, Dallas, TX 75001-4839, to participate in a panel discussion on "Office Communication." You would like to do so, but your current work load is extremely heavy, and your employer feels he needs you on the job. Write a letter to Mr. Rowse saying no to his request. Any standard letter

style may be used. Use the letterhead provided on page 307. Do not address an envelope for this letter. Sign your own name.

3. One of your friends, Ms. Monica Sanchez, has just received a promotion to office manager for Roger Steel, 309 Mockingbird Avenue, Arlington, TX 76010-2674. Write a letter of congratulations to her, using an appropriate letter style. Assume that you will use your own stationery and sign your own name. Select an appropriate size and weight of paper.

robert & jones inc. ①

811 eighth avenue   fort worth, tx 76107-2235

November 15, 19-- ②

RJ Computer Corporation
Attention Mr. Jack Navarate ③
813 Marsh Lane
Dallas, TX 74220-1604 ④

Ladies and Gentlemen ⑤

Subject: Purchase Order 8790 ⑥

Thank you for your order of November 10 for 100 executive desks
and 75 model D chairs. The chairs will be shipped within ten days.

A supply of the executive desks is usually kept in our warehouse;
however, our last shipment contained several damaged desks. These ⑦
damaged desks are being replaced, so we should be able to fill your
order within the next three weeks.

You will be pleased with your selection of desks and chairs; they
are most comfortable and attractive.

Sincerely ⑧

George Horton

George Horton ⑨
Manager

lm ⑩

cc Ms. Ruth Smart ⑪

For Use in Office Application 7-4

301

RJ COMPUTER CORPORATION

813 Marsh Lane
Dallas, TX 75220-1604
214-555-2016

For Use in Office Application 7-6

RJ COMPUTER CORPORATION

813 Marsh Lane
Dallas, TX 75220-1604
214-555-2016

RJ COMPUTER CORPORATION

813 Marsh Lane
Dallas, TX 75220-1604

RJ COMPUTER CORPORATION

813 Marsh Lane
Dallas, TX 75220-1604
214-555-2016

813 Marsh Lane
Dallas, TX 75220-1604
RJ COMPUTER CORPORATION

813 Marsh Lane
Dallas, TX 75220-1604
214-555-2016

RJ COMPUTER CORPORATION

For Use in Office Application 7-7

CHAPTER 8

OFFICE APPLICATIONS

Office Application 8-1   (Objective 1)

Call a local travel agency and find out what services are available for planning a trip. Write your findings in a short report.

Office Application 8-2   (Objective 2)

Your employer, Mr. Navarate, is planning a business trip to Florida on October 5, 6, and 7. He needs to be in Florida for a noon meeting on October 5 with Peter Irwin. He will return on October 7 after a 3 p.m. meeting with Marcia Mudd; the meeting with Marcia is planned for 2 hours. Get flight information by calling local airlines; then prepare an itinerary for Mr. Navarate. In addition to the two meetings mentioned, he will be attending a management conference at the Patterson Hotel on October 6 from 9 a.m. until 3 p.m. and continuing from 9 a.m. until noon on the 7th.

Office Application 8-3   (Objective 3)

You are secretary of the Arlington chapter of the Professional Secretaries Association. One of your jobs is to prepare the minutes and agendas for the meetings. Last evening, October 7, you attended a meeting held at Rimrock Inn in Arlington at 7:30 p.m.

The meeting was called to order by Beverly Cox, president. Three members of the chapter were absent—Carl Grosset, Evelyn Pitman, and Eunice Woolworth. The minutes from the previous meeting (a month ago) were read and approved. Three committees reported. The Fun and Games Committee reported that a party is planned for December, with toys to be brought which will be given to Lena Pope Children's Home. The Seminar Committee reported that plans are underway for the annual seminar to be held in April. Two sites are possibilities—Rimrock Inn in Arlington and The Woodbine in Grand Prairie. The members were asked to send any speaker and topic possibilities to Lou King by the first of next month. The committee reported that work is proceeding with MacArthur High School on the establishment of a Future Secretaries chapter. The high school teachers are interested; they are polling their students to see if student interest exists. One committee was appointed—a fund raising committee to seek scholarship funds for high school students planning to enter the secretarial profession. Eileen Lynch was appointed chairperson of the committee; Jeana Remington and Nancy Olsen were appointed as committee members. The meeting adjourned at 9 p.m.

Office Application 8-4   (Objective 3)

You have the responsibility of sending out the agenda for the next meeting of the Professional Secretaries Association. The meeting will be held at the Oakland Plaza in Arlington on November 10. Committee reports are to be given by the Fun and Games Committee, the Seminar Committee, and the Service Committee. The treasurer will give a financial report before the business meeting. There will be a dinner beginning at 6:30 p.m. and a presentation by Diana Vela on time management. Prepare the agenda in appropriate format.

Office Application 8-5 (Objective 4)

Using reference sources from the library, look up the following information. Record your answers, giving the reference sources you used.

1. Who were the U.S. senators from your state in 1985?
2. What was the gross national product of the United States in 1982?
3. How many women are employed in management positions today?
4. How many minorities are employed in white-collar positions today?
5. What is the average education of individuals in the U.S. today?
6. List two jobs where the employment possibilities for the next 5 years is expected to increase.

Office Application 8-6 (Objective 5)

You are working for one day in the Sales Department. Edgar Robinson, assistant sales manager, asks you to prepare an interoffice memorandum. The copy is given below. Prepare your own interoffice communication form, centering "Interoffice Communication" at the top of the form and using the guide words "To, From, Date, and Subject." Select an appropriate subject and prepare three copies. The memorandum is to be sent to all salespersons. (You will find a list of these persons in the table given in Office Application 8-8.)

Several of the sales personnel have found it difficult to attend our regular sales conference on the first Monday of each month. Some have told me that Monday morning seems to be an ideal time to call on most customers. Effective next month, therefore, our monthly

sales conference will be held on the first Friday afternoon of each month at three o'clock in the conference room.

R. S.

Office Application 8-7 (Objective 6)

The office employees at RJ Computer have problems with identifying spelling errors in their work. Mr. Robinson asks you to send them the information on pages 313–316. Prepare the material in report form; correct any spelling errors you find in the copy.

Office Application 8-8 (Objective 7)

Mr. Robinson requests that you prepare the following table for a sales meeting. Use leaders between the columns and total the sales figures. Make two copies.

RJ COMPUTER CORPORATION
Sales 19--

Salesperson	Amount of Sales
Evans, John	$130,000
Fujiwara, Jun	250,000
Godkin, Ralph	351,000
Hart, Sue	110,000
Inge, Ann	150,000
Johnson, Mike	290,000
Kalhelms, George	375,000
Mitchell, Albert	230,000
Nowlin, Ruth	395,000
Patrick, David	160,000
Rose, Travis	227,000
Stevens, Ida	332,000
Total:	

Office Application 8-9 (Objective 7)

Mr. Robinson gives you the handwritten data on pages 317–318 and asks that you prepare a table for his sales meeting. Mr. Robinson asks that you rule the table and make two copies. Total each column.

Office Application 8-10 (Objective 8)

Research ways in which computer graphics are used in business. Prepare a report of your findings, giving the reference sources that you used.

Office Application 8-11 (Objectives 5 and 9)

You are working temporarily in the Finance Department because one of the employees in that area is ill. On page 319 there is a form to use in preparing a statement of account for Rutgers Company, 6743 Pryor Street, Duncanville, TX 75116-2234. Prepare two copies of the statement. The statement should contain a summary of information as follows:

The date on the statement should be October 12, current year. On July 12, Rutgers purchased merchandise amounting to $2,515; on July 23, additional purchases amounted to $3,789.15. On August 1, a payment amounting to $2,900 was received from them. On August 13, additional purchases amounted to $5,892, and on September 15, additional purchases amounting to $1,115.75 were made. The statement should show a summary of this information and the balance of the account after each transaction as well as the current balance.

After preparing the statement that is to be sent to Rutgers, prepare the following interoffice memorandum to L. C. Knox. Prepare your own form by placing "Interoffice Memorandum" at the top of the page and using the guide words "To, From, Date, and Subject." Select an appropriate subject to be inserted in the memorandum. Make two copies of the memorandum.

Attached is a statement of account for Rutgers Company. We have sent Rutgers our regular credit follow-up letters during the past month but so far have not received any reply from them. Since they are one of your customers, I thought perhaps you could give us some suggestions for collecting this account. Are you planning to call Rutgers very soon? Please return this statement to me with your suggestions.

J. T. McCoy

Office Application 8-12 (Objective 9)

On page 321 are two orders received from customers. These orders have been interpreted by workers in the Sales Department. Make the extensions on the Orion, Inc. order by multiplying the number of units ordered times the price. Check the extensions on the Raytherson Company order for errors. Total both orders.

Using the interpreted orders as a basis for billing information, you are to prepare an invoice for each of the two orders. Use the invoice forms on pages 323–325. Both invoices should be dated October 12. Keep your work until you have finished Office Applications 8-13.

Office Application 8-13 (Objective 9)

In Office Application 8-12 you prepared an invoice to Orion. On October 19 Orion returned 1 package of coding forms which they had ordered. Prepare a credit memorandum. The number of the memorandum is 20. Use the forms on page 327; prepare two copies.

Office Application 8-14 (Objective 9)

You are asked to fill out a purchase requisition for the supplies given here. When the supplies are delivered, Jane Edwards is to be notified. Use the forms on page 329; make two copies.

5 reams	20#, 50% cotton content, 8½" x 11" plain white bond paper
5 reams	8½" x 11" second sheets, canary yellow
2 dozen	No. 2 pencils
2 dozen	Typewriter ribbons, cartridge type, IBM, black

Office Application 8-15 (Objective 9)

You have been asked to prepare a purchase order using the following information taken from the purchase requisition:

Order from: Rockridge Corporation, 212 West Airport Freeway, Carrollton, TX 75006-3422.

Delivery date: November 26, 19--. Ship via: Truck. Order date: October 26, 19--. Terms: 2/10, n/30. Items: 100 Diskettes, flexible, 8", DSDD, soft sector, part No. 67-5840 @ $1.85 ea.; 100 pkgs. Coding forms, COBOL format, 50 sheets per pad, 10 pads per pkg., part No. 9M-38 @ $15.50 per package; 100 shipping labels, perforated, 1 across format 4" wide by 2 ¾", 500 labels per roll, part No. 8N-87B @ $6.50 per roll.

1. Ordinarily the purchase order would consist of several copies, but for the purpose of this job you are asked to prepare only two copies. Use the purchase order forms on page 331.
2. Insert the quantities, descriptions, prices per unit, and necessary information from that given above.
3. Make the extensions.
4. Sign your name as purchasing agent.
5. Proofread carefully.

Office Application 8-16 (Objective 10)

Prepare the copy on pages 333–334 making all the corrections indicated. Use an unbound report format and double space the body of the report. Double space before the subheadings and underscore them. Make an original and one copy.

Correct Spelling—Important For The Office Employee

Perfection in spelling is a prerequisite for success as an office worker. Poor spelling can be a serious handicap and will be a drawback in your business career. Executives frequently judge the office employee's ability to do one task by his or her performance on another. A misspelled word in business corespondence suggests carelessness. If you demonstrate carelessness in your business writing, you may be suspected of the same qualities in other office activities. Perfect spelling is essential for every professional office worker!

Proofread

Always proofread your work carefully before taking it from your typewriter. Make it a habit to read your work at least twice. Read through one time for grammatical correctness and completeness. Use the paper bale method as you read your copy. Roll your paper down until the first line of type is above the paper bale. Read that line and then roll up until the next line is above the paper bale. Read that line carefully too. Then read through a second time, reading from right to left rather than from left to right. Concentrate on each word to see that it is spelled correctly and that there are no typographical errors. Keep a dictionary in a convenient spot on your desk. <u>Do</u> take the time to look up words when you are not sure of their spelling.

<u>Memorization</u>

You may find memorization is helpful to you in spelling. Obviously you cannot memorize the spelling of all the words in the English language. But you can memorize some of the most commonly misspelled words. Table I presents a list of these words. Start now to memorize this list. Strive to memorize at least ten words a day for the next ten days.

<u>Develop Your Own List</u>

In addition to memorizing the most commonly misspelled words, begin now to develop your own list of words that you frequently misspell or have to look up. Keep a notebook on your desk in which you write down all the words you have trouble with. When you have a few spare moments, study this list. Soon you will find that you have mastered it.[1]

---

[1] JoAnn Hennington, "Back to Basics — Spelling," <u>The Secretary</u> (August/September, 1979), pp. 40-42.

TABLE I
Commonly Misspelled Words

1. absence
2. accommodate
3. achievement
4. acquiesce
5. allotted
6. analyze
7. approximate
8. argument
9. assistant
10. attendance
11. beginning
12. believe
13. changeable
14. colossal
15. commitment
16. committee
17. concede
18. conscientious
19. consensus
20. controversy
21. criticize
22. desperate
23. develop
24. dictionary
25. disappoint
26. discriminate
27. drastically
28. efficiency
29. eligible
30. embarrass
31. exaggerate
32. existence
33. forty
34. friend
35. fulfill
36. grammar
37. immediately
38. inadvertent
39. infallible
40. insistent
41. intercede
42. interesting
43. interfered
44. knowledge
45. license
46. liquefy
47. loneliness
48. maintenance

49. management
50. millionaire
51. misspelled
52. mortgaged
53. nickel
54. niece
55. ninety-ninth
56. occasionally
57. occurrence
58. paralyze
59. permissible
60. persistent
61. persuade
62. Pittsburgh
63. preceding
64. predictable
65. preferable
66. presumptuous
67. privilege
68. psychological
69. publicly
70. pursuit
71. questionnaire
72. quizzes
73. receive
74. recipient

75. recommend
76. referred
77. repel
78. repetition
79. rhythm
80. safety
81. seize
82. sincerely
83. sincerity
84. skillful
85. souvenir
86. specimen
87. suing
88. superintendent
89. supersede
90. surprise
91. their
92. transferable
93. truly
94. unparalleled
95. usage
96. vegetable
97. vicious
98. Wednesday
99. weird
100. writing

RJ Computer Corporation
Sales of Selected Items
1984–1987

Item	1984	1985	1986	1987
Diskette Organizer, 100 Capacity, 5¼"	$ 9,800	$ 10,300	$ 14,600	$ 14,200
Diskette Organizer, 100 Capacity, 8½"	2,500	2,100	2,900	2,700
Anti-static Mat	14,600	17,300	19,000	21,700
CRT Turntable	17,000	15,900	17,200	19,800
Equipment Locking Device	4,200	6,300	9,400	9,200
Bulk Diskette Eraser	8,400	4,600	3,600	3,800
Diskette, 5¼" DSDD Hard Sector	12,800	11,800	10,400	13,200
Printerwheel, Metal, Elite 12	1,200	3,100	5,100	5,800

Coding Forms, BASIC Format	16,200	14,900	15,600	14,800
Printer Ribbon Cartridge	10,500	11,600	13,500	19,500
Modem, Internal, 1200 BAUD	24,600	33,300	44,000	49,600
Modem, External, 300/1200 BAUD	35,900	31,800	32,100	38,300
Printer, Printerwheel, 25 cps	36,000	39,000	56,000	54,100
Printer, Dot Matrix, 100 cps	54,000	68,000	71,000	79,600

RJ COMPUTER CORPORATION

813 Marsh Lane
Dallas, TX 75220-1604
214-555-2016

WE RENDER MONTHLY STATEMENTS ON THE 25th OF EACH MONTH
ALL BILLS DUE 30 DAYS FROM DATE OF INVOICE

DATE	CHARGES	CREDITS	BALANCE

RJ COMPUTER CORPORATION

813 Marsh Lane
Dallas, TX 75220-1604
214-555-2016

WE RENDER MONTHLY STATEMENTS ON THE 25th OF EACH MONTH
ALL BILLS DUE 30 DAYS FROM DATE OF INVOICE

DATE	CHARGES	CREDITS	BALANCE

ORDER INTERPRETATION

Sold to *Orion, Inc.*
369 Country Club Road
Farmers Branch, TX 75234-4997

Order dated *Oct. 7, 19--*

Received *Oct. 9, 19--*

Interpreted by *Grace*

Ship to

Our Inv. No. *4720*

Terms	*net 30*	Ship Via	*Truck*	Cust. Ord. No.	*A-69*	Salesperson	*Hart*

Quantity	Stock No.	Description	Price	Totals
2	*Nesco 488*	*Polarized CRT glare filters, 10½" x 12½"*	*105.00*	
3 pkgs.	*9N-38*	*Coding Forms, BASIC format, 50 sheets per pad, 10 pads per package*	*26.50*	
10	*67-5852*	*Diskette, flexible, 8", DSDD, hard sector*	*4.60*	

Remarks :

RAYTHERSON COMPANY   3487 West Division • Grand Prairie, TX 75208-2843

October 6, 19--

RJ Computer Corporation
813 Marsh Lane
Dallas, TX 75220-1604

Ladies and Gentlemen:

Please send immediately by truck the following materials on Raytherson Order 6317:

2	Anti-static mats, 24" x 28", with 10' grounding card, Part No. Nesco 582	$ 9.95	$20.90
2	Bulk diskette eraser, 8" x 5¼", diskette capability, Part No. Nesco 496	36.50	76.50

If you cannot make immediate shipment, please let me know as soon as possible.

Sincerely,

A.J. Bartlett

A. J. Bartlett

AJB:rv

our order no. 4719
terms 2/10, n30
salesperson - mitchell
E.R.

RJ COMPUTER CORPORATION

813 Marsh Lane
Dallas, TX 75220-1604
214-555-2016

SOLD TO

DATE

YOUR ORDER NO.	DATE OF ORDER	OUR ORDER NO.	SHIP VIA	TERMS	SALESPERSON	
QUANTITY	STOCK NO.	D E S C R I P T I O N			PRICE	TOTAL

813 Marsh Lane
Dallas, TX 75220-1604
214-555-2016

RJ COMPUTER CORPORATION

SOLD TO

-
-
-

DATE

YOUR ORDER NO.	DATE OF ORDER	OUR ORDER NO.	SHIP VIA		TERMS	SALESPERSON	
QUANTITY	STOCK NO.	D E S C R I P T I O N				PRICE	TOTAL

RJ COMPUTER CORPORATION

813 Marsh Lane
Dallas, TX 75220-1604
214-555-2016

CREDIT MEMORANDUM

No. _____

Name _____

Street _____ City _____

QUANTITY	DESCRIPTION	PRICE	EXTENSION

DATE	AUTHORIZED BY	REC'D IN STOCK BY	DATE OF SALE	AMOUNT OF SALE

RJ COMPUTER CORPORATION

813 Marsh Lane
Dallas, TX 75220-1604
214-555-2016

CREDIT MEMORANDUM

No. _____

Name _____

Street _____ City _____

QUANTITY	DESCRIPTION	PRICE	EXTENSION

DATE	AUTHORIZED BY	REC'D IN STOCK BY	DATE OF SALE	AMOUNT OF SALE

Purchase Requisition

REQUISITION
NO. B-211

RJ COMPUTER CORPORATION

813 Marsh Lane
Dallas, TX 75220-1604
214-555-2016

Required for Department

Advise _____ on delivery

Date Issued

Date Required

DESCRIPTION

Approved by _____

Requisition placed by _____

PURCHASING AGENT'S MEMORANDUM

Purchase Order No. _____

Issued to _____

Date _____

_____

Purchase Requisition

REQUISITION
NO. B-211

RJ COMPUTER CORPORATION

813 Marsh Lane
Dallas, TX 75220-1604
214-555-2016

Required for Department

Advise _____ on delivery

Date Issued

Date Required

DESCRIPTION

Approved by _____

Requisition placed by _____

PURCHASING AGENT'S MEMORANDUM

Purchase Order No. _____

Issued to _____

Date _____

_____

PURCHASE ORDER

813 Marsh Lane
Dallas, TX 75220-1604
214-555-2016

No. ___185___

RJ COMPUTER CORPORATION

To

Deliver

Date

Ship Via

FOB

Terms

QUANTITY	DESCRIPTION	UNIT PRICE	TOTAL

PURCHASE ORDER

813 Marsh Lane
Dallas, TX 75220-1604
214-555-2016

No. ___185___

RJ COMPUTER CORPORATION

To

Deliver

Date

Ship Via

FOB

Terms

QUANTITY	DESCRIPTION	UNIT PRICE	TOTAL

Team Work and the Office Worker

Team work is important for all office employees, but it is particularly important for the supervisor-office worker relationships. Several office workers were asked to state what factors they felt contributed to a good team relationship. Their responses are below listed.

Smooth Supervisor-Office Worker Relationship

1. Clear Expectations

2. Mutual goals and objectives

3. Good judgment

4. Respect for others

5. Open communication

6. Loyalty, integrity (each to the other)

7. High motivation

8. Maturity in interpersonal relationships

These office workers were also asked to identify factors that lead to a poor supervisor-office worker relationship. Here are the factors they identified.

Poor Supervisor-Office Worker Relationship

1. Lack of motivation (unhappy with job duties; no incentive to do better)

2. Lack of time with company

3. Personality conflict between boss and worker

4. Lack of respect

5. Lack of communication

6. Pressure deadlines of

7. Manipulation by boss

How do you move from a poor team relationship to a good one? Here are some suggestions.

1. Accept yourself as a worthy, dignified member of the human race; speak out; state how you feel.

2. If you have a personality conflict with your supervisor, the two of you should talk about it. Say what is troubling you, and ask your employer what is troubling him or her.

3. Listen openly to what other people are saying.

4. Plan your work well so that pressure periods are *is* kept to a minimum.

5. Set priorities.

6. Do not make assumptions; get the facts.

7. Ask for clarification when you do not understand a job instruction.

8. Be sensitive to the other persons needs.

OFFICE APPLICATIONS

Office Application 9-1   (Objective 1)

Read at least three articles in current periodicals on trends in telecommunications. The periodicals you choose should not have been published more than six months ago. Summarize your findings in report form listing your reference sources. Some suggested periodicals are *Administrative Management, The Office, Modern Office Technology, Words,* and *PC World.*

Office Application 9-2   (Objective 2)

Read the telephone responses below. Indicate a better manner of responding. Place your answers on a separate sheet of paper.

1. "Hold the line."
2. "Her line is busy."
3. "Call back later."
4. "Mr. Navarate isn't in."
5. "Mr. Navarate is playing golf."
6. "What did you say?"
7. "Who's this?"
8. "I don't know where Mr. Navarate is."
9. "Your call is being transferred."
10. "I am not responsible for the mistake; don't raise your voice at me."

Office Application 9-3   (Objective 2)

Indicate what your response would be in each of the following situations.

Situation 1

Assume that you are handling the incoming calls for Ms. Marjorie Ott, office manager of RJ Computer Corporation. Ms. Ott left the office at 12:30 p.m. for an important luncheon engagement at the Continental Restaurant in the Plaza Hotel. Before leaving, she told you that she would return at 2 p.m. At 1 p.m. Mr. Hayworth, an important customer in a local concern, calls and asks to speak to Ms. Ott. Mr. Hayworth tells you he is leaving town at 1:30 p.m. and must reach Ms. Ott before then. How would you respond?

Situation 2

At 2:15 p.m. Ms. Ott is back in the office and is in conference with several other executives of the business. The conference should not last more than a half hour. A few minutes after the conference begins, Mr. Stewart, chairperson of a civic committee of which Ms. Ott is a member, calls and asks to speak to her. How would you respond?

Situation 3

At 3 p.m. Ms. Ott leaves the office to play golf at her country club. Mr. Wittaker, a good customer, calls at 4 p.m. to ask Ms. Ott to stop in to see him the first thing the next morning. How would you handle this call?

Situation 4

At 9:20 the next morning, while Ms. Ott is calling on Mr. Wittaker as requested the previous afternoon, another customer, Mr. Chan of Hilltop Corporation, telephones and asks that Ms. Ott call him at 555-0400 at 2 p.m. to discuss an order. How would you respond to Mr. Chan?

Office Application 9-4 (Objective 2)

Carlos Perez has worked for RJ Computer Corporation for one month. During that time, you heard him make numerous mistakes over the telephone. How should you or Carlos handle the following situations? Use a separate sheet of paper to prepare your answers.

Situation 1

A customer calls who is upset due to an overcharge on his account. The customer, in a loud and discourteous voice, tells Carlos what he thinks of RJ Computer Corporation and accuses all employees of being incompetent. After the customer gets out the first two sentences, Carlos interrupts him and says: "Just wait a minute. There is no reason to be unhappy with me, and don't call me an incompetent. I am extremely competent. Perhaps you are the one who is incompetent."

Situation 2

Carlos goes to lunch each day at 11:30 a.m. You answer his phone while he is out. He not only leaves without telling you where his supervisor is or when his supervisor is expected back, he leaves without telling you when he will be back from lunch. Even though the company policy is a one-hour lunch, many times it is 1 p.m. or later when Carlos comes back.

Situation 3

Carlos does not usually take a break in the morning. He goes to the cafeteria, gets a doughnut and juice, and brings the food back to his desk. He then eats while he works. When Carlos is busy keying a project, he will often let the phone ring at least six times before picking it up. When he does pick it up, he often answers with a curt, "RJ Computer Corporation." Many times Carlos has had his mouth full of food. He seems to get irritated when the caller asks him to repeat something. He usually ends his conversation by hanging up the telephone with a loud click.

Office Application 9-5 (Objective 3)

Indicate how you would handle the following situations. Place your answers on a separate sheet of paper.

1. Mr. Navarate asks you to call Claudia Pearson and Erick Strickland to inform them of a meeting tomorrow.
2. Mr. Navarate asks you to call the local chapter of the American Management Association. He tells you that he thinks the number is 555-2000.
3. Mr. Navarate asks you to get Earl Carvell of Carvell Manufacturing on the line.
4. It is 4:30 p.m. in Texas and Mr. Navarate asks you to call William Roth in New York.
5. Assume that you are directly handling all incoming telephone calls for RJ Computer Corporation. Indicate the proper response that you should make in answering these calls.

Office Application 9-6 (Objective 3)

1. Locate telephone numbers for each of the following. Prepare the names and telephone numbers in tabular form. Make one copy.
   A. Public library
   B. Internal Revenue Service
   C. Police department
   D. Post office
   E. Your state's employment commission
   F. Weather bureau
2. Locate one company name and telephone number under each of the following categories. You will need to check the Yellow Pages for this information. Prepare the information in tabular form. Include the heading under which you found the information in the Yellow Pages plus the name and telephone number of the company.
   A. Company that sells reprographic equipment
   B. Office supply company
   C. Certified public accountant
   D. Lawyer
   E. Company that sells computers
   F. Company that sells word processors

336

Office Application 9-7 (Objective 3)

On page 339 are four copies of a form used to report telephone calls. For each of the situations listed below, use one of the forms. Be sure to give Mr. Navarate complete information about the calls he received while away from his desk. It is assumed that you place the forms on Mr. Navarate's desk after you prepare them. At the bottom of each form, sign your name. Do not separate the four forms. Hand in the entire sheet to your instructor.

1. Mr. Navarate's wife calls at 3 p.m. and asks you to remind him to pick up his daughter at the doctor's office on his way home.
2. Mr. Murphy calls at 10 a.m. to ask Mr. Navarate to attend a conference of office executives at 4 p.m. today.
3. Ms. G. M. Smith of the Gre-Pak Company, with whom Mr. Navarate has an appointment tomorrow at 11 a.m., calls at 1 p.m. to say that she has been called out of the city and will not be able to keep the appointment tomorrow.
4. Mr. Chan of Hilltop Corporation calls at 11:05 a.m. to discuss an order Mr. Navarate has placed with Hilltop. Mr. Chan will be out of the office from noon until 4 p.m. today. His number is 555-4842.

Office Application 9-8 (Objective 4)

In the following situations, indicate the type of telephone service you would recommend. Record answers on a separate sheet of paper.

Situation 1

Your company makes numerous long-distance calls. You recently heard your supervisor say that the telephone bill is excessive. Is there a possibility of cutting the cost of the long-distance calls? What would you suggest?

Situation 2

Mr. Navarate travels a great deal and frequently calls in to check on what is happening at RJ Computer Corporation. Is there a telephone service that he might find helpful? If so, what is it?

Situation 3

There is no one available to sit at your desk and answer phones while you eat lunch. Is there some special telephone feature that can help you in this situation?

Office Application 9-9 (Objective 4)

To become more familiar with telephone equipment and services, visit a large company in your area and determine what types of telephone equipment are used; summarize your findings in report form. Report your findings to the class.

Office Application 9-10 (Objective 5)

Read at least two articles in current periodicals on the latest written message and image communication systems. Some suggested periodicals are *Administrative Management, The Office,* and *Modern Office Technology.* Summarize your findings in report form listing your reference sources.

WHILE YOU WERE OUT

TO _____

DATE _____ TIME _____

M _____

OF _____

PHONE _____

TELEPHONED ☐   PLEASE CALL ☐

CAME TO SEE YOU ☐   WILL CALL AGAIN ☐

WANTS TO SEE YOU ☐

RETURNED YOUR CALL ☐

MESSAGE _____

_____

_____

_____

By _____

WHILE YOU WERE OUT

TO _____

DATE _____ TIME _____

M _____

OF _____

PHONE _____

TELEPHONED ☐   PLEASE CALL ☐

CAME TO SEE YOU ☐   WILL CALL AGAIN ☐

WANTS TO SEE YOU ☐

RETURNED YOUR CALL ☐

MESSAGE _____

_____

_____

_____

By _____

WHILE YOU WERE OUT

TO _____

DATE _____ TIME _____

M _____

OF _____

PHONE _____

TELEPHONED ☐   PLEASE CALL ☐

CAME TO SEE YOU ☐   WILL CALL AGAIN ☐

WANTS TO SEE YOU ☐

RETURNED YOUR CALL ☐

MESSAGE _____

_____

_____

_____

By _____

WHILE YOU WERE OUT

TO _____

DATE _____ TIME _____

M _____

OF _____

PHONE _____

TELEPHONED ☐   PLEASE CALL ☐

CAME TO SEE YOU ☐   WILL CALL AGAIN ☐

WANTS TO SEE YOU ☐

RETURNED YOUR CALL ☐

MESSAGE _____

_____

_____

_____

By _____

OFFICE APPLICATIONS

Office Application 10-1 (Objective 1)

You receive the incoming mail listed below for Mr. Navarate, Ms. Ott, and Mr. Strickland. Identify the procedures you would go through in (1) the preliminary sort; (2) the priority arrangement of items for the individual's mail; (3) the general procedures followed in opening the mail; (4) the special handling procedures (e.g., retaining envelopes); and (5) the arrangement of mail in individual folders after the final sort. To assist your instructor in grading your work, place the number of the correspondence in parentheses after the listing; see the example given below under Mr. Navarate's mail. Your paper should have the following headings:

OPENING THE MAIL

Preliminary Sort Procedures
Items Arranged in Priority Order

   Mr. Navarate's Mail
   1. Special delivery letter (#17)
      (List the remaining items in priority order)
   Ms. Ott's Mail
      (List items)
   Mr. Strickland's Mail
      (List items)

General Procedures for Opening Mail
Special Handling Procedures
Arrangement of Mail in Individual Folders

   Mr. Navarate's Mail
   Ms. Ott's Mail
   Mr. Strickland's Mail

Here is the list of incoming mail you are to handle.

1. Confidential letter addressed to Ms. Ott.
2. *The Wall Street Journal* addressed to Mr. Navarate.
3. A new product advertisement addressed to the manager of RJ Computer Corporation.
4. A letter addressed to Regina Kinseth; she is no longer with RJ Computer Corporation.
5. A letter addressed to Mr. Strickland with enclosures.
6. A certified letter addressed to Mr. Navarate.
7. An insured letter addressed to Mr. Strickland.
8. An interoffice memorandum addressed to Mr. Navarate.
9. A catalog of computer supplies addressed to Mr. Navarate.
10. A letter with no letterhead address sent to Mr. Navarate.
11. An interoffice memorandum addressed to Ms. Ott.
12. A letter addressed to Ms. Ott. The envelope has an incorrect address for RJ Computer Corporation.
13. A letter addressed to Mr. Navarate which states that a check is enclosed. No check is enclosed.
14. A letter to Mr. Strickland. The letter is dated two weeks ago; however, the postmark date is only two days ago.
15. A letter to Mr. Navarate that refers to a letter written two weeks ago by Mr. Navarate.
16. A bill addressed to Mr. Navarate from Carvell Manufacturing.

17. A special delivery letter to Mr. Navarate.
18. *U.S. News & World Report* addressed to Ms. Ott.
19. A memorandum from Jo Fowler addressed to Mr. Navarate.
20. A memorandum from Alan Raye to Mr. Navarate.

Office Application 10-2 (Objective 1)

On pages 345–346 are two letters that you received in the morning mail. Date and time stamp, read, underline, and annotate these letters. In Letter 1 you discover that no check has been enclosed. You have checked with the Accounting Department regarding Letter 2 and discovered that the check for $332.56 has been received, but the check for $224.22 has not been received. Write the procedure for handling this correspondence directly on each letter.

Office Application 10-3 (Objective 1)

You keep a record of all incoming mail. On page 347 is a register to use in recording today's mail (November 16). The mail arrived at 9:30 a.m. and included the following:

1. A special delivery letter from Heun, Incorporated, Boston, Massachusetts, dated November 12, addressed to Mr. Jack Navarate. It refers to materials that are being sent in a separate envelope.
2. A registered letter addressed to the Sales Department in care of Ms. Ramona Stanley, from B. C. Mainze of Chicago, dated November 13. The letter is ordering computer supplies and should be filed in the orders file.
3. A memorandum received from Alan Raye and addressed to Jack Navarate. The memorandum concerns a change in a purchase order. The memorandum is dated November 13.
4. A first-class letter from Rineair and Company dated November 14 and addressed to Ms. Marjorie Ott in Central Services; however, it should be referred to Marketing.
5. A letter from RAF Corporation, Dallas, Texas, asking for bids on a large order of computers. The letter is dated November 14 and is addressed to Miss Jo Fowler.
6. The materials sent under separate mail (for No. 1 above) are received on November 20.

Office Application 10-4 (Objectives 1 and 2)

Mr. Navarate asks you to mail the correspondence listed below. How will you prepare each item for the outgoing mail?

1. A letter with enclosures that must be sent in a separate envelope.
2. Five memorandums to be sent to Greco Company.
3. A letter that is to be sent SPECIAL DELIVERY.
4. A memorandum to be sent to the Sales Manager.
5. A first-class letter that is to be sent with a package that weighs more than 16 ounces.
6. A memorandum to be sent to the vice-president.
7. A letter that has two enclosures.
8. A letter that is confidential.
9. A first-class letter to be sent with third-class material.
10. An outgoing letter that has Mr. Navarate's name and title on it, but no signature.

Office Application 10-5 (Objectives 2, 3, and 5)

Indicate the class of mail or special service that should be used in sending the items listed below. Set up a three-column table with the special headings (1) Correspondence, (2) Mail Classifications, and (3) Shipping Service.

1. A newspaper.
2. A periodical.
3. A photocopy of a letter.
4. A booklet that weighs 15 ounces.
5. A catalog that weighs 24 ounces.
6. An important letter that weighs 14 ounces.
7. A $75 check.
8. An important package that has a value of $5,000.

9. Two books with a value of $25.
10. A box of coding forms weighing 10 pounds to be shipped as quickly as possible.
11. Computer systems that weigh 1,000 pounds to be shipped to London, England.
12. A letter for which Mr. Navarate wants proof that it has reached its destination.
13. A package that weighs 10 pounds and is valued at $150. The receiver is to pay for the goods upon receipt.
14. A box of perishable items weighing 5 pounds.
15. A package that weighs 200 pounds and is to be sent to a small town where there is no airport. The parts should arrive as soon as possible.
16. A package that weighs 50 pounds and is 100 inches in length and girth combined. It is being shipped from California to Maine; it is necessary that the package be received within two days.

Office Application 10-6 (Objective 4)

Mr. Navarate gives you the following note:
Send the shpt via RR frt to Cincinnati to the consignee indicated. Payment is to be C.O.D., parts shipped FOB Dallas. Transportation charges will be more expensive than normal, since it is a LCL shpt. Prepare a BL.
What is he talking about? Rewrite the note, using terms to indicate what each abbreviation means.

Office Application 10-7 (Objective 5)

Determine the express and freight services available in your city or town. Check the business pages in your local telephone directory. Make a list of the companies that offer such services.

EDWARDS CORPORATION

2456 Abrams Avenue
Arlington, TX 76010-2674

November 12, 19--

Mr. Eric Strickland
RJ Computer Corporation
813 Marsh Lane
Dallas, TX 75220-1604

Dear Mr. Strickland

On November 1, we ordered ten anti-static mats at $58 each
and twenty rolls of shipping labels at $9.95 each. You
informed us that the anti-static mats would be delivered
next month, but you stated that you were sending us the
shipping labels. We received an order from you today but
only ten rolls of shipping labels were received.

Will you please check into the matter? A check for $99.50
is enclosed for the ten rolls of shipping labels that we
received.

Sincerely yours

Michael Edwards

Michael Edwards

pt

Enclosure

①

AIRCRAFT SUPPLY

5689 South Jefferson   Dallas, TX 75210-4838

November 12, 19--

Mr. Eric Strickland
RJ Computer Corporation
813 Marsh Lane
Dallas, TX   75220-1604

Dear Mr. Strickland

Your past-due notice on Account 4567 in the amount
of $556.78 was received today. Apparently there is some
mistake. On October 11, we sent you a check for $332.56
to cover Invoice 89. On November 1, we sent you a check
for $224.42 to cover Invoice 95. According to our records,
our account should be paid in full.

Would you please check your records immediately to
see if you have not received these payments? We have
always paid our bills promptly, and we would like to have
this matter cleared up immediately.

Sincerely yours

R. W. Criton

R. W. Criton

say

②

MAIL REGISTER

Name _____

Dates this page _____

| RECEIVED | | FROM | DATED | ADDRESSED TO | | DESCRIPTION | SEP MAIL | REFERRED | | WHERE |
Date	Time	Name/Address		Dept	Person	Kind of mail/enc/sep cov	RECEIVED	To	Date	FILED

OFFICE APPLICATIONS

Office Application 11-1   (Objective 1)

Prepare four voucher checks. Use the information below and the forms provided on pages 353–355.

December 2 Issued Check 114 for $159.34, payable to Maynard Office Company, 3781 Beech Street, Duncanville, TX 75116-1846, for office supplies, Invoice 34890.

December 4 Issued Check 115 for $2,416.85, to John T. Snyder & Sons, 1872 Harrison Road, Tucson, AZ 85730-5872, for computer supplies, Invoice 7891.

December 5 Issued Check 116 for $58.93, payable to Trucking Express, 35 First Street, Dallas, TX 75210-4838, for freight charges, Invoice 48314.

December 6 Issued Check 117 for $100, payable to Cash, to replenish the petty cash fund.

Office Application 11-2   (Objective 2)

1. On a separate sheet of paper, identify the types of endorsement shown at the right.
2. Explain what type of endorsement you would use in each of the following situations:
   a. RJ Computer Corporation received a check from J. T. McElroy in payment of a bill. You plan to send the check to the bank through the mail. What type of endorsement should you use?
   b. You are depositing your payroll check. You are at the bank and are personally handing the check to the bank teller. What type of endorsement should you use?

Office Application 11-3   (Objective 3)

Using the forms on pages 357–358, prepare a deposit slip for each of the following deposits.

1. On December 4 the deposit was:
   Currency $240.00
   Coin   3.62
   Checks: Lincoln National Bank of Denver,

$4,192.90; Merchants Bank of Nashville, $3,822; Central Trust Co. of Decatur, GA, $2,761.10.

2. On December 8 the deposit was:
   Currency $270.00
   Coin   6.92
   Checks: Central Trust Co. of Decatur, GA, $821.64; Farmers' Bank & Trust Co. of Des Moines, IA, $348; Chicago Trust Co., $310.16.

3. On December 11 the deposit was: (The numbers before the amounts of the checks are the ABA transit numbers that should be used in preparing the deposit tickets.)

Currency		$ 93.00
Coin		4.21
Checks:	21-52	2,714.00
	84-118	3,186.05
	73-633	319.75
	19-130	249.15

Office Application 11-4 (Objective 4)

On page 359 is a statement from the Bank of the South for the checking account of the Dallas chapter of the Administrative Management Society for the month of December. After verifying the canceled checks with your check stubs, you find that Checks 48 ($15) and 49 ($18.75) are outstanding. In the space below the bank statement, reconcile the bank balance with the check stub balance of $891.78. Take into account the service charge and interest on the statement.

Office Application 11-5 (Objective 5)

Explain which method you would use to transmit payment in each of the following situations. Prepare your answers on a separate sheet of paper.

1. RJ Computer Corporation is buying materials from Keith Industries. RJ Computer has not previously done business with Keith Industries, and Keith Industries has asked for a guaranteed payment. Keith Industries is located in Dallas. The materials are to be picked up at Keith. What type of service would you use to transmit payment?
2. RJ Computer Corporation is purchasing office forms from Martin Supply Company which is located in Baltimore, Maryland. RJ Computer Corporation has not established credit with Martin Supply Company, and the company has asked for guaranteed payment. What type of service would you use to transmit payment?
3. Your supervisor, Mr. Navarate, is planning a business trip to England. He needs to take $1,000 with him for expenses. What type of service would you use?

Office Application 11-6 (Objective 6)

Mr. Navarate gave you the responsibility of keeping the petty cash record for the AMS chapter. Instead of writing checks for small expenditures, a petty cash fund is used for making such payments.

On page 361 is a petty cash record that is used to keep account of petty cash. You are to enter the petty cash transactions listed below and keep a running balance.

December 1 A petty cash fund is started by issuing Check 41 for $100. You are not to prepare the check, but you should make an entry in the petty cash record.

December 4 Paid $22.00 for postage stamps.

December 4 Paid $4.00 for special cards to be sent with an announcement of a meeting.

December 5 Paid $8.40 to the mail carrier for postage on business reply envelopes and cards that were returned.

December 7 Paid $5.80 for express charges on a shipment of letterheads.

December 8 Paid $20.50 for miscellaneous supplies ordered for use in AMS business.

December 9 Paid $25 for flowers sent to Miss Roush, one of the members of the activities committee.

December 13 Paid $10.00 for office supplies delivered by Pounsford Stationery Company.

December 13 Issued Check 45 to replenish the petty cash fund to its original amount of $100. Compute the amount of the check and make the appropriate entry in the petty cash record. You are not required to prepare the check to replenish the fund.

Office Application 11-7
(Objectives 7 and 11)

1. On page 363 are copies of a Condensed Comparative Statement and a Condensed Comparative Balance Sheet for RJ Computer Corporation. Use a calculator to determine the answers for the blanks and the percentage increase or decrease on each item. Indicate a decrease by enclosing the number in parentheses. (See Appendix D for help in your calculations.) After all calculations are made, prepare the income statement and balance sheet in proper form. Use a separate sheet of paper for each.
2. Explain each of the following terms as used on the balance sheet and income statement:
   a. Current Assets
   b. Plant and Equipment
   c. Current Liabilities
   d. Long-Term Debt
   e. Capital
   f. Gross Profit on Sales
   g. Net Income

Office Application 11-8   (Objective 8)

Read two current articles on electronic banking procedures. Summarize your articles on 5″ × 3″ cards. List the source of your article at the top of each card.

Office Application 11-9
(Objectives 9 and 11)

You earn $8 an hour and are paid overtime at 1½ times your hourly pay. All hours over 40 are considered overtime. You are paid every two weeks. During the last two weeks you worked 42 hours the first week and 40 hours the second week. Calculate the following problems on a separate sheet of paper.

1. What are your gross earnings for this two-week period?
2. If the FICA tax rate is 7.51 percent and there is a $121.20 federal income tax deduction, what are your net earnings for the two-week period?
3. RJ Computer Corporation pays unemployment tax on your gross salary. The tax rate is 3.4 percent. What is the total amount of unemployment tax for this two-week period?

Office Application 11-10   (Objective 10)

Mr. Navaraté gave you the receipts on page 364 when he returned from a business trip. In addition to these receipts, Mr. Navarate spent the following amounts. Prepare an expense report; use the form on page 365.

Sunday Dinner, December 7	$ 15.50
Breakfast, December 8	3.75
Lunch, December 8	8.25
Dinner, December 8	12.50
Breakfast, December 9	4.50
Lunch, December 9	5.50
Dinner, December 9	14.50
Breakfast, December 10	3.50
Lunch, December 10	8.75
Dinner, December 10	20.50
Breakfast, December 11	5.25
Lunch, December 11	6.50
Dinner, December 11	12.25
Breakfast, December 12	3.50
Lunch, December 12	5.75
Air Fare, December 7	384.48
Taxi Service, December 7	12.00
Taxi Service, December 12	14.00

Office Application 11-11   (Objective 11)

Determine the selling price of the products listed on page 367. The markup percentage is based on the cost price. See Appendix D on page 250 for tips on how to perform the mathematical calculations.

Key the information as a table. Entitle it "Selling Prices."

No. 114

$\dfrac{32\text{-}56}{3110}$

RJ COMPUTER CORPORATION

813 Marsh Lane
Dallas, TX 75220-1604
214-555-2016

_____ 19 _____

PAY TO THE
ORDER OF _____ $ _____

(For Classroom Use Only)

_____ DOLLARS

BANK OF THE SOUTH
Dallas, TX 75211-1135

RJ COMPUTER CORPORATION

⑆311009990⑆ 130⑈456⑈7⑈

_____

INVOICE NUMBER	NET AMOUNT	DESCRIPTION

DATE	VOUCHER NO.	CHECK NUMBER	RJ COMPUTER CORPORATION Dallas, TX

DETACH AND RETAIN THIS STATEMENT - IF NOT CORRECT, PLEASE NOTIFY US PROMPTLY.

No. 115

$\dfrac{32\text{-}56}{3110}$

RJ COMPUTER CORPORATION

813 Marsh Lane
Dallas, TX 75220-1604
214-555-2016

_____ 19 _____

PAY TO THE
ORDER OF _____ $ _____

(For Classroom Use Only)

_____ DOLLARS

BANK OF THE SOUTH
Dallas, TX 75211-1135

RJ COMPUTER CORPORATION

⑆311009990⑆ 130⑈456⑈7⑈

_____

INVOICE NUMBER	NET AMOUNT	DESCRIPTION

DATE	VOUCHER NO.	CHECK NUMBER	RJ COMPUTER CORPORATION Dallas, TX

DETACH AND RETAIN THIS STATEMENT - IF NOT CORRECT, PLEASE NOTIFY US PROMPTLY.

No. 116

32-56
3110

RJ COMPUTER CORPORATION
813 Marsh Lane
Dallas, TX 75220-1604
214-555-2016

_____ 19 _____

PAY TO THE
ORDER OF _____ $ _____

(For Classroom Use Only)

_____ DOLLARS

BANK OF THE SOUTH
Dallas, TX 75211-1135

RJ COMPUTER CORPORATION

⑆311009990⑆ 130⑈456⑈7⑆

_____

INVOICE NUMBER	NET AMOUNT	DESCRIPTION
DATE	VOUCHER NO.	CHECK NUMBER	RJ COMPUTER CORPORATION Dallas, TX

DETACH AND RETAIN THIS STATEMENT - IF NOT CORRECT, PLEASE NOTIFY US PROMPTLY.

No. 117

32-56
3110

RJ COMPUTER CORPORATION
813 Marsh Lane
Dallas, TX 75220-1604
214-555-2016

_____ 19 _____

PAY TO THE
ORDER OF _____ $ _____

(For Classroom Use Only)

_____ DOLLARS

BANK OF THE SOUTH
Dallas, TX 75211-1135

RJ COMPUTER CORPORATION

⑆311009990⑆ 130⑈456⑈7⑆

_____

INVOICE NUMBER	NET AMOUNT	DESCRIPTION
DATE	VOUCHER NO.	CHECK NUMBER	RJ COMPUTER CORPORATION Dallas, TX

DETACH AND RETAIN THIS STATEMENT - IF NOT CORRECT, PLEASE NOTIFY US PROMPTLY.

CHECKING ACCOUNT DEPOSIT TICKET

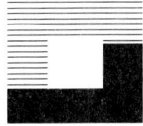

813 Marsh Lane
Dallas, TX 75220-1604
214-555-2016

RJ COMPUTER CORPORATION

DATE _____ 19 _____

_____

CASH	CURRENCY		
	COIN		
C H E C K S			
TOTAL FROM OTHER SIDE			
TOTAL			
LESS CASH RECEIVED			
NET DEPOSIT			

32-56
3110

USE OTHER SIDE FOR
ADDITIONAL LISTING

BE SURE EACH ITEM IS
PROPERLY ENDORSED

◆ **BANK OF THE SOUTH**

⑆3110099901⑆ 130⑈456⑈71⑆

CHECKS AND OTHER ITEMS ARE RECEIVED FOR DEPOSIT SUBJECT TO THE TERMS AND CONDITIONS OF THIS BANK'S COLLECTION AGREEMENT

CHECKING ACCOUNT DEPOSIT TICKET

813 Marsh Lane
Dallas, TX 75220-1604
214-555-2016

RJ COMPUTER CORPORATION

DATE _____ 19 _____

_____

CASH	CURRENCY		
	COIN		
C H E C K S			
TOTAL FROM OTHER SIDE			
TOTAL			
LESS CASH RECEIVED			
NET DEPOSIT			

32-56
3110

USE OTHER SIDE FOR
ADDITIONAL LISTING

BE SURE EACH ITEM IS
PROPERLY ENDORSED

◆ **BANK OF THE SOUTH**

⑆3110099901⑆ 130⑈456⑈71⑆

CHECKS AND OTHER ITEMS ARE RECEIVED FOR DEPOSIT SUBJECT TO THE TERMS AND CONDITIONS OF THIS BANK'S COLLECTION AGREEMENT

CHECKING ACCOUNT DEPOSIT TICKET

813 Marsh Lane
Dallas, TX 75220-1604
214-555-2016

RJ COMPUTER CORPORATION

DATE _____ 19 _____

_____

CASH	CURRENCY		
	COIN		
C H E C K S			
TOTAL FROM OTHER SIDE			
TOTAL			
LESS CASH RECEIVED			
NET DEPOSIT			

32-56
3110

USE OTHER SIDE FOR
ADDITIONAL LISTING

BE SURE EACH ITEM IS
PROPERLY ENDORSED

◆ **BANK OF THE SOUTH**

⑆3110099901⑆ 130⑈456⑈71⑆

CHECKS AND OTHER ITEMS ARE RECEIVED FOR DEPOSIT SUBJECT TO THE TERMS AND CONDITIONS OF THIS BANK'S COLLECTION AGREEMENT

Table 1

CHECKS LIST SINGLY	DOLLARS	CENTS
1		
2		
3		
4		
5		
6		
7		
8		
9		
10		
11		
12		
13		
14		
15		
16		
17		
18		
19		
TOTAL		

ENTER TOTAL ON THE FRONT OF THIS TICKET

Table 2

CHECKS LIST SINGLY	DOLLARS	CENTS
1		
2		
3		
4		
5		
6		
7		
8		
9		
10		
11		
12		
13		
14		
15		
16		
17		
18		
19		
TOTAL		

ENTER TOTAL ON THE FRONT OF THIS TICKET

Table 3

CHECKS LIST SINGLY	DOLLARS	CENTS
1		
2		
3		
4		
5		
6		
7		
8		
9		
10		
11		
12		
13		
14		
15		
16		
17		
18		
19		
TOTAL		

ENTER TOTAL ON THE FRONT OF THIS TICKET

BANK OF THE SOUTH
Dallas, TX 75211-1135

Checking Account Statement

ACCT. 203-924-4
DATE 12/1/--
PAGE 1

Administrative Management Society
Dallas Chapter
Dallas, TX 75201-1132

BALANCE FORWARD	NO. OF CHECKS	TOTAL CHECK AMOUNT	NO. OF DEP.	TOTAL DEPOSIT AMOUNT	INTEREST	SERVICE CHARGE	BALANCE THIS STATEMENT
750 53	8	292 00	1	467 00	5 25	4 20	926 58

CHECKS AND OTHER DEBITS		DEPOSITS AND OTHER CREDITS	DATE	BALANCE
42	25.00	467.00	11/05	1,192.53
43	50.00		11/07	1,142.53
44	75.00		11/15	1,067.53
45	100.00		11/16	967.53
46	12.00		11/18	955.53
47	5.00		11/22	950.53
50	10.00		11/25	940.53
51	15.00 4.20SC	5.25INT	11/31	926.58

PLEASE EXAMINE AT ONCE.
IF NO ERRORS ARE REPORTED WITHIN 10 DAYS, THE ACCOUNT WILL BE CONSIDERED CORRECT.
PLEASE ADVISE US
IN WRITING OF ANY CHANGE IN YOUR ADDRESS.

KEYS TO SYMBOLS

AD - AUTOMATIC DEPOSIT	DM - DEBIT MEMO
AP - AUTOMATIC PAYMENT	EC - ERROR CORRECTED
AR - AUTOMATIC REVERSAL	INT - INTEREST
CB - CHARGE BACK	OD - OVERDRAWN
CC - CERTIFIED CHECK	RC - RETURN CHECK CHG
CM - CREDIT MEMO	RT - RETURN ITEM
CO - CHARGE OFF	SC - SERVICE CHARGE

PETTY CASH RECORD

DATE		DESCRIPTION	RECEIPTS	PAYMENTS	BALANCE

RJ COMPUTER CORPORATION
Condensed Comparative Income Statement
December 31, 1988, and December 31, 1989

	December 31 1988	December 31 1989	Percent Increase or Decrease
Net Sales.............................	$ 3,400,000	$ 3,800,000	
Cost of Goods Sold	2,100,000	2,200,000	
Gross Profit on Sales...................	$	$	
Selling Expenses......................	665,000	800,000	
General and Administrative Expenses...	350,000	375,000	
Total Operating Expenses	1,015,000	1,175,000	
Net Profit from Operations	$	$	
Other Income........................	21,000	19,000	
Total Net Profit plus Other Income......	$	$	
Other Expenses.......................	12,000	20,000	
Net Income Before Federal Income Taxes	$	$	
Federal Income Taxes	82,500	100,000	
Net Income After Federal Income Taxes .	$	$	

RJ COMPUTER CORPORATION
Condensed Comparative Balance Sheet
December 31, 1988, and December 31, 1989

	December 31 1988	December 31 1989	Percent Increase or Decrease
Assets			
Current Assets	$ 1,200,000	$ 1,400,000	
Investments	250,000	300,000	
Plant and Equipment	1,800,000	2,200,000	
Total Assets	$	$	
Liabilities			
Current Liabilities.....................	350,000	450,000	
Long-Term Debt	800,000	700,000	
Total Liabilities.......................	$	$	
Capital			
Capital and Surplus...................	2,100,000	2,750,000	
Total Liabilities and Capital...........	$ 3,250,000	$ 3,900,000	

MAXWELL HOTEL

Customer _Jack Navarate_   Room No. _210_

Date	Charges	
12/10	$90.00	
12/11	$90.00	
TOTAL	$180.00	

Paid _One hundred eighty_ ⁰⁰⁄₁₀₀ _____ Dollars

Cash ☒   Check ☐   Credit card ☐   Other ☐

MAXWELL HOTEL
555-8900

Jessica Capps
Clerk

18245

Room _311_   **Manhattan Manor**
New York • 555-6200

Customer _Jack Navarate_

Date	Charges	Balance
12-7	$105.00	
12-8	$105.00	
12-9	$105.00	$315

R. H. Goldford
Signed

Allen Rent-a-CAR
555-7100

Name _Jack Navarate_

Date _December 8, 19--_   PAID   Car _1987 Monte Carlo_

Charges _$104.00_   Salesperson _Denise Wagner_

Rj Computer Corporation

WEEKLY EXPENSE REPORT

ENTER ONLY ONE AMOUNT PER LINE, PER DAY.

NAME _____

SAVE NO. ___ ENDING SPEEDOMETER ___ CHANGED DRIVER'S LICENSE NO. ___ TR NO. ___ S ___

WEEK ENDING	SUNDAY	MONDAY	TUESDAY	WEDNESDAY	THURSDAY	FRIDAY	SATURDAY	TOTALS
SATURDAY								
PERSONAL								
MOTEL OR HOTEL								
CITY								
STATE								
ROOM CHARGE (ATTACH RECEIPT)	11							
BREAKFAST								
LUNCH								
DINNER								
TOTAL MEALS →	12							
OTHER PERSONAL	13							
COMPANY OWNED AUTOMOBILE	14							
GAS-OIL								
OTHER OPERATING (INCLUDE PARKING TOLLS, TAXES, AND FEES)	15							
PARTS AND REPAIRS	16							
MISCELLANEOUS (EXPLAIN-ATTACH RECEIPT IF OVER $25.00)								
ENTERTAINMENT	17							
OTHER TRANSPORTATION (AIR FARE CAR RENTAL)	18							
MISC. OTHER (EXPLAIN-ATTACH RECEIPT IF OVER $25.00)	19							
TOTAL FOR DAY								WEEK'S EXPENSES

EXPLANATION OF ENTERTAINMENT AND MISCELLANEOUS

INCREASE MY ADVANCE 21
DECREASE MY ADVANCE 22
ISSUE CHECK 23

PLEASE SIGN _____

Product	Cost Price	Markup Percentage	Selling Price
Printwheel, Metal	$11.00	10	_____
Polarized CRT Glare Filters	69.00	20	_____
Coding Form, BASIC Format	15.50	8	_____
Anti-static Mat	33.40	20	_____
Bulk Diskette Eraser	26.00	15	_____
Printer Cable	17.00	20	_____
Shipping Labels	6.50	15	_____
Diskette, 5¼"	1.47	20	_____
Diskette, 8"	1.85	20	_____
Printwheel, Plastic	3.10	15	_____

OFFICE APPLICATIONS

Office Application 12-1 (Objective 1)

Read and summarize on 5″ × 3″ cards two articles on the types of records systems used in offices today. Indicate the source of each article at the top of the card.

Office Application 12-2 (Objective 2)

Do library research on careers available in records management. You might wish to check the *Dictionary of Occupational Titles* and publications by The Association of Records Managers and Administrators, Inc. This association published *Records Management Quarterly* which also might be of some help to you. Write a report of your findings, giving your sources.

Office Application 12-3 (Objectives 1 through 7)

Interview one office worker on records management functions used in his or her office. Ask the questions listed below. Write your findings in a short report.

1. What filing classification is used?
2. What type of equipment is used? Are automated systems used? If so, what are they?
3. Is a records-retention schedule available?
4. How are materials transferred and stored?
5. Does the company have full-time positions in records management. If so, what are they and what are the job duties? Obtain a copy of the position descriptions if possible.

Office Application 12-4 (Objective 3)

Indicate the subject you would use in filing the following correspondence. Place your answers on a separate sheet of paper.

1. A reminder notice for the next weekly meeting of the Administrative Management Society.
2. A notice of a seminar on leadership.
3. A job application from Martin Irwin.
4. A copy of Mr. Navarate's expense account.
5. A blueprint of a new product.
6. A commercial script on a new product.
7. A copy of RJ Computer's financial report.
8. A copy of Mr. Navarate's sick leave form.
9. A report on past due accounts.
10. A research project on a new piece of equipment.

Office Application 12-5 (Objective 3)

Assume that you are setting up a numeric file. Assign numbers for the following correspondence; begin your numbers with 100. Then prepare 5″ × 3″ cards for the alphabetic card file and alphabetize the cards. Study the alphabetic filing rules in Appendix H, pp. 264–270. Prepare a list showing how the numbers would be placed in a numeric file. Place the company name opposite the number assigned. Turn in your list of numbers plus your 5″ × 3″ cards to your instructor.

Dave Marley Ford, Incorporated
McCoy-Hoving and Associates
Maritime Telecommunications Corporation
Marek Auto Service
Paul Marco and Associates
George W. McCormick Insurance Agency
Mark IV Systems
Margo's Coiffures
Marlin-Rockwell Division

J. A. McBride, Inc.
Margie's Florist & Gift Shop
Marsalis Avenue Garage
Maresa's
Marquee East Apartments
McCrackin Carpet Service

Office Application 12–6   (Objective 4)

On pages 373–374 are 21 groups of names. In the space provided at the right of each group, show how the names would be indexed by units and alphabetized within each group. The first group is given as a sample.

Office Application 12-7   (Objective 4)

Before you begin this job, you may wish to study the alphabetic filing rules in Appendix H. For this activity, use 5″ × 3″ cards. Write or key the name and address of the individual or business firm in proper indexing form on the 5″ × 3″ card. Place the number given by the name in the upper right hand corner of the card. Then, alphabetize the cards. Once you have finished the alphabetizing, take a sheet of paper and list in proper order the card numbers that would be filed under each letter of the alphabet. Turn in this sheet to your instructor. Retain your cards for use in Office Application 12-8.

(1) Donald L. Sells, Jr.
4329 Mountain Drive
Juneau, AK 99801-2573

(2) San Diego Supply Co.
1181 Jefferson Road
San Diego, CA 92110-9837

(3) Russell J. Sells
600 South 29th
Arlington, VA 22202-3422

(4) Vinson Supply Company
3804 Wood Street
Hastings, NE 68901-4789

(5) Mrs. James D'Ilvetta
1405 Knoxville Avenue South
Tulsa, OK 74112-7835

(6) MacAbbott Corporation
412 Broadway
Montclair, NJ 07043-2384

(7) Capt. John Frase
427 Grand Avenue
Princeton, WV 24720-3839

(8) M. M. Stans & Co.
4500 Fifth Avenue
Pittsburgh, PA 15213-7865

(9) Ima L. McCormick
719 Superior Avenue
Cleveland, OH 44116-5684

(10) Tolbert Aircraft Shop
1800 Tremont South
Kansas City, KS 66103-4755

(11) John Lipinski & Sons
83 Main Street
Peoria, IL 61611-3892

(12) The L & S Lane Company
875 Willow Road NW
Albuquerque, NM 87107-8932

(13) Jones & Hardin Mfrs.
208 Holona Place
Honolulu, HI 96817-2428

(14) Universal Company
81 Branch Avenue
Portales, NM 88130-5679

(15) 7th Street Supply Company
Fall River, WI 43932-8273

(16) Capital Services
Insurance Building
Houston, TX 77012-3492

Office Application 12-8
(Objectives 3 and 4)

In addition to the 16 cards you prepared in Office Application 12-7, you will now need to prepare additional cards. Prepare the cards just as you did in Office Application 12-7. Write or key the name and address of the individual or business firm in proper indexing form on the 5″ × 3″ card. Place the number given by the name in the upper right hand corner of the card. Then, alphabetize all cards (the cards from Office Application 12-7 and the cards from this job). Once you have finished the alphabetizing, take a sheet of paper and list in proper order the card numbers that would be filed under each letter of the alphabet. Turn in this sheet to your instructor. Retain your cards for Office Application 12-9.

(17) Glenn Overman Company
3020 23rd Street NW
Tucson, AZ 85703-5868

(18) Mays & Suter
351 Ludlow Street
Chicago, IL 60612-3472

(19) A. L. George, Jr.
3842 Texas Avenue
Baton Rouge, LA 70805-9747

(20) D. George MacBeth
1142 Market Street
Charlotte, NC 28202-7985

(21) L. T. Stinson
2960 Flagler Street
Tampa, FL 33607-2385

(22) A. L. George, Sr.
3842 Texas Avenue
Baton Rouge, LA 70805-9747

(23) O'Neal Office Services
1710 Hampton Avenue
Columbia, SC 29204-9542

(24) Ammond Supply Co.
Decatur, GA 30016-4379

(25) Northwest Suppliers
911 Flowers Avenue
Helena, MT 59602-6589

(26) Nevada Products Company
6182 Main Street
Carson City, NV 89701-2548

(27) O'Keefe Rubber Company
1674 Chestnut Street
Decatur, AL 35601-2376

(28) Wm. A. Prangle
1800 Brooks Drive
Miami, FL 33112-2892

(29) R & W Raymond
1016 Riverside Avenue
Concord, NH 03301-9483

(30) L. M. Doutt
106 Granite Avenue
Montpelier, VT 05601-4855

(31) Western Export Corp.
Golden Gate Drive
San Francisco, CA 94107-6765

(32) Dr. Georgia Ammon
210 Doctor's Building
Hartford, CT 06107-1538

(33) Cantor–Cantor
1419 South Street
Cheyenne, WY 82001-2388

(34) J. T. Crow
1231 Sixteenth Street
San Francisco, CA 94107-0856

(35) J. T. Crow
1231 Sixteenth Street
Seattle, WA 98106-3652

(36) Department of Health
State of Kentucky
Frankfort, KY 40601-5752

(37) Department of Parks
State of Idaho
Pocatello, ID 83202-3899

(38) Graham Department Store
412 East Street
Madison, WI 53704-7814

(39) Olivia S. Young
21 Ocean City Drive
Atlantic City, NJ 08401-9532

(40) Barnes and Batts
4726 Wilmore Street
Decatur, GA 30012-4415

(41) San Rafael, Inc.
1708 Tremont Street
Springfield, MA 01105-8962

(42) Bertke and Young, Attorneys
Norton, KS 67654-2435

(43) Jane's Bootery
Meadville, PA 16335-3984

(44) The Oriental Company
12 Michigan Boulevard
Chicago, IL 60611-4725

(45) Bartons' Importers
Hanover and Spring Streets
Binghamton, NY 13902-6581

(46) Leppert and Carter Company
Carlon and Lacey Streets
St. Paul, MN 55101-7785

(47) Wilson Electric Company
Redfield, SD 57469-8992

(48) McFeatter Box Company
200 East Sixth Street
Little Rock, AR 72203-5483

(49) KRLD Television Station
1990 Stuart Avenue
Des Moines, IA 50301-9235

(50) James and Company
Fifth and Main Streets
White Plains, NY 10604-8765

(51) Bowers Show Store
119 Limestone Street
Lexington, KY 40503-7443

(52) Twelve Plus One Apartments
123 Erie Avenue
Cincinnati, OH 45205-2316

(53) 12 Step AA Club
Front Street
Columbus, OH 43210-3467

(54) 12 Hills Apartments
444 Foster Street
Boston, MA 02110-4812

(55) At Home Grocery
666 North Avenue
Kalamazoo, MI 49002-3954

(56) Deland Cigar Company
Ida Avenue and Smith Road

(57) Knoxville Supply Co.
100 University Street
Knoxville, TN 37906-5506

(58) Hammond Inn
Hammond, LA 70402-6812

(59) Dr. Harold Owens
504 Medical Arts Building
Johnstown, PA 15902-3495

(60) Daniel's Supply Store
1400 Cleveland Place
Denver, CO 80202-8294

(61) H. E. V. Thomasen
890 Hill Road
Rapid City, SD 57702-6275

(62) Randall Book Store
3413 Linwood Street
Davenport, IA 52802-8254

(63) Harold C. Duffy
Bristol, GA 31518-8534

(64) Helen LaMarr
3 Bond Place
Bismark, ND 58502-4892

Office Application 12-9
(Objectives 3 and 4)

You will use the same cards in this job as were used in Office Applications 7 and 8. Follow these instructions for completing this job.

1. Arrange the 64 cards in geographical order by states; then in alphabetical order by cities within each state; and finally, in alphabetical order by names within each city.
2. After arranging the cards properly, take a blank sheet of paper to prepare your solutions. On the left side, list the names of the states. After each state, list in proper order the card numbers within each state.
3. Hand in your sheet to your instructor.

Office Application 12-10   (Objective 5)

Sometimes correspondence may be called for under more than one name. It may be filed under the name of a company or filed under the name of an individual who signed a particular letter. When there is such a possibility, a cross-reference sheet should be made. On page 375, you will find four cross-reference sheets. Using the following information, fill out the sheets with a pen or pencil. Use the current date.

1. A letter from Vinson Supply Company, Hastings, NE 68901-4789, regarding discount from list price (File V-6). Letter signed by Anne L. Frazier (File F-12).
2. A letter from Ronald L. Selzer (File S-3), National Airport Services Co., Washington, DC 20013-3942 (File N-2), regarding their last order.
3. Telegram from P. R. Eads (File E-1), Stillwater Products Company, Stillwater, OK 74074-8526 (File S-12), asking that delivery of their last order be speeded up.
4. Letter from Torres and Mills, Minneapolis, MN 55660-2839 (File T-8), signed by Benjamin Torres (File T-3), asking for advice in planning a promotional campaign.

Office Application 12-11   (Objective 6)

Read and summarize two recent articles on filing equipment and supplies. Information may be obtained from such periodicals as *The Office* and *Records Management Quarterly*. Summarize the articles on a plain sheet of paper, giving the sources.

Office Application 12-12   (Objective 7)

Visit your college or public library. Locate two items that are stored on microfilm or on microfiche. Use the microfilm reader and make a hard copy of one of the items.

Office Application 12-13   (Objective 7)

Using current periodicals, read and summarize two articles on office use of micrographics. Prepare your summaries on a plain sheet of paper, noting the sources.

Office Application 12-14   (Objective 7)

Read and summarize two articles in current periodicals on automated filing systems. Prepare your summaries on a plain sheet of paper, noting the sources.

Names		Indexed by Units and Alphabetically Arranged			
		Indexing Units			
		1	2	3	4
(a) John T. Baur	1.	Bauer	Mary	Ellen	
Henry Elison Bowers, Jr.	2.	Baur	John	T	
Mary Ellen Bauer	3.	Bower	C	L	
C. L. Bower	4.	Bowers	Henry	Elison	Jr
(b) Z. T. Glasier, II	5.	Glasier	II	ZT	II
Z. T. Glasier, Jr.	6.	" "	JR		
Alice Glazier	7.	Glazier	Alice		
Gleason Company	8.	Gleason	Gleason		
(c) Helen Clara McBeth	9.				
David F. MacCormack	10.				
Mildred MacBeth	11.				
L. B. Maple	12.				
(d) D. A. Schwartz	13.				
M. Robert Swartz	14.				
Katherine Schwarz	15.				
Ethel M. Schwarzkoff	16.				
(e) Edward C. Albert	17.				
Albert's Ice Cream Shoppe	18.				
Alberts' Grocery Store	19.				
E. Charles Albert	20.				
(f) John T. Schklar, Jr.	21.				
John L. Schlanger, Sr.	22.				
Judge Julia Schleicher	23.				
Mary B. Schlick	24.				
(g) Five Hundred Ervay Bldg.	25.				
500 Cafeteria	26.				
5 Dollar Diner	27.				
The 500, Inc.	28.				
(h) Francis Q. Bourque	29.				
Patricia Boark	30.				
Patrick O'Reilly Burke	31.				
Iris Burk	32.				
(i) Moore Supplies & Equipment	33.				
Moore-Town Boat Repair	34.				
Frank H. Mohr	35.				
Betty Geneva Mohr	36.				
(j) George M. Lloyd	37.				
Amelia E. Lollar	38.				
Eugene Bahr Loyd	39.				
Mrs. Carmen C. Lopez	40.				

Names		1	2	3	4
(k) O. Edwards Shop	41.				
Mrs. Mary McClellan O'Connor	42.				
Jacqueline O. Odum	43.				
George Felix Oden	44.				
(l) Jos. A. O'Neill	45.				
J. George O'Neal	46.				
Harriet R. O'Neill	47.				
J. Gerald O'Neal	48.				
(m) The SP Printing Company	49.	52			
The Standard Oil Company	50.	49			
Standard Clothing Company	51.	51			
SFAX Television Station	52.	50			
(n) Joseph Parker	53.				
Allen Parks & Sons	54.				
Inman D. Parker, Attorney	55.				
O. A. Park	56.				
(o) Sister M. Bernadine	57.				
St. Louis City Library	58.				
San Francisco State Univ.	59.				
St. John's School	60.				
(p) M. L. DeBrum	61.				
Mrs. Robert G. De Spain	62.				
Mayor Ronald W. DeBerry	63.				
Carolyn De Baca, M.D.	64.				
(q) The V & V Deli	65.				
Prof. H. S. Vallery	66.				
Thal's & Thal's, Inc.	67.				
Thomasen Brothers	68.				
(r) Thomas Hardy Syrgley	69.				
Syndicated Newspaper Corp.	70.				
Sylvan Park Service Station	71.				
Jeannette K. Sylvia	72.				
(s) U.S. Department of Agriculture	73.				
U.S. Playing Card Company	74.				
United Dairy Farmers	75.				
Union Bank & Trust	76.				
(t) Herbert N. Jahncke	77.				
E. H. Jakes	78.				
Helen O'Toole Jackson	79.				
Jack & Jill's Shop	80.				
(u) T. W. O'Poole	81.				
Martin Y. Pryszanski	82.				
Belva D. Pyrtle	83.				
O. R. Poole, Sr.	84.				

374

CROSS-REFERENCE SHEET

Name _____ Date

Subject _____

File Number _____

Regarding

SEE

Name _____ Date

Subject _____

File Number _____

CROSS-REFERENCE SHEET

Name _____ Date

Subject _____

File Number _____

Regarding

SEE

Name _____ Date

Subject _____

File Number _____

CROSS-REFERENCE SHEET

Name _____ Date

Subject _____

File Number _____

Regarding

SEE

Name _____ Date

Subject _____

File Number _____

CROSS-REFERENCE SHEET

Name _____ Date

Subject _____

File Number _____

Regarding

SEE

Name _____ Date

Subject _____

File Number _____

OFFICE APPLICATIONS

Office Application 13-1 (Objective 1)

The purpose of this activity is to help you consider the type of company for which you would like to work. Choose three other members of your class to work with you on this project. Select four businesses in your city where you would like to work. Your instructor will review your list of companies to make sure that other class members have not chosen the same companies. By phone, letter, or personal contact, obtain the information listed below. After receiving the information, determine which company would provide you with the most challenging opportunities. As a group, write and submit your report to your instructor.

1. Name and address of company
2. Size of company
3. Duties of general office worker (or duties of the job in which you are interested)
4. Office hours
5. Opportunities for promotion
6. Vacation policy

Office Application 13-2 (Objective 2)

Where can you get information concerning job opportunities in your city? Answer the following questions by doing the necessary research.

1. Does your school have a placement office? If so, what process do you go through to apply for a job?
2. Do you have private employment agencies in your city? If so, give the names of two and the fee they charge for placing an employee.
3. What types of jobs are available in your city? Check your Sunday newspaper for five classified advertisements for office employees. Determine the qualifications necessary for each job listed and the salary given.
4. Is there a state employment agency in your city? If so, what process do you go through to apply for a job?

Office Application 13-3 (Objectives 3, 4, and 7)

You see the following advertisement in the newspaper.

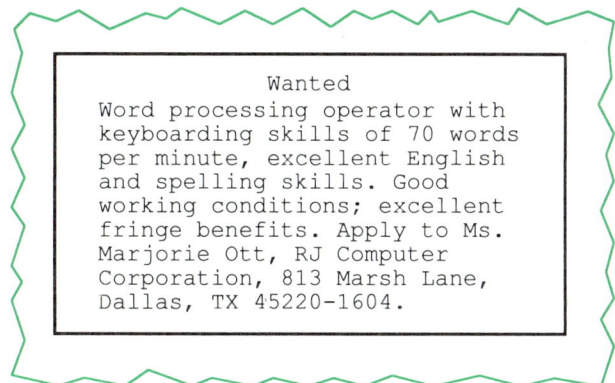

```
            Wanted
Word processing operator with
keyboarding skills of 70 words
per minute, excellent English
and spelling skills. Good
working conditions; excellent
fringe benefits. Apply to Ms.
Marjorie Ott, RJ Computer
Corporation, 813 Marsh Lane,
Dallas, TX 45220-1604.
```

Write a letter of application and include a resumé. Assume that you have an interview with Ms. Ott; write a follow-up letter. Make an original and one carbon copy of each item.

Office Application 13-4 (Objective 5)

In order to assist you in the interviewing process, do some library research on interviewing. Check for recent books or periodicals on the interviewing process. Write a review of one article on 5″ × 3″ cards. Your review should include the following:

1. Source of the article
2. Summary of important points of the article
3. Short paragraph of what you learned from the article

Office Application 13-5 (Objective 6)

Fill out the application form on pages 379–380 for RJ COMPUTER CORPORATION.

RJ COMPUTER CORPORATION

813 Marsh Lane
Dallas, TX 75220-1604
214-555-2016

Name _____ Social Security Number _____

         LAST   FIRST   MIDDLE

Present Address _____ Tel. No. _____

                  NO.   STREET   CITY   STATE   ZIP

U.S. Citizen? _____

Have you ever been convicted of a crime? _____ If yes, describe in full: _____

Have you ever been employed by RJ Computer Corporation? _____ When? _____

Have you ever had or do you now have a worker's compensation claim pending for an injury while working for any employer? _____

If yes, give date and nature of accident _____

List relatives working for RJ Computer Corporation

_____

                NAME   RELATIONSHIP

List acquaintances now employed for RJ Computer Corporation

_____

_____

Person to be notified in case of emergency: _____

                                      NAME

Home Address _____ Tel. No. _____

Business Address _____ Tel. No. _____

SCHOOL	NAME & ADDRESS OF SCHOOL	COURSE OF STUDY	DATES ATTENDED	CIRCLE LAST YEAR COMPLETED	DID YOU GRADUATE?	DIPLOMA, DEGREE, OR CERTIFICATE
High				1 2 3 4	☐ Yes ☐ No	
College				1 2 3 4	☐ Yes ☐ No	
Other (Specify)				1 2 3 4	☐ Yes ☐ No	

EMPLOYMENT RECORD

Present or Last Employment:

Name of Firm		Type of Business	Your Dept. Manager	Your Job Title	Salary
Address	Phone	Date Started	Date Left	Reason for Leaving	

Previous Employment:

Name of Firm		Type of Business	Your Dept. Manager	Your Job Title	Salary
Address	Phone	Date Started	Date Left	Reason for Leaving	

Previous Employment:

Name of Firm		Type of Business	Your Dept. Manager	Your Job Title	Salary
Address	Phone	Date Started	Date Left	Reason for Leaving	

List Other Employers:

_____

_____

_____

U.S. Military Experience: Branch of Service _____ Date Entered _____

Do you have a valid Drivers License? _____ Type _____ Was it ever suspended? _____

Have you ever been bonded? _____

REFERENCES (not former employers or relatives)

NAME AND OCCUPATION	ADDRESS	PHONE NUMBER

I hereby authorize any former employer or any other person given as reference to answer any and all questions that may be asked concerning me. The facts set forth in my application for employment are true and correct. I understand that any false statements on this application shall be considered sufficient course for dismissal. RJ Computer Corporation is an equal opportunity employer.

Applicant's Signature _____

Applicant Leave This Area Blank

INTERVIEW EVALUATION

CHAPTER 14

JOB KNOWLEDGE

OFFICE APPLICATIONS

Office Application 14-1 (Objective 1)

You interview for a position as a secretarial employee at RJ Computer Corporation. During the interview, you are told that your duties will include using a microcomputer, handling the mail, managing records, and receiving callers. Two days after the interview, you receive a call from Ms. Ott, the office manager with whom you interviewed. She asks you to report for work on the following Monday. Answer the following questions:

1. What additional information do you need from Ms. Ott before reporting to work?
2. What should you do before Monday morning to prepare for work?

Office Application 14-2 (Objective 2)

Find out about the organizational structure of your college. If there is an organizational chart available, examine it to determine the lines of responsibility. If one is not available, interview a secretary to find out the following information:

1. Who is the president?
2. Who reports to the president?
3. Is there a dean or vice-president of instruction? If so, who reports to this person?
4. Is there a dean or vice-president of student services? If so, who reports to this person?

Office Application 14-3 (Objective 3)

You have learned in this chapter that it is important to understand the formal policies of a company. The personnel policies of RJ Computer Corporation are being revised by Marjorie Ott. She asks that you prepare a revised copy of the policies which appear on pages 382–385. As you prepare these policies, become familiar with them. Make two copies of the policies.

Office Application 14-4 (Objective 3)

For two days you have worked at RJ Computer Corporation and you have several questions concerning the informal policies of the company. Here are your questions.

1. May I have food and drinks at my desk?
2. May I receive personal phone calls at work?
3. Are morning and afternoon breaks provided?

Here is what you have observed during the past two days.

Your employer drinks coffee at his desk; you have seen two or three other people with soft drinks at their desks. People are away from their desks for certain periods of time, but you do not know if they are on personal or company business. You have received two personal telephone calls from friends congratulating you on getting the job. You felt uncomfortable when they called, but you hated to be rude to them. You kept the calls brief and got back to work quickly.

How should you get answers to your questions? What should you have done when your friends called? What if friends call in the future? How should you handle the situation?

Office Application 14-5 (Objective 4)

The performance review on page 386 is used to evaluate employees at RJ Computer Corporation. Rate yourself in relation to the work you do in this class. In what areas do you need improvement? What are your strengths?

381

PERSONNEL POLICIES AT RJ COMPUTER CORPORATION

PROBATIONARY PERIOD *as*

Your first three months at RJ Computer will be considered a probationary period during which your supervisor will see how ~~well you take up~~ *you progress with* the new work. During this period your employment may be terminated without notice.

A merit rating report will be made by your supervisor at the termination of the probationary period and periodically thereafter. This report is used as the basis for salary increases and advancement. *promotions*

PROMOTION

When vacancies occur at RJ Computer, they are filled through the appointment of the best qualified candidates available. Whenever possible, this is done through promotion from within RJ Computer ~~Corporation~~. Your demonstrated ability to perform your job well, your attendance and punctuality record, and your relationships with employees will all have a bearing when considering you as a candidate for promotion. Any outside courses of study which result in skills in addition to those already noted on your application should be recorded with the ~~Comptroller's~~ *Personnel* office to insure complete information when jobs are to be filled.

HOURS OF WORK

The basic week totals 40 working hours-- ~~8 hours a day for 5 days~~. *8 a.m. to 5 p.m. Monday through Friday.* Your department head will arrange your rest and lunch periods. Time cards are used as a means of recording your attendance and punctuality.

OVERTIME

ten minutes or one-sixth
Overtime salary is paid for units of ~~one-half~~ hour. ~~Lesser~~ fractions ~~of a half~~ *less than one-sixth* hour of overtime are not reported.

~~If your salary is less than $1,000 a month,~~ compensation for work authorized by the department in excess of 40 hours is at the rate of time and one half beyond 40 hours in any week, or for work on Saturdays, Sundays, and holidays.

HOLIDAYS

You will have the following legal holidays with pay:

New Year's Day
Memorial Day
Independence Day
Labor Day
Thanksgiving
Christmas

When a religious or other holiday is to be observed, announcement will be made in advance.

VACATIONS

The vacation period extends from ~~May~~ *april* 1 to September 30. If you were employed on or before September 1, you will be entitled to one week of vacation after completing six months of continuous employment.

A legal holiday falling on a ~~working~~ day within your vacation adds one day to your vacation time.

Vacation salary is paid to you in advance on the latest regular salary payment date before your vacation.

ABSENCES AND LEAVES

your department head

Regular attendance and punctuality are necessary for the smooth functioning of the organization, and your record in this respect will be considered in determining your advancement and salary adjustment. There are, however, certain absences which are unavoidable and for which provisions are made. In each case, ~~the Comptroller's secretary~~ should be notified in advance whenever possible, or before 9:30 on the day of your absence. If you fail to make proper notification, the unadvised absence will be counted as absence without salary.

Sick Leave ^For Your Own Confining Illness

(For absence due to illness of others, no leave with salary is provided.)

When absence is for your own illness, salary is paid for up to one day for each month of employment, cumulative within the current year only. If you need sick leave in addition to the above, you may apply for additional time without pay.

Court Duty

If you are required to serve as a juror or witness, your absence is considered as leave with salary.

Marriage

If you marry after having been employed for one year or more, five days' leave with salary is granted, if you continue in your position after marriage.

Death in the Immediate Family

If a member of your immediate family dies, up to three days' leave may be granted with salary.

Leave of Absence for Other Reasons

If you request a leave of absence for other reasons, or for a longer period than is provided with salary, various factors will be taken into consideration, including your previous work and attendance record, the length of leave you are requesting, the work needs of your department, and any other pertinent points.

SALARIES

Payment of your salary is by check on a weekly basis, covering salary through Wednesday of the current week. Salary checks are distributed each Friday.

Salary increases are considered periodically. The quality of your work, the amount of responsibility you carry, your attendance and punctuality record, your attitude, and your length of service are factors which enter into consideration.

Deductions from salary regularly include withholding tax and social security; deductions for savings bonds, group insurance, hospital care, and other benefits are made only on your written request.

Assignments or garnishee of salary is not permitted, and may result in your release from RJ Computer Corporation. However, a reasonable amount of time will be given to you to satisfy any judgment before such action is taken. If you have personal financial difficulties, you are urged to seek the advice of the ~~Assistant~~ Personnel manager.

INSURANCE

To help provide security in times of sickness, hospitalization, old age, and so forth, insurance of various kinds is available as follows:

Hospital care membership is available to all employees on a payroll deduction basis. If you are married, you may include your husband or wife and dependent children under 19 years of age in your hospital care contract. Deductions for hospital care are made on the *first* ~~second~~ payday of each month.

Group insurance is available to you if you wish to participate. RJ Computer Corporation contributes to the cost to the extent of a little more than half of the premium. Each employee is permitted to take $25,000 worth of life insurance. This insurance can be obtained without a physical examination if you apply for it within 30 ~~thirty~~ days of your employment. ~~at RJ Computer Corporation.~~ It becomes effective immediately. Deduction for group insurance are made on the ~~first~~ *second* payday of each month.

Under the provisions of the Texas State Unemployment Insurance Law, unemployment insurance is available at no cost to you if you lose your position.

Social security is provided through payments by you and RJ Computer Corporation to the federal government. Your share of the cost is deducted from each salary payment.

TERMINATION OF EMPLOYMENT

<u>Resignation</u>

You are asked to give two weeks' notice of resignation. If you have been employed for six months or more and resign during the vacation period, having given two weeks' notice, you will be compensated for your vacation according to the vacation schedule.

<u>Release</u>

If you are released form your position for reasons other than misconduct--in which case no notice is given--you will have notice or salary in lieu of notice as follows:

If you have been employed for: 6 months but less tha 12--1 week
12 months or more--2weeks

Name _____ Department _____

Quality of
Work

| 15 | 16 | 17 | | 18 | 19 | 20 | | 21 | 22 | 23 | | 24 | 25 | 26 | | 27 | 28 | 29 |
Unsatisfactory   Below Average   Average   Above Average   Superior

Comments _____
_____

Volume of
Work

| 15 | 16 | 17 | | 18 | 19 | 20 | | 21 | 22 | 23 | | 24 | 25 | 26 | | 27 | 28 | 29 |
Unsatisfactory   Below Average   Average   Above Average   Superior

Comments _____
_____

Knowledge of
Work

| 5 | 6 | 7 | | 8 | 9 | 10 | | 11 | 12 | 13 | | 14 | 15 | 16 | | 17 | 18 | 19 |
Unsatisfactory   Below Average   Average   Above Average   Superior

Comments _____
_____

Initiative

| 5 | 6 | 7 | | 8 | 9 | 10 | | 11 | 12 | 13 | | 14 | 15 | 16 | | 17 | 18 | 19 |
Unsatisfactory   Below Average   Average   Above Average   Superior

Comments _____
_____

Work
Attitude

| 5 | 6 | 7 | | 8 | 9 | 10 | | 11 | 12 | 13 | | 14 | 15 | 16 | | 17 | 18 | 19 |
Unsatisfactory   Below Average   Average   Above Average   Superior

Comments _____
_____

Attitude
Toward Others

| 5 | 6 | 7 | | 8 | 9 | 10 | | 11 | 12 | 13 | | 14 | 15 | 16 | | 17 | 18 | 19 |
Unsatisfactory   Below Average   Average   Above Average   Superior

Comments _____
_____

Promotional
Potential

| 5 | 6 | 7 | | 8 | 9 | 10 | | 11 | 12 | 13 | | 14 | 15 | 16 | | 17 | 18 | 19 |
Unsatisfactory   Below Average   Average   Above Average   Superior

Comments _____
_____

Add points in each area to determine total rating; check appropriate rating below.

55 - 69 points _____ Unsatisfactory
70 - 90 points _____ Below Average
91 - 111 points _____ Average
112 - 132 points _____ Above Average
133 - 153 points _____ Superior

Date _____

Manager _____

OFFICE APPLICATIONS

Office Application 15-1   (Objective 1)

When working in a business office, you will encounter many situations requiring tact and common sense on your part. This is true whether you are an experienced or inexperienced worker, but it is particularly true when you are new on the job. There are no predetermined answers to use in most situations; you must use your best judgment.

The following situations are typical of those that you may encounter in an office. Read each one carefully, think about it, visualize yourself in the situation, and then write your answer. Make your answer brief but to the point.

Situation 1

You are allowed a 15-minute coffee break in the morning and in the afternoon. Some of your fellow workers abuse this privilege by staying longer than 15 minutes in the cafeteria. When you get ready to leave, one of them says, "Oh, come on and stay a couple of minutes longer while I finish my cigarette. The boss doesn't mind." What should you do?

Situation 2

The man who works at the desk next to yours and who does work similar to yours comes in late an average of once a week. Since efficient office help is hard to get, this tardiness apparently is overlooked. He, however, asks you to help him catch up with his work so he can leave on time at the end of the day. What should you do?

Situation 3

In your office it seems that someone is always "passing the hat" to buy a present for the boss's birthday, a wedding anniversary, or for some other occasion. You feel that these frequent collections are an imposition. What should you do?

Situation 4

A member of the opposite sex stops by your desk at every opportunity. It seems that an excuse is made to do so. You were popular in school and you like the attention. Others are beginning to notice, and you do have work to do. What should you do?

Situation 5

During your first day on a new job, two of your fellow employees asked you to have lunch with them. During lunch they talked unkindly about several people in the office. If they ask you to have lunch with them again, what should you do?

Situation 6

There are 50 people in your office. Although you have been in the office a month, you have been concentrating on learning your immediate job well and have not made any special effort to learn co-workers' names. Anyway, you have difficulty remembering names. The result is that you call Mr. Brown, Mr. Boone; Miss Grant, Miss Brant; and so on. What should you do?

Situation 7

You have been planning an important date for two weeks—a fine restaurant for dinner and then the theater. In fact, the theater tickets have already been purchased. At noon on the day of the big event, your boss requests you to work overtime that night to get out a special order. What should you do?

Situation 8

You have been working for a year and are entitled to a two-week vacation with pay. You have always gone on vacation with the members of your family. This year the family vacation is planned for the last two weeks of June and you have asked your boss for vacation during this period. Your boss delays approval until all requests are in and then tells you that you will have to take your vacation the first two weeks of August. The other members of your family cannot rearrange their plans, however. What should you do?

Situation 9

Some time ago your boss asked you to entertain a small group of customers who had just placed sizable orders with your firm. As a token of appreciation, the boss presented you with a nice but inexpensive gift. This was the first time a token of appreciation had been given to an employee. What should you do?

Situation 10

You have been working for the same company for five years. You know your work, do it efficiently, and apparently get along well with other employees. Others, however, have been promoted over you, even though they have been with the company a shorter time. What should you do?

Situation 11

For some time you have been working on an idea that involves changing one of the office clerical routines. You believe your idea will save the company money. Although you have discussed your proposal many times with your supervisor, nothing has been done about it. What should you do?

Situation 12

You are well-liked by your fellow employees and apparently have the confidence of your boss. One day a committee of employees comes to you with a petition for you to present to your employer which requests that the lunch hour be lengthened from an hour to an hour and fifteen minutes. You feel that the boss will be strongly opposed. The boss has said many times that "an hour for lunch is too long with all the other time that employees are away from their desks." What should you do?

Office Application 15-2   (Objective 2)

Do one of the following activities:

1. Visit a local company to determine how an exit interview is conducted; if they use a form, ask to see a copy of it. Write a report of your findings.
2. Do library research on leaving a job. Read at least two articles, and prepare summaries of the articles on 5″ × 3″ cards, giving the sources.

Office Application 15-3   (Objective 3)

You have worked for Mr. Navarate for six months. You feel you do a fairly good job, but you are concerned because you never seem to get everything done. You talked with Mark Valentino, the office worker who had the job before you, and he told you that he had no problem getting all the work done. Your keyboarding ability is above average, and you have never considered yourself slow in performing any type of job. Yet, something is wrong.

New employees are evaluated every six months at RJ Computer Corporation. When Mr. Navarate talked with you about your evaluation recently, your inability to keep up with the job was discussed. You told Mr. Navarate that you realized it was a problem, but you couldn't seem to identify where you could improve. The two of you determined that you should analyze your time carefully, establish priorities, and organize your work area. In order to improve in these areas, perform the following activities.

1. Write a plan of action for analyzing your time. Itemize each step you plan to take.

Prepare one copy of this plan; present it to your instructor.

2. You are given the following jobs one morning. Establish priorities for performing all these jobs. Prepare an original only.
   a. Quarterly report that must be prepared for a meeting at 2:00 p.m. It will take you approximately 40 minutes to complete the report.
   b. Morning mail to sort, open, date and time stamp, and distribute. (Mail is delivered to your office at approximately 10:00 a.m.)
   c. Regular filing (requires about one hour).
   d. Copy of letter requested by the president of RJ Computer Corporation. The president's secretary called at 8:45 a.m. and requested a copy of the letter.
   e. Unhappy customer calls at 9:15 a.m. Customer has not received supplies ordered two weeks ago. The sales department at RJ Computer Corporation had promised the customer that the supplies would be delivered the previous day.
   f. Mr. Navarate gives you a rush memo to prepare at 8:42 a.m.
   g. Ms. Ott, office manager at RJ Computer Corporation, gives you a letter. She tells you the letter should go out sometime that day.
   h. Mr. Navarate dictates three letters for you to transcribe from a transcribing machine at 10:00 a.m. He needs the letters as soon as possible.

3. You have the responsibility for ordering the supplies for your department. What steps would you take to keep the supplies in the supply cabinet organized? Prepare an original only of these steps.

N

O

Notes